BUDDHISM, CONFLICT AND VIOLENCE IN MODERN SRI LANKA

Buddhism, Conflict and Violence in Modern Sri Lanka explores dilemmas that Theravāda Buddhism faces in relation to the continuing ethnic conflict and violence in recent decades. In this book, prominent scholars in the fields of anthropology, history, Buddhist Studies and Pāli examine multiple dimensions of the problem. It discusses in detail various Buddhist responses to the crisis and suggests ways how resources found within Buddhism and Buddhist institutions can help create peace in Sri Lanka. Evaluating the role of Buddhists and their institutions in bringing about an end to war and violence, this collection puts forward a critical analysis of the religious conditions contributing to continuing hostilities.

Mahinda Deegalle is Senior Lecturer in the Study of Religions at Bath Spa University. His research interests are Buddhist Preaching, Mahāyāna Buddhism in Sri Lanka and Violence and Peacebuilding. He is the co-editor of Pāli Buddhism (Curzon, 1996), and is currently researching on Buddhist monks' involvement in Parliamentary Politics.

ROUTLEDGE CRITICAL STUDIES IN BUDDHISM

General Editors:
Charles S. Prebish and Damien Keown

Routledge Critical Studies in Buddhism is a comprehensive study of the Buddhist tradition. The series explores this complex and extensive tradition from a variety of perspectives, using a range of different methodologies.

The series is diverse in its focus, including historical studies, textual translations and commentaries, sociological investigations, bibliographic studies, and considerations of religious practice as an expression of Buddhism's integral religiosity. It also presents materials on modern intellectual historical studies, including the role of Buddhist thought and scholarship in a contemporary, critical context and in the light of current social issues. The series is expansive and imaginative in scope, spanning more than two and a half millennia of Buddhist history. It is receptive to all research works that inform and advance our knowledge and understanding of the Buddhist tradition.

A SURVEY OF VINAYA LITERATURE
Charles S. Prebish

THE REFLEXIVE NATURE OF AWARENESS
Paul Williams

ALTRUISM AND REALITY
Paul Williams

BUDDHISM AND HUMAN RIGHTS
Edited by Damien Keown, Charles Prebish and Wayne Husted

WOMEN IN THE FOOTSTEPS OF THE BUDDHA
Kathryn R Blackstone

THE RESONANCE OF EMPTINESS
Gay Watson

AMERICAN BUDDHISM
Edited by Duncan Ryuken Williams and Christopher Queen

IMAGING WISDOM
Jacob N. Kinnard

PAIN AND ITS ENDING
Carol S. Anderson

EMPTINESS APPRAISED
David F. Burton

THE SOUND OF LIBERATING TRUTH
Edited by Sallie B. King and Paul O. Ingram

BUDDHIST THEOLOGY
Edited by Roger R. Jackson and John J. Makransky

THE GLORIOUS DEEDS OF PURNA
Joel Tatelman

EARLY BUDDHISM – A NEW APPROACH
Sue Hamilton

CONTEMPORARY BUDDHIST ETHICS
Edited by Damien Keown

INNOVATIVE BUDDHIST WOMEN
Edited by Karma Lekshe Tsomo

TEACHING BUDDHISM IN THE WEST
Edited by V.S. Hori, R.P. Hayes and J.M. Shields

EMPTY VISION
David L. McMahan

SELF, REALITY AND REASON IN TIBETAN PHILOSOPHY
Thupten Jinpa

IN DEFENSE OF DHARMA
Tessa J. Bartholomeusz

BUDDHIST PHENOMENOLOGY
Dan Lusthaus

RELIGIOUS MOTIVATION AND THE ORIGINS OF BUDDHISM
Torkel Brekke

DEVELOPMENTS IN AUSTRALIAN BUDDHISM
Michelle Spuler

ZEN WAR STORIES
Brian Victoria

THE BUDDHIST UNCONSCIOUS
William S. Waldron

INDIAN BUDDHIST THEORIES OF PERSONS
James Duerlinger

ACTION DHARMA
Edited by Christopher Queen, Charles Prebish and Damien Keown

TIBETAN AND ZEN BUDDHISM IN BRITAIN
David N. Kay

THE CONCEPT OF THE BUDDHA
Guang Xing

THE PHILOSOPHY OF DESIRE IN THE BUDDHIST PALI CANON
David Webster

THE NOTION OF *DITTHI* IN THERAVADA BUDDHISM
Paul Fuller

THE BUDDHIST THEORY OF SELF-COGNITION
Zhihua Yao

MORAL THEORY IN ŚĀNTIDEVA'S *ŚIKṢĀSAMUCCAYA*
Barbra R. Clayton

BUDDHIST STUDIES FROM INDIA TO AMERICA
Edited by Damien Keown

DISCOURSE AND IDEOLOGY IN MEDIEVAL JAPANESE BUDDHISM
Edited by Richard K. Payne and Taigen Dan Leighton

BUDDHIST THOUGHT AND APPLIED PSYCHOLOGICAL RESEARCH
Edited by D. K. Nauriyal, Michael S. Drummond and Y. B. Lal

BUDDHISM IN CANADA
Edited by Bruce Matthews

BUDDHISM, CONFLICT AND VIOLENCE IN MODERN SRI LANKA
Edited by Mahinda Deegalle

The following titles are published in association with the
Oxford Centre for Buddhist Studies

Oxford Centre for Buddhist Studies
a project of The Society for the Wider Understanding of the Buddhist Tradition

The *Oxford Centre for Buddhist Studies* conducts and promotes rigorous teaching and research into all forms of the Buddhist tradition.

EARLY BUDDHIST METAPHYSICS
Noa Ronkin

MIPHAM'S DIALECTICS AND THE DEBATES ON EMPTINESS
Karma Phuntsho

HOW BUDDHISM BEGAN
The conditioned genesis of the early teachings
Richard F. Gombrich

BUDDHIST MEDITATION
An anthology of texts from the Pāli Canon
Sarah Shaw

BUDDHISM, CONFLICT AND VIOLENCE IN MODERN SRI LANKA

Edited by Mahinda Deegalle

Routledge
Taylor & Francis Group
LONDON AND NEW YORK

First published 2006
by Routledge
2 Park Square, Milton Park, Abingdon, Oxon OX14 4RN

Simultaneously published in the USA and Canada
by Routledge
270 Madison Ave, New York, NY 10016

Routledge is an imprint of the Taylor & Francis Group

Transferred to Digital Printing 2009

Typeset in Times New Roman by
Newgen Imaging Systems (P) Ltd, Chennai, India

British Library Cataloguing in Publication Data
A catalogue record for this book is available from the British Library

Library of Congress Cataloging in Publication Data
Buddhism, conflict, and violence in modern Sri Lanka / edited by Mahinda Deegalle.
p. cm. – (Routledge critical studies in Buddhism)
Includes bibliographical references and index.
1. Buddhism and social problems – Sri Lanka. 2. Reconciliation – Religious aspects – Theravada Buddhism. 3. Violence – Religious aspects – Theravada Buddhism. 4. Nonviolence – Religious aspects – Theravada Buddhism. 5. Ethnic relations – Religious aspects – Theravada Buddhism. 6. Ethnic conflict – Sri Lanka. I. Deegalle Mahinda, Ven. II. Series.

HN40.B8B83 2006
294.3′372′095493–dc22 2005022413

ISBN10: 0–415–35920–1 (hbk)
ISBN10: 0–415–54441–6 (pbk)

ISBN13: 978–0–415–35920–7 (hbk)
ISBN13: 978–0–415–54441–2 (pbk)

A TRIBUTE TO
MEN AND WOMEN WHO ARE
PROACTIVE IN CREATING PEACE
AROUND THE WORLD

CONTENTS

CONTRIBUTORS

George Bond is Professor of Religion at Northwestern University, USA. He is the author of *Buddhism at Work: Community Development, Social Empowerment, and the Sarvodaya Movement* (2004).

Chandra R. de Silva is Dean of College of Arts and Letters at Old Dominion University, USA. He is the author of *Sri Lanka: A History* (1987) and the co-editor of *Buddhist Fundamentalism and Minority Identities in Sri Lanka* (1998).

Mahinda Deegalle is Senior Lecturer in the Study of Religions, School of Historical and Cultural Studies, Bath Spa University, UK. He is the co-editor of *Pāli Buddhism* (1996) and the author of *Popularizing Buddhism: Buddhist Preaching in Sri Lanka* (State University of New York Press, 2006).

Richard Gombrich was Bowden Professor of Sanskrit at University of Oxford and Fellow of Balliol College. He is the author of *Precept and Practice* (1971), and *Theravada Buddhism: A Social History from Ancient Benares to Modern Colombo* (1988).

R.A.L.H. Gunawardana is Emeritus Professor of History at University of Peradeniya, Sri Lanka. He is the author of *Robe and Plough: Monasticism and Economic Interest in Early Medieval Sri Lanka* (1979) and *Historiography in a Time of Ethnic Conflict* (1995).

John Clifford Holt is Professor of Religion at Bowdoin College, USA. He is the author of *Buddha in the Crown: Avalokiteśvara in the Buddhist Traditions of Sri Lanka* (1991), *The Religious World of Kīrti Śrī* (1996) and *The Buddhist Viṣṇu: Politics, Religion and Culture* (2005).

Gananath Obeyesekere is Emeritus Professor of Anthropology at Princeton University, USA. He is the author of *Medusa's Hair* (1981), *The Cult of the Goddess Pattini* (1984), *A Meditation on Conscience* (1988), *The Work of Culture* (1990), and *Imagining Karma* (2002).

Mahinda Palihawadana is Emeritus Professor of Sanskrit at Sri Jayawardhanapura University, Sri Lanka. He is the co-translator of *The Dhammapada* (with John Ross Carter, 1987) and author of *The God of War and Lavishness* (1996).

P.D. Premasiri is Professor and Head of Pali and Buddhist Studies at University of Peradeniya, Sri Lanka. He has published numerous articles on Buddhism and Buddhist Ethics in the *Encyclopedia of Buddhism*.

Peter Schalk is Professor of Religious Studies at University of Uppsala, Sweden. He is the author of *Der Paritta-Dienst in Ceylon* (1972) and co-author of *Buddhism among Tamils in Pre-Colonial Tamiḷakam and Īḻam* (2002).

Bardwell Smith was *John W. Nason* Professor of Asian Studies at Carleton College, USA. He has edited a number of volumes including *The Two Wheels of Dharma* (1972), *Religion and Social Conflict in South Asia* (1976), and *Religion and Legitimation of Power in Sri Lanka* (1978).

Asanga Tilakaratne is Professor and Head of Buddhist Philosophy at the Postgraduate Institute of Pali and Buddhist Studies at University of Kelaniya, Sri Lanka. He is the author of *Nirvana and Ineffability: A Study of the Buddhist Theory of Reality and Language* (1993).

Alvappillai Veluppillai is Professor of Religious Studies at Arizona State University, USA. He is the co-author of *Buddhism among Tamils in Pre-Colonial Tamiḷakam and Īḻam* (2002).

Ananda Wickremeratne teaches at Loyola University of Chicago, USA. He is the author of *The Genesis of an Orientalist* (1984), *Buddhism and Ethnicity in Sri Lanka* (1995) and *Roots of Nationalism: Sri Lanka* (1995).

ACKNOWLEDGEMENTS

This book would not have been published without the support and help of many individuals. Initial preparation for this book began at the time of the International Conference on *Buddhism and Conflict in Sri Lanka* held at Bath Spa University on 28–30 June 2002. My thanks to the sponsors of the conference – the Buddhist Federation of Norway – speakers, respondents, the other three members of the conference organizing committee – Professor Peter Harvey, Dr Rupert Gethin and Ms Rita Langer, the United Kingdom Association for Buddhist Studies, conference participants and especially the contributors who have enriched the quality of this volume. Editing of the book was undertaken while carrying out regular teaching and administrative tasks at Bath Spa. My thanks to Dr Fiona Montgomery, Head of School of Historical and Cultural Studies and Professor Denise Cush, Head of Study of Religions, for supporting research. Professor Peter Harvey has continuously encouraged me on this project and Professor Damien Keown has supported this project on several levels by making sure the book get printed in timely manner. Over the last two decades, several friends and teachers at The University of Chicago, Harvard University, University of Peradeniya, Kyoto University, Aichi Gakuin University, International College for Advanced Buddhist Studies (Tokyo), McGill University and Bath Spa have inspired me, supported my education and scholarship and enriched my academic career. I am grateful for all those who went out of their ways to help me and contributed in countless ways for my growth. On this occasion, it is with great pleasure that I mention the support and guidance that I received from Professor Frank E. Reynolds and Professor Wendy Doniger at The University of Chicago and Professor Diana Eck at Harvard University. May all of you, mentioned and not mentioned here, achieve Buddhahood for your selfless *bodhisattva* acts!

ABBREVIATIONS

A	*Aṅguttaranikāya*
BCE	Before the Common Era
BEP	Bauddha Eksat Peramuṇa
CE	Common Era
CP	Communist Party of Sri Lanka
D	*Dīghanikāya*
DB	*Dialogues of the Buddha*
DDC	District Development Councils
Dhp	*Dhammapada*
Dv	*Dīpavaṃsa*
EPRLF	Eelam People's Revolutionary Liberation Front
GoSL	Government of Sri Lanka
HSZ	High Security Zone
IPKF	Indian Peace-Keeping Force
ISGA	Interim Self-Governing Authority
J	*Jātaka*
JHU	Jathika Hela Urumaya
JVP	Janatha Vimukti Peramuṇa
LSSP	Laṅkā Samasamāja Party
LTTE	Liberation Tigers of Tamil Eelam
M	*Majjhimanikāya*
MLS	*Middle Length Sayings*
MoU	Memorandum of Understanding
Mv	*Mahāvaṃsa*
NBF	National Bhikṣu Front (Jathika Bhikṣu Peramuṇa)
NSA	National Saṅgha Assembly (Jathika Saṅgha Sammēlanaya)
NSC	National Saṅgha Council (Jathika Saṅgha Sabhāva)
P	Pāli language
PA	People's Alliance
PLOTE	People's Liberation Organization of Tamil Eelam
PTA	Prevention of Terrorism Act
PTS	The Pali Text Society

S	*Saṃyuttanikāya*
Sin	Sinhala language
Skt	Sanskrit language
SLFP	Sri Lanka Freedom Party
SLMC	Sri Lanka Muslim Congress
SLMM	Sri Lanka Monitoring Mission
Sn	*Suttanipāta*
SU	Sihala Urumaya
Sv	*Sumaṅgalavilāsinī*
TELO	Tamil Eelam Liberation Organization
TNA	Tamil National Alliance
TULF	Tamil United Liberation Front
Ud	*Udāna*
UF	United Front
UKABS	United Kingdom Association for Buddhist Studies
UNP	United National Party
v	verse
Vin	*Vinaya Piṭaka*
vv	verses

1

INTRODUCTION

Buddhism, conflict and violence

Mahinda Deegalle

> 'Blind is the world
> Few are those who clearly see'
> *Dhammapada* v. 174

Buddhism, Conflict and Violence in Modern Sri Lanka explores the dilemmas that Theravāda Buddhism faces in relation to the continuing ethnic conflict. Fifteen contributors from Sri Lanka and abroad examine canonical and cultural resources found within the Theravāda Buddhist tradition that can be effectively used in seeking a viable solution to the problem through reconciliation and transformation of violent elements that endanger peace in Sri Lanka.

The current ethnic conflict in Sri Lanka between the majority Sinhalese (represented by the Sri Lankan Government) and the minority Tamils (primarily by the Liberation Tigers of Tamil Eelam) has lasted over two decades. The catastrophic event, which destroyed the friendly relations between the two ethnic groups, occurred in July 1983. Since then, for the last twenty years, Sri Lankan government forces have been fighting a guerrilla war orchestrated by the Liberation Tigers of Tamil Eelam (LTTE).[1]

This civil war has resulted in the loss of thousands of lives from all ethnic and religious groups; many Sinhalese, Tamils and Muslims have been displaced and religious places have become ruins. Recent estimates suggest that over 64,000 died in the events related to the war and more than two millions are displaced. This war has caused serious economic, political, social and moral damage to this primarily Theravāda Buddhist society, which is proud of its liberal cultural heritage and tolerant values cultivated on the basis of Buddhist teachings and Aśokan principles[2] in incorporating non-Buddhists and non-Sinhalese into its cultural and religious ethos.

The LTTE claim that they are fighting for a separate homeland called 'Eelam'[3] which covers the Northern and Eastern regions of Sri Lanka on behalf of the minority Tamils since it is the only way in which Tamils can overcome what they conceive as 'injustice' and discrimination perpetuated on them by the Sinhalese majority; they have written widely and publicized in the Western media that the

Sinhala majority has continuously restricted the rights of Tamils as Sri Lankans in educational and employment policies. All these accusations need detailed investigation and analysis in order to understand the problem that Sri Lanka has faced in recent decades.

Sri Lanka's 19 million population is diverse both in ethnicity and religious adherence. By birth, the ethnic majority, the Sinhalese (74%) are primarily Buddhists (69.3%). The major minority ethnic group, Tamils (both Sri Lankan and Indian) constitute 18.1% of the total population. The majority of Tamils are Hindus and constitutes about 15.5% of the entire Sri Lankan population. A small proportion of the Sinhalese and Tamils are Christians (7.6%), with a majority Roman Catholic constituency. Muslims and Burghers constitute 7% and 0.8% of the population respectively. As a small nation in South Asia, Sri Lanka thus has adherents of four main world religions.

A majority of the Sinhalese claim not only that Sri Lanka has, throughout a known history traced to the fifth century BCE, been one country, but also has historically been primarily a Sinhala Buddhist country. As the papers in this volume illustrate, ideologically, among Sinhalese and Tamils, there are irreconcilable religious, ethnic, political and nationalistic positions, which have continuously fed into further misunderstandings and accusations of injustice resulting in the bloody conflict now witnessed in modern Sri Lanka.

In the context of terrorism and brutal provocations of the LTTE, over the last two decades rather marginal groups such as Mavubima Surakīme Vyāpāraya (Movement for the Protection of the Motherland),[4] Sihala Urumaya (Sinhala Heritage),[5] Janatha Vimukthi Peramuna (JVP) (People's Liberation Front),[6] being a few of the vocal groups, have put forward a reactive agenda. Some Sinhala leaders in these marginal nationalist groups favour war as the solution to the problem.[7] They also see and express forcefully the potential threats to the future survival of Buddhism in Sri Lanka. Fear of threats to their identity as Sinhalese and Buddhists in their historical homeland seems to be one of the dominant factors that encourage the need to combat terrorism. Some groups such as the Sihala Urumaya (Sinhala Heritage) maintain that in Sri Lanka there is no ethnic problem at all since Sinhalese, Tamils and Muslims live in harmony in the West and South but the real problem is Tamil terrorism rather than ethnicity.[8] Recently, the Chief Patriarch of the Asgiriya Chapter of the Siyam Nikāya also expressed this view,[9] which denies that there is an ethnic problem in Sri Lanka.[10]

When some nominal Buddhists advocate war against the LTTE in the context of the current conflict, observers, often Westerners, raise an important question, which has serious implications for the accumulative tradition that we identify as Buddhism. Can Buddhists, who claim to follow the teachings of the Buddha, advocate war as a solution to the ethnic problem? How could people who profess to be Buddhists advocate war? Are they betraying Buddhism?[11] These ethical and moral issues related to war, violence and conflict have given birth to dilemmas in contemporary Buddhism in Sri Lanka.

Contextualizing violence and conflict in relation to Theravāda teachings

Buddhiṣt scriptures, whether they are in Pāli or Sanskrit, are crucial and indispensable resources in understanding the theoretical side of violence from a religious perspective and in elucidating the non-violent path prescribed by the Buddha. This book gives priority to the examination of views on violence as found in the Theravāda scriptures in the Pāli canon. Several papers in this book explore material from the Pāli canon to understand and analyse the attitudes towards violence and conflict in a specific Theravāda context in Sri Lanka. The papers identify a selection of scriptures in the Pāli canon in elucidating canonical perspectives towards violence. They examine what the scriptures state about nature of violence, different manifestations of violence as noted by the Buddha, his reasons for denouncing violence, the fundamental roots of violent actions as analysed by Buddhism, and more importantly the Buddhist message for the contemporary world in transforming all forms of violence both within individuals and society at large.

To a large extent, there is an exploration of Theravāda Buddhist attitudes in preventing physical violence as understood by the Pāli canonical literature and finding ways in creating peace in Sri Lanka. To a limited extent, the chapters explore the continuity of ideas about violence and non-violence from scriptures to practising communities. The papers, however, do not make the presumption that what the Pāli canon states is exactly what Buddhists have been doing over the centuries in Theravāda Buddhist communities. The immediate purpose here is to examine the potential of Buddhist scriptures as guidelines for non-violent human action.

It is possible to identify two key texts – the *Dhammapada* and the *Cakkavattisīhanāda* Sutta – to demonstrate that Theravāda Buddhism has a sound basis in denouncing violence and its condemnation of violence is founded on strong moral and ethical teachings as taught by the Buddha.

In Buddhist scriptures, all forms of mental, verbal and physical abuse, whether directed towards oneself or others, are defined as possible examples of 'violence'.[12] In any society, including Theravāda Sri Lanka, violence can manifest in various forms and can have many dimensions with varying degrees of severity of harm. Causes of violence are not necessarily singular and violence as a threatening modern social phenomenon can have many causes and its agency can be plural. As evident even from a superficial observation of modern phases of violence related to Sri Lankan ethnic problem, violent contexts are complex and it is hard to come up with a single explanation of its root causes.

One of the problems in understanding the conflict in Sri Lanka is that most try to attribute the current problem to one cause (e.g., as a result of poor economic conditions, a result of Sinhala Buddhist chauvinism, or due to terrorist acts of the LTTE). It appears that phases of violence are multivalent and can have pluralistic explanations. The Bath conference itself suggested diverse dimensions of violence and the complex nature of violent activities. Depending on the given context, the severity of violent activities changes. Given that Sri Lanka is proud of being the home of Theravāda Buddhism, it is incomprehensible how and why within the last two decades it has experienced various forms of violent activities perpetuated by either extremists, terrorists, or government soldiers.

Though various forms of violent activities in Sri Lanka have no direct link with Buddhist teachings, the phenomenon of violence in Sri Lanka has challenged and tested the sustainability of Buddhism in Sri Lanka and its continuing influence in Sri Lankan society. No Buddhist can ignore the implication of violence on Buddhist monks, Buddhist laity, Buddhist institutions in Sri Lanka and the daily practices of Buddhists. The unhealthy and violent conditions in modern Sri Lanka have caused all Sri Lankans – irrespective of their ethnic or religious boundaries – to suffer. Moderate people in Sri Lanka have witnessed that extreme groups on both the Sinhala and Tamil sides have continuously gained more power in perpetuating violence. Day by day, neutral voices get undermined and ignored both in the political process as well as in social and religious spheres. As anywhere else in the world, in Sri Lanka, too, extreme groups resort to violence as a means of solving social and political problems, which are perceived as based on economic, ethnic, racial and religious prejudices.

The perpetuation of violent activities in the name of one's own religion and nationhood also has increased dramatically in recent decades. In Sri Lanka, however, various forms of violent activities are perpetuated, not necessarily in the name of religion but mostly in the name of nationhood, either Tamil or Sinhala. While the perpetrators of violent acts justify their violent activities, for example, by using narratives found in the Pāli chronicles, the nature of violence and quantity of violent acts have increased dramatically within the last two decades. Certain forms of violence such as the exploitation of labour are also embedded in the economic order itself and exploitation becomes a basis for animosity between ethnic groups leading to the breakdown of law and order. For Buddhists, the real challenge in the modern world is finding a way to avoid getting bogged down in various forms of violence either in the name of nationhood or religion.

A glance at the Pāli canonical literature such as the *Dhammapada* demonstrates that certain verses there reveal basic attitudes of the Buddha towards violence and his position in overcoming violence both on the individual and social levels. These teachings can be used as a foundation in formulating a clearly defined Buddhist view of non-violence. Such popular scriptures, which had been quite accessible for both lay and monastic communities in Theravāda countries, are important in understanding the Buddhist perspectives towards violence. An outline of this Buddhist perspective can demonstrate that Buddhism condemns violence. However, this demonstration of the non-violent Buddhist point of view itself is not adequate. As practising religious persons, Buddhists have an obligation to show how that message is reflected upon and translated into Buddhist lives. Furthermore, the modern challenge for Buddhists is that they have to demonstrate that the Buddhist message can transform violent contexts into more creative positive actions that are suitable for creating genuine peace. Buddhist scholars also have an ethical as well as an academic responsibility to interpret the nature of violence, the root causes of violent actions, and show a path to the general public which will enable those who are resorting to violence to transform their violent actions into peaceful ones.

Physical torture, verbal abuse and written accusations are forms of violence. On the whole, the Pāli canon gives clear indications that physical violence cannot be accepted even as a means of solving human and social problems. Its rejection of physical violence is based upon a strong conviction and reflection on the severity of the violent acts. The *Dhammapada* verses 129–30 draws our attention to a common human situation and reaction in the face of all forms of violence:

> All tremble at violence[13]
> All fear death…
> Life is dear to all
> Comparing oneself with others
> One should neither kill nor cause to kill.

This popular Theravāda scripture, the *Dhammapada*, draws our attention to several important factors with regard to violence and human reactions in the face of suffering. It states that

1. all sentient beings fear violent activities. When a rod or any form of violent act falls on them, they become frightened,
2. it states, in particular, that all living beings are scared of death,[14]
3. all living beings value their own lives,
4. when one is faced with violence, one has to reflect that one's situation is similar to that of others (P. *ṣattānaṃ upamaṃ katvā*) because of the fact that as human beings we want our own lives to be secure,
5. thus, the motivation to avoid violence and protect the lives of others comes from the conviction that one's life is also 'sacred' or precious. Abstention from violent activities comes from a reflection on the fact that everyone has a similar position towards one's own life. Thus, the Buddhist notion of protecting all forms of life and avoiding violent activities derives from the fundamental conviction that as one's life is worthy for oneself, others also have a similar position with respect to their own lives.

In the above *Dhammapada* verses, the Pāli term *daṇḍa* (punishment or rod) has been translated as 'violence'. The original context, which led the Buddha to recite these two verses are important. The Buddha had recited these verses when it was reported that the groups of six monks had assaulted the group of sixteen monks (Narada Thera 1978: 123) on a dispute in possessing a temple constructed by the group of sixteen monks: when the latter objected to the intrusion of the former, the former assaulted the latter. Thus, it was basically a dispute in the construction and the possession of a material property. However, the focus in the verses has nothing to do with monks' possession of buildings and houses. Rather it centres on the aspect of violence in the incident and encourages abandoning violent activities. The encouragement for abstention from violence comes from a real practical context in which monks had resorted to violence in resolving a dispute on a physical property that they themselves had constructed. While the dispute was between two groups of monks, from the context, it is clear, that physical assault is not acceptable in resolving disputes.

On another occasion, in the *Dhammapada* vv. 131–132, when the Buddha witnessed some young children were injuring a snake with sticks, the Buddha advised them not to do so by stating:

> Seeking one's own happiness, [s]he, who harms other pleasure-seeking sentient beings with a rod, will not experience happiness hereafter. Seeking one's own happiness, [s]he, who does not harm other pleasure-seeking sentient beings with a rod, will experience happiness hereafter.

In this case, too, violent actions – using a rod to harm other living beings – are rejected because such violent acts cannot be justified as a means of deriving one's own happiness.

In general, Theravāda Buddhism holds the opinion that extreme violent activities, for example, war and conflict among groups, arise due to sensual desires. The *Mahādukkhakkhandha Sutta*, in particular, identifies sensual desires as the leading factor in creating disputes among various segments of society:

> Monks, when sense-pleasures are the cause, sense-pleasures the provenance, sense-pleasures the consequence, the very cause of sense-pleasures, kings dispute with kings, nobles dispute with nobles, brahmans dispute with brahmans, householders dispute with householders, a mother disputes with her son, a son disputes with his father, a brother disputes with a brother, a brother disputes with a sister, a sister disputes with a brother, a friend disputes with a friend. Those who enter into quarrel, contention, dispute and attack one another with their hands and with stones and with sticks and with weapons, these suffer dying then and pain like unto dying. This too, monks, is a peril in the pleasures of the senses that is present... the very cause of pleasures of the senses.
>
> (*The Middle Length Sayings* I.113–4)

This *Sutta* suggests that as long as human beings are driven by sensual desires, violent activities such as using sticks and weapons to harm one another, verbal and physical abuses of each other, are unavoidable. The total overcoming of violent activities seems to be impossible as long as human beings have not completely eliminated their sensual desires. In violent circumstances, generating a relatively peaceful state is the only lasting possibility for creating peace.

In creating a violence-free-context, Theravāda Buddhist teachings propose a causal point of view. Since all phenomena are conditioned, there is nothing in this world that can be claimed to be independent. Because of this interdependent nature, various forms of violence are also conditioned by other activities. By analysing those causes, which lead to violence, and transforming violent contexts into non-violent social realities, Buddhism shows the potential of breaking down the vicious circle of violence.

Some Buddhist discourses such as the *Cakkavattisīhanāda Sutta* analyse conflicts which lead to extreme forms of violence by showing their interdependence and conditionality. In those discourses, the complexity of issues is discussed and the importance of distributing wealth to the poor is emphasized. Once income is not distributed fairly among all the communities, the potential for crimes increase among the poor and as a result, communities encounter various forms of violence. In this context, in a traditional society, the role of the king in resolving conflicts and violent activities becomes crucial.

In a mythological framework, the *Cakkavattisīhanada Sutta* suggests that, though the king had provided 'rightful shelter, protection and defense' he failed to 'give money to the poor' (Collins 1998: 606). Because of the king's inability in providing a means of right living, which creates wealth for the poor, in that society, poverty increased creating a violent context. A poor man 'intentionally took from others what [they] had not given [him].' When taken and brought to the king, the king gave him wealth because he had stolen since he could not make a living. Hearing that the king gave wealth to thieves, others began stealing. When the king heard that some stole because he gave money to thieves, he revised his policy and began punishing thieves with death. However, to avoid being reported to the king, thieves began to carry swords and kill those victims whose property they had stolen. As a result crimes increased. The *Sutta* states:

> In this way, monks, money not being given to the poor, poverty flourished; because poverty flourished, theft flourished; because theft flourished, weaponry flourished; because weaponry flourished, murder flourished; because murder flourished, these beings' vitality decreased, as did their beauty...

Violent conditions lead to decrease in life span:

> When people live for (only) ten years, the ten Good Deeds... will completely disappear... the idea of 'good' (*kusala*) will not exist... [men will not recognize women as] 'mother,' 'mother's sister,'.... the world will become thoroughly promiscuous... fierce mutual violence will arise among these beings, fierce ill-will, fierce hatred, fierce thoughts of murder, in a son for his mother... Just as now when a hunter sees an animal fierce violence... fierce thoughts of murder arise in him... there

> will be a seven-day period of war, when people will see each other as animals; sharp swords will appear in their hands and they will murder each other, each thinking 'This is an animal.'

The *Sutta* further states a transformation of these violent contexts through self-reflection and by the practice of non-violent means:

> 'Let me kill no-one, let no-one kill me'. . . 'It is because we have undertaken Bad Deeds that we have for so long been murdering our (own) relatives. Why don't we start doing good?. . . Why don't we abstain from killing?'
>
> (Collins 1998: 606–11)

This self-realization to do good and engage in non-violent actions, from a Theravāda perspective, can be seen as the most important step towards transcending the vicious circle of violence.

Further, this *Sutta* suggests that the State has an important duty to provide sufficient means of earning wealth for all sections of society in order to prevent unhealthy social problems and secure law and order. If we analyse problems such as the ethnic problem in Sri Lanka, it is clear beneath terrorism, extremism, war and the abuse of human rights lie key issues: the growing unemployment among the youth, the lack of resources to provide a decent living, healthcare and education for all sections of the population, the severe imbalance in distributing wealth, the corruption in the political system and the lack of public accountability in relation to national problems, a lack of sensitivity to the religious concerns of the people on private and public levels and the misuse of religion for political and personal gain. The last five decades after Independence in 1948 demonstrate that all the governments, which came to power continuously, failed to provide adequate and sufficient resources for the self-improvement of the poor. These conditions intensified subconscious ethnic prejudices and animosity towards each other that are ethnically and religiously different.

What some of the canonical *Sutta*s such as the *Cakkavattisīhanāda Sutta* demonstrate is that there is a close link between a righteous rule, fair, distribution of wealth and providing adequate ways of earning a living for the masses. Once unemployment has grown, poverty leads to stealing and all other forms of violent activities that lead to the downfall of society.

In examining the nature of violence from a Buddhist perspective, another important factor is the role of psychological factors. As the *Dhammapada* (vv. 1–2) states, the mind precedes all verbal and physical actions. Thus, the leading factor even in an extremely violent event can be an unhealthy psychological state of mind. From a Buddhist point of view, thoughts of violence and violent activities are defilements. They defile oneself and others. Once defiled, they lead to negative effects. From a Buddhist point of view the transformation of defilements in positive thinking is very much needed. This transformation is essential for healthy communities.

The vision of a peaceful life portrayed in the Pāli canon can thus be useful for contemporary Buddhist communities to understand the nature of human conditioning and realize the danger of emotional involvement in conflicts. A close examination of the Pāli canon demonstrates that Theravāda Buddhism has a negative view towards violence. In the scriptures, while there is an analysis of violence and its causes as psychological as well as external, it does not recommend violence in resolving human conflicts and social problems. The issue of defensive violence, however, needs to be addressed; even then what matters most is the protection of human lives, property and the environment, and employing relatively less harmful, peaceful means to arrive at a solution.

In terms of the violence in Sri Lanka, it is clear that its roots are based on economic factors, linguistic issues, matters of equal opportunities and human rights, land ownership, democratic representation in the political system and misunderstandings generated over the centuries. In this practical context, the challenge to modern Buddhists is to explore ways of transforming violent contexts in order to bring peace to all religious and ethnic communities.

Buddhism in diplomacy: peacemaking and reconciliation

In the third millennium, Sri Lankan Buddhism has entered an important and provocative phase in Buddhist history. With respect to the *saṅgha* as an institution, the years 2001 and 2004 are significant mileposts. Both years signify an active engagement of Buddhist monks in politics in relation to the ethnic conflict and current violent climate in Sri Lanka.

The General Election held on 5 December 2001 for the first time elected a Buddhist monk to the Sri Lankan Parliament.[15] Venerable Baddēgama Samitha, abbot of Duṭugämuṇu Vihāra, was elected as a Member of Parliament from the Galle District from People's Alliance (PA).[16] As I have noted in Chapter 15, Venerable Samitha has actively worked for peace in Sri Lanka during his Parliamentary term.

The year 2004 marked another milestone. Two events occurred: (i) In February 2004, over 260 Buddhist monks affiliated with the Jathika *Saṅgha* Sammēlanaya (National *Saṅgha* Assembly) and vowed to save Sri Lanka from the ethnic turmoil by standing in the General Election held on 2 April 2004. Buddhist monks of the National *Saṅgha* Assembly (NSA) contested the election under a newly formed all-monk political party, the Jathika Hela Urumaya (National Sinhala Heritage Party). They were quite successful and nine Buddhist monks were elected to Parliament.

Another disastrous event, which affected the lives and economy of Sri Lanka, was the Tsunami. The tidal waves in the morning of 26 December 2004 took the lives of 31,000 Sri Lankans from Sinhala, Tamil and Muslim communities and displaced millions. The social work and relief efforts of Buddhist monks along the coastal area stretching over several hundred miles were a blessing in healing the Tsunami victims. Temples became temporary residences for Buddhists and non-Buddhists. Once again, in the context of Tsunami relief efforts and rebuilding, Buddhist monks' role and influence as healers became prominent in the affected communities.

Apart from Tsunami relief efforts, the active political involvements, in particular with regard to the Jathika Hela Urumaya (JHU), are extremely significant events, which have repercussions on ethnic tensions. It is worth exploring why a section of Buddhist monks decided to contest the general election. One of their justifications in contesting the elections is that lay politicians have been unjust and corrupt and failed to address religious and national issues concerning Buddhists and Sinhalese. As religious practitioners, they see the necessity and importance of becoming involved in politics. Their interference in secular politics has significant implications on the role of the *saṅgha* as a Buddhist institution in Sri Lanka. The impetus for their active political involvement lies in the unhealthy social and religious climate created by two decades of ethnic conflict.

In Sri Lanka, on various occasions, religious groups have invoked religion to justify their actions in relation to the ethnic problem. Also religious issues in Sri Lanka have made the political life of the country difficult. What some proponents identify as 'unethical' conversions carried out by home churches and evangelical groups has created a religiously tense atmosphere. Interreligious dialogue and cooperation has broken down as a result. The monks of the JHU contested the election by promising to take action against those who actively convert Buddhists and Hindus to Christianity. As a result, there are two draft bills in the Sri Lankan Parliament, one sponsored by the Sri Lankan Government and the other by the JHU (*Prohibition of Forcible Conversion of Religion (Private Member's Bill) by Omalpe Sobhita* 2004) to deal with the issue of unethical conversions.[17]

People are inclined to recognize now that the world's religious traditions are involved in complex ethnic and religious conflicts. The solution to most of these conflicts can be detected within the living traditions. In that process, the observers have to recognize the religion's potential for both making peace and in creating immense violence. A conference dedicated to the exploration of 'Religion in Diplomacy and Peacemaking' was held in Oslo on 7–9 February 2005.[18] Scholars and practitioners of all major religious traditions whose members were affected by worldwide conflicts had been invited to the conference. Persons who are actively involved in reconciliation efforts discussed their frustrations as well as successes in peace efforts around the world.

In *Violence in God's Name* (2003), Oliver McTernan has drawn the attention to the power of religion in aggravating conflicts around the world. They are cases where religious practitioners misuse religion by creating violence going against their fundamental religious convictions and textual canons. Rather than creating peace, religious symbols, institutions and doctrines are manipulated to perpetuate violence. On 9 February 2005, at the workshop of Religion in Diplomacy and Peacemaking conference Oliver McTernan clearly indicated that Tamil terrorists are clearly with the Roman Catholic Church. At the Bath Conference one Tamil female participant clearly indicated that the LTTE leader Velupillai Prabhakaran is Roman Catholic.[19] These connections are not coincidental. The LTTE is not purely a secular, liberation movement, as it is perceived to be. It could have hidden religious affiliations and agendas. If similar religious factors and religiously charged events are occurring in Sri Lanka, they have to be taken into account.

The current ethnic conflict in Sri Lanka thus cannot be simply characterized as a 'Sinhala Buddhist war with Tamil Hindus'. It is much more complex and a wide range of issues are at stake. Recent events clearly indicate that the 'religion' and 'religious concerns' of the ethnic groups are also contributing factors in the Sri Lankan conflict. These implicit and explicit religious interests need to be investigated rather than just accusing Buddhist extremists and chauvinists. At the same time, however, the conflict cannot be merely explained on materialistic terms by reducing it to a conflict arising from poor economic conditions.[20] One can argue that its roots lie in the failure of a majority Parliamentary structure to give minorities a say over their own affairs. Into this issue has entered the 'religious', particularly the 'holy land' myth of the *dhammadīpa* invoked by some who are eager to assert their religious identity.

In finding a viable solution to the Sri Lankan problem, the religious resources found within the Buddhist tradition should be explored. At the same time, one should be aware of the cases where some marginal but influential groups abuse religion to support their violent activities by using religious texts to support defensive violence against other ethnic and religious groups. It is important to discover resources within the Buddhist tradition for resolving the conflict in Sri Lanka; it is also equally important to identify potential hurdles for peacemaking. The areas where Buddhism can create problems for diplomacy and peacemaking with Tamils should be explored and analysed. For example, already scholars have argued that the notion of the island of *dhamma* has contributed to a *Sinhalatva* notion where Sinhala nationalism flourishes at the cost of minorities. Dilemmas within the Buddhist tradition in relation to the Sri Lankan polity, the constitutional status of Buddhism, and the issues related to nationalism and fundamentalist trends need further exploration.

Bath conference on 'Buddhism and conflict in Sri Lanka'

In the spring of 2001, The Buddhist Federation of Norway requested The United Kingdom Association for Buddhist Studies (UKABS) to organize a three-day conference on Buddhism and Conflict in Sri Lanka. As a result, the international conference on 'Buddhism and Conflict in Sri Lanka' was held at Bath Spa University, 28–30 June 2002. The purpose of the Bath conference was to explore the potential of using Buddhist teachings, practices, monks and institutions in creating peace, harmony and reconciliation in Sri Lanka.

An important objective of the conference was to examine the way Buddhist communities in Sri Lanka were actually coping with the issues of promoting peace and reconciliation. At the very outset, the participation of Buddhist monks and Sri Lankan Buddhist scholars was desired in the hope of engaging them in an intellectual exchange with Western Buddhist scholars in an academic setting.

The conference papers were organized under four headings: (i) Material from the Pāli Canon relevant to an analysis of the place of armed conflict, human rights, and conflict resolution, (ii) The Pāli chronicles, and the way that they have been used by some parties to the conflict, (iii) The roots of the Sinhalese-Tamil conflict in as much as these indicate factors which may aid a solution, and (iv) Voices, perspectives, fears and aspirations that feed into the conflict.

The conference included 15 presentations and 15 responses. Sixty-nine participants attended the Bath conference: 22 scholars from the United Kingdom, 11 Buddhist monks from Sri Lanka (9 had arrived in England for the conference alone), 9 lay scholars from Sri Lanka, 9 scholars from the United States of America, 5 scholars from Germany, 2 scholars from Sweden and 1 scholar from Denmark. There were 24 Sinhalese, 3 Tamils and 10 women in the audience. Six Buddhist monks, 1 Tamil scholar and 6 Sinhala scholars gave presentations. Five of the respondents were Sri Lankans.

A Sinhala version of the conference proceedings entitled *Budusamaya saha Śrī Laṅkāvē Janavārgika Ghaṭṭanaya* (Deegalle 2003) was published and released on 20 December 2002 at Mahaveli Centre, Colombo. It contained 19 chapters including a summary of the discussion at the conference. An English edition of the conference proceedings containing 19 papers (12 paper presentations and 7 responses) were published in the *Journal of Buddhist Ethics* (vol. 10) under the title 'Bath Conference on "Buddhism and Conflict in Sri Lanka"' (Deegalle 2003). A selection of revised versions of those papers is included in this volume of essays.

This collection of essays

Prominent scholars in the fields of Anthropology, History, Buddhist Studies, Pāli and Religious Studies use several interdisciplinary approaches in uncovering the multi-faceted aspects of the current ethnic problem in Sri Lanka and the negative impact of violence on the Buddhist institutions and practices. The volume evaluates the role of Buddhists and their institutions in creating peace as well as in aggravating the ethnic tensions. It puts forward a critical analysis of the religious conditions contributing to continuing violence. It attempts to discern any relationships that Theravāda Buddhism has to current atrocities. One of the themes explored extensively is the notion of *ahiṃsā* (non-violence) and the way the concept of peace can be cultivated for reconciliation by employing resources found within the Buddhist tradition.

This volume presents a strong argument with regard to Buddhist involvement in the ethnic conflict. Leading experts maintain that the conflict in Sri Lanka cannot be simply characterized as a Buddhist war against Tamils but a civil war in which the Sri Lankan government forces are involved in combating Tamil terrorists. Rather than purely Buddhist or Hindu religious distinctions contributing to the problem directly, the religious involvement in the conflict is diverse and complex since the other two non-Asian world religions also play a role as a religious agency. Inefficient, corrupt and dated political structures, linguistic, ethnic and religious concerns and socio-economic factors such as poor economic conditions are the roots of the present ethnic problem that aggravate misunderstandings leading to political and communal tensions.

The volume aims to challenge those who use Buddhism to justify violence. It recognizes that at least indirectly certain religious factors on both sides of the conflict – whether it is a cultural version of Theravāda Buddhism from the Sinhala majority side or Roman Catholicism from sections of the Tamil minority rebel side[21] – have contributed to the ethnic conflict in Sri Lanka by intensifying misunderstandings and misperceptions of potential threats to the Buddhist tradition.

The role of the *saṅgha* in the peacebuilding process is an important concern of this volume. Several contributions have focused on the *saṅgha*'s role in creating peace. Some recent publications have maintained that the *saṅgha*'s exclusivist worldview narrowly defined with emphasis on the Sinhala language, Sinhala nation and Buddhism is largely responsible for non-accommodation and discrimination against the ethnic and religious minorities. They see the *saṅgha*'s interference in the affairs of the state after Independence as an important reason that led groups such as the LTTE to take up arms against Buddhists and the Sri Lankan government. Several contributors challenge this broad generalization on the role of the *saṅgha* in the ethnic conflict.

Contributions in this volume

This volume includes eight contributions (4, 5, 6, 7, 9, 11, 13, 14) presented at the 'Buddhism and Conflict in Sri Lanka' conference held at Bath Spa University (28–30 June 2002) and subsequently, published in the *Journal of Buddhist Ethics* (vol. 10, 2003) and revised for this volume. Seven new essays (2, 3, 8, 10, 12, 15) have been added to cover a wide range of perspectives and to tackle the complex issue of Buddhism and violence in Sri Lanka from more than one perspective.

Chapter 2 by Richard Gombrich presents an impartial view on the civil war in Sri Lanka by identifying important phases that relate to some aspects of Buddhist tradition. It raises the question whether there is a fundamentalism in Sri Lanka. It argues that Sinhala Buddhists are not fundamentalists. It also stresses that Buddhism is not responsible for the civil war.

In Chapter 3, John Clifford Holt examines the way Hinduism inscribed its influences on Sri Lankan Buddhist beliefs and practices. Focusing on the period between the twelfth and sixteenth centuries, it explains how and when Hinduism made a significant impact on Sinhala religious culture. It illustrates the integration of Hindu constructs such as the incorporation of Viṣṇu within the popular Buddhist pantheon. It maintains that Hindu deities were eventually assimilated – they were 'Buddhacized' and 'Sinhalized.' This assimilation process, however, did not go through smoothly without protest from Sinhala Buddhists. Nevertheless, it highlights how elements of Hinduism were absorbed meaningfully into Sinhala Buddhist culture.

Chapter 4 by Mahinda Palihawadana examines the Buddha's teachings on conflict and its causes. It identifies deep psychological roots that manifest as social and political problems. It maintains that conflicts are rooted in flawed perception, which includes prejudices and unhealthy mental propensities. It presents a number of resources found within Buddhist doctrine that can be used effectively in understanding conflicts and in resolving them in a realistic manner.

Chapter 5 by P.D. Premasiri attempts to answer the question how war could be advocated by practising Buddhists. It argues strongly and rightly that there is no room for the concept of a righteous war in the canonical Buddhist teachings. Nevertheless, Buddhist discourses recognize that war is sometimes a necessary evil. But participation in any kind of violence is absolutely against the pursuit of *nibbāna*. Buddhists should struggle to win over those who are cruel and violent through kindness and compassion. War cannot be prevented where the roots of evil, greed, hatred and delusion determine human behaviour and interaction. It argues that Buddhist teachings explain war in a realistic manner by recommending a sense of morality and a concern for justice and fair play in situations where even pious Buddhists are compelled to fight wars.

In Chapter 6, Peter Schalk examines in detail the historical development of the concept of the 'Island of the *Dhamma*'. It argues that though there is no canonical or chronicle support for the *Dhammadīpa* concept it has often been used to construct the notion that Sri Lanka belongs to the Sinhalese. He maintains that the single mention of the *Dhammadīpa* in the *Mahāvaṃsa* (1:84) can be alternatively translated as 'light' rather than as a reference to an 'island'. He further argues that although *Dhammadīpa* is a *tatpuruṣa* compound, some have taken it as a *bahuvrīhi* compound and subsequently interpreted it as a reference to the Sinhalese. According to him, it refers to Buddhists who lived virtuously having *dhamma*. Schalk points out that the twentieth-century transformations of the *Dhammadīpa* concept by Dharmapāla and his *Sinhalatva* followers have become a continuing obstacle for creating peace in Sri Lanka.

Chapter 7 by Alvappillai Veluppillai explores the social and political difficulties that Tamils have faced after Independence in 1948. It maintains that today Tamils have lost hope in negotiations and Sinhalese have not tried genuinely to build trust among the Tamils. Differing from the other contributors of this volume, Veluppillai characterizes the civil war in Sri Lanka as a Buddhist–Tamil war rather than a Sinhala–Tamil war. He criticizes the two major political parties, the post-Independence political policies and the role that *saṅgha* has played in the conflict. With respect to creating peace in Sri Lanka, he privileges the LTTE against other Tamil groups and discusses the importance of the LTTE in political negotiations in finding a solution to the crisis.

In Chapter 8, Ananda Wickremeratne argues that none of the stereotypes survive historical evaluation in the light of comparisons with other countries, especially with regard to the putative paradox of Buddhism and violence.

He identifies as stereotypes the views that the Sinhala Buddhists were mindlessly and irrationally enamored with pseudo-historical myths, obsessed with the past, untouched by the sophistications of nationalism, were exclusive rather than inclusive, and maintained a spurious symbiosis between church and state. Wickremeratne points out that some Western scholars, being unable to access indigenous primary sources in their original languages, have repeated without discrimination the threadbare shibboleths of local scholarship. His dialogue with modern heads of state and prominent Buddhist monks show how secular thinking plays a part in decision-making. The essay concludes with the observation that the projected amalgamation of the Northern and Eastern provinces leads not to resolution, but to the perpetuation of the conflict.

Chapter 9 by Gananath Obeyesekere shows the necessity of spiritual revival and religious transformation as it was at the time of Colonel Henry Steel Olcott (1832–1907) and Anagārika Dharmapāla (1864–1933) by asserting that during the past three decades both the JVP and the successive governments in Sri Lanka have contributed to the escalation of violence. It stresses the importance of placing Buddhist nationalism in the context of the LTTE's provocations. The essay discusses in detail the obligatory pilgrimage around the sacred space of Mahiyaṅgana and demonstrates convincingly that the term *sāsana* has multiple meanings in its usage in Sri Lanka. Focusing primarily on the manner in which Buddhism was instituted, it documents how primordialism in identity formation was created and sustained. It draws attention to the relationships that existed between the Sinhalas and Väddās on the one hand and Sinhalas and Tamils on the other hand.

In Chapter 10, Bardwell Smith examines some of the ingredients of sustained strife as they affect Sri Lanka's conflictive forms of ethnic, cultural, economic, and religious identities. It focuses on the perplexing nature of what constitutes 'identity' in a society in which communalism becomes the reflexive means by which personal and social identity is shaped. When cast in these terms, identity becomes inflammatory, deeply centripetal, creating ever-smaller circles of exclusivity. The task of how to engage in more inclusive, self-critical sorts of identity is always difficult, often dangerous, yet remains imperative. While most people possess multiple senses of identity, these coexist harmoniously only when others are included within one's more generous visions of identity. How to envision and coexist within a more expansive reality of interdependence is the ongoing societal task. The problem lies in relating to others in ways that are not mutually destructive.

Chapter 11 by R.A.L.H. Gunawardana identifies the absence of national agreement as the main obstacle for creating peace in Sri Lanka. It maintains that the issue of language is extremely important in the current ethnic problem. The Government's inability to grant an equal status to the Tamil language has prompted and aggravated the current ethnic problem. It asserts the necessity of multi-linguality as well as measures to establish trust among the Tamils. It points out that the LTTE have resorted to violence and provocation to establish an

Eelam. In multi-ethnic Sri Lanka, it has been difficult to materialize the concept of 'homeland' that the LTTE proposes and the aspiration for a separate state has become a double-edged sword. What multi-ethnic and multi-religious Sri Lanka needs is neither a unitary system nor separatism but a penetrating wisdom that can foresee and identify things that fit into particular historical occasions. The essay also discusses the important role that Buddhist monks can play in the peace process.

In Chapter 12, Chandra R. de Silva argues that a durable peace in Sri Lanka needs the support of Buddhist monks who are held in respect by the Buddhist majority but nevertheless perceive themselves and Buddhism as marginalized. Many of them are suspicious of political devolution because of their vision of the past associated with political division and the destruction of Buddhism in Sri Lanka. Their lived experience is one of struggling to combat fissiparous tendencies within the *saṅgha* and this makes many of them cautious about weakening the centre. It also argues that if the members of the *saṅgha* are to play a meaningful role in the peace process and in the contemporary context, more attention needs to be paid to providing the monastics with a broader education.

Chapter 13 by Asanga Tilakaratne evaluates two recent monographs by Seneviratne (1999) and Bartholomeuz and De Silva (2001) on the role of the Buddhist monks. It points out that the *saṅgha* has played a key role in the evolution of the ethnic conflict and that there are many areas in the *saṅgha*'s life that need to be rethought in the context of current crisis. It also challenges some of the broad generalizations made regarding the role of the *saṅgha*. The essay questions the casual explanation often given as a justification of the current ethnic conflict. It also maintains that the manner of the *saṅgha*'s involvement in the process needs to be seen not necessarily as an instance of Sinhala Buddhist chauvinism but as one of their grappling with an inner moral problem of their concern for the country and the people on whom they depend for the protection of their religion, on the one hand, and the challenges of multi-ethnicity and multi-religiousness, on the other.

In Chapter 14, George Bond examines the effectiveness of Sarvōdaya's discourse on peace and social revolution. Sarvōdaya identifies the non-violent revolution as the basis for long-term peace. By self-transformation, it expects to create peace and thus emphasizes the importance of grass-root communities focused on villages. To counter the structural violence at the root of the present social order, Sarvōdaya's peace movement stresses the need to restore the human spirit by adopting a bottom-up approach. The philosophy of peace that Sarvōdaya advocates derives from Buddhist doctrines such as the Four Noble Truths. In addition, Sarvōdaya's peace plan has blended Buddhist elements with Gandhian idealism and Victorian spirituality.

Chapter 15 by Mahinda Deegalle examines the most recent radical development that occurred in the Sri Lankan Theravāda Buddhist *saṅgha*. Marking a historic moment, in April 2004, nine Buddhist monks of the newly formed political party – JHU (National Sinhala Heritage) – were elected to the Sri Lankan Parliament. The Chapter discusses the history of Buddhist monks' involvement in politics and analyses the political and religious events that led Buddhist monks of the JHU to contest the election and become professional politicians. It contextualizes the history, development and problems of the JHU by identifying its predecessors, in particular, the Sihala Urumaya. It explains Buddhist fears of potential threats to Buddhism in the context of two decades of ethnic turmoil and 'unethical conversions' and shows the impact of the controversial death of Gangoḍavila Sōma for the birth of the JHU. In understanding the political ambitions and real intentions of the Buddhist monks who are now actively involved in Sri Lankan politics, Deegalle examines the JHU's religious rhetoric of establishing a 'righteous state' (*dharmarājya*) as a solution to the corruptions in the present political system, increased terrorist violence that spreads ethnic atrocities and the alleged 'unethical conversions' of the evangelical Christians.

Limitations and way forward

In no sense does this volume pretend to be comprehensive and all-encompassing in the examination of the current ethnic conflict and violence in Sri Lanka. There are limitations both in its scope and in its available space to include more contributions covering unexplored areas of the problem. This book has primarily concentrated on the Buddhist and Sinhala side of the problem and briefly touched upon some aspects of Tamil grievances in the problem. The current Sri Lankan ethnic problem is complex and one cannot advance a one-sided causal explanation of the problem. To cover fully the multifaceted aspects of the problem, several volumes like this are necessary.

The strength of this book is that it sheds some light upon the religious factors that are contributing to the conflict and violence. At present, religious concerns play a significant role in the problem and understanding them fully is crucial in searching for a resolution. Religious concerns and religious agents have both positive and negative contributions. While recognizing the indirect contributions of some Buddhists in aggravating the problem, the volume also identifies resources found within the Buddhist tradition that are useful in creating peace in Sri Lanka. Though this volume does not pretend to cover all the minute details of the current Sri Lankan ethnic conflict and its relationship to Buddhists and their institutions, it provides a plethora of narratives and contexts to enable one to fully comprehend the limitations of the stereotypical characterization of Sri Lankan problem as purely a Buddhist or Sinhala problem.

There are several dominant religious and ethnic agents in the current ethnic conflict. Most studies of Sri Lanka have undermined the diversity of religious agency in the conflict by overemphasizing some forms of Sinhala Buddhist extremism as rhetoric of justification for the conflict. There is no doubt that those extremist elements in Tamil communities where the LTTE as the self-appointed sole representative of Tamils have taken the leading role in creating a violent climate throughout the island by their terrorist campaigns stretching over two decades. A critical treatment of the LTTE that outlines its secular Marxist ethos and religious leadership needs full investigation. A comprehensive understanding of the Tamil extremist contribution to the problem is essential for reconciliation and a proper diagnosis of the problem. This volume, however, has not undertaken that critical task, which is left to future scholarship to embark on.

The Muslim minority, though small compared to the Tamil population, is also not a neutral agency. In the Eastern Province a substantial number of the population is Muslim. There are genuine fears of potential conflicts in future when power-sharing and devolution is implemented as a solution to the conflict by privileging the LTTE and by recognizing its demands and its supremacy over other ethnic and religious minorities. The likelihood of possible fundamentalist Muslim reactions is apparent in the context of likely Tamil oppression in the region when the Eastern and Northern Provinces are united as one governing body. Muslim responses to the ethnic problem in the midst of Sinhala and Tamil communities need examination.

In the last decade, accusations and allegations against Christian evangelists have multiplied in Sri Lanka. A decade ago it was rare to find any details on religious conversions in the newspapers. Today there are plenty of reports and grievances on 'unethical' conversions. Similar accusations of unethical conversions can be found in Iraq, Israel, Indonesia, Pakistan and India and some of these countries have sought the power of the legislature to overcome religious threats. In Sri Lanka, evangelists are accused of using the ethnic turmoil and poor economic conditions of the Buddhist and Hindu communities as fertile ground for recruiting new members. The newly arrived evangelical groups from the West and South Korea were taking advantage of the war situation and were ready to exploit the war victims. Their predominant concern is the growth of their numbers; they are less concerned with the welfare of either Sinhala or Tamil communities. Largely, the evangelical groups are culturally insensitive to local norms and practices of the Buddhist and Hindu traditions; they appear to abuse people's good will, trust, tolerance and traditional hospitality. Now, allegations of 'unethical conversions' from official and unofficial channels have emerged from both Buddhist and Hindu quarters.[22] There are also several cases on these matters in Sri Lankan courts. Foreign-funded, current evangelical Christian missionary activities in Sri Lanka have created a religiously tense and unhealthy environment. As mentioned, as a result of public demand on the issue of unethical conversions, there are two bills against the alleged 'unethical conversions' in the Sri Lankan Parliament waiting for approval. All these recent events demonstrate that religious concerns and fears of losing one's religious identity to encroaching non-governmental organizations have become contributing ingredients to the already fragile peace process and gruesome ethnic conflict. Proper comprehension and contextualization of these religious trends in the Sri Lankan ethnic conflict is an essential area that future scholarship can undertake.

Notes

1 Recently an Indian journalist, M.R. Narayan Swamy (2004) has published a biography of the LTTE leader, Velupillai Prabhakaran (b. 1954). Prabhakaran formed the LTTE in the 1970s to create a separate state in the Northern and Eastern Provinces of Sri Lanka called Eelam (T. Īḷam). By the mid 1980s, the LTTE was able to dominate other militant Tamil groups and now claim to be the authentic voice of the Tamil people by successfully eliminating dissenting voices among the Tamils through assassinations of democratic Tamil political leadership.

2 Sri Lankan Buddhists appreciate very highly ideas of religious tolerance and harmony found in the Aśokan inscriptions. For example, see the elaboration of these ideals in Walpola Rahula's *What the Buddha Taught* (1959: 4–5). In designing a Buddhist leadership based on Buddhist principles, several have invoked Aśoka's ideas of righteous ruler (Bond 1998: 42–43). One could observe this tendency even in the JHU 12 principles of the 'righteous state' (item no. iv) that is discussed in Chapter 15.

3 Eelam (T. Īlam) is a Tamil name, meaning 'Sinhala', used as a reference to Sri Lanka. Currently, it is a popular word that generates fear for the Sinhalese since it denotes still pending separate homeland for Tamils covering the areas of the North and Northeast regions of Sri Lanka.

4 See Tambiah (1992: 80–94) and Amunugama (1991) for contextualized explanations of the Mavubima Surakīme Vyāpāraya (Movement for the protection of the motherland (MSV).

5 See Chapter 15 of this volume for more explanations of Sihala Urumaya and its relationship with the monk politicians of the Jathika Hela Urumaya in the context of ethnic conflict in Sri Lanka.

6 In general, the Marxist JVP has been critical of peace negotiations. The JVP vehemently criticized the permanent ceasefire agreement signed in 2002 between the Sri Lankan government and the Liberation Tigers of Tamil Eelam as surrender to the LTTE. In the two-day Parliamentary debate on truce held on 4–5 March 2002, the JVP parliamentarian Mr Anura Dissanayake said that with the signing of the agreement with the government, the LTTE had laid a foundation to establish a separate state in the island. http://www.tamilnet.com/art.html?catid=13&artid=6753 (accessed on 1 October 2005). Since the time of signing the Indo-Sri Lanka Accord on 29 July 1987, the JVP has attacked the peace process. The JVP affiliated monks of the National Bhikṣu Front (NBF) have carried out several demonstrations against the peace process. When the ceasefire agreement was signed in February 2002, the NBF joined the protesters against a Norwegian mediated peace. When Norwegian ceasefire monitors prepared to meet Prabhakaran, the reclusive leader of the LTTE, in a letter to Norwegian Ambassador Jon Westborg, the NBF insisted: 'We earnestly request of you to leave the country instead of interfering in our internal affairs.'

7 In a newspaper article in *Daily Times* that portrays the JHU and Buddhist monks in negative light, on 15 March 2005, Simon Gardner reported that the leader of JHU, Venerable Medhānanda advises to crush the LTTE rebels rather than have peace negotiations. He insisted:

> Affairs of the state and religion are two different things. Buddhism does not teach us to keep quiet and pretend to be blind to all the injustices in the world... We follow the middle path, that's what the Buddha wanted us to do. We are not fundamentalists or extremists, we tread a path of non-violence... But that does not mean Buddhists can't act in self defence... If the peace talks are not yielding the desired results and the next best thing to do is to go back to war.

8 For an analysis of such denials of the ethnic problem by Sihala Urumaya, see my forthcoming paper entitled 'Buddhist Monks as Foot Soldiers in Political Activism: War and Peace in Contemporary Sri Lanka'. In *Can Faiths Make Peace? Holy Wars and the Resolution of Religious Conflicts from Historical and Contemporary Perspectives*, edited by Philip Broadhand and Damien Keown, London: I.B. Tauris, 2006, pp. 135–53 (Deegalle forthcoming).

9 On the occasion when the Norwegian Special Peace Envoy Erik Solheim paid a courtesy call to Venerable Buddharakkhita's residence on Sunday 27 February 2005, the Chief Patriarch expressed this view to the BBC Sinhala programme *Sandeshaya* reporter on 28 February 2005. See also *Daily News* for Mr Solheim's visit to the Mahānāyaka of Malvatta Chapter of Siyam Nikāya. http://www.dailynews.lk/2005/02/28 (accessed on 1 October 2005). This is the first time such a visit is made to the prominent Buddhist clergy in Sri Lanka since the beginning of peace talks. Norway has now realized the importance of consulting Buddhist religious leadership in finding a solution to the ethnic problem. Such religious interactions are also recommended by the recent report published by the International Peace Research Institute, Oslo (PRIO): 'Norway would benefit from building up networks with Buddhist actors and becoming more visible on the "Buddhist scene" through participation in public ritual events' (Frydenlund 2005: 34). Mr Solheim himself stated,

> Lasting Peace in Sri Lanka is our fervent hope. What we hope is peace with dignity for the survival of all ethnic groups in Sri Lanka... We are always devoted to forge ahead the peace process in Sri Lanka and committed to listen to the Buddhist clergy and accept their advice and guidance in our mission.
> (http://www.dailynews.lk/2005/02/28/new02.html)

10 At the Bath Conference, now the JHU Parliamentarian, Venerable Athuraliyē Rathana (2003) attempted to express his view on the artificiality of the notion of ethnic conflict in following words:

> Today there is a discourse about 'peace' in Sri Lanka. It is an extremely artificial exercise and one that is clearly being orchestrated under the threat of terrorist attack. Our responsibility is to ensure that the *jathika sammuti* is given voice and the lie of the 'ethnic conflict *sammuti*' is exposed.

11 For example, Tambiah's book (1992) asks: 'How can committed Buddhist monks and lay persons in Sri Lanka today actively take part in the fierce political violence of the Sinhalese against the Tamils?'

12 For more detailed elaborations on violence and its potential justifications within the Sri Lankan tradition, see my article 'Is Violence Justified in Theravada?' (Deegalle 2002).

13 Here the Pāli term *daṇṣa* is translated as 'violence'. It literally means 'stick' or 'punishment'.

14 The *Dhammapada Commentary* (Carter and Palihawadana 1987: 202) makes it clear that only four are not frightened in the face of death: (i) the thoroughbred horse, (ii) the thoroughbred elephant, (iii) the thoroughbred bull, and (iv) the influx-extinct [Arahant]. An *arahant* does not fear death because of the very fact that the very notion of 'self' is extinct in him.

15 The issue of a Buddhist monk becoming a Member of Parliament became a heated debate in the newspapers. Amarasiri Weeratne (2001), writing to the *Island*, argued

> Rev. Samita has made a serious error of judgement. He has taken the gospel according to Rev. Walpola Rahula as his scripture and religious text. It is a litany of apostasies and corrupt practices of erratic monks of a by-gone age.

16 The PA led by President Chandrika Kumaratunga is a coalition government of several political parties who won the elections of 1994 and 2000. The coalition led by the

Sri Lanka Freedom Party (f. 1951) included the Laṅkā Sama Samāja Party (f. 1935), Communist Party of Sri Lanka (f. 1943) and Mahajana Eksath Peramuna (f. 1956). Although Sri Lanka Muslim Congress (f. 1981), a minority party, was in the coalition, it withdrew in 2001.

17 See http://lankaliberty.com/bills.html (accessed on 1 October 2005) for a private member's bill introduced by Venerable Ōmalpē Sōbhita, a member of JHU parliamentary group and the Sri Lanka government's bill introduced by the Minister of Buddhist Affairs, Ratnasiri Wickremanayake.

18 *Mapping the Terrain: Religion in Diplomacy and Peacemaking* conference was held at Holmenkollen Park Hotel Rica, Oslo on 7–9 February 2005. It was organized by the PRIO and was funded by the Norwegian Ministry of Foreign Affairs. The conference aimed at exploring the role and potential of religion in peacemaking processes. It gathered over 100 individuals engaged in peacemaking efforts. http://www.prio.no/page/Project_detail/News_details/9244/46152.html (accessed on 1 October 2005).

19 On 28 June 2002, the discussion in the afternoon of the first day of the Bath Conference.

20 In the Bath Conference several speakers maintained that the root cause of the Sri Lankan conflict is the poor economic conditions. Venerable Māduḷuvāvē Sōbhita (2003), for example, stated

> the current conflict has economic issues as its main cause. It is therefore incumbent on everybody to come together and make a concerted effort to remove this cause, which has been the biggest source of irritation to all communities. Economic development will give everyone a sense of expectation.

21 In her unpublished paper 'Roots of Resistance: The Role of Jaffna Catholic Schools in the Formation of the Tamil Youth Organization in Sri Lanka, 1960–72,' Agnes P. Thambynayagam (n.d.) claims that in the formative period the roots of the LTTE lies in the responses of Tamil secondary school students in the Roman Catholic schools in Jaffna in the 1960s, where the Tamil Youth Movement emerged. She writes:

> Jaffna town alone had ten Roman Catholic schools; eight of them were now government schools and two were privately run . . . Many intelligent and articulate young students from the two privately run Catholic schools in Jaffna [St Patrick's College and Holy Family Convent], now entering adulthood, questioned the government's actions of the past two years. The deep sense of resentment gave birth at St. Patrick's College to the first organized non-violent movement, the *Eela Thamil Elanger Eyakam* (ETEE) – Eelam Tamil Youth Movement . . . One of Liberation Tigers Tamil Eelam's (LTTEs) central committee members, Mr. Thilakar (alias Christy John), and late Mr. P. Sivakumaran [the first Tamil youth to end one's life by biting a cyanide capsule to avoid capture, which became the hallmark of the LTTE] are from this initial movement . . . the movement changed its name in 1970 to *Mannavar Parravai* . . . In October 1972 the first underground movement was formed under the name of Tamil Tigers . . . . In May 1976, the Tamil Tigers changed its name to the Liberation Tigers of Tamil Eelam (LTTE) . . . *Eela Thamil Elangar Eyakam*, which began as a non-violent student movement had transformed itself into a formidable disciplined army.
>
> (pp. 7–9)

22 Here I am reminded of the fact that the former Hindu Affairs Minister T. Maheswaran had challenged the former Prime Minister Ranil Wickremasinghe that he would resign if 'the government did not bring in an act to prevent Hindus being converted to Christianity before the 31st of December' 2003. http://www.spur.asn.au/News_2003_Dec_31.htm (accessed on 1 October 2005).

2

IS THE SRI LANKAN WAR A BUDDHIST FUNDAMENTALISM?

Richard Gombrich

Sri Lanka is a secular state whose constitution recognizes Buddhism as the foremost religion while recognizing the equality of other religions.[1] At least since 1983, Sri Lanka has been embroiled in a civil war. Though the civil war has been far more complex, the protagonists fighting today are on the one hand the state, in which the Sinhalese form an ethnic majority and Buddhists the religious majority, and on the other a Tamil organisation called the Liberation Tigers of Tamil Eelam (LTTE), who are fighting for a separate Tamil state. Accordingly, the questions, which will principally concern me, are the following:

1 Is Buddhism, as distinct from Buddhists, in any sense responsible for this war?
2 Does their religious tradition predispose Buddhists to being less violent than other people?
3 What meaning can reasonably be attached to the concept of 'Buddhist fundamentalism', and does it play any part in the current situation?

Background of the Sri Lankan civil war

Let me begin with the linguistic and religious composition of Sri Lanka. According to the census of 1981, Sri Lankan population was under 19 million. Of these, about 74% are defined, primarily by their mother tongue, as Sinhalese, 18.1% as Tamil, and 7% as Muslim. Most of the Muslims have a form of Tamil as their first language, though the majority of them live in predominantly Sinhala-speaking areas. Dividing the population by religion: 69.3% are Buddhist, 15.5% Hindu, 7.6% Christian (mostly Roman Catholic), and 7% Muslim. Almost all of the Buddhists are Sinhalese and all the Hindus are Tamils. The Christians, both Roman Catholics and Protestants, are fairly equally divided between Sinhalas and Tamils.

Though this paper is about Buddhists, it is necessary to explain that while the Sinhalese Buddhists form a population homogenous in terms of language and culture, the Tamils do not. The Tamil population divides into two clear-cut groups, which used to be known in English as 'Ceylon Tamils' and 'Indian Tamils'.

The latter, about a third of the total, are descended from immigrant labour brought from India, mostly in the second half of the nineteenth century to work in the estates. Soon after Independence from Britain, which took place in 1948, the Ceylon Tamils voted in Parliament with the Sinhalese to disenfranchise the Indian Tamils. Since then the two groups have been politically at odds, and the leader of the Indian Tamils has usually been a member of the cabinet, whichever Sinhalese party was in power. The Indian Tamils have played no part in the civil war of the last two decades.

Only 20 miles of water, the Palk Strait, divide Sri Lanka from Tamilnadu (formerly Madras State) on the Indian mainland. There are historical records to show that there have been Tamils in the northern part of Sri Lanka since before the beginning of the Christian era. There have also been Tamil invasions into Sri Lanka at many times in the past two millennia. To say that whenever there was a war one side was a 100% Tamil and the other side a 100% Sinhalese would be a gross over-simplification. However, it is a fact that at the end of the first millennium CE invasions by the Tamil Cōḷa Empire (tenth–thirteenth centuries) brought an end to the classical Sinhalese Buddhist civilisation, which had been based on Anurādhapura as its capital city for more than a millennium.

Modern Sri Lanka is divided into nine provinces. The Northern Province is centred on the town of Jaffna and is almost entirely Tamil after late 1970s. The Eastern Province, a long thin strip down the east coast of the island, has a population of one third Tamil, one third Sinhalese, and one third Muslim. Tamil separatists claim the Eastern as well as the Northern Province. Since they seem to have no political appeal to the Muslims, they are undoubtedly claiming territory in which they do not constitute a majority of the population, and this has been one of the major stumbling blocks in all negotiations. It is also important to understand that about half of the 'Ceylon Tamils', including many who have ties with Jaffna, live in the predominantly Sinhalese parts of the island, especially in Colombo and in the second largest city, Kandy, which was the late medieval Sinhalese capital and lies in the centre of the island.

Sinhalese Buddhists constitute the largest single group, though they have never voted as a single block; indeed, the two largest parties both aim primarily to represent Sinhalese Buddhist interests. While many of these interests are of course economic, issues of religion and language have played a major part in politics since Independence. The constitution at Independence effectively gave equal protection to all religions, but a new constitution in 1972 gave Buddhism pride of place, and this was repeated in the constitution of 1978, which is still in force. Tamil interests since the Federal Party (f. 1949) and its successor, the Tamil United Liberation Front (TULF), which have always been committed to democratic politics and long received electoral support from the great majority of Tamils in the Northern and Eastern Provinces, have mainly represented politically Tamil interests since the 1950s.

Both Sinhalese and Tamils accuse the other side of having started the present conflict. Politically, however, 1956 was a watershed. In that year S.W.R.D.

Bandaranaike (1899–1959) won an election on a Sinhalese nationalist programme. Thereafter for over 20 years the two largest parties, usually called the United National Party (UNP) and the Sri Lanka Freedom Party (SLFP), vied with each other in their attempts to placate, even foment, Sinhalese nationalist sentiment. Though their bark when in opposition was sometimes worse than their bite when in power, there can be no doubt that many of their policies and actions were politically inept, some of them unjust. The Tamil opposition remained firmly within the rules of parliamentary democratic politics until the beginning of the 1980s, though sporadic violence by small separatist groups began in the 1970s. In 1981 Sinhalese thugs burnt down the Jaffna Public Library, a famous institution, while the police did nothing. Nobody was ever punished for this appalling act of vandalism. Terrorist activity began to increase. At this stage there were two Tamil terrorist organisations of any importance, the LTTE and the Tamil Eelam Liberation Organization (TELO), both of them effectively operating out of Madras. Soon these organisations multiplied to four, but the LTTE had effectively eliminated their rivals by the end of the 1980s; in 1986, for example, they blew up the entire leadership of the TELO, some thirty men, in a house in Madras.

The beginning of both the civil war and large-scale Tamil terrorism can be dated to July 1983. A jeep carrying thirteen Sinhalese soldiers was blown up in a combat area in the north by a Tamil landmine, and their remains were brought to Colombo for cremation. This sparked off terrible riots in Colombo. Initially the President, J.R. Jayewardene (1906–1996), was not unhappy that Tamils should be 'taught a lesson', but he lost control of the situation and even seems to have feared for his own life. The riots spread to Kandy and other predominantly Sinhalese areas. Many Tamils were murdered and there was a vast amount of arson and looting of Tamil property.

The Sri Lankan government has prosecuted the war almost entirely by conventional military means. It still regards itself as the government of the whole island – essentially, that is what the war is about – and to substantiate this claim it has continued to pay the salaries of the Tamil administration of Jaffna and has done its best to maintain civic institutions and the machinery of government, including the health and education systems.

In 1987 the Sinhalese army were poised to take Jaffna and seemed likely to win the war by doing so. The LTTE engaged in successful black propaganda, claiming that the Sinhalese were bombing Jaffna hospital – which later proved to be entirely untrue. This facilitated the intervention of the Indians. Up to this point the Indian government had been ambivalent. Tamil separatist nationalism was sufficiently important in India to make the government turn a blind eye when the Tamils set up several military training camps, which were used also as a base from which to seek and obtain arms from overseas, for example, from Libya and the PLO, to aid the Tamil cause in Sri Lanka. On the other hand, the same Tamil separatism meant that the Indians did not want to see Sri Lanka politically divided, lest it serve as a precedent. Now, however, Indian Prime Minister Rajiv Gandhi (1944–1991) decided to intervene to halt the attack on Jaffna with an

Indian Peace-Keeping Force (IPKF). Nominally the Sri Lankan government agreed to this intervention, but it was obvious to all that this was *force majeure*. The Indians mainly favoured not the LTTE but another Tamil organisation, the Eelam People's Revolutionary Liberation Front (EPRLF).

When the Indians withdrew, two years later, their 125,000 troops had achieved less than nothing. Their intervention had provoked a Sinhalese terrorist uprising against the Sri Lankan government by the Janatha Vimukti Peramuṇa (JVP), an organisation that, like the LTTE, combined extreme chauvinism with extreme leftist ideology. The JVP began to kill members of the police and the armed forces, as well as other government employees and supporters. This provoked terrible and partially indiscriminate reprisals. Thus there were three civil wars raging on the island at the same time: the Sinhalese versus the Tamils, the JVP versus the Sinhalese government, and the LTTE versus the other Tamil militants.

The LTTE drew a line under the episode of Indian intervention by assassinating Rajiv Gandhi in 1991 when he visited Tamilnadu to give an election speech. The means of assassination was a woman who detonated a bomb strapped to her body. Since then the LTTE has successfully used the same means to assassinate President R. Premadāsa of Sri Lanka (1924–1993), two Ministers of Defence, and many other prominent opponents; recent attempt (1999) on the life of the present President, Mrs Kumaratunga, failed, though she sustained an eye injury and bystanders were killed. Mostly, however, the LTTE have killed Tamils known to be working for reconciliation, including at least 10 MPs and 2 mayors of Jaffna. This excludes their many savage attacks, often indiscriminate, on humble civilians.

No words are adequate to describe the toll in terms of suffering and loss of life. Figures for those killed and disabled in the war are not available, but certainly huge; an unofficial estimate is that 60,000 people have been killed. Amnesty International has vast dossiers on atrocities committed by both sides. The LTTE seem to take no prisoners, the Sinhalese very few. Tigers who are captured are supposed to bite on a cyanide capsule, and evidently many follow instructions. They may be wise to do so, for Sri Lankan forces evidently torture on a considerable scale. While I was preparing the first draft of this article (June 2000) I received an appeal from a British charity, The Medical Foundation for the Victims of Torture, saying: 'Last year more survivors of torture came to us from Sri Lanka than from any other country.' Though they do not make this explicit, Sri Lankan soldiers carried out that torture on Tamils.

Violence breeds violence, and despair. It is interesting to look at the suicide statistics; the picture is so dramatic that it does not matter that these figures do not differentiate between Sinhalese and Tamils. In 1960, the rate for males in Sri Lanka was 13.2 per 100,000, for females 6.0. Now, Sri Lanka has one of the highest suicide rates in the world. According to figures issued by the World Health Organisation the rate of suicide among males in 1995 was 44.7 (16.6 for females). Only a few countries, almost all of them parts of the former Soviet Union, have higher rates. For comparison, the rate for India is 11.4 (women 8.0), Thailand 5.6 (2.4), Japan 24.3 (11.5), and UK 11.0 (3.2). (Not all the figures are for the same year.)

What is the relationship between Buddhism and ethnicity?

In 1956, the year in which Mr S.W.R.D. Bandaranaike came into power, Buddhists were celebrating the 2,500th anniversary (by traditional dating) of the Buddha's passing away. However, the part of his programme, which inflamed civil discord mainly, concerned language, not religion. He had a policy known as 'Sinhala only', by which Sinhala was to become the sole official language, whereas until then it had been understood that English was to be replaced as the official language by both Sinhala and Tamil. In the mainly Sinhala-speaking areas Sinhala was to replace English as the medium of instruction in higher education and elite secondary schools. Sinhalese chauvinists obliterated the Tamil writing on some road signs. This led to the first serious Sinhala–Tamil riots in 1956 and, worse, in 1958.

In *Nations and Nationalism* (1983), Ernest Gellner has argued that as an economy modernises the issue of language assumes paramount importance for those seeking employment. White-collar jobs, both in public and in private enterprises, demand competence in the language of the state, and this in turn will be the language of the public education system. The group, which can make their language the medium of instruction, will gain a great economic advantage. In a democracy with universal suffrage that group is of course likely to be the majority. The 'Sinhala only' programme of Bandaranaike and his supporters, and their successors, was surely a textbook example to corroborate Gellner's analysis. It was also a tragic miscalculation. The local economy is far too small to flourish independently; English, the main world language, is bound to be the main avenue to white-collar employment. University graduates educated in the Sinhala medium found themselves unemployed while English 'tutories' flourished in most villages. The frustrated expectations of the Sinhala-educated led to their armed uprising in 1971, and their unemployment has only been mitigated by the demands of the war.

The hypothesis that language, not religion, has been the relevant marker for affiliation in this terrible conflict can be tested by looking at the only large religious group to include speakers of both Sinhala and Tamil: the Roman Catholics. On this, let me quote R.L. Stirrat:

> Since the early 1980s there has been an increasing gap between the church in the north of Sri Lanka and that in the Sinhala-dominated south of the country. The result has been in effect a split between a Tamil Church and a Sinhala Church. During the 1983 riots Catholics were involved alongside Buddhists in attacking Tamils, no matter what the latters' religious affiliation. In the north, the Catholic Church is closely identified with the LTTE (Liberation Tigers of Tamil Eelam) and many individual priests and members of the laity identify themselves with what they see as a war of liberation against the Sri Lankan state. The

> statements of the Catholic bishops calling for peace have little impact on the generality of the laity . . . Thus throughout even the most uniformly Catholic areas of southern Sri Lanka, people see themselves first and foremost as Sinhala; only secondly do they identify themselves as Catholics. So as far as the war is concerned, most Sinhala Catholics are much more shocked by reported LTTE atrocities against Sinhala than they are by government military attacks on churches in the north or the deaths of Tamil Catholics. Whilst a shared religious affiliation is recognized, this does not generate any strong sense of identification with the Catholics of the north.
>
> (1998: 151–52)

One should also look at the statements of the combatants themselves. Neither the LTTE nor their opponents identify them as Hindus, and indeed they appear to be largely secular. While being Buddhist is a major component of the Sinhalese identity, as we shall see later, and the Sinhalese do make allusions to their Buddhist tradition, nobody seems to have said that this war is being fought for Buddhism as against other religions: it is being fought for the Sinhalese.

Why, then, do people brand the civil war in Sri Lanka as an example of Buddhist violence? Before I answer this question, I need to say more about my own understanding of communal violence, and how I would apply it to contemporary Sri Lanka.

It is clear throughout the animal kingdom that if one starts from equilibrium, violence is not the normal means of getting one's way – it is too risky. Violence is rather used as a defence, a response to what is perceived as a threat. If I think that you are coming to kill me, or to burn my house down, I may well take violent action to forestall you. In a word, violence is commonly *pre-emptive*. And this is especially so when general law and order has broken down and one sees no chance of protection but 'to take the law into one's own hands', as the saying goes.

The pre-emptive violence of a whole group will often be a response to a perceived threat to that group. Repeatedly throughout the last few centuries of European history, groups ranging from bands of thugs to whole societies have attacked Jews because they were perceived as a threat, even though they were a weak and helpless minority. I must here ignore many aspects of the history of anti-Semitism. It remains true that because the Jews were held to have murdered Jesus, they were believed to prey on Christians whenever the opportunity arose, and fantastic conspiracy theories were widely believed, from the story that they stole children for ritual sacrifice to the forgery of the 'Protocol of the Elders of Zion', a document purporting to show that Jewish financiers were planning to take over the world. Like mediaeval witch-hunters, the persecutors felt themselves to be in imminent danger from their victims.

What is it that causes a social group to be perceived as a threat, so that it elicits a pre-emptive strike? I do not pretend that human affairs can be reduced to any kind of mathematical formula. But one cannot help noticing how many large-scale conflicts within states follow one particular pattern. This is that within a given political boundary the majority community has a minority complex, because the largest minority within that boundary has the same social identity as the community, which is in the majority next door. One finds this situation all over the place, and it is evidently very hard to deal with, not least because it tends to replicate itself. Moreover, the fears of majorities in this position may even be realistic.

In Ireland we have a double dose of this problem: the Irish Catholics who form two thirds of the population of the island are afraid of the Protestant minority in Ulster whose loyalty lies with the rest of Britain, but then within Ulster the Protestants who are in a similar majority are frightened of their Catholic minority, who identify with the Catholics in the rest of the island. I regard it as no accident that the appallingly violent break-up of the former Yugoslavia has shown this pattern again and again.

In Sri Lanka the Sinhalese account for nearly three quarters of the population, which is still well under 20 million, while the Tamils account for less than a quarter; but the Sinhalese are acutely conscious that just across a narrow stretch of water there are over 50 million Tamils. Moreover, the Sinhalese are well aware of their historical tradition, which goes back to ancient times, that they took possession of the island in the time of the Buddha, while the Tamils were later invaders and a constant threat. In fact many Tamils must have settled peaceably and relations have been good far more than they have been bad. Nevertheless, Sinhalese fears of violent interference from the Indian mainland are by no means unrealistic. There is no doubt in my mind that the Tamil Tiger insurgency could only establish itself in the early 1980s because the leaders found a safe haven in Tamilnadu (South India). They would come across to the Jaffna peninsula by boat at night to recruit and perform acts of violence. As already mentioned, the Tigers established training camps in India and collected arms from that base, none of which could have taken place without the connivance of the Indian government.

A particularly relevant concept that we owe to modern psychology is that of *displacement.* Most people nowadays know about the worker who is given a hard time at work by his boss, comes home in a foul mood, and hits his wife. Hitting the person who has made him angry would have disastrous consequences, so he displaces his anger and vents his violence on someone who cannot hit back. In choosing a victim simply by availability, such displacement is opportunistic. Not all displacement of anger is opportunistic, but very often it is.

This simple and by now well-understood mechanism is surely of enormous importance for the study of mass violence. Let me take what I think would be a little contested example. Black people in the United States suffer many indignities, and it is hardly surprising if many of them often feel angry. This applies particularly to the many blacks that are also poor and live in run-down neighbourhoods. Black people in the United States commit a lot of violent crimes; the majority of their targets, however, are other black people. Similarly, and perhaps even more tellingly, when a black neighbourhood erupts into violence, the main sufferers are the local people. The rioters do particularly target non-black local shopkeepers; but by and large their anger is vented on the most available victims, those who are defenceless and near at hand.

The riots of July 1983 marked a decisive stage in the outbreak of the Sinhala–Tamil civil war. The popular impression, not surprisingly, and the impression conveyed by the foreign media, was that the riots were an act of revenge wrought by the Sinhalese on their Tamil neighbours. From many eyewitness accounts, however, it is evident that that picture is so over-simplified as to be virtually false. True, it was the funeral of Sinhalese troops killed by Tamil Tigers, which provided the occasion for the riots. The rioting began among the Sinhalese crowd at the cemetery, who had passive support from the authorities, and it seems that an important reason why it was not brought under control was that some of the senior police officers were Tamils and were frightened of trying to take firm action against them. Moreover, it was reliably reported that during the ensuing days of arson and looting Sinhalese thugs, henchmen of nationalist politicians, used electoral registers to identify Tamil homes and property. Even so, I believe that what followed was less a race riot than an uprising of the slums against the propertied classes. Colombo contains vast areas of filth and degradation in which poor people of all communities live side by side. Like other capital cities, it also contains relatively wealthy residential areas, and in fact the wealthiest are quite central. It appears that most of the looting and arson was opportunistic. The perpetrators were Tamils as well as Sinhalese, and the victims were the wealthy, not just the Tamil wealthy. Gangs stopped and burned, or at least damaged, many cars, often without bothering to inquire whether the owner or occupier was Tamil or Sinhalese. They simply wanted to profit from a time when the forces of law and order were incapacitated to vent their rage on those they perceived as their rich oppressors. And some of the aggression was clearly displaced onto available targets.

Once we start to examine the motives of the perpetrators of violence, we find that the kinds of mass violence are not actually organised typically by governments but are full of *opportunism*, some of it perfectly rational, however nasty. When law and order breaks down so that criminal behaviour seems likely to go unpunished, people seize the opportunity not merely to give vent to their frustrations, as by burning any car within reach, but also to get rich quick or to pay off old scores. I have heard detailed accounts from impeccable sources of how, during the atmosphere of terror in 1958, Tamil landlords took the opportunity to get rid of inconvenient Tamil tenants by sending them anonymous threats which they would assume came from Sinhalese thugs. (I hope I need not say that I do not wish to single out the Tamils or any other group; I just happen to know of these cases.)

The longer the breakdown in law and order persists, the more opportunism of this rational criminal kind will flourish. If your unscrupulous neighbours have got away with sacking a shop, you may overcome your usual inhibitions and take a chance likewise. This is clearly what has been happening in many parts of the former Yugoslavia.

This leads to an important point. When criminal violence goes unpunished, a vicious circle will develop, so that more and more people are tempted – or, in the case of initial victims, even forced – into further violence. For this to happen, the breakdown of law and order need not be total. If the government allows violence against a particular social group to go unpunished, this too will suck more and more people into the vortex. In such cases of discrimination by the government, the violence may not be technically criminal, in the sense of illegal, but it is still criminal by generally accepted norms.

I suggest that violent conflict between religious groups is mostly pre-emptive and/or opportunistic in origin, and that displacement of aggression onto scapegoats and available victims often plays a part. There must be many marginal cases, as when an act by one community is seen as a provocation by the other – for Muslims to kill a cow or Hindus to carry an idol in noisy procession through a Muslim quarter will provoke the other community, and one can argue about the extent to which a violent reaction would be defensive or what I have called preemptive. Nevertheless, I think it is a valid generalisation that the kind of violence that concerns us here is rarely the result of unprovoked and premeditated aggression – except by governments or comparable political powers.

It is often thought that violence breeds war, but the reverse is more often the case. Once your government (or the LTTE, where it is in control) has told you to fight, you usually have little choice. If you refuse, you will be severely punished, perhaps even shot as a mutineer or deserter, and you will probably lose the respect of your peers and be socially ostracised. Here again, violence breeds violence.

Is Buddhism responsible for this war?

At this point I feel I am in a position to answer the first of my three questions. Buddhism is not responsible for this war. But let me turn to consider why people think that it might be. Sri Lanka has a national chronicle, written in Pāli by Buddhist monks in several instalments over the centuries. It is called the *Mahāvaṃsa*, which simply means 'Great Chronicle'. Sometimes this name is reserved for the first part of the chronicle, which was probably completed early in the sixth century CE. The *Mahāvaṃsa* regards the Sinhalese people as the rightful owners and rulers of the entire island of Sri Lanka, and identifies their fortunes with the fortunes of Theravāda Buddhism. The Buddha, the *Mahāvaṃsa* (7: 3–5) tells us, paid three flying visits to the island during his lifetime, and on his deathbed entrusted the fortunes of the island, people, and religion to the king of the gods (who in turn put the god Viṣṇu in charge). The dominant figure in this first part of the chronicle, to whose achievements many chapters are devoted, is a king called Duṭṭhagāmaṇī (Sin. Duṭugämuṇu), first century BCE. When Duṭṭhagāmaṇī was born, a Tamil king called Elāra ruled Anurādhapura, the capital of Sri Lanka. Duṭṭhagāmaṇī waged a successful war against Elāra, killed him, and ruled in great pomp and piety from Anurādhapura.

While the whole *Mahāvaṃsa* is written in a nationalistic spirit, and the Tamils frequently figure in it as enemies of the Sinhalese and *hence* of Buddhism, the most famous/notorious passage in it comes shortly after Duṭṭhagāmaṇī has won his war. His new luxurious life gives him no pleasure because something is on his mind. He asks a Buddhist monk:

> 'How can I be consoled? For I have caused the slaughter of a huge army.' The monk replies: 'That deed is no obstacle on your path to heaven. You know, O King, that you have caused the death of one and a half men. One had taken the refuges,[2] the other the five precepts as well. The rest had wrong views and bad morals; they are considered to be on the level of domestic animals. And you will illuminate Buddhism in many ways. So stop worrying, O King.'[3]
>
> (25: 108–11)

I am not aware that anyone has previously pointed out that this episode has a kind of model or precursor earlier in the same chronicle. The chronicle relates that when the great Indian Emperor Aśoka (*c.*300–232 BCE) had been converted to Buddhism he was worried about events in the principal monastery in his capital, Pāṭaliputra (modern Patna), and sent a minister to tell the monks to perform a communal ceremony together. For valid reasons the monks refused – whereupon the minister had some of them beheaded. On learning of this Aśoka was deeply concerned and asked the chief monk, Tissa Moggaliputta, whether he had incurred evil *karma* because of his employee's act. The monk reassured him: 'Without evil intention, there is no karmic result' (*Mahāvaṃsa* 5: 264).

I am not equating the two incidents or the two verdicts. No humane person today can regard the monk's statement to Duṭṭhagāmaṇī that non-Buddhists are no better than animals without disgust. The historian however must recognise that the idea that the ends may justify the means, and the further idea that the preservation of Buddhism is a supremely worthwhile end, are both quite widely found in the Buddhist tradition.

With this in mind we turn to our second question: whether their religious tradition predisposes Buddhists to being less violent – that is, in public affairs – than other people. When one looks at the historical record one begins to wonder how anyone ever came by the idea that it might. Robert Heinemann writes of mediaeval Japan:

> The state had lost its formerly strict control over the Buddhist clergy . . . many roamed through the land in armed groups plundering. Some temples raised their own armies from the so-called *Sōhei*, 'warrior monks', to protect themselves . . . and to settle their disputes with other temples. Often temples were set on fire and destroyed. At the beginning of the 12th century the most influential temples and Shinto

> shrines...would storm the capital in thousands to force the court to grant their demands. Often on these occasions the *Sōhei* would carry with them the precious litter...containing the Shinto divinity, which Buddhism equated with a Buddha or bodhisattva.
>
> (Bechert and Gombrich 1984: 221)

When the Japanese invaded Korea in the sixteenth century they killed Buddhist monks and pillaged monasteries on a massive scale. In fact, most of the masterpieces of early Korean Buddhist sculpture to survive are now in Japan.

If we turn from Far Eastern to Northern Buddhism we find that in Tibet, as recently as the first half of the twentieth century, 'Even such areas as military command were divided [between religious and secular authorities] and the army had two commanders-in-chief, one a lama, the other a civilian' (Bechert and Gombrich 1984: 250).[4]

What about the Theravāda Buddhist tradition? When the Theravāda Buddhists from the kingdom of Ava (in modern Burma) destroyed the Theravadin city and kingdom of Ayutthaya in Thailand in 1767, they sacked the monasteries and broke open all the magnificent *stūpa*s to extract the valuables there enshrined. This example, like that of the Japanese invading Korea, is a clear case of ethnicity overriding religious affiliation.

Even more remarkable is the story of how Theravāda Buddhism gained a firm footing in Burma. According to the chronicles, a Mon monk converted the king of Pagan, Anuruddha (B. Anawrahta) to Theravāda Buddhism soon after he gained the throne in 1044. He sent to Thaton, the Mon capital in southern Burma, for copies of the Pāli scriptures. When the Mon king refused to send them, Anuruddha invaded his kingdom, destroyed Thaton (in 1057), 'and brought back to Pagan not only the scriptures, but Buddhist monks, and the Thaton royal family.' (Keyes 1977: 71).

King Anuruddha's success was of cardinal importance for the history of Theravāda Buddhism. At that time Sri Lanka had been so devastated by the Cōḷa invasions that it was no longer possible to assemble the five monks necessary for holding a valid ordination ceremony. So the Sinhalese king, Vijayabāhu I (1055–1110 CE), borrowed monks from Anuruddha to restore the Sri Lankan tradition.[5]

One could multiply instances of how violent Buddhists have been in practice, but maybe one rather different example will suffice:

> According to the *Dipavaṃsa* [another ancient chronicle], the *yakkhas* [ghouls] were the original inhabitants of the island. At the time of the first visit of the Buddha they had all assembled at Mahiyaṅgana. The Buddha appeared in the sky over the assembly and afflicted the *yakkhas* with rains and cold winds. Then he addressed them to ask for a place to sit in return for dispelling these calamities. The *yakkhas* readily consent to this and beseech him to provide heat to overcome the cold. The Buddha sits on his rug and makes it diffuse heat, unbearable in its intensity,

> compelling the *yakkhas* to flee...In the variant version found in the *Mahāvaṃsa*, the *yakkhas* offer the Buddha the whole island if he would only relieve them of their distress.
>
> (Gunawardana 1978: 97)

As Gunawardana (1978: 98) points out, this story is in sharp contrast to stories in the Pāli canon in which the Buddha invariably wins over *yakkha*s by displaying tolerance and kindness towards them.

Yet again, we have to turn the question round and ask why anyone should assume that Buddhists might be less violent than others. My answer to this question has three parts: (1) non-violent, or at least moderate, elements in the Buddhist tradition; (2) the monastic/lay distinction; and (3) the fundamentalism of modern scholars.

Non-violence in the Buddhist tradition

The tradition of Buddhism in politics and public life goes back to the Indian Emperor Aśoka, who ruled over most of the sub-continent in the middle of the third century BCE. It was Aśoka who was primarily responsible for the success of Buddhism and its diffusion beyond the part of Northeast India where it began. He left a series of edicts inscribed on rocks and pillars. The most famous one of all is Rock Edict XIII. He begins this edict by telling of a war he has waged against Kāliṅga, in eastern India, in which thousands of people have been killed, deported, and caused great suffering; and he declares how deeply he regrets this. He does not wish to wage war. He says of himself:

> The beloved of the gods thinks that even if someone does him harm, he should tolerate it if it can be tolerated. The jungle-dwellers in his realm he also wishes to conciliate...but points out to them his power, so that they may be modest and not get killed.

In this remarkable edict, Aśoka is not entirely abjuring the use of violence. What he seems to promise is the renunciation of *aggressive* violence. This distinction between violent aggression and violence in self-defence seems to me to be crucial. Though they acted badly in many ways before the war began, and since it began have committed many atrocities, I think one could at least argue that the current Sinhalese war against the LTTE is not an aggressive but a defensive war. Moreover, though there is one claim in their chronicles that the Sinhalese invaded the Tamils on the mainland (under Gajabāhu (1132–1153)), this is probably mythical, and usually it has been the Tamils who have invaded Sinhalese areas, not vice versa.

The arrival of Buddhist pacifism in public affairs I believe to be quite modern. The Prime Minister of Burma, U Nu constructed in the early 1950s a 'World Peace Pagoda on the edge of Rangoon. Through the construction of this pagoda, it was believed that peace would come not only to Burma but to the whole world'

(Keyes 1977: 296). In Japan, Buddhism lost power in the late nineteenth century in the Meiji Restoration, and some of the smaller sects became pacifist; some Buddhist leaders were even imprisoned for this reason during the Second World War. Undoubtedly the most famous Buddhist pacifist in modern politics, however, is the Dalai Lama; he is the most impressive figure whose values, to say nothing of his intellect, fit him much better to be regarded as a hero in the West than would those of his predecessors. Aung San Suu Kyi in Burma has over the last decade adopted a similar stance, probably learning more from Gandhi (1869–1948) than from her native Buddhism. I do not wish to decry the courage and nobility of these pacifist figures when I point out that, unlike Aśoka, they are in any case in no position to gain anything by resorting to force.

Lay/monastic distinctions

More fundamental to this misunderstanding is the Protestant assumption that norms and values are the same for all adherents of a religion. A modern reading of what the Buddha taught would assume that his prescriptions apply to everyone. If one is more alert to historical clues, however, one sees that he expected those who really wanted to aim for salvation (*nirvāṇa*) in this life to join the *saṅgha*, the community of monks and nuns; much less was expected of the laity. To Protestants, this made no sense, and under their influence some Buddhist laity in Sri Lanka started to develop a more Protestant view of their own role. The monastic hierarchy reacted to this so strongly that in 1904 they stated, in a Memorial to King Edward VII, 'By the laws of Buddha the laity forms no part of religion.' I would call this an exaggeration, but I quote it to show what was at stake.

I have already written extensively on this topic in chapter three of my book *Theravāda Buddhism: A Social History from Ancient Benares to Modern Colombo* (Gombrich 1988). I showed there that from the outset Buddhism provided for the laity what Max Weber came to call an 'insufficiency ethic', and that it was assumed that at best the good layman would go to heaven. It was only monks and nuns who could lead such lives that they would attain *nirvāṇa*. Note that the sycophantic monk only promised even King Duṭṭhagāmaṇī heaven, not *nirvāṇa*. Moreover, I assume that the Emperor Aśoka in his edicts mentions the attainment of heaven, not of *nirvāṇa*, for much the same reason. I have shown in my book that although Buddhists in ancient times were as aware and concerned as anyone with the difference between a good king and a bad king, they considered that his royal duties, since they involved such things as condemning criminals to death, precluded the attainment of *nirvāṇa*.

Monks have certainly taken part in public affairs, and some have even argued that they should do so. In Sri Lankan elections it has become normal to find monks on public platforms and they tend to believe that they have an influence, while politicians flatter them by seeking their support. My own investigations, however, suggest that such participation costs monks the respect of the voters, and I have found that their influence on votes cast is probably zero (Gombrich 1973: 257–66). In the present crisis monastic leaders are able to command publicity in the media, at home and even abroad, and those who oppose any concession to Tamil separatism allow the politicians who do not want to make the concessions to plead the opposition of 'Buddhism' as an alibi, but my own conjecture (alas unverifiable) is that it is no more than that: the politicians really care next to nothing for monastic opinion.

If we look at the modern Buddhist pacifists I have mentioned we note that the XIVth Dalai Lama is first and foremost a spiritual leader, whose lack of temporal power may save him from certain acute dilemmas. In Japan, some of the leading pacifists have been monks. But in modern Japan the protestanisation of Buddhism advanced further than elsewhere, in line with the advance of the modern Japanese economy, so that lay Buddhist leaders arose in a way impossible in other Buddhist countries, and correspondingly assumed certain values, which had traditionally been monastic. U Nu of Burma is an interesting case, which leads me into my final topic: fundamentalism.

The fundamentalism of modern scholars

My second question at the beginning of the chapter was whether the Buddhist tradition is non-violent, and I have answered it in the negative. My third question concerned the concept of 'Buddhist fundamentalism' and how it could be applied to the current situation. At the same time, a discussion of the same concept constitutes the third and final part of my answer to the counter-question: why do people think of Buddhists as non-violent?

The term 'fundamentalism' is derived from Christianity. There it has much the same meaning as the more modern term 'inerrantism': it is a claim that the Bible, the foundation of the Christian religion, is a sufficient guide for all aspects of a Christian's religious life, and is to be understood as literally true. Even if one gives to 'fundamentalism' a somewhat weaker sense, the term refers not merely to a claim to return to the foundations of a religion, as embodied in its earliest sacred texts – for probably all religious reform movements claim to do that – but at the same time a rejection of tradition. Nor is fundamentalism mere idealisation of the past; that again is extremely common, and probably part and parcel of every nationalist movement.

Fundamentalists seem to be just what most Sinhalese Buddhists are *not*. In so far as they use any text or charter, it is a local chronicle which all acknowledge to have been composed a millennium after the time of the Buddha and the foundation of Buddhism. In so far as they are aggressive we can describe them as 'militant' or even 'chauvinist'. But to call them 'fundamentalist' when they are just the opposite not only deprives the term of all heuristic value but, to my mind, offers a completely misleading picture of the situation.

The fundamentalists here are we western scholars and our acolytes, the too much maligned 'Orientalists', who have exhumed from manuscripts and published for all to read the inspiring and noble words in which the Buddha preached how to live an ideal life and escape the cycle of rebirth. It is quite understandable that in the nineteenth century Protestant missionaries to Sri Lanka attacked the Buddhists by the standards of their own scriptures and accused them of not practising what they preached. It is perhaps not quite so permissible more than a hundred years later to confuse the ideal code of ethics laid down for renunciates with the real historical tradition of Buddhist politics and societies. Perhaps it is the ecologists who have particularly romanticised Buddhism, a form of flattery to which the Buddhists themselves are naturally not immune.

I am not entirely denying that fundamentalism exists in modern Buddhist societies. Western missionaries and scholars have influenced the bourgeoisie in Theravāda societies. Gustaaf Houtman has shown how in Burma the revival of Buddhist 'insight' meditation associated with the *Mahā Satipaṭṭhāna Sutta* has been intertwined with political developments:

> The experience of dispossession of domain coincided with an emphasis on the quest for enlightenment in the company of skeletons…The Le-di Hsa-ya-daw [a leading monk] withdrew for the first time in the forest to practise mental culture in 1887 in direct reaction to the 1886 British annexation of Upper Burma, when he expressed fear of the 'destruction of the era'. He wrote and preached a lot about insight and had many pupils who became themselves nationally renowned and was thereby indirectly responsible for a substantial number of the insight centres that populate Burma today.
>
> (1993: 5)

U Nu was a devoted practitioner and member of this movement,[6] and tried hard to bring Buddhist values into public life. Unfortunately his fate – in 1962 he was deposed by a military coup under Ne Win – illustrates all too vividly why this idealism will not work in practice; indeed, Burma has suffered the consequences ever since.

How will Buddhism be preserved?

A final word. I do not wish to leave the impression either that I condone the misbehaviour of Sinhalese Buddhists or that it is entirely the work of the laity. The 'religious' militancy that we are witnessing in many parts of the world is first and foremost political, that is, concerned with power, and has usually arisen as a reaction to what is seen as a threat. Sinhalese Buddhists have long felt threatened by Christian colonial powers, and later by India and by those (the Tamils) whom they consider to have close ties with India. Their aggressive response has indeed hurt the Tamils, and to a lesser extent other minorities so that they have suffered the usual fate of paranoids and made real, or aggravated, the dangers they feared. They have set up a vicious circle.

As for the parts played by the Sinhalese Buddhist clergy today, they are as varied as any sensible person might expect. There are monks who are doing all they can to achieve peace and reconciliation. But alas, it is not they who catch the headlines. My friend Professor H.L. Seneviratne, a Sinhalese Buddhist, has recently published a fine book entitled *The Work of Kings: The New Buddhism in Sri Lanka* (1999) in which he bitterly criticises the chauvinism of certain individual monks. One in particular, Elle[7] Guṇavaṃsa, seems to defy all traditional monastic norms by composing songs for soldiers to sing in battle. It is enough to quote:

> My brave, brilliant soldier son
> Leaving [home] to defend the motherland
> That act of merit is enough
> To reach Nirvana in a future birth.
> When you march to battle
> Like the son of Vihara Maha Devi
> May the gods of the four directions protect you
> My son, defender of the land
>
> (Seneviratne 1999: 272)

The son of Vihāra Mahādēvī was Duṭṭhagāmaṇī. The idea that defending the motherland (not, note, defending Buddhism) may lead one to *nirvāṇa* – albeit only in a future life – is certainly alien and repulsive to the mainstream of Buddhist tradition. But even Buddhists are only human.

Notes

1 Initially, this paper was presented at the symposium on 'Religion and Violence in South Asia' organized by Professor Axel Michaels of the Südasien Institute of Heidelberg University in July 2000.
2 The three refuges are the Buddha, the Dhamma, and the Saṅgha. Taking the three refuges one declares himself to be a Buddhist.
3 All translations are my own.
4 By 'civilian' I assume 'laymen' is meant.
5 Geiger and Rickmers (1980: 214–15).
6 See Houtman (1994: 16–21).
7 Though he is thus spelt in the book, I believe that the first name should strictly be Älle.

3

HINDU INFLUENCES ON MEDIEVAL SRI LANKAN BUDDHIST CULTURE

John Clifford Holt

> Some of our nationalists resent the assertion that Sinhalese culture is made up of and developed from elements borrowed and adapted. The readaptation of foreign elements is a sign of the originality and the virility of a given culture rather than a weakness.
>
> (Martin Wickramasinghe 1992: 21)

If Sri Lanka were to be identified on a contemporary world map depicting the geography and history of religions, it would no doubt be shaded categorically, along with Burma, Thailand, Cambodia, and Laos, as a predominantly Theravāda Buddhist country. Characterizing Sri Lanka's religious culture exclusively in this way, however, would be quite innocent, even less apt than categorizing Indonesia, for instance, as a Muslim country. Although the majority (approximately two thirds) of Sri Lankans are indeed Buddhist, like the vast majority of Indonesians in that country are now certainly Muslim, religious and cultural constructions in both contexts are extraordinarily complex and multilayered indeed. Deeper inquiries reveal how these two remarkable religious cultures continue to bear the stamp of how other religions (particularly Hinduism) have inscribed their influences upon them over many centuries of history.[1]

In this paper, I will make use of some of the extensive research conducted by various Sri Lankan historians and anthropologists in the recent past to explain how and when Hinduism has made its salutary impacts on Sinhala Buddhist religious culture. I will also explore, in general, some of the reasons for why this impact has taken place and then cite some instances of Sinhala Theravāda monastic resistance to its occurrence. Specifically, I will limit this general historical review primarily to the period of the twelfth through the sixteenth centuries CE. This is not only an historical period when many communities from the South Indian Coromandel and Malabar coasts were migrating to Sri Lanka, but it also provides the general historical background for understanding how elements of Hinduism came to be absorbed meaningfully into the evolving matrix of Sinhala Buddhist culture.

Generations of immigrants and mercenaries representing a plethora of castes from various regions of South India have brought with them a kaleidoscope of religious myths and rites reflective of Hindu worldviews contemporary in the locales of their origins. In time, some of these have been found congenial and have been "Buddhacized" (or "Sinhalized"): accepted into but subordinated to the evolving structures and values, or principles and assumptions of Sinhala religious culture grounded in the soteriology of the Buddha, but at the same time extending the heterogeneity of the very culture into which they have been absorbed.[2] For instance, Kataragama Deviyo, whose cult many scholars have studied in depth,[3] known to the Sanskrit *purāṇa*s as Skanda, the mythic son of Śiva and Pārvatī, in turn conflated with the indigenous Tamil ecstatic cult of the mountain god Murugan in South India, remains one of the most powerful and popular deities venerated by Sinhala Buddhists on the island today.

Shrines to the goddess Pattini, the heroine of the Tamil epic *Cilappatikāram*, are also prevalent in most Sinhala cultural areas. Obeyesekere's massive study (1984) of Pattini documents the monumental extent to which her cult was incorporated and further developed within the ritual life of Sinhala villages in various parts of the island.

Viṣṇu *dēvālaya*s are also ubiquitous in Sinhala Buddhist culture areas throughout the island. These three gods of Hindu origins, together with the Mahāyāna-derived Nātha Deviyo (Avalokiteśvara), came to be regarded as the four guardian deities of Sinhaladvīpa during the late medieval Kandyan period (eighteenth century CE), substituted for another set of guardian deities who had been established a few centuries earlier (fourteenth century).[4] Within the traditional metaphysics and soteriology of emerging Sinhala Buddhist worldviews, all four deities are regarded as *bodhisattva*s on the path to *nibbāna*.[5] Today, their local temples in the sacred area of the old traditional Kandyan capital in proximity to the Daḷadā Māḷigāva (Temple of the Tooth Relic) remain important, if not the most conspicuous, foci for Sinhala Buddhist deity veneration in the upcountry region of the island.

Moreover, since the eighteenth century reign of the Nāyakkar king, Kīrti Śrī Rājasiṅha (1751–1782), each of these gods has been accorded a formal place of honor and recognition in the annual ritual processions of Sri Lanka's most famous religiocultural pageant, the *äsaḷa perahära*.[6] As H.L. Seneviratne (1978) illustrated, one of the primary functions of this royally sponsored public rite was to express, in orderly and symbolic fashion, the hierarchy of divine and social identities constitutive of the Kandyan socio-cosmos.

What is interesting about this particular selection of incorporated Hindu deities (and the Mahāyāna Bodhisattva Avalokiteśvara) is that, when regarded as a whole, they represent the major currents (*Vaiṣṇava*, *Śaiva*, *Śakta*, and *Mahāyāna*) of South Indian religion that have been contemporary in India to most of the history of Theravāda Buddhist tradition in Sri Lanka, at least since the later centuries of the first millennium. Thus, the incorporation of these deities indicates that the Buddhist culture of Sri Lanka has been historically inclusive of the major trajectories of religious development that have occurred in South India concomitantly, though not without periodic resistance.

In this chapter, then, what follows is a brief survey of some of the important historical evidence of the ideological, literary, and material types that indicate periodic flows of Brāhmaṇic and Hindu presence among the Sinhalas primarily from the twelfth up through the sixteenth century CE. By presenting and discussing this evidence, I aim to illustrate why the influence and integration of Hindu constructs in the late medieval period of Sinhala history was very thorough on the one hand, and that Viṣṇu's incorporation, in particular, was but a part of a larger process of assimilation-made-meaningful on the other. I will also take note of evidence indicating a resistance to Viṣṇu's assimilation.

Vaiṣṇava ideology of kingship at Poḷonnaruva

If there is any traditional literary source that might be expected to mute or de-emphasize an acceptable place and positive influence of the Brāhmaṇic and Hindu presence in the history of a predominantly Sinhala Theravāda Buddhist religious culture, it could be the Pāli *Mahāvaṃsa* and its continuation, the *Cūlavaṃsa*, as dubbed by its translator, Wilhelm Geiger (1973). These traditional sources are essentially an orthodox Buddhist monastic seriatim or Theravāda-minded apologetic narrative about how the *Buddhasāsana* has fared under the reigns of Sri Lanka's long line of royalty. The narratives of this chronicle, beginning with mythic accounts of the Buddha's three visits, the immigration of the prototypical Sinhalas to the island, and the celebrated arrival of institutional Buddhism, consist almost entirely of either elaborate accounts of what various hero-kings have allegedly accomplished to defend, support, and glorify the religion of the Buddha, or briefer accounts which roundly condemn the damaging affects of heretical others who were judged hostile to the religion.

The fundamental apologetic of this literature articulates an ideal model of reciprocating *saṅgha* – state relations,[7] relations deemed primordial, even predestined.[8] The work was written, so it proclaims, "for the serene joy and emotion of the pious." But a close reading of this spectacularly "pro-Theravāda," often melodramatic source leaves little doubt that Sri Lankan or Sinhala kings presided over a rather cosmopolitan populace from at least the twelfth through the eighteenth centuries and that many of these kings seemed disposed to accept and nurture the reality of that cosmopolitan character as part of their kingdoms' cultural make-up. Insofar as kingship often reflects the reality it rules, it is not surprising that Sinhala kingship during this era of increasing social variegation tended to become ever more eclectic in its symbolic expression, more composite or aggregated in its ideology and appeal.

Searching through the *Mahāvamasa* – *Cūlavaṃsa* for clues about the presence of Hinduism, however, is a bit like reading Confucian histories to learn about the presence of Taoism. It is somewhat of a dubious historical exercise *per se*, especially since the *Mahāvaṃsa-Cūlavaṃsa* that we can read today in search of various indications for the presence of Hinduism is, undoubtedly, a compilation that was assembled in at least four different historical settings over a period of some thirteen hundred years[9] and contains much that is legendary and folkloric. It is one source among others, primarily the inscriptional and the artistic that requires examination.

Because myth, eulogy, and political history are thoroughly intertwined throughout, the *Mahāvaṃsa–Cūlavaṃsa* may be a fascinating source to study in search of cultural meaning, but it is also a source that can strain historical credulity as well. In spite of these caveats, however, the important point I stress here is that the *Mahāvaṃsa–Cūlavaṃsa* contains numerous references to the presence of Hinduism; and among those references, it has constructed profiles of Buddhist kingship which unmistakably reflect the accommodation of Hindu conceptions of royalty (in relation to Hindu notions of the divine).

In his indices to the *Mahāvaṃsa–Cūlavaṃsa*, Geiger lists exactly 100 references made to gods of *Brāhmaṇic* or Hindu origins within the 100 chapters that form the completed text. Among the divinities who figure in various passages are Brahma, Viṣṇu, Śiva, Lakṣmī Indra, Kuvera, Skanda, Viśvakarman, Bṛhaspati, and Sarasvatī. The vast majority of these occur in the last three (post-twelfth century) installments of the text.

The *Mahāvaṃsa* (the first 37 chapters attributed to the fifth century CE) contains only three references to the royal office of the Brahmin *purōhita*, an official advisory post in the king's court. The first occurs in the mythic story of Paṇḍukābhaya's consecration (Mahānāma Thera 1908: 10.79, 1950: 73), the second within the context of Devānampiyatissa's consecration in the third century BCE (Mahānāma Thera 1908: 11.26, 1950: 78–9), and the third in the story about how the passionate, philanderous, and murderous Queen Anulā (early first century CE), who is credited with poisoning several lover-kings, had made a *brāhmaṇa* her temporary king before poisoning him only six months later (Mahānāma Thera 1908: 34.15–31, 1950: 239f).

While these three instances might indicate that *Brāhmaṇic* practice and knowledge were accorded some scope during the early centuries of kingship in Sri Lanka, there are also indications that Brāhmaṇic traditions were, at times, rejected and condemned. For instance, King Mahāsena, whose disastrous reign for the Mahāvihāra *saṅgha* forms the concluding segment of the text, is said to have completely destroyed temples dedicated to the *Brāhmaṇic* gods (Mahānāma Thera 1908: 37.41, 1950: 270). While the literary evidence for the ancient pre-Poḷonnaruva period is scant, it seems to indicate an ambivalent attitude for the presence of *Brāhmaṇic* tradition: sometimes *brahmins* serve the court, sometimes their temples are ransacked.

That *brāhmaṇas* were recognized, supported through royal donations, and served in the courts of various later Sri Lankan kings, can be noted in several other places in the second installment of the *Mahāvaṃsa–Cūlavaṃsa*. For instance, King Kassapa III [717–724] is said to have "encouraged the way of life fitting for laity, *bhikkhus* and *brāhmaṇas*" [1: 112; 48.23]. Included in the list of his benefactions, King Sena II [851–885] is said to have

> [H]ad a thousand jars of gold filled with pearls and on top of each he placed a costly jewel and presented it to a thousand *brāhmaṇas* whom he had fed with milk rice in pure jewelled goblets, as well as golden threads.
> (Mahānāma Thera 1908: 1.153, 51.65–66)

What *may be* noteworthy about these last two references, if they can be regarded as roughly accurate references to the royal activities of this era, is that they would appear to indicate the ascendancy of Brahmins at royal courts precisely during the time that, as Inden (1998) has indicated, the ideology of kingship in many parts of India was shifting away from the cult of the cosmic Buddha to Vaiṣṇava or Śaivite orientations. There is, of course, no indication in our text that such a shift actually occurred in Sri Lanka during this time period, only that *brahmins* were favorably regarded during specific royal reigns.

Royal rhetoric reflecting the presence of Hindu conceptions of kingship at work does not seem to appear graphically in the text until the Poḷonnaruva period (eleventh through thirteenth centuries), and then only after a period of intense military invasions and occupations by South Indian imperial armies.[10] Regarding the *Mahāvaṃsa–Cūlavaṃsa*'s characterization of kingship in the twelfth century Poḷonnaruva era, however, indications of state-sponsored Hindu cultic practices and Sanskrit literary activity are much more readily apparent (Wijesekera 1973). Vikramabāhu II (1116–1137), for instance, is reported to have actually held the ancient Vedic *sōma* sacrifice "performed by the house priest and other *brāhmaṇas* well-versed in the *Vedas* and the *Vedangas*" [1: 234; 62.33]. More significantly, he is also depicted as having his son's bodily marks read "by *brāhmaṇas* versed in the lore of bodily marks" [1: 234; 62.45–7] to determine if the prince was destined for kingship. This latter instance is very important; for, it seems to be a clear signal that Hindu conceptions of kingship had formally come into play in determining royal successions.

Parākramabāhu I (1153–1186), widely remembered in Sri Lankan history as one of the greatest patrons of Theravāda Buddhist tradition, owing in part to the *Cūlavaṃsa*'s lengthy and laudatory account of his support for Buddhism, including his restoration and unification of the Buddhist monastic *saṅgha* under Theravāda auspices, is reported to have been given the *upanayana* (thread investiture) ceremony by his uncle, Kīrti Śrī Megha, assisted "by *brāhmaṇas* versed in the *Veda*" [1: 244; 64.13–17]. Since the *upanayana* is a *Brāhmaṇic* rite performed to negotiate the transition in identity from childhood to adulthood, it would appear that Parākramabāhu's *kṣatriya varṇa* was being affirmed in the process of preparing him for his role as an acceptable king according to Brāhmaṇic standards, that is, at least in a manner that would be clearly understood by Hindu observers.

In describing Parākramabāhu's consolidation of rule in Rōhaṇa (the south and southeastern swaths of the island), the *Cūlavaṃsa* makes analogical allusions to the great mythic victories won in the Sanskrit epics *Mahābhārata* and *Rāmāyana*. Here is one descriptive example:

> Thereupon the best soldiers of the two parties fought a severe action in the middle of the river. Now raged between the two armies a terrible battle like to that of the gods with the *Danavas* [2: 49; 75.54]... They fought an exceedingly terrible battle like the monkeys who leapt over the ocean in the combat between Rama and Ravana [2: 49; 75.59].

Parākramabāhu, himself, is compared to Kāma, the god of love, later in the narrative recounting the wonders of his reign [2: 100; 77.106]. His chief consort, Queen Rūpavatī, is said to have loved him "as Sītā loved Rāma" [2: 17; 73: 137].

Since the compiler of this section of the *Cūlavaṃsa* may have been, according to Kemper (1992: 34–47), from the Cōḷa country in India, he would likely have been well versed in classical Hindu conceptions of kingship and epic literature. It would appear that his appeals to Hindu imagery and practice, which also seem designed to flatter his royal patron (Parākramabāhu I 1153–1186), are either a reflection of the religious proclivities of the royal court and/or the king's own empathy for those *Brāhmaṇic* traditions; possibly a reflection of the need to present the king's power and accomplishments in as variegated a fashion as might be appropriate to the king's similarly variegated social and political constituencies; or, more bluntly, a measure of propaganda dished out in language that his political and military foes from South India would surely understand. Likely, all of these reasons and perhaps others came into play.[11]

The extent to which Parākramabāhu I (1153–1186) patronized things Hindu – brahmins, temples and their gods – arises in relation to how the *Cūlavaṃsa* credits him with erecting 13 *dēvālaya*s [2: 117; 79.19] and repairing some 79 more in the *rājaraṭṭha* region [2: 117; 79: 22], while erecting another 24 temples to the gods in southern Rōhaṇa [2: 123; 79: 81. From this account, it would appear that the compiler of this section of the *Cūlavaṃsa* wanted to record the fact that Parākramabāhu supported *both* Hindu and Buddhist constructions within the country's religious culture. The portrayal, therefore, is of a kingship with an inclusive ethic. Or to put the matter bluntly again in another way: Parākramabāhu was to be regarded as the master patron of both Buddhist and Hindu establishments, the supreme imperial overlord of all communities.

It is likely that several of the temples dedicated to Viṣṇu and Śiva at Poḷonnaruva, shrines studied by historians and archaeological teams in the twentieth century, are among those being referred to in the *Cūlavaṃsa* account. But as Liyanagamage (1968: 121) points out:

> [t]he Śaiva and Vaiṣṇava *dēvālas* in Poḷonnaruva are generally regarded as monuments erected in the [time of] Cōḷa occupation of [the] Rājaraṭṭha (1017–70). In many cases, this view is confirmed by Tamil inscriptions of the time of the Cōḷa kings like Rājarāja I and Rājendra I, found at the sites of these monuments[12] [brackets mine].

While Liyanagamage seems to be correct in this instance and, as such, casts some doubt on the *Cūlavaṃsa*'s implication that all of these Hindu temples were built or repaired by Parākramabāhu I (1153–1186), the fact remains that the *Cūlavaṃsa*, though a Theravāda-inspired text, is articulating an inclusive or transcendent model of kingship by indicating Parākramabāhu's supportive disposition to Hindu cults as well as Buddhist. That is, Parākramabāhu lays claim to patronizing all religious establishments – he is to be regarded as their chief support.

Parākramabāhu's own inclusive or imperial disposition *may be* reflected in other instances of material culture as well. For example, at Poḷonnaruva's magnificent *Gal Vihāra*, allegedly constructed under the patronage of Parākramabāhu I, a seated Buddha in the artificially excavated *Vijjādhara guhā* is flanked by two figures who, it has been argued, may be either the *bodhisattvas* Manjuśrī and Vajrapāṇi, or even less likely, the *bodhisattva*s Maitreya and Avalokiteśvara. Between and above the Buddha (whose identity, according to von Schroeder may be Akśōbhya) and these two respective flanking *bodhisattva*s, are two more figures identified as a four-headed Brahma and a four-armed Viṣṇu (von Schroeder 1990: 363, 368). The identification of these Hindu deities was first made by H.C.P. Bell in 1907.

The identification of Viṣṇu in this particular setting is of paramount importance: it could signal the first attempt, in the evidence of material culture available at this time, to incorporate Viṣṇu into a Buddhist cosmology. But, unfortunately, there is a possible complication and confusion. Von Schroeder and others before him (e.g. Fernando 1960) have asserted that the ensemble of sculptures in the *Vijjādhara guhā* cave at Gal Vihāra is Tantric in nature, and thus the assimilation of Viṣṇu, if that identification holds, would have been made into a Mahāyāna or Tantric context of symbol and cosmology, and not that of Theravāda.

However, Mudiyanse (1967: 107–19) has rebutted in great detail most of Fernando's observations warranting an identification of Tantric symbolism in this sculptural constellation, and seems to have anticipated Von Schroeder's similar observations (1992) as well, thus casting some doubt on the matter. Furthermore, in my own previous and extensive research on the cult of the Mahāyāna *bodhisatva* Avalokiteśvara in Sri Lanka, I did not find any instances of Hindu assimilations of this nature into the Mahāyāna. Because of that, I am inclined to agree with Mudiyanse, and chiefly for the reason he advances: a *Tantric* construction at the *Gal Vihāra* master site of Parākramabāhu I would have run completely counter to the ethos of the king's religious enterprise to purify and unite the Buddhist *saṅgha* under the Theravāda Mahāvihāra umbrella. That is, it seems unlikely that his "master piece" at *Gal Vihāra* would be meant to articulate the rival Mahāyāna cosmology and soteriology. Beyond this reason, aside from this specific sculptural "evidence," there is no other indication of the Mahāyāna in the Poḷonnaruva archaeological complex dating to this general historical period. Moreover, the iconography of the two flanking *bodhisattva*s in question is so indistinct that I have had a difficult time distinguishing them at all from similar types of fly-whisk bearers frequently found in various Buddhist caves throughout Deccan India.

On the other hand, in the absence of any other explanation by Mudiyanse regarding the identity of the two deities in question, Von Schroeder's identification of the two as Brahma and Viṣṇu, confirming Bell's earlier finding, is very much a distinct possibility. The identification of Viṣṇu is based upon the presence of a hand held *saṅkha* (conch), one of Viṣṇu's four traditional attributes. What makes me hesitant to accept this suggestion as final and conclusive, however, is that in every other instance in which images of Hindu deities have been found within the entire Poḷonnaruva archaeological complex, they were enshrined within specifically identifiable Hindu temples. That is, the cultic practices of Buddhists and Hindus at Poḷonnaruva seem to have been kept quite consciously separate from one another.

There also does not seem to be any evidence unearthed at the massive monastic Alahana Parivena (built by Parākramabāhu I) archaeological site that indicates the presence of Hindu deities, or Purāṇic practices in relation to Hindu deities, within the confines of this huge monastic university (Prematilleke 1981). Later literary sources in both Pāli and Sinhala depict the presence of Brahma and Viṣṇu at the Buddha's moment of enlightenment. In these instances, they appear with fly whisks and *saṅkha* respectively. Perhaps the sculpture at Vijjādhara was a harbinger of this depiction.

If Viṣṇu is indeed the identity of the sculpture in question, then my sense is that it represents an experimental anomaly, or as I have said, a harbinger at best. The sculpture in question, an attendant deity to the Buddha, would probably not have been an object of worship *per se*. Indeed, it is an object that only represents a deity worshipping the Buddha (here *devātideva*, "the god beyond the gods"). If the Viṣṇu figure at *Gal Vihāra* is, after all, a Viṣṇu figure, it is a remarkable "find" or "marker."

It is still some distance from the thoroughly integrated "Buddhist Viṣṇu" of the sort who appears and is worshipped as a Buddhist deity several centuries later in the upcountry regions of the island. But what this Viṣṇu represents in this sculptural constellation, if it is Viṣṇu at all, is a subordinated Hindu presence within a predominantly Theravāda Buddhist composition. As such and beyond its specific religious meaning, it may be taken (and perhaps charitably so) as symbolically characteristic of either the inclusive liberality of Parākramabāhu's Poḷonnaruva kingship or a statement of propaganda, the message of which would be clear: as Viṣṇu worships the Buddha, Cōḷa Hindus venerate a Sinhala Buddhist king. At least this is what might constitute its "political reading."

Such a reading of this material prompts a deeper consideration of the ideology and rhetoric of kingship at Poḷonnaruva. S. Pathmanathan (1982) has written extensively about Hindu influence from India on Sri Lanka in the medieval Poḷonnaruva and Koṭṭē eras respectively. He notes that, in the case of kingship at Poḷonnaruva (eleventh through thirteenth centuries), significant cultural influence came about due to intensive political contacts with the Cōḷa, the Pāṇḍyan, and

Kāliṅga dynasties in South India. Some of this influence was also the direct result of strategic marriage alliances forged by Poḷonnaruva kings, alliances that had the international affect of creating balances of power and the domestic effect of fostering the presence of various South Indian factions in the Poḷonnaruva royal court, once it had been established as the capital.

Before that, Poḷonnaruva had been a provincial capital city under Cōḷa sovereignty for at least the first 70 years of the eleventh century. The long-standing (13 centuries) capital of Anurādhapura to Poḷonnaruva's northwest had been sacked in the late tenth century by Cōḷa armies. Subsequently, the new Cōḷa imperial center had been established to the east in Poḷonnaruva, a strategic location that helped to extend control, as much as possible, to the south and east regions of the island where disestablished Sinhala royalty had fled. It is probable that the archaeological remains of the several Viṣṇu and Śaiva shrines at Poḷonnaruva served the cultic proclivities of these South Indian Cōḷa officials. Later, after the Sinhalas had regained power at Poḷonnaruva, these shrines served the religious orientations of the South Indian factions at court, possibly the relations and courtiers of the king's South Indian queens.

Pathmanathan (1982: 123) mentions, as I have already cited, how during the Poḷonnaruva period, the *Cūlavaṃsa* begins to cite the influence of the same types of Purāṇic Hindu and classical *Brāhmaṇic* conceptions of kingship at work. Specifically, he also notes how the *Cūlavaṃsa* refers to Parākramabāhu I as having mastered Kauṭilya's *Arthaśāstra*, the classical Indian treatise on the dynamics of political power which is sometimes compared to Machiavelli's work in the West, and the *Yuddharnava*, a classic Sanskrit treatise concerned with military science. Pathmanathan also cites textual and inscriptional evidence to indicate how the powerful Sinhala king who closely followed Parākramabāhu I (1153–1186), Niśśaṅka Malla (1187–1196), seem to have appealed to *dharmaśāstra* texts to publicly articulate the ideology of his kingship. Moreover, Pathmanathan also points out how the *Cūlavaṃsa* refers to *Manusmṛti* as a treatise frequently consulted by Vijayabāhu II (1186–1187), Parākrama Paṇḍu (1212–1215), and then Parākramabāhu II (1236–1270).

At some length Pathmanathan (1982: 124–126) explains the increased use of epithets such as *cakravartī* (P. *cakkavatti*, "universal monarch") and *rājādhirāja* ("supreme sovereign") during this time period. He hastens to add that *cakravartī* does not signal the revival of the term as it was deployed in the ancient Buddhist ideology of kingship context,[13] but rather the fact that Sinhala rulers had been influenced by conceptions of kingship then articulated in neighboring South Indian states where the term *cakravartī* connoted supreme overlord, an emperor-*avatāra* who rules by *daṇḍa* (the stick), as opposed to the Pāli Buddhist conception wherein the *cakkavatti* rules by *dhamma*. What differentiates its usage here from its ancient Buddhist usage, of course, is that the cosmology within which it is deployed is thoroughly Purāṇic. This is how the term was also deployed by Āriyaccakkaravarttis (çinkāiāriyān) in the Tamil kingdom of late fourteenth century Jaffna.

The conception of kingship that emerged in the Poḷonnaruva period, therefore,

> was a consequence of the combined effect of three conceptions, the *dhammic* conception rooted in Buddhist idealism, the heroic ideal depicted in the *Arthaśāstra* and the epic tradition and the conception of the divinity of kingship as expressed in the *dharmaśāstra* literature.
>
> (Pathmanathan 1982: 126)[14]

This mix is earlier apparent in the Ambagamuva inscription of Vijayabāhu I (1055–1110):

> He has surpassed the Sun in the majesty inherent in him, Maheśvara (Śiva) in prowess, Viṣṇu in haughty spirit, the Chief of the Gods (Indra) in kingly state, the Lord of riches (Kuvera) in exhaustible wealth, Kitisiru in (bestowing) happiness to living beings, the Preceptor of the Gods (Bṛhaspati) in the fertility of wisdom, the Moon in gentleness, Kandarpa in the richness of his beauty and the Bodhisatta in the fullness of his benevolence.
>
> (Pathmanathan 1982; Wickremasinghe 1928: 215–16)

Vijayabāhu I, of course, is the Sinhala king who overthrew Cōḷa power at Poḷonnaruva and set the stage thirty years later for the magnificent construction activities of Parākramabāhu I (1153–1186) which signal a revived efflorescence of Sinhala and Theravāda fortunes.

Pathmanathan certifies that the Brāhmaṇic and Hindu rhetoric noted above in relation to Vijayabāhu was also used to depict Parākramabāhu I in the Devanagala inscription (Paranavitana 1933: 323–24). Even before this, during the reign of Vikkama Paṇḍu (1029–1043), a Sinhala king in Rōhaṇa coping as best as he could with the powerful Cōḷa presence established in Poḷonnaruva, the ideology of the king as a divine *avatar* had been articulated. With specific reference to what is clearly the classical conception of the king as an *avatar* of Viṣṇu, Pathmanathan says:

> The adoption of the terminology expressive of the notion of divinity of kingship in the inscriptions of other rulers of Polonnaruwa may suggest that the expression *rājanārāyana* used in connection with Vikramabāhu was intended to convey the same idea in a more developed form . . . [i]t should not be ignored as mere metaphor purely on account of the eulogistic manner of the inscription in which it occurs. The expression could be interpreted in a literal sense as referring to the king as Viṣṇu and this idea had become familiar to many Indian rulers long before the tenth century . . . . The connection of a saviour was partly derived from the theory of *avatāra* associated with Vaishnavism and propagated by later versions of the *Rāmāyana* and the *Purāṇnas*.
>
> (1982: 139)

Pathmanathan's detailed studies of Hindu influence on Buddhist kingship at Poḷonnaruva are of great salience to this discussion. They not only complement the findings of my own research, but they also provide a warrant in this context for one of the central assertions of my thesis: that religiocultural assimilations or purifications are often the consequence of political dynamics or political expediency. The rhetoric deployed in relation to these Sinhala kings represents a co-option of their rivals' legitimating claims to power. It is language making a claim in the language of the rival's own framework and hence, it is language whose intention would be surely understood.

The Buddhist king, in this medieval context, was also often regarded as a kind of microcosmic symbol of his kingdom, or at least of his royal court. Engaging the conceptions of kingship of South India contemporaries and from Cōḷa predecessors at Poḷonnaruva, conceptions rooted within Vaiṣṇava and Śaiva cosmologies, meant that the king could be regarded compositely as a type of *axis mundi cum avatār*. The apparent mix so evident in the rhetoric of kingship ideology articulated in relevant inscriptions and in the *Cūlavaṃsa* account I have been noting may also reflect, in fact, the political and cultural plurality of this time and place: a mixture of Hindu and Buddhist peoples whose principals of legitimization and hierarchy were deemed complementary.

If the king's constituency was a mix of Hindu and Buddhist peoples, it makes complete political sense, in *Arthaśāstra* fashion, that his mythic public profile of legitimization be constructed in such a composite manner to appeal to as many constituents as possible. Or further within the context of the *Arthaśāstra* mindset, the rhetoric expresses imperial and absolute power in language clearly understood by the king's Hindu-oriented supporters and/or enemies. The claim that the king was an *avatār* of Viṣṇu was tantamount to claiming total suzerainty.

That the rhetoric of royalty during the Poḷonnaruva period registered negatively on some of the *literati* of the Theravāda monastic *saṅgha* in Poḷonnaruva is evident in the *Amāvatura* (The Flood of Nectar) written by Guruḷugōmī. This Sinhala text is regarded as "the earliest example of [Sinhala] connected prose writing" (Reynolds 1970: 32), having been produced around 1200 CE following the reigns of Parākramabāhu I (1153–1186) and Niśśaṅka Malla (1187–1196) during the apex of Poḷonnaruva's glories. "The language of the *Amāvatura* eschews Sanskrit words almost entirely, and sticks to 'pure' Sinhalese" (Reynolds 1970: 32).[15] It has no concession to the Hindu *weltenschaung*.

The substance of one of the major stories comprising the *Amāvatura* is especially relevant to my argument regarding the antipathetic side of Sinhala ambivalence to religious assimilations, Hindu ones in particular. It is concerned with how Sakka, king of the gods (the *Brāhmaṇic* Indra), was approached by Mahāmoggallāna, one of the Buddha's most powerful disciples (known for his cosmological tours of heavens and hells). The setting for the exchange is the splendor of Sakka's heaven. Cleverly, Mahāmoggallāna asks Sakka to preach a *sūtra*, which the Buddha had previously made known to him. Sakka's response and Mahāmoggallāna's rejoinder is this:

> "My lord, we are very busy. Though my own business be little, great is the business of the gods. Even such things as we learn well truly escape quickly from our memory and are no more seen, as pictures in a darkened room. Therefore I am not able to declare what my lord asks of me." Then the great elder reflected thus: "Wherefore does the king of gods remember not this matter?" and he thought "The gods are very foolish; for they are overcome by the things of the six senses which press upon them by the six doors. They know not whether they have eaten or whether they have not eaten, nor whether they have drunk or whether they have not drunk." And he saw how the gods were bemused and did forget.
>
> (Reynolds 1970: 78)

Mahāmoggallāna proceeds to perform a wondrous miracle that so frightens and amazes Sakka and all of the other deities in his assembly that they then beg to hear the *sūtra* they had forgotten. The text clearly represents an attempt to indicate how, from a Theravāda Buddhist perspective, the gods and their activities are subordinate to the Buddha's *dhamma*, and that they, too, are in need of following its realization to gain the final spiritual goal of *nibbāna*. Later in the text (Reynolds 1970: 88–89), Sakka directly asks the Buddha why it is that the gods are bound to the cycle of birth and death. The Buddha's response is:

> King of gods! Whatever gods there be, whatever men or *asuraṣ* or *nāga*s or heavenly musicians, in fine whatever creatures there be, each among them gives gifts and offers worship with earnest resolution, saying "Let us divide whatsoever we can hold in our hands, and thus let us enjoy it without hatred, without violence, without enemies, without ill-will, and without wrath towards any." And yet they live lives of hatred, of violence, with enemies, with ill will; for they are bound to the fetters of envy and avarice.

The text concludes with this:

> Thus because the Buddha is the subjugator of rude mankind, he subdued Sakka the king of gods; and whereas it is spoken of others also, know that he sat also in four and twenty places and preached the Law four and twenty times and subdued thereby a million times a million gods at each time that became of the ranks of the Worthy, and countless millions at each time that entered the Paths, or advanced in the Paths, or attained the Middle of the Paths; and he brought them all to the immortal greatness of nirvana.
>
> (Reynolds 1970: 89–90)

Ostensibly, this critique of the gods is made precisely on grounds of doctrinal orthodoxy, but it is not difficult to imagine that it also reflects political sentiments of the monastic literati to royal aggrandizement occasioned by the Vaiṣṇava ideology of divine kingship.

Hindu saturation in the "drift to the Southwest"

Sri Lankan historians often refer to the historical period following the demise of Poḷonnaruva, wrought by the devastating invasion of Māgha (1215–1236) from Kāliṅga and his mercenaries from Kerala in the early thirteenth century, as "the drift to the Southwest." It was an epoch of immense political turmoil. Except for the veritably exceptional reign of Parākramabāhu VI (1411–1466), when all of Sri Lanka fell under his single sway (the only time of such single rule between the reign of Parākramabāhu I (1153–1186) and the Kandyan capitulation to the British on March 2, 1815), the island was frequently invaded from without and divided by sometimes as many as four different rulers simultaneously within. Sinhala kings often adopted primarily a defensive political posture in these difficult circumstances.

Referring to the substantial transformations occurring within Sinhala Buddhist religious culture during this time of stormy and turbulent political sea changes, Pathmanathan in underscoring the legacy of this era, says:

> The period under consideration [the three centuries prior to the Portuguese conquest of the maritime provinces in the early sixteenth century] is of special significance as it was then that Buddhism in the form in which it has come down to modern times attained many of its characteristics.
>
> (1986: 81)

To emphasize the more precise nature of these enduring transformations, he quotes the work of Lynn de Silva who states:

> The recourse to the gods is a place where Hinduism has flowed into Buddhism and . . . has given it a new vitality. Indeed, when one sees Buddhism in actual practice one is surprised by the amount of conscious Hinduism, which lies within Buddhist ritual and ceremonial practices. There is hardly a place of Buddhist devotion where one will not find images of Hindu gods and shrines.
>
> (1974: 21)

One conventional interpretation [Ilangasinha's and many others] of this development is that Sinhala kingship was so often in a state of enervation and often so impoverished that it simply lacked the means to be able to support the Theravāda *saṅgha* in a manner similar to its backing by the state during the Anurādhapura and Poḷonnaruva periods. While there may be some truth in this assertion, the more likely reality is that kings, understanding their predicaments in terms of power relations, lent their sanction of and support to religious institutions in light of the exigencies of the contemporary real *politik*. Given the increasing number of Hindus living within their kingdoms, it is likely that their awareness of constituency contributed to their congeniality for Hindu ideologies of kingship. Rājasiṅha I (1581–1593) actually went so far as to banish the Buddhist *saṅgha* from his capital at Sītāvaka and formally embraced Śaivism.[16]

The practice of kings stylizing themselves, as divinely ordained and divine-like kings would have held a special appeal to them, especially if they reigned in perilous conditions inducing bouts of personal insecurity. Certainly the epithets deployed by kings in the late Kandyan period *sannasa*s (sixteenth to eighteenth centuries) that they had inscribed on copper plates reflect a penchant for an inflated and eclectic rhetoric (in comparison to the reality of their tenuous holds on power).

It would seem to be the case that political conditions were heavily responsible for the manner in which elements of Hinduism, especially the cult of Viṣṇu, were incorporated. I have just illustrated how the manner in which kingship was conceived and represented during the Poḷonnaruva period supports this thesis. In the period of Sri Lankan history following the demise of Poḷonnaruva in the thirteenth century until the conversion of King Dharmapāla (1551–1597) to the Roman Catholicism by the Portuguese missionaries, conceptions of kingship remain an important port of entry for the increasing Hindu influence in Sri Lanka. But during this later period, Hindu influence becomes much broader in scope and intensity, transcending the rhetoric of Sinhala kingship and court politics while becoming suffused into many other aspects of culture.

I will first show that Vaiṣṇava Hinduism remained an important conceptual force in play at the royal courts of the time, but I will also go on to cite its easily discernible presence in some exemplary compositions of classical Sinhala literature, in the design and ornamentation of architecture, and in the popular cultic practices of Buddhist monasticism. I will suggest that Hindu permeation of Sinhala culture was not just a by-product of royal scenarios of legitimization, but also a consequence of the island's changing demography, owing to the nature of the many military campaigns that were waged, and to the transformation of the political economy itself during this period.

As late as the date of Bhuvanekabāhu VII (1521–1551), there is evidence (from the Portuguese in this instance), of Brahmin pandits serving as royal advisors to Sinhala kings (Ilangasinha 1992: 196). It is believed, indeed, a Brahmin advisor was selected to travel to Portugal on behalf of the Sinhala King Bhuvanekabāhu VII to represent royal interests in negotiations with the King of Portugal. Ilangasinha is of the view that with the passing of Parākramabāhu VI in the 1460s

> The influence of the Saṅgha on the kings and nobles of Koṭṭē [the capital from 1411–1597 just southeast of modern Colombo] steadily waned, and that of Brahmins gained ground until by the time of the arrival of the Portuguese [in 1505], the upper strata of Sinhalese society were more or less becoming Hinduized.
>
> (1992: 375)

The trajectory that Ilangasinha identifies had been, in fact, long in-the-making. As Pathmanathan (1986: 82) points out: ". . . . documents recording royal grants or proclamations issued in this period refer to Hindu gods along with the *triratna* [Buddha, *dhamma*, and *saṅgha*] in their concluding portions." That is, gods of Hindu origin were, during the time frame with which I am now concerned, thoroughly integrated in the rhetorical language of power officially proclaimed by a royalty articulating a rhetoric of legitimation. Moreover, the presence and importance of Brahmins at court, from the reign of Parākramabāhu II (1236–1270) at Dambedeṇiya until Dharmapāla's conversion to Catholicism at Koṭṭē (1551–1597), is evident from any number of sources, both literary and inscriptional. For example, I cite Pathmanathan's (1986: 99–100) summary description of Parākramabāhu II's daily routine as it was recorded in the thirteenth century *Kandavuru Sirita*:

> The king was met at dawn by the Brahmin *purohita* from whom he received the sacred *kusa* grass, a conch shell filled with sanctified water and blessings. The *purohita*, it is said, made inquiries about his dreams at night and made recommendations for the performance of appropriate ceremonies in case they were considered auspicious.

That more than one type of Brahmin attended the king, and that they had attained degrees of specialty beyond their purely ritual roles, is evident in what Pathmanathan adds in commenting on the *Kandavuru Sirita* passage just cited:

> Parākramabāhu II, who had a concern for the promotion of knowledge and learning is known to have made provision for the maintenance of a Brahmin scholar who had a specialized knowledge of Sanskrit and medicine. Brahmins were also consulted on matters relating to astrology.

There is another compelling reference that occurs in the *Cūlavaṃsa*'s description of the events that occurred during Parākramabāhu II's long reign at Dambedeṇiya (1236–1270). The *Cūlavaṃsa* (83: 46), in describing Prince Vīrabāhu's defeat of Chandrabhāṇu and his *Jāvaka* mercenaries, alludes to Vīrabāhu in the following manner: "Going forth to the combat like Rāma, Prince Vīrabāhu slew numbers of Jāvakas, as Rāma (slew) the Rakkhasas" (Geiger and Rickmers 1980: 152). Since Vīrabāhu then repaired to Devinuvara to worship Uppalavaṇṇa after his victory, there is some reason to explore further the identity of the god as Rāma. The royal visit to Devinuvara at this time was also critical for the establishment of the cult of Viṣṇu at upcountry Aluthnuvara.

Brāhmaṇic influence at the Sinhala royal court, moreover the specific presence of a Vaiṣṇava ideology of kingship, is clearly an evident aspect of the Kurunägala reign of Parākramabāhu IV (1302–1326) who, in addition to being a patron of continuing the *Cūlavaṃsa*, is depicted in *Caracotimalai*, a Tamil handbook on astrology, as "the incarnation of Viṣṇu who churned the ocean to obtain the nectar"

(Pathmanathan 1986: 102). This would be the second documented specific instance, then, that a Sinhala king had been literally referred to as Viṣṇu's *avatar* (the first being Vikramabāhu I (1111–1132) who had claimed Poḷonnaruva for Sinhalas following their history-reversing defeat of the Cōḷas). Another explicit reference to the application of a Vaiṣṇava ideology to Sinhala kingship with reference to Parākramabāhu VI (1412–1467) is found in Śrī Rāhula's *Sälaḷihiṇi Saṅdēsaya*:

> There, friend, feast your gaze on the great Lord Parākramabāhu
> Who is to the Sun's Race as the sun is to the lotus-pond
> In whose bosom-home Lakshmi the goddess lies always;
> Radiant, his beauty unblemished, like Ramba's lord.
> Wearing all sixty-four kingly insignia, including the crown,
> Like Vishnu incarnate, he graces the lion throne.
> Bow low at his gracious feet and take leave of this King
> Who came down from Manu in unbroken line.
>
> (Reynolds 1970: 286)

In the years following Parākramabāhu VI's reign (1411–1466), the political situation continued to deteriorate for Sinhala rulers, while the strength and presence of Brahmins at court, as well as the veneration of Hindu deities, seems to have increased. Ilangasinha observes at length the nature of this peculiar dynamic:

> The latter part of the fifteenth century and the whole of the sixteenth century are marked by political instability, chaos and constant warfare in the country. Preoccupied by these political troubles, the rulers of the country could not extend the necessary patronage to religious affairs. The growing influences of Brahmins not only at the royal court but also on society of this time caused in some ways diminish the relationship between the state and the Saṅgha. The *Nikāyasaṅgrahaya* records that Vīrabāhu Ādipāda gave slaves, male and female, cattle, houses, elephants and villages to Brahmins. The latter seem to have come in increasing numbers from India to benefit from the liberality of the Sinhalese rulers of the day. This influx of Brahmins to Ceylon from India no doubt was due to the fact that Muslim inroads deprived many of them of their livelihood. A few of these Brahmins were converted to Buddhism, but most practised the forms of religion to which they were accustomed, and gained adherents from among the Buddhists. The prestige of Brahmins seem to have grown stronger in the course of time . . . It is perhaps not too wide a guess to suggest that this growing influence of Brahmins on the royal court weakened the relationship of the state and Saṅgha after the reign of Parākramabāhu VI. This may be further supported by the fact that after Vīdāgama Maitreya in the reign of Bhuvanekabāhu VI we do not hear any member of the Saṅgha holding the title of *rājaguru*, "adviser to the king."
>
> (1992: 211–12)[17]

In relation to the influence of Hinduism on the literature of the court and of the *literati* of the time, Pathmanathan complements the general view just advanced by Ilangasinha:

> Through Hinduism the ruling classes and the *literati* in the Sinhalese kingdoms gained access to the secular branches of learning developed in India. The study of Sanskrit and Tamil languages along with Pāli and Sinhalese at the court and some of the monastic establishments tended to promote inter-cultural communication and gave access to several varieties of Indian literature.
>
> (1986: 82)

Commenting on the profusion of references to Sanskrit myths in the classical Sinhala literature of this era, Pathmanathan continues:

> The churning of the ocean by Viṣṇu with the aid of the Mandara mountain, Agastya's reduction of the ocean, the extraordinary prowess and feats of Ravana, the piercing of Mount Meru by Skanda . . . are among the most important Purāṇic myths and epic legends alluded to in the Sinhalese poetic works produced during this period.
>
> (1986: 105)

In the *Girā Sandēsaya*, one of the many *dūta kāvyas* which was written during the reign of Parākramabāhu VI (1411–1466), poems that beseech the powers of various deities for divine assistance, there is a description (vv. 217–27) of the Vijayabāhu Pirivena (located between modern Ambalaṅgoḍa and Hikkaḍuva) which was presided over by the famous *gāmavāsi* (P. "village-dwelling") poet-monk Śrī Rāhula. It is quite detailed. From this, it appears that the academic curriculum of this Buddhist educational institution was quite diverse and included not only the teaching of Pāli, but also Sanskrit, Tamil, prosody, logic, drama, and astrology.

Ilangasinha (1992: 40) notes that students at this institution included Brahmins from India who studied the *Vedas* along side of Buddhist texts and speculates that many may have come to the *pirivena* owing to the fame of Śrī Rāhula's erudition as a master of six languages (1992: 239). He adds: "It may be assumed that the famous Brahmin scholar, Sri Ramacandra Bharati, who learnt Buddhism under Śrī Rāhula, was a teacher of Sanskrit at the Vijayabāhu Pirivena. He composed the Sanskrit *sataka* poem, the *Bhakti-sataka* in honour of the Buddha" (Ilangasinha 1992: 250). Ilangasinha further cites references in the Pāli text from Northern Thailand, the *Jinakalamālī*, to note that students were also coming from Southeast Asia in the fifteenth century to study Buddhist texts under the guidance of Sinhalese *Mahātheras*. Moreover, to underscore the cosmopolitan character of the era's educational institutions, he cites a variety of sources (Ilangasinha 1992: 250–52) in which it becomes apparent that Buddhist monastic educational institutions during the Koṭṭē period even offered the study of Tamil drama. Summarizing the *Cūlavaṃsa*'s distanced account of the royal education of kings during this period, Ilangasinha writes:

> [t]he influence which Sanskrit learning exerted on the political and social spheres may be judged from the statements in the chronicles with regard to the education of princes like Parākramabāhu [VI] and the references therein to authorities like Kauṭilya and Manu.
>
> (1992: 248)

With regard to the production and style of material culture during this same era, some of the Buddhist architectural monuments of this period actually had closer affinities with Hindu architectural forms and conceptions than with Buddhist monuments of the preceding centuries. In architectural form and conception, the *dēvālaya*s built for the guardian deities of the island were distinctively Dravidian.

Laṅkātilaka and Gaḍalādeṇiya, important to the later Kandyan ritual cult of Viṣṇu, were built in the early years of the Gampola period (1341–1410). Their importance lies in the fact they are the first Buddhist monuments that thoroughly integrate the presence of Hindu deities with the worship of the Buddha. Pathmanathan has this to say about the Hindu influence exerted on both:

> [T]he monuments of Lankatilaka and Gadaladeniya in the interior parts of the island, which are representative of the architecture of the period under consideration, provide sufficient evidence of influence exerted by the Hindu tradition on the construction of Buddhist monuments. In the preceding periods the influence of the Hindu tradition on the Sinhalese monuments was marginal ... with the notable exceptions of Nalanda Gedige and the shrine of Upulvan described as the *galge* ... [I]n the Lankatilaka [monument] which was of brick construction except for the base and door frames, the Dravidian influence is remarkable but also restrained. The exterior walls of the *garbhagrha* at Lankatilaka in the niches of which the images of the guardian deities have been accommodated merit attention on account of their resemblances with those of the corresponding architectural components of Hinduism ... The Gadaladeniya monuments represents a distinct stage in the evolution of the Sinhalese architectural tradition characterised by the architectural design of a Hindu temple with suitable modifications for the purposes of Buddhist religious worship. It is also significant that such a development synchronised with a phase in the development in Buddhism characterized by the incorporation of the cult of guardian gods and *devale* worship into its tradition.
>
> (1986: 108–09)

These considerations beg the obvious question: aside from the royal court, from where did these cultural flows originate and by what processes? With regard to how and where the cultural flow from Hindu India was occurring, Pathmanathan says:

> Another noteworthy feature was the prominence attained by coastal towns as centres of constructional activity and cultural interaction. Dynastic capitals lost their pre-eminence as centres of constructional and cultural activities as dynastic power declined and its resources diminished.

One of the major differences in accounting for Hindu influence in the post-Poḷonnaruva period is that rather than matrimonial alliances being forged with powers based in South India, Sinhala royalty adopted Hindu practices and traditions through the influence of "matrimonial connections made with locally established families of South Indian extraction" (Pathmanathan 1986: 83). The Alakeśvara family, who dominated Sinhala kingship for about a century, was a primary example of this pattern. Their influence was such that in the last half of the fourteenth century, claims to kinship (and therefore the succession of kingship) were sometimes based on principles of matrilineal descent. This societal trait is probably the consequence of heavy migration from Kerala, the place of origins of the Alakeśvaras. It is a pattern still discernible in Kerala today (Agarwal 1994: 168–79) and one that lasted for a long era in the Kandyan region of Sri Lanka too.

What also distinguishes this era from the Poḷonnaruva period is that "Hindu influence on Buddhism operated chiefly through the medium of commerce and emanated mostly from Malabar and the Vijayanagara empire..." (Pathmanathan 1986: 83). This was an era of intensified seaborne trade and consequently coastal ports were the most dynamic venues for cultural flows (Roberts 1995: 22–23).

> Native inhabitants and foreigners of diverse ethnic groups and faiths were participants in these enterprises. Some of them established permanent communities and also fostered craft-production in which artisan communities became permanently involved. Hindus from Southern India and Gujarat and Muslims from India, Persia and Arab countries were among the foreigners involved in the process. Some of them had settled down in some principle towns like Galle, Devinuvara, Colombo, Negombo and Chilaw.
>
> (Pathmanathan 1986: 83)

Trade and commerce were not the only factors leading to the increasing heterogeneity of Sinhala religious culture. Liyanagamage (1986) points out that Kerala mercenaries formed a large contingent of Parākramabāhu's army which dislodged the Cōḷas from Sri Lanka finally in the late twelfth century and that some of these mercenaries were quite possibly the Vēläikkāras who were charged with guarding the Tooth Relic of the Buddha, which by this time had become the ritual symbol or palladium of the Sinhalese kings.

In his assessment of the presence of Keralas from the Malabar coast in medieval Sri Lanka during the period within which I am concerned, Liyanagamage (1986) notes, with irony, how the Keralas had formed the entirety of Māgha's contingent which ransacked Sinhala-ruled Poḷonnaruva in the mid-thirteenth century, and yet about a hundred years later were enlisted by Sinhala rulers in the Gampola period (1341–1411) to defend the kingdom against invasions by Āryacakravartī of Jaffna (Liyanagamage 1986: 68–70). Probably the Alakeśvaras, who were the dominant political family of the time and whose own origin was clearly in Kerala, recruited them. Their increasing power during the Gampola period is known from a number of inscriptions and literary texts.[18] Their great wealth was derived from merchant activities, chiefly trade between Sri Lanka's southwest coast and Kerala. They had parlayed their position as successful merchants to gain control over vast amounts of land bordered by the ocean on the west and the mountains around modern Ratnapura to the east.

Before Āryacakravartī's invasion, the Alakeśvaras had established power so deep into the upcountry, around the royal capital in Gampola itself, that they had colluded with the Tamil Āryacakravartī of Jaffna in allowing him, in the regions just north of Kandy, to force payment of transport dues to *brāhmaṇas* acting on the Āryacakravartī's behalf (Liyanagamage 1986: 72). Whatever terms of collusion had been reached, they must have been abrogated by one party or the other; for the Alakeśvaras and the Āryacakravartī were locked in a bitter war toward the end of the fourteenth century. The Alakeśvara defeat of the Tamil king not only brought the family enormous prestige, but also underscored their thorough identification with Sinhala economic and political interests.

In discussing the political significance of the Alakeśvara family, Liyanagamage (1986: 73) confirms through inscriptional evidence that they were originally from a caste of traders in Kerala. He provides an extensive translation of a tract from the *Alakeśvara Yuddhaya*, a sixteenth century text upon which the later *Rājāvaliya* seems quite dependent in parts, which details in laudatory fashion the heroic accomplishments especially of Niśśaṅka Alagakkonāra, the head of the family credited with the Āryacakravartī's defeat.

Liyanagamage has added his own commentary on the revelations and perspectives of this interesting source: how the stature and ability of Nissanka Alagakkonara stands out in contrast to the weakness and cowardice of the Sinhalese king Bhuvanekabāhu; how the latter is portrayed as having deserted his people in the hill country while seeking refuge with the Alakeśvaras at Raigama during the peak of hostilities with the Jaffna Āryacakravartī; and how, once the Alakeśvaras had defeated the Āryacakravartī, Bhuvanekabāhu was able to return to his capital in Gampola. The image proffered is one of a great political savior. On his historical significance for the political fortunes of Sinhala royalty, Liyanagamage writes:

> Alagakkonara built the fortress of Jayawardhanapura [which eventually became the royal palace in the Koṭṭē era], stored adequate food and other requisites, collected troops and thus created an effective overall defense

> strategy... It is the fortifications erected by Alagakkonara and the sense of confidence and morale created by him during his stewardship that enabled Parākramabāhu VI, at a later stage, to [entirely] subjugate the Jaffna kingdom thereby effecting the unification of the island, for the last time prior to the arrival of Western nations to the Island. In passing it may be noted that although medieval chroniclers had highlighted the achievements of the Alakeśvaras, modern historians, possibly in their enthusiasm to underline the greatness of Parākramabāhu, seem to bypass the significant contributions of the Alakeśvaras, but for which the Sinhalese rulers task would have been more difficult, if not impossible. (1986: 75)

In addition to this commentary by Liyanagamage regarding the Alakeśvara legacy for Sinhala political history, I would now note specifically the symbolism of the Koṭṭē fortification that Alakeśvara had erected. On each of the four corners of the fortification wall was located a *devalaya* to the then regarded national guardian deities of the time: Vibhīsana, Saman, Upulvan, and Skanda.[19]

What I am suggesting is that the Alakeśvara family, with its roots in Hindu Kerala, played a significant role in propagating the cosmological idea that four divine guardian deities protected the island from invasion. The idea, itself, seems to have surfaced for the first time in the mid-fourteenth century Laṅkātilaka inscription when the Alakeśvara's had already begun to assert their power upon the weakening Sinhala kingship of the Gampola era.

In the conclusion to his article on the place of Keralas in medieval Sri Lankan history, Liyanagamage (1986: 76) reflects on the ironies of history regarding how various factions of Kerala immigrants, including the Alakeśvaras, became acculturated to Tamil or Sinhala culture. Noting how Keralites had been mercenaries for Magha in the thirteenth century and had later fought for the Alakeśvaras against the Jaffna Āryacakravartī, Liyanagamage underlines how allegiances and identities can shift so quickly within a brief period of tumultuous history.

> It is quite natural that in the face of growing Dravidian settlements in the Jaffna peninsula and adjacent areas, the Sinhalese who were at one time the majority community in those parts, were reduced to a minority and were eventually submerged, retaining but faint traces of their Sinhalese identity. In other words, it may well be said that they had come to be "Tamilized" in the course of time. Undoubtedly the same process may have taken place in reverse order in the areas further south where the Sinhalese formed the majority. Tamil minorities living among the Sinhalese in those parts of the Island would have been "Sinhalized" with the passage of time. The Alakeśvaras were no exception to this historical process. Though their Kerala origins were not forgotten, for all intents and purposes the Alakeśvaras had virtually become Sinhalese... It is the irony of history that when the Sinhalese and Tamils confronted

> each other in the battlefield, as indeed they did in the fourteenth century, the former would scarcely have known that they were not quite so "Sinhala" as they thought they were, much as the latter would hardly have known that they were ultimately not quite so "Damila" either.
>
> (1986: 75)

Then adding his own twist of irony, since Liyanagamage was writing his piece in the immediate aftermath of the 1983 ethnic pogrom and the militancy it spawned among both Tamil and Sinhala communities, he says: "It is by no means fitting that this knowledge should continue to be the prerogative of the historians."

While Pathmanathan, Ilangasinha, and Liyanagamage have written extensively on the social, political, and historical dynamics contributing to Hinduism's influence on Sinhala Buddhist culture, Obeyesekere's (1984) anthropological studies of the cult of Pattini are very instructive in gaining insight into how domesticated Sinhalas have come to construct an understanding of their migrations from India to Sri Lanka through, as Obeyesekere has followed Eliade, the process known as the "historicization of myth."

Following the widespread implications of Obeyesekere's discussions, I have also attempted, previously, to analyze 'colonization myths' within the context of the cult of a regional Sinhala deity, Pitiye, and his mythic conflict with Nātha (Avalokiteśvara) Deviyo in the Dumbara region of Kandy (1991: 125–50) while Roberts (1995: 18–32) has analyzed how migration myths (or "myths of origins") of the *karava* caste and others (including the *durava*s and *salagama*s) reflect community conceptions of identity within a newly adopted milieu. What I want to mention in this context specifically is what Obeyesekere (1984: 361–75) has determined on the basis of his detailed analyses of the Gajabāhu "colonization myth."

In summary, the Gajabāhu myth describes how the second century Sri Lankan king Gajabāhu avenges a moral wrong by kidnapping Solī king's widow's two sons among 12,000 others. Gajabāhu takes with him a giant named Nīla, parts the waters of the ocean separating Laṅkā from Solī (Cōḷa Country of South India) and visits the Solī king while Nīla gathers together the elephants of the royal city and kills them by banging them together! Following such an act of intimidation, Gajabāhu visits the Solī king who at first refuses to let the captives go. Gajabāhu not only demands the 12,000, but another 12,000, or else, he says, he will destroy the city. To make his threat more forceful,

> Nila squeezed out water from sand and showed it; squeezed water from his iron mace and showed that. Having in this way intimidated the king of Solī he received the original number supplemented by an equal number of men, making 24,000 persons in all. He [Gajabāhu] also took away the jewelled anklets of goddess Pattini and the insignia of the gods of the four devalas, and also the bowl-relic which had been carried off in the time of king Valagamba; and admonishing the king not to act thus in the future, departed. On arrival he landed the captives; sent each captive

> who owned ancestral property to his inherited estate, and caused the supernumerary captives to be distributed over and settle in these countries, viz., Alutkuruwa, Sarasiya pattuwa, Yatinuwara, Udunuwara, Tumpane, Hewaheta, Pansiya pattuwa, Egoda Tiha, and Megoda Tiha. The king ruled 24 years, and went to the world of the gods.
>
> (Gunasekara 1900: 40–41; Obeyesekere 1984: 364)

Obeyesekere has made a number of astute observations regarding the historical, social, and religious significance of this myth.

In general, Obeyesekere points out in relation to its many versions (which begin with the thirteenth century *Pūjavaliya*'s imaginative embellishment of the *Dīpavaṃsa* and *Mahāvaṃsa* accounts of the historical second century king and continue through expansions in the sixteenth and seventeenth century *Rājaratnākara* and *Rājāvaliya*), "the Gajabāhu myth has been a continually viable one, justifying and explaining the existence of South Indian settlers in Sri Lanka" (1984: 367). It has not only functioned as a myth of origins for a number of migrating communities, but it has also served as a myth of origins for the pre-eminently significant religiocultural pageant, the *äsala perahära*. Obeyesekere also suggests that one way to read the Gajabāhu story is as a myth of "reversal" generated during the Dambedeṇiya dynasty in the aftermath of Māgha's invasion:

> If I am right about the fantasy in the myth as the opposite of reality, the period of the depredations of Magha was probably the time when the myth evolved... When we compare the Gajabāhu myth and the Magha account, we realize again that the former is a myth that is the opposite of the latter "reality"; Magha invades Sri Lanka with twenty-four thousand (or twenty thousand Kerala troops); Gajabāhu brings back twenty-four thousand; Magha plunders and terrorizes the Sinhalas, killing their king; Gajabāhu terrorizes the Cōḷas; Magha populates Sinhala villages with Tamil *conquerors*; Gajabāhu does it with Tamil *captives*. Even more important than these polarities are the social-psychological functions of the myth, which are to boost the self-esteem of people whose "morale" had sunk low in an era of troubles.
>
> (1984: 371–72)

This is but a segment comprising Obeyesekere's rich analyses of the myth. Within this context, what I want to underscore relates to two matters. The first is that Obeyesekere has shown that the part of the story about recovering the "insignia of the four *dēvālayas*" does not occur until the *Rājāvaliya*'s version in the seventeenth or eighteenth century (Obeyesekere 1984: 368).

I want to emphasize this now because it has a bearing on when it is possible to identify the "Buddhist Viṣṇu" *per se*, as a Hindu deity who has been thoroughly assimilated into Sinhala Buddhist culture. Second, Obeyesekere's interpretation is completely complementary and congruent with Pathmanathan's and

Liyanagamage's historical discussions of how many Kerala peoples were pouring into the upcountry and coastal regions of the island from the thirteenth through the fifteenth centuries as mercenaries and traders. It is very likely that this migration in reality was responsible for the importation and assimilation of many Hindu traditions. While it is impossible to determine with any great degree of accuracy, I would speculate that much of the Śaiva presence in Sri Lanka originated with the Cōḷas from the tenth and eleventh centuries, and much of the Vaiṣṇava presence with the Keralas from the thirteenth and fourteenth. Even to this day, some people of *salāgama* caste, who originate from the Malabar Coast (Kerala) in a popular recension of their origin myth, celebrate Viṣṇu as a kind of primordial progenitor.

The antipathetic response

In the preceding pages, I have indicated the various ways in which, from the thirteenth through the sixteenth centuries, Sri Lanka was somewhat awash in *Brāhmaṇic* and Hindu influence. Earlier in this chapter, I mentioned how the thirteenth-century *Amāvatura* in the Poḷonnaruva period seems to reflect a Buddhist antipathy. Here, I want to briefly discuss the fifteenth century *Buduguṇālaṅkāraya* that contains, perhaps the wittiest and rebuking protest of all.

In opposition to the proliferation of veneration for Hindu deities, the eminent monastic leader and royal tutor of Parākramabāhu VI (1411–1466) and Prince Sapumal (who became Bhuvanekabāhu VI), Vīdāgama Maitreya, wrote a stinging castigation of those who worship the gods in his *Buduguṇālaṅkāraya*. It was, no doubt, a text for the consumption of the educated *literati* of the court and for the *gāmavāsi* segment of the monastic fraternity, the likes of Śrī Rāhula. As Ilangasinha notes (pp. 45–46), much of the text is composed to extol the virtues of the Buddha on the one hand and to argue the inferiority of *Brāhmaṇic* gods and the ineffectuality of Hindu priest craft on the other. In this respect the work is significant not only because it depicts the attempts by some members of the *Saṅgha* in this period to decry the worship of Hindu deities, a practice which had attracted as adherents even some of the most distinguished monks of the day, but it also raises the specter of an antipathetic response to the Sinhala Buddhist inclusion of deity veneration. It is clear that Vīdāgama's ruthless and sarcastic condemnation of *Brāhmaṇic* practice and belief emerged as a result of immense Hindu influence on the royal court and society-at-large during this period.

The *Buduguṇālaṅkāraya* (Ornament of the Buddha's Virtues), written in 1470 by Vīdāgama Maitreya, must have been the author's final work. Peiris and Van Geyzel, who have translated a portion of the *Buduguṇālaṅkāraya* refer to Vīdāgama Maitreya as:

> The author [who] belonged to a strict puritan sect and [who] spends much energy in preaching against brahmins and other worshippers of gods. In the first extract given here, the king has just been advised by one of his counselors to seek aid for the plague-stricken city from Jains.

> Another counselor now pours scorn on the Jains, and recommends instead the Brāhmaṇic offerings to Agni the fire-god. Another counselor pours scorn on this suggestion also, but recommends the worship of Śiva. Yet another counselor thinks is that Vishnu is a worthier object of worship, but he in turn is attacked by another. All the descriptions are full of sarcasm.
>
> (Reynolds 1970: 269)

The context of the narrative is a story known first in Sinhala literature through the *Butsaraṇa* (thirteenth century). It is about a plague that occurred during the time of the Buddha at Vesāli originally recounted in the commentary of the *Ratana Sutta*. It cannot be taken as definitive evidence for the thriving cults of Brāhmaṇic deities in Laṅkā on the face of it, because it is referring back purportedly to the time of the Buddha. However, most Sri Lankan scholars (Ilangasinha and Ariyapala, for instance) have read the text in that way.

What it certainly does record is Vīdāgama Maitreya's observations that such worship is fruitless in comparison to veneration of the Buddha. In that sense, it represents an attempt not only to close out deity veneration, particularly of the Hindu gods, but also seems to represent the assertion that worship of the Buddha is a powerful device for managing *laukika* (this-worldly) matters of grave concern. The specific passage regarding the cult of Viṣṇu is as follows:

> "As God of the three Worlds, there is but Vishnu. No other is like him. He alone is worthy of sacrifices," said the minister. "Then let rich offerings be made to him."
>
> When that minister had uttered those words, which proclaimed the special power of Vishnu, another minister who stood nearby spoke in the assembly in this fashion:
>
> "You speak as one who fetches salt water for a thirsty man to drink. Is it because there's too little sorrow here that one should add a further mountain of it?"
>
> "You fear not mockery in this world, and you say what you will in your ignorance, but have you ever heard that anyone has obtained blessings by making offerings to Vishnu?"
>
> " 'Vishnu is present everywhere! Never has he been separated from Sita! There was a war on account of this!' – Now to what end has this lying tale been spread?"
>
> "Rama, who could not get across a sea which a monkey hopped over, is believed to have built a bridge to get himself here. Could a god's power be so small in this world?"
>
> "Listen to my words of truth, for you do not understand! Rama was overtaken by fear, and that is why he started that war with clubs of iron."

> "He blew on his conch, and yet could not expel ill-feeling and appetite from his heart. Since he is in terror himself how could he expel the terrors of men?"
>
> "The sacrifical rites performed for him with a prayer to win salvation in the future are like striving to obtain sweet ghee by setting camel's milk to curdle!"
>
> (Reynolds 1970: 274)

The *Buduguṇālaṅkāraya* continues on to a praise of the Buddha emphasizing his mastery over all the worlds, including heavens and hells, how his followers will not be made to suffer from various calamities:

> All deep pain borne by all species that have life,
> Human or animal, found in the ten thousand universes
> —Of all this, on the day when the Lord
> Attained Buddhahood, not even a trace remained.
> (Reynolds 1970: 277)

Two interesting points are raised in these passages. In addition to the obvious general antipathy expressed in relation to things Hindu, the power of the Buddha is now framed in a decidedly more this-worldly (*laukika*) fashion inadvertently lending support to later Buddhist monastic practices which have not been, traditionally speaking, the wont of the Buddhist *bhikkhu*, for example, trying to assert, through ritual practices, the powers that also, traditionally speaking, were the wont of the gods. I mention this now because it is an issue that comes up in a very different context, political at that, in the twentieth century. That is, that the *Saṅgha* can do for the country what was previously thought to be the prerogative of the gods (Seneviratne 1999: 333–48).

Second, passages like those from the *Amāvatura* and the *Buduguṇālaṅkāraya*, and from the *Saddharmaratnāvaliya*[20] as well, are frequently cited by historians of a nationalist bent to characterize the *Saṅgha* as heroically defending the faith on the one hand and to marginalize the contributions of assimilated communities on the other. Thus, antipathetic sentiment toward the presence of assimilated Hindu deities would also appear to have a deep historical vein within some sections of the Theravāda Buddhist monastic community.

In summary, the period of the twelfth through the sixteenth century in Sri Lanka was one of great political instability and religio-cultural transformation, owing in part to the importation of many Hindu ideas and practices first seen in relation to kingship but also as a by-product of a shifting demography and the burgeoning development of seaborne trade. This Hindu presence is seen not only in the ideology of kingship articulated symbolically by Sinhala kings, but also in the literature and architecture of the period. It is a time in which the popularity of deity veneration was on the ascent. Nonetheless, such veneration of Hindu deities by Sinhala Buddhists met with periodic resistance expressed by eminent Buddhist monks of the orthodox Theravāda *Saṅgha*. But these Hindu deities were eventually "Buddhacized" (or "Sinhalized") in the same manner in which migrating Hindus from South India, especially from Kerala, accommodated themselves and were accommodated by incumbents into a new culture.

As is so often the case, patterns of change in religion stand in reflexive relation to larger patterns of change taking place in society. The inclusion of Hindu elements in Buddhist cultic practice and the resistance to this inclusion may very well indeed reflect the more general social patterns of immigration, assimilation, accommodation, and, consequently, reactions to these very processes of social change. This penchant for inclusion and the reaction it sometimes generates is a pattern that seems to be sustained within Sri Lanka's Sinhala Buddhist culture to this day.

Notes

1 For a general historical description of Sri Lanka's variegated religious culture, see Holt (1991: 4–11).

2 Roberts' (1995) study of the *karāva* caste is one of the most lucid accounts that identifies the manner in which arriving immigrants found their cultural and social niches in an increasingly variegated Sri Lankan social milieu.

3 For an account of the reasons why Kataragama remains such an important deity for Sinhalas, see the best study of this deity to date by Obeysekere (1978).

4 The earlier formulation of the four guardian deities included Saman, Vibhīsana, Upulvan, and Skanda, a selection that seems somewhat dependent upon the epic vicissitudes of the *Rāmāyana*.

5 Obeyesekere's discussion (1984: 50–70) of the dynamics of change within the Sinhala Buddhist pantheon of deities is an excellent portrayal of the principles and hierarchies at work in relation to deities, their functions, and their relative roles *vis-à-vis* one another.

6 For a discussion of the religious and social significance of the *perahära* see Seneviratne (1978: 136–70) and Holt (1991: 176–201). For a study of Kīrti Śrī's reorganization of public ritual and Buddhist monasticism, see Holt (1996: 15–40).

7 For an illuminating discussion of this relationship, see Smith (1978: 73–95).

8 R.A.L.H. Gunawardana and K.N.O. Dharmadasa have debated on the issue of just when Sri Lankan royalty can be identified as "Sinhala" royalty *per se*, or more generally when a genuine self-conscious Sinhala identity emerges historically in Sri Lanka. Gunawardana (1990: 45–86) argues that such an identity cannot, without precision, antedate the twelfth century CE. More precisely, his argument is much more subtle than what I have rather baldly inferred. Dharmadasa has written an extensive and detailed critique of Gunawardana's argument. Dharmadasa (1992: 55) finds certain "salient themes" such as the *Sinhaladvīpa* concept articulated at least four or five centuries before the twelfth. This is a very instructive debate about the issues involved and the strategies deployed in determining the nature of ethnic and religious identities.

9 The first section is generally attributed to the Theravāda monk Mahānāma who lived in Anurādhapura in fifth century CE, the second to the monk Dhammakitti who lived in Poḷonnaruva in the twelfth during the reign of Parākramabāhu I, the third to yet another Dhammakitti Thera who lived in Kurunägala in the fourteenth century in the reign of Parākramabāhu IV, and finally the fourth installment written by Tibboṭuvāvē Buddharakkhita of Ridīgama Vihāra who lived in Kandy in the eighteenth century during the reign of Kīrti Śrī Rājasiṅha. Kemper (1991: 42–43) has noted traditions

regarding both of the Dhammakittis that allege that they were foreign monks, possibly from the Cōḷa country of South India.

10 One of the best sources for gaining an effective overview of the religious, artistic, political, and social aspects of culture in the Poḷonnaruva period is Saparamadu (1973). See also Seneviratna (1998).

11 It is difficult to overemphasize the historical importance of Parākramabāhu's reign for the history of Theravāda fortunes specifically and for Sinhala Buddhist culture in general. Not only is the *bhikkhusaṅgha* reconstituted according to the principles of the Pāli *Vinaya*, but the *bhikkhuṇīsaṅgha* was not reconstituted at all. In terms of political history, the preceding 3–4 centuries in India had witnessed a complete shift away from Buddhist ideology in the manner in which kingship had been envisaged. The conversion to Hindu or *purāṇna* related imagery and Kautilyan models of statecraft had been almost complete. In the twelfth century, on the eve of Muslim invasions, it had reached its zenith in prevalence. The Sinhala recovery and re-establishment of a Buddhist kingship at Poḷonnaruva following the Cōḷa invasions was, therefore, an extraordinary development that resisted the larger tides of political and cultural change on the subcontinent. Indeed, unless Tibet is regarded as part of the Indian sub-continent, the Sinhalas were the only Buddhist peoples in South Asia to retain a Buddhist lineage of royalty.

12 Von Schroeder (1990: 671–76) provides very brief discussion of 2 and a blue print plan for 1 of 5 Viṣṇu "devales" [sic] whose remains are still found at Poḷonnaruva. There are some 7 Śiva "devales" and a temple to Kali which have been archeologically surveyed.

13 See Reynolds (1972) and Tambiah (1976) for detailed analyses explicating the Buddhist nuances of understanding this critically important term.

14 Holt (1996) has shown that *Nāyakkar* kings in the late eighteenth century deployed not only these conceptions, but also the concept of *bodhisattva*.

15 P.B. Meegaskumbura points out [private communication] that pure Sinhala was used by Guruḷugōmī for the "narrative elegance of creative writing," but also that Guruḷugōmī culled material for the *Amāvatura* from the *Aṭṭhakathā*s, such that *Amāvatura* can be regarded really as more of a work of editing and translation than as a truly creative work.

16 Here is part of the *Cūlavaṃsa's* account for Rājasiṅha's conversion to the cult of Śiva: "But one day the King, after he had brought a gift of alms, asked the Grand Theras full of anxiety: 'How can I undo the crime of my father's murder?' Then the wise Theras expounded to him the doctrine, but could not win over the wicked mind of this fool. They spoke: 'To undo this crime is impossible.' Full of fury like some terrible poisonous snake, which had been struck with a stick, he asked the adherents of Śiva. The answer they gave him that it was possible, was received like ambrosia, smeared his body with ash and adopted the religion of Śiva" (II: 225–26; 93.6–10).

While the focus of my inquiry is especially directed to Viṣṇu, it is clear that during this time frame significant Śaiva forces made their presence felt, especially in coastal towns, but also in the dynastic capitals as well. Śrī Rāhula's *Sälalihini Sandēsaya* (Reynolds 1970: 286) contains explicit references to a Śiva temple and rituals performed therein. It is also known that Śiva temples existed in Munnesvaram and Devinuvara (Pathmanathan 1986: 85–86).

17 It is interesting to note that Bhuvanekabāhu VII of Koṭṭe (1521–1551), who was the last of the Sinhala kings before Dharmapāla converted to the Roman Catholicism of the Portuguese, signed all of his official proclamations in Tamil. I have learned this from a private communication with Alan Strathern, currently writing his doctoral dissertation on Bhuvanekabāhu VII at Trinity College, Oxford, UK.

18 Sagama rock inscription of 1380 CE (Paranavitana 1943: 310–11); for a brief overview of the Alakeśvara's role in the political dynamics of the late fourteenth and early fifteenth centuries, see Holt (1991: 102–03, 109–10); see also Suravira (1962).

19 Somaratne (1984: 3) cites the *Nikāyasaṅgraha* reference to the four guardian deities as Kihiräli, Saman, Vibhīsana, and Skanda Kumāra, whose respective *dēvālaya*s were located at the four corners of the rampart of the fortress at the Koṭṭe capital of Jayawardhanapura and ritually attended to by *brahmin*s who were provided with accommodation within the royal fort.

20 Ariyapala (1956: 185).

4

THE THERAVĀDA ANALYSIS OF CONFLICTS

Mahinda Palihawadana

The Buddha appeared at a time of political, social, and spiritual unrest in ancient India. Theravāda canonical texts provide testimony to the prevalence of wars between kings and the republican states. The texts also show that the Buddha reflected upon social conflicts arising from crime and poverty, and interminable disputes and confrontations among the many competing religious and philosophical schools of the time.

A striking example of the Buddha's comments on conflicts is found in the *Sakkapañha Sutta* of the *Dīghanikāya*. Sakka tells the Buddha that all people wish to live in peace "without hate, harming, hostility or malignity." In spite of this, they actually live in "hate, harming one another" (Walshe 1996: 328). When Sakka asked why this is so, the Buddha begins the discourse tracing the cause of conflict and hostility to bonds of jealousy and avarice, likes and dislikes, and finally to *papañca*[1] (distortion of perception). Here the Buddha is concerned with revealing the deeper psychological roots of what may manifest itself as a social or political phenomenon. On another occasion, in the *Suttanipāta* (vv. 862–74), too, the Buddha traces the origin of disputes to sense perception and to its distortion (or the condition) of *papañca* (Norman 1984: 144).

How perceptions lead to error is the theme of the *Madhupiṇḍika Sutta* (M.I.108) where the Buddha gives a terse summary of his teaching. Interestingly, in this summary the Buddha teaches how to handle perceptions so that they do not lead to latent tendencies; this is the art of living without conflicts. When this is referred to the Elder Mahākaccāna for a fuller explanation, he gives an analysis of the various stages of sense perception as they occur in any ordinary person. He points out that "thinking" (P. *vitakka*) follows perception and it is this that leads to distorted perception (P. *papañca*) and thence to violence and conflict.

When one frequently thinks some kind of thought, a thought-habit or a tendency develops[2] and remains latent in the mind. But why does one think such a thought in the first place? The *Vāseṭṭha Sutta* (Sn. 115) has the answer to this question. One thinks as others do, that is, one follows the conventions of thought found in one's surroundings. As this happens again and again, one becomes habituated to such thought; it becomes so strong that the mind becomes "bent" on thinking in that way, a simple explanation of how biases, prejudices, and stereotypical notions are unconsciously imbibed by us in the course of growing up in society. This is flawed perception, which really amounts to ignorance or delusion. We can therefore conclude that in the contexts mentioned, the Buddha sees ignorance or flawed perception as the factor that is responsible for all conflicts.

Theravāda canonical texts often trace the origin of conflicts to opinions, beliefs, and ideologies. The question arises, are they any different from "distorted perception" discussed in the previous paragraph? The umbrella term for beliefs, opinions, and ideologies is *diṭṭhi*. The Pāli term *diṭṭhi* derived from the root *dis* (to see) means "view." Although in some contexts the word stands for religious views, in its actual usage at the hands of the Buddha, it has acquired a far more complex significance. According to this usage, a habitually held view becomes a latent tendency of the mind (P. *diṭṭh'ānusaya*), something invested with emotional content. The classic example is the idea of me and my self; compounded with other conventional "views," an entire list of things such as my clan, my country, my language, my nation, and my creed emerge.

In the *Vāseṭṭha Sutta* (Sn. 594–656), the epic exposition of the Buddha's teaching of the biological indivisibility of humankind analyses methodically how the notion of "difference-by-birth" has come to occupy such an important place in our consciousness. It is a "designation" that has arisen by common usage in the world. In four words – *dīgharattaṃ anusayitaṃ diṭṭhi-gataṃ ajānataṃ* – verse 649 of the discourse brilliantly sums up the unconscious evocative power of the idea of "difference-by-birth." Here "view" (P. *diṭṭhi*), "ignorant persons" (P. *ajānataṃ*), and "latent tendency" (P. *anusaya*) are interlinked. A mistaken view has remained in memory for a long time and has become a mental habit. An example of this is the notion of *nāma-gotta* or name-and-clan, that is, the common assumption "I am of such-and-such lineage." The last word, *ajānataṃ*, a negative form from the root *na* (to know) indicates how, unconsciously or without knowledge,[3] the notion of differentiation by birth has taken root in the mind. Racial consciousness is unexceptionably an expression of this differentiation by birth, which the *Vāseṭṭha Sutta* determinedly exposes as a misconception, a designation formulated from place to place.[4]

In *diṭṭhi*, one can detect the flawed cognitive aspect of human consciousness. The cognitive aspect is, however, not the only dimension that needs attention but also other mental tendencies such as craving, pride and arrogance, ill will, and aggression (S.III.254). The canonical texts of Theravāda identify these more complex affective characteristics of the flawed consciousness as common causes of social conflict and violence. The *Aṅguttaranikāya* (I.201) states that greed, hate, and ignorance create misery for others. The thoughts of hunger for power and the thinking that "I have power, I want power" (P. *balava'mhi, balattho iti)* propels belligerent conduct. According to the *Majjhimanikāya* (I.86f), it is due to lust (P. *kāma*) that kings, Brahmins, householders, parents, children, brothers, sisters, and friends and colleagues get into disputes and conflicts (P. *kalaha/viggaha/vivāda*) and end up fighting with destructive weapons.

So this is how distortions of perception lead to cancerous mental habits; yet this is a development of which we are wholly unaware. It is part of the ignorance or delusion, which is said to be the origin of the whole cycle of human suffering. A perceptive person may discover this, as did the Buddha. He then points it out to others, bringing awareness where there was none before. Such awareness, carefully nurtured, weakens the power of the tendencies and in the fullness of time liberates the mind from their grip.

To sum up, there is in us a habitual tendency to distorted perception, which causes the intrusion of all kinds of prejudice into our relationships. But we are not aware of this constant interference of the past. Because of this unawareness, which is our ignorance or our delusion, we see humanity fragmented as "me" and others, us and them, and in various other stereotypes – skin color, ethnicity, language, ideology included. When we are trapped in these conceptual moulds, we lose our natural sensitivity and compassion, and become prone to violence and excessive attachment to separative notions such as "our people," "our homeland," etc. We become hardened and lose the ability to see the essential similarity of human beings, which the Buddha sums up in the saying "as I am, so are they; as they are, so am I" (Sn. 705). We thus remain in ignorance of a very important aspect of our humanity. This is the ultimate source of the micro- and macro-conflicts among human beings.

On this model, conflict originates from the same root as suffering. For that very reason, the way to the resolution of conflicts cannot be different from the Noble Eightfold Path which the Buddha recommended for the "pacification" of suffering.

It seems to me that this would be an approximation to a valid Buddhist approach to the causation of conflicts. However, Buddhism does not adopt the skeptical and pessimistic view that we are destined to remain in this state. The Buddha explained that change is a very difficult process but not an impossible one. In fact the whole of Buddhism is an enterprise "to transform" human beings from what they are to what they "ought to be" (Jayatilleke 2000: 52), or rather to what he has the potential to be. Aṅgulimāla, the serial killer is an example of one who underwent a sudden change of heart. Usually however, there are no such short cuts, only a systematic, long-term program of moral education. It is for such change in society that the Buddha gave his discourses and founded the *saṅgha*.

> The stress on a gradual process of change and training, beginning with moral habits, stretches like a thread across the Buddhist texts. There is a firm belief that discipline, education and the taking of one step at a time can lead people from a state of relative ignorance to greater wisdom. The possibility of gradual change must be admitted alongside the sudden change of Angulimala.
>
> (Harris 1994: 38)

The *Dhammapada* (v. 183) recommends: "To abstain from what is morally bad, to do what is wholesome and to purify one's mind – this is the teaching of Awakened Beings." The last, cleaning up one's mind, is inward change and the liberation of Buddhism, which the Buddha declared to be the essence and flavor of his teaching (V.II.239; A.I.198). It implies a new mode of perception and a new kind of relationship with the world – which necessarily signifies the absence of that antagonism toward others from which we cannot escape under normal circumstances. To be free in this manner is to have that strength of character that can be at ease with persons of all types and ideas, viewpoints and perceptions that differ from our own. From the Buddhist point of view, the direct way of achieving a real difference lies on these lines.

Causation in large-scale social and political conflicts

In the Theravāda Canon, there are instances where the question of social and political conflicts on a mass scale has been addressed. Two of such examples are the discourses named *Cakkavattisīhanāda Sutta* (D.III.58–79; Walshe 1996: 395ff) and *Kūṭadanta Sutta* (D.I.127–49). In these cases, the roots of conflict lie not only in individual consciousnesses, but also that it is the very structure of society that encourages those roots to grow.

Although obviously mythological in character, these two discourses mirror important Buddhist ideas on the relationship between violence and poverty. The *Cakkavattisīhanāda* shows how successive "universal monarchs" kept social problems at bay by following the sage dictum "whosoever in your kingdom is poor, to him let wealth be given." Ultimately there came a king who disregarded this advice and allowed poverty to continue. Only when he found that the poor got into the habit of breaking the law by stealing, did he give them wealth, hoping that they would set up businesses and lead a stable life, without resorting to crime. But this did not happen. Now more and more people resorted to stealing, in order to get assistance from the king. When the king found this out, he changed his tactics. He decided to punish the wrongdoers with extreme severity; in fact he completely wiped them out. But, instead of fulfilling the king's wish that this should serve as a deterrent and make his subjects remain within the law, the latter decided that it would be good for them to do as the king did. They obtained weapons and "launched murderous assaults on villages, towns and cities" and indulged in highway robbery and violent murder. Once they got accustomed to this kind of violence, every thing started going wrong, resulting in killing, deliberate lying, evil speech, adultery, incest, covetousness and hatred, false opinions, lack of respect for parents, clan elders, and the religious, in short the breakdown of all social norms (D.III.70f).

The *Kūṭadanta Sutta* (D.I.134–36) also speaks of a king whose kingdom was ravaged by thieves and brigands. His Brahmin adviser advocated him that:

> This situation will not be solved by executions, imprisonments or other repressive measures, for those who survive such measures will continue

> to cause problems (as often happens in anti-guerrilla measures today). He then gives an alternative plan to "completely eliminate the plague," which involves granting grain and fodder to those who cultivate crops and keep cattle; granting capital to traders; and giving proper living wages to those in government service.
>
> (Harvey 2000: 198)

Peter Harvey sums up the key message of these texts: "[I]f a ruler allows poverty to develop, this will lead to social strife, so that it is his responsibility to avoid this by looking after the poor, and even investing in various sectors of the economy" (2000: 198). Where this is not done, the result will be crime and lawlessness, as is shown in the *Cakkavattisīhanāda Sutta*.

In the contribution "How to Reform a Serial Killer: The Buddhist Approach to Restorative Justice," David R. Loy offers some illuminating insights on the *Cakkavattisīhanāda Sutta*:

> In spite of some fanciful elements, this myth has important implications for our understanding of crime and punishment. The first point is that poverty is presented as the root cause of immoral behaviour... Unlike what we might expect from a supposedly world-denying religion, the Buddhist solution has nothing to do with accepting one's "poverty karma." The problem begins when the king does not give property to the needy, that is, when the state neglects its responsibility to maintain what we call distributive justice. According to this influential *sutta*, crime, violence and immorality cannot be separated from the broader questions about the justice or injustice of the social order... the king's violent attempt at deterrence sets off an explosion of violence that leads to social collapse... If punishment is sometimes a mirror-image of the crime... in this case the crime is a mirror-image of the punishment. The state's violence reinforces the belief that violence works. When the state uses violence against those who do things that it does not permit, we should not be surprised when some of its citizens feel entitled to do the same... The emphasis on nonviolence within so much of the Buddhist tradition is not because of some other-worldly preoccupations; it is based upon the psychological insight that violence breeds violence. This is clear example, if anything is, of the maxim that our means cannot be divorced from our ends. There is no way to peace; peace itself is the way.
>
> (2000: 152–54)

Loy's assessment that, ends are not separable from means, is a necessary conclusion, stemming from the Buddhist portrayal of the causal process. The opinion of some who take Buddha's reference in the *Abhayarājakumāra Sutta* (M.III.195) to the unavoidability of giving pain when removing an obstruction in a child's throat, as an endorsement of the notion of the end justifying the means is, as far as I can see, a misunderstanding. There is no comparability between pain in a lifesaving treatment and the lifedestroying violence that occurs in war. The pain involved in the removal of the obstruction is in any case not the means to the child's recovery. It is an incidental side effect, which would and should be avoided if a better way could be found (which eventually anesthesia has done). In social terms Buddhism is that search for a better way to replace violence.

In her assessment of these discourses, Elizabeth Harris comments:

> The *Cakkavattisīhanāda Sutta* presents a disturbing picture of how a society can fall into utter confusion because of a lack of economic justice. The extremes reached are far greater than anything envisaged in the *Kūṭadanta Sutta* and they stem from the state's blindness to the realities of poverty.
>
> (1994: 23)

Harris goes on to show how according to the *Sutta*, criminality in society spirals to the point when people behave as if they see one another as wild beasts: it is as if an evolutionary drift toward extreme violence has taken place.

> It is significant that the *sutta* does not concentrate on the psychological state of the people. The obsessive cravings, which overtake them, are traced back to the failure of the state rather than to failings in their own adjustments to reality. The root is the defilement in the state – the *rāga, dosa* and *moha* in the king, which afflict his perception of his duty.

One cannot preclude the fact that the psychological state of the people had indeed deteriorated and that in this instance the *sutta* emphasizes the responsibilities of the state. The *sutta* does not suggest that the deteriorated psychological condition of the people can be restored and radically improved merely by the state adopting the correct social and economic policies. Such a (Marxist) conclusion would run counter to the Buddhist teaching that that there can be no external source of liberation.

Can there be a world without wars?

War is one of the great curses of humanity. But are we doomed to live with it? What does Buddhism say on this? It would seem that Buddhism recognizes war as a fact of life, even as it projects the possibility of an ideal world of peace and sanity.[5] Nowhere in the canonical texts can we find an instance where the use of military force is justified or the role of the fighter idealized.[6] The conduct that is idealized as befitting a true follower of the Buddha is that of the person who never thinks a thought of anger, even when subjected to extreme torture: "Bhikkhus, even if bandits were to sever you savagely limb by limb with a two-handled saw, he who gave rise to a mind of hate towards them would not be carrying out my teaching" (M.I.129). This most extreme rejection of the use of force is certainly exceptional, but what reason is there to think that it was not meant to drive home a message?

The Buddha's comments on hearing of the wars between Ajātasattu and Pasenadi Kosala do not appear to be an endorsement of war; rather they portray his considered opinion that war only leads to misery and degradation: "Victory breeds hatred, the defeated live in pain. Happily the peaceful live, giving up victory and defeat" (S.I.83). "The slayer gets a slayer (in his turn), the conqueror gets a conqueror… Thus by evolution of kamma, he who plunders is plundered" (S.I.85).

When Sakka defeats his adversary Vepacitti in battle he does not even retaliate verbally when Vepacitti insults him in the presence of his subordinates (S.I.221). This is not because he is afraid or weak, but because, being a wise person, he knows that one who does not react in hate toward a hater wins a victory hard to win, which serves the true interests of both contestants.

The question of war cannot be discussed without considering the social significance of the ethical precepts, because the necessity of war involves the violation of the first precept. It would be a mistake to assume that the importance given to the observance of the precepts is solely because it is a means of personal, moral improvement. We should note that two things are said about the precepts: (1) one should observe them (P. *samādāna*) and (2) one should also advocate and applaud their observance by others (P. *samādāpana* and *samanuñña*, A.I.194–96). Because of the long held prejudice that Buddhism is predominantly concerned with individual "salvation," the social significance of such Buddhist views tends to be ignored. The so-called "military option" becomes even more incompatible with Buddhism when we realize that the precepts are invested with this wider significance.

The message of Buddhism is that it is possible for individuals to achieve, and abide in, peace and sanity.[7] On the other hand, the Buddha did not even pursue the noble doubt that arose in him once, as to whether it would be possible to run a state righteously, without killing, conquering, or creating grief to self and others (S.I.116). It is true that the *cakkavatti* king is portrayed as going about with the "fourfold army," bringing "rival" rulers under his nominal suzerainty (D.III.62), but he achieves this without firing a single arrow and he does not do so for power or glory but for the promotion of ethical values. Yet it is not unreasonable to infer from this passage that Buddhism found it impossible, even under the best of circumstances, to visualize a state that functions without the backing of an army. It is only a commentary on the human condition, not an endorsement of war.

Buddhist resources for conflict resolution

Following are some of the resources found within Buddhist tradition, which could help in our quest for peace:

1 *The first necessity is the investigation and understanding of the ground reality with all its ramifications*. This is none other than observing the principles of

dependent origination.[8] Buddhist thought stresses the importance of investigating the ground reality (*tathiya* or *yathābhūta*) as comprehensively as possible, not forgetting its vital psychological and socioeconomic implications. We saw how these implications were taken into account in the *Kūṭadanta Sutta* and *Cakkavattisīhanāda Sutta*. In the *Kūṭadanta Sutta*, the king was able to restore peace by addressing the grievances of the impoverished people and taking timely action after being alerted to the social reality by wise counsel.

On the long-term view, Buddhism offers an important insight by pointing out that peace cannot be achieved as long as the seeds of war rule human minds. That is why the investigation of the psychological realities of our situation is important. The Buddhist ethical training is based on the conviction that hidden propensities lose their potency to dominate the mind when brought under the light of observation. The corollary is that a society that is keen on peace must learn to promote that kind of self-education among its citizens.

It would also be quite in keeping with the Buddhist spirit of understanding facts as they really are to recognize that ethno-nationalism is one of the most potent forces in the world whose power we must never underestimate. The reality may even be that the problems created by it are simply too complex to be "solved" by appeal to reason and morality.

2 *There must be the ability to review and leave out, or at least mollify, exclusivist and rigid positions*, which in conflict discourses appear in the guise of "unnegotiable" conditions. Clinging to opinions tenaciously, holding that this "alone is the truth" (Sn. 895; Jayatilleke (2000: 53) has been repeatedly shown in the Theravāda canon as a reason for conflicts among people. "Emotional attachment to dogmatic views…disrupts the harmony of social relations and brings about results which are socially harmful" (Premasiri 1972: 18). The abandonment (*pahāna*) of such attitudes is hailed as a sign of a developed mind or of maturity of character. There cannot be peace as long as people – that is to say the various contending parties – remain irrevocably "fixated" on divisive and exclusive conceptions of nationality, creed, language, culture, and territory.

Where self is not solid and absolute, but is seen as a (changeable) product of the experiences of a person's consciousness, and identification on the part of such a relative self with dogma and ideology is seen as a major cause of social conflict. Buddhism requires that every aspect of behavior be critically investigated: all socially, culturally acquired traits of behavior, etc. will have to pass that test. *The Kālāma Sutta* (A.I.189) advises that one should inquire "Are they free from faults? Do they not conduce to harm?" and if found wanting, they should be abandoned. This procedure is applicable to every aspect of culture. The culture that Buddhism accepts is defined as the "noble tradition," the "noble discipline," etc., but these are really radical innovations, not things picked up from tradition and accumulated.

In this context the Buddha's attitude toward language is instructive. The *Araṇavibhaṅga Sutta* (M.III.234) shows that the Buddha considered language primarily as a tool of communication, not to be elevated to a higher pedestal.

Attachment to territory or 'homelands' is entirely similar to the attachment to culture, language, and nation.

3 *No solution is possible through war, violence, or the vindictive approach.* This has been discussed earlier in some detail and is too obvious to need any further elaboration. The *Dhammapada* (vv. 3–5) states that those who "arm" themselves with memories of harm done to them in the past will never be able to allay hostility. Hostilities are allayed by "not continuing to hate" (one possible interpretation of which is by forgiveness) are actually illustrated in the *Vinaya* (I.342)[9] by a truly remarkable and dramatic story of Prince Dīghāyu who in the face of great temptation resolved an aching personal crisis not by taking revenge but by overcoming the urge to take revenge.

There is a practical implication arising from this. In all conflict situations, both, or all, contending parties have (real or imagined) grievances stemming from historical experience. The observation of the Buddha about past memories of conflict means that this "burden of the past" must be shed in order for peace to be a reality.

4 *The importance of right speech and saying what is true and what promotes unity at the right time.* The Buddha does not advocate "free speech." In discourses such as *Sāleyyaka Sutta* (M.I.285; Nanamoli 1995: 379) and *Sevitabbasevitabba Sutta* (M.III.45; Nanamoli 1995: 913), what he emphasizes is "right" and responsible speech. Right speech is gentle, pleasing to the ear, reasonable, and moderate. Among the many qualities attributed to right speech, the predominant place goes to the consideration that it should promote unity and concord and friendship among people. The speaker of right speech is "not one who divides people, but one who reunites those who are divided, a promoter of friendships" (Nanamoli 1995: 282). But there is a significant proviso attached to right speech. While it must be truthful and factual, it must also be "timely."

In the *Abhayarājakumāra Sutta* (M.I.396), the Buddha enunciates the principles that he follows when speaking:

> He does not say what is unbeneficial to others whether it is true, untrue, correct, incorrect, agreeable, disagreeable, welcome or unwelcome. He says what is beneficial to others if it is true and correct, whether agreeable and welcome or disagreeable and unwelcome, but he says it only at the proper time.

Thus while truth and correctness are important criteria, they are not the only criteria. Nor is agreeability or disagreeability a criterion. The decisive criteria are whether what one says is beneficial to others and whether it is said at the proper time. The lesson that we can learn from this is that, if what we say is true and factual, but is likely to arouse disunity among people, we must wait till the time comes when saying the truth will not arouse any passions like fear and hatred.

5 *Until mutually beneficial and mutually acceptable solutions are found, there should be patient discussions.* This derives from the Buddhist conviction that the improvement of character can be achieved only through an arduous and

carefully nurtured process. All those involved in the peace process have to strive to bring about a change of heart in the population. A solution is possible only when the people are ready to go with it. Peace activists may talk, but change will come only when a critical mass of change has occurred in the minds of the people. No outsider can really change us, says the Buddha; only those who have come thus far will communicate the message that change is indeed possible. Why mutual benefit and mutual acceptability? It is a cardinal principle in Buddhist Ethics that we must strive for not what is good for oneself only; the best course is to strive for what is beneficial to both self and others. Conversely, what is conducive to the injury and oppression of self and others is to be avoided at all costs.

6 *The devolution of authority is a practical model of administration*. This is a resource that can be derived from Buddhist monastic organization. It is clear from the *Vinaya* texts as well as present day practices in the Buddhist monasteries that though the *saṅgha* was essentially envisaged as a universal institution, the practical day-to-day administrative unit was always the local *saṅgha*. It is necessary, however, to emphasize that the local administration was not expected to be capricious or arbitrary; on the contrary it was to be based firmly on the principle that every action had to be consonant with the *dhamma* and the *vinaya*, the *saṅgha*'s central "constitution."

Concluding thoughts

The principles and procedures proposed for personal regeneration in Buddhism are applicable to the path of social regeneration. A resolution to conflicts is possible if one is able to realize the necessity to learn how to loosen the grip exerted by the unwholesome roots. As discussed earlier the attachment (*lobha*), aggression (*dosa*), and delusion (*moha*) are the three roots of unwholesome action. Sooner or later, humanity has to make a valiant struggle toward loosening the grip exerted by these unwholesome roots. This struggle is necessary to escape from the spiral of hate and criminality in which the humanity is now engulfed.

Notes

1 We can broadly accept Ñāṇānanda's explanation of *papañca* as conceptual proliferation (1986). It refers to all that we "think" about a person or an object perceived, all that we associate with that person (e.g., his or her class, caste, race, color, etc.). Such "proliferation" amounts to misperception or distorted perception. On the other hand, authentic perception is not colored by "expansion" or "proliferation"; the Buddha describes the nature of that experience as: "In the seen, there will be just the seen" (Ud.8).

2 What a *bhikkhu* frequently thinks and ponders upon will become the "bent" of his mind (M.I.116).

3 It is not that one is ignorant and thus holds the mistaken view; rather, both ignorance and the view are mutually causative.

4 "For what has been designated name and clan in the world is indeed a mere name. What has been designated here and there has arisen by common assent" (Norman 1984: 107).

5 In A.IV.90, the Buddha stated that he, as a *cakkavatti* of Jambudīpa in a past birth, won this earth without resorting to weapons and ruled it non-violently and in peace.
6 For example, the Buddha is compelled to dispel *yodhājīva*'s mistaken idea of divine company after death (S.IV.308).
7 The *Dhammapada* (v. 197) maintains that persons of insight live in harmony and happiness, even though society is full of haters. Verses 103 and 104 of the *Dhammapada* state that no divine force can overturn the victory of the person who conquers self, not others.
8 The *Suttanipāta* (v. 653) describes the wise as those who see the dependent origination.
9 The king Brahmadatta conquers the kingdom of Didhiti and executes Didhiti and his wife. Just before dying, Didhiti advises his son Dīghāyu not to seek revenge because enmity will never be allayed by enmity. Dīghāyu lives in disguise and manages to find employment at Brahmadatta's court and wins his trust. He gets a chance to avenge his parents' death when Brahmadatta falls asleep on his lap during a hunting expedition. He takes the sword to kill Brahmadatta but thrice desists, remembering the father's words. Brahmadatta awakens and learns what happened. They forgive each other. The king returns the kingdom to Dīghāyu and gives his daughter in marriage to him.

5

A 'RIGHTEOUS WAR' IN BUDDHISM?

P.D. Premasiri

Sri Lanka has been experiencing the agonies of war for almost two decades resulting in the death and maiming of thousands of her citizens. Despite recent moves for a peaceful resolution of the conflict, tension has not eased and the country is not completely free from the dangers of a resumption of hostilities. There are two major parties to the conflict, each of which is convinced about the justifiability of its own cause. Those who advocate LTTE (Liberation Tigers of Tamil Eelam) militancy are strongly of the opinion that this organization is fighting a 'just' or 'righteous' war against oppression of the minority Tamil community by the majority Sinhalese who control the legislative and executive power of the state. They claim that a separate state carved out of the present territory of Sri Lanka is the only solution to their problem, and that since this is not possible by peaceful means, it has to be achieved by means of armed struggle.

The majority Sinhalese in general claim that Sri Lanka has been one country throughout known history, and that under no circumstance should the territorial integrity of the Sri Lankan state be sacrificed in the interests of peace. There is also a much stronger opinion expressed by those who have been advocating the restoration of Sinhala-Buddhist supremacy in the country since gaining independence from colonial rule. They contend that Sri Lanka should not only safeguard her territorial integrity but also remain as a predominantly Sinhala-Buddhist state. It is the demand for separation on the one hand and the demand for the establishment of Sinhala-Buddhist supremacy on the other that seriously hinder a peaceful settlement of the Sri Lankan ethnic conflict.

The two main parties to the conflict also represent people who inherit two of the world's most ancient religious traditions. Buddhism is the religion of a large majority of the Sinhala community. It is also evident that the most prominent among the Sinhala community who advocate war as a solution to the problem are leading people belonging to the Buddhist lay and monk communities. They perceive the Tamil militant movement as primarily a threat to the stability and survival of Buddhism in Sri Lanka. Sri Lankan historiography has created a distinct Sinhala-Buddhist ethnic identity assigning the historical role of the protection of the Buddha *sāsana* to the Sinhala leaders of the lay and monk communities. The majority of the Tamils in Sri Lanka are Hindus, but they rarely perceive any religious connection to the present conflict except that they consider the attitude of the Sinhala-Buddhist lay and monk perceptions of it as a great hindrance to the fulfilment of their aspirations.

Buddhism is a religion well known for its teachings about love and compassion. The ultimate goal of a person treading the path of Buddhism is the attainment of perfect inner peace. Whatever the worth of a desired end may be, the Theravāda canonical scriptures, considered to be the primary source of the Buddhist system of moral values of the Sinhala-Buddhist community of Sri Lanka, contain absolutely no instance in which violence is advocated as a means of achieving it. This is in clear contrast to Hindu scriptures like the *Bhagavadgītā* that contain a concept of a 'righteous war' (Skt. *dharmayuddha*). Buddhism considers war and conflict as evil and teaches how an individual could transcend the universal tendency to engage in conflicts, debates, disputes and wars. However, in the early periods of Sri Lankan history as well as in the ongoing ethnic conflict, those who profess to be Buddhists do not seem to have seen any contradiction in advocating war for the purpose of safeguarding Buddhism.

Concerning this apparent contradiction the opinion has been expressed that Sinhala-Buddhist nationalism has transformed the character of Buddhism from being religion as moral practice to religion as a cultural and political possession (Tambiah 1992: 59). It is argued that the original soteriological function of Buddhism emphasizing the cultivation of moral virtues has been replaced by a different social and political function conceived in terms of parochial interests concerning racial and ethnic identity. Those who see the historical development of Buddhism in Sri Lanka in these terms believe that this transformation has been a great contributory factor to the present ethnic conflict. Tambiah observes that even in the case of Buddhist monks 'important tenets of the religion regarding detachment, compassion, tranquillity and non-violence and the overcoming of mental impurities are subordinated and made less relevant to Sinhala religionationalist and social reform goals' (Tambiah 1992).

As some of those who seek to justify the attitudes connected with Sinhala-Buddhist nationalism would like to put it, Buddhists are confronted with two kinds of enemies to battle against. The first kind is that Gotama Buddha, the founder of the religion pointed out as the unskilled mental states, and personified as the armies of death (P. *mārasenā*). The second kind are those external forces that constantly conspire to destroy Buddhism by weakening the Sinhala race, recognized as the very custodians of the religion who preserved Buddhism in its pristine purity. They perceive the present militant movement of the Tamils (LTTE) as one supported by the enemies of Buddhism including those of the Western world who desire to attack the Buddhist heritage of Sri Lanka and to Christianize the Sinhala people. Therefore, they perceive the war against Tamil terrorism as a just, righteous and necessary one.

This chapter will not attempt to come to any conclusions about the justifiability of the claims of the two contending parties. Its objective is to go back to the canonical Buddhist sources and to examine whether the normative principles of canonical Buddhism can be invoked in favour of a righteous war involving the protection of Buddhism. An attempt will be made to present as far as possible all the material relevant to the issue. When all the material is presented one might find that it is not surprising that people who profess to be Buddhists also advocate war and directly participate in war. It is not a new phenomenon but one that Buddhism implicitly recognized as a possibility even during the canonical period.

There is no doubt that the ultimate goal of Buddhism is to overcome conflict primarily at the level of individual consciousness. This is evident from the answer that the Buddha had given to a person who questioned him about the doctrine he propounded. The doctrine of the Buddha is such that one who lives in accordance with it succeeds in living in the world without coming into conflict with anyone (M.I.109). The Buddhist path of moral development is described as the noble and incomparable path of peace (P. *anuttaraṃ santivarapadaṃ*). The requirements of the Buddhist path are to be fulfilled when one's mind attains perfect peace. *Nibbāna*, the ultimate attainment can be described as the attainment of inner peace.

According to Buddhism, the foremost truth about the human condition is the existence of *dukkha*. The term *dukkha* connotes all disappointments, frustrations, discontents, unhappiness as well as the unsatisfactory state of affairs characteristic of the world of mental and physical nature. The persistence of *dukkha* in all its different forms is dependent on the activity of unwholesome mental processes referred to in Buddhism as *āsava* (influxes), *anusaya* (latent evil) and *kilesa* (psychological defilements). All inner psychological conflicts as well as conflicts produced in society are traced in Buddhism to these psychological causes. All wars, according to the Buddhist view, originate in the minds of people. Buddhist teachings maintain that the mental processes referred to as unskilled or unwholesome (P. *akusala*) determine the behaviour of the large majority of living beings. Conflict in society is therefore, considered in Buddhism to be endemic. The *Sakkapañha Sutta* draws attention to this as follows:

> Devas, men, Asuras, Nagas, Gandhabbas and whatever other different kinds of communities are there, it occurs to them that they ought to live without mutual hatred, violence, enmity and malice. Yet for all they live with mutual hatred, violence and malice.
>
> (D.II.276)

The intensity of the miseries produced when conflicts arise in human society is described in the *Mahādukkhakkhandha Sutta* as follows:

> Having taken swords and shield, having girded on bow and quiver, both sides mass for battle and arrows are hurled and knives are hurled and swords are flashing. Those who wound with arrows and wound with knives and decapitate with their swords, these suffer dying then and pains like unto dying.
>
> (Horner 1954: 114; Trenckner 1888: 86)

In several other contexts such as the *Kalahavivāda Sutta*, *Madhupiṇḍika Sutta* and *Mahānidāna Sutta*, the Buddha explains the psychological origins of such conflict. Conflict is explained in these instances as a consequence of an unenlightened response to one's sensory environment. As long as people lack an insightful understanding of the mechanical nature of the reactions to the sensory environment produced by unwholesome roots of psychological motivation conflict in society cannot be avoided. Buddhism traces conflict in society to certain instinctual responses of people such as the attraction to what is pleasant, the repulsion against what is unpleasant, the pursuit of what gives pleasure, the psychological friction against what produces displeasure, the great desire to protect one's own possessions, the irritable feeling experienced when other persons enjoy possessions that one is incapable of acquiring, competing claims on limited resources, ideological disagreements involving dogmatic clinging to one's own view and so on. The selfish pursuit of sense pleasures (P. *kāma*) is considered as the root cause of conflict. Where there is sympathetic concern, compassion, sharing, charitableness and generosity conflict can be minimized. The latter attitudes, however, are not instinctive. They need to be cultivated through proper reflection and insightful understanding.

It is evident that in instances such as the one mentioned in the previous paragraph where Buddhism refers to conflicts, their source as well as their consequence is considered to be evil and undesirable. The unwholesome impulses that generate conflict as well as the unwholesome psychological states and patterns of behaviour that grow and become manifest in situations of violent conflict negate righteousness. It would, therefore, imply that there could not be a righteous war from the Buddhist point of view.

The only instance in which Buddhist canonical sources speak of victory or conquest through righteousness is where reference is made to the political principles of a *cakkavatti* who conquers territory not with the force of arms but through principles of morality. The idea of a just or righteous war involving the use of weapons of war and violence is conspicuously absent in the Buddhist canon. The Buddha countered the prevailing belief that soldiers of war who fight for a cause could, as a consequence of their rightful performance of duty, aspire to attain a heavenly rebirth if they succumb to their injuries while in combat. According to the Buddha one who fights a war does not generate wholesome thoughts but thoughts of malice and hatred, which are absolutely unwholesome (S.IV.308). Therefore, their future destiny will be a woeful one, which is in accordance with their unwholesome *kamma*.

The *Aṭṭhakavagga* of the *Suttanipāta* speaks of conflicts, debates and disputes prevalent among people who pursued the religious life, dogmatically clinging to mutually contradictory opinions or theories on the nature of the good life. Although the context in which such disputes are mentioned did not involve any armed combat, the Buddhist analysis of the psychological conditions that determined them can be seen to be applicable to all situations in which disputes arise. The Buddha's observations on the psychological and behavioural processes that operate in situations of conflict are very relevant to instances in which people argue in favour of righteous wars.

There is no doubt that in the modern civilized world, war or aggression motivated by imperialist and expansionist intentions is subjected to universal condemnation. Similarly deprivation of human rights and oppression of the weak by the strong is also widely open to moral condemnation. However, it is to be noted that each party currently engaged in war attempts to show that violence is the only alternative available to achieve what is perceived to be the righteous cause. The point made by the Buddha in this connection is that people are psychologically incapable of forming opinions about what is right and wrong, just and unjust, righteous and unrighteous while being immersed in their defiled psychological condition. They may express strong convictions about what is just and right, but when objectively examined they turn out to be mere rationalizations of their pre-conceived notions, desires, cravings, likes and dislikes. When the unwholesome roots of motivation are removed conflicts and disputes no longer arise. When people make decisions about what is right and wrong, just and unjust while they are still affected by the roots of evil, greed, hatred and delusion their judgements are mere rationalizations. What we may conclude from this is that Buddhism allows no place for righteous wars.

The Buddhist canonical standpoint elucidated in the previous paragraph shows clearly that the psychology of war is antithetical to the psychology of Buddhist liberation. Liberation is ensured only by the elimination of greed, hatred and delusion. Greed, hatred and delusion and other ramifications of these basic roots of unwholesome behaviour produce war, whatever form it takes. This would imply that if every Buddhist pursued the Buddhist goal of liberation there should be no wars in Buddhist communities. But can we reasonably expect this to happen? The Pāli canon itself bears evidence that even the Buddha did not expect it to happen. It would be totally unrealistic to entertain such an expectation.

A Buddhist community, like any other one consists of people of different degrees of moral development. Ordinary lay Buddhists are referred to as persons who enjoy the pleasures of sense (P. *kāmabhogino*). Here we should note that the pursuit of *kāma* (sense pleasures) is seen in Buddhism as the most proximate psychological cause of conflict. Disputes arise even between members of the same family, of the same caste, race or social group, between nations, etc. due to the pursuit of *kāma*. People who are engaged in this pursuit are not liberated beings in the Buddhist sense; since they are not free from the roots of evil, greed or lust, hatred and delusion.

The *Mahānidāna Sutta* describes, in terms of the Buddhist doctrine of dependent origination, how people are driven to conflicts as a result of seeking to secure their cherished possessions. People are strongly attached to their material possessions, their cultural traditions, their belief systems, their values, etc. If they perceive a threat to any of these things to which they are attached the natural tendency is to be drawn into conflict. This is why Buddhism considers conflict as an unavoidable evil in society. Even the *cakkavatti* ruler who rules according to the principles of justice does not disband his armies. For, he too had secular duties to perform as the guardian of his citizens. This shows that Buddhism does not envisage a society in which the necessity for engaging in war never arises. Perhaps the implication is that even a righteous *cakkavatti*, who will not engage in wars of imperialist aggression, would need to fight in self-defence.

In Buddhist canonical mythology there is reference to two types of celestial beings, one representing the righteous, the *devas*, and the other representing the unrighteous, the *asura*s. The two groups are mentioned as engaging in war from time to time. Sakka, the most devout Buddhist deity led the battlefront of the *deva*s against the evil *asura*s. Sometimes Sakka is represented as ordering the leaders of his armies like Suvīra and Susīma to act vigilantly and effectively against the aggressive enemy forces. However, in such instances Sakka concedes the fact that the Buddhist goal of *nibbāna* is of much greater worth than the victory over a mundane conflict (S.IV.216). Sakka himself, advices the combatants on his side that when they are overcome with fear in the battlefield, confronted by the advancing enemy forces, they should take courage by looking towards the might and glory of Sakka or that of any of the other powerful deities in order to be rid of their fear. The Buddha says that by this means they will not always be rid of their fear because neither Sakka nor any of the other deities is free from lust, hatred and delusion. They can all be overcome by fear and flee in the face of a threat to their lives.

The Buddha says that his *bhikkhu* disciples who may be overcome by fear when they battle against the inner foes of the mind meditating in desolate places may look towards the Buddha to be rid of their fear. In this case they would indeed succeed, for the Buddha is free from lust, hatred and delusion and therefore would not be overcome by fear, or flee in the face of danger. In another instance Sakka speaks to the Buddha about the joy and happiness he experienced by becoming victorious over *asura*s after engaging them in war But Sakka says that the joy he experienced then was associated with the victory obtained from violent armed conflict and therefore did not conduce to the Buddhist goal of liberation. He contrasts that joy with the joy, which is free from any associations with violence that he experienced after listening to the good teaching of the Buddha. That, he says, is joy that leads to disenchantment with all worldly things and to the ultimate peace of *nibbāna* (D.II.285). In these instances it is implied that armed conflict is not compatible with any serious commitment to the Buddhist goal of liberation, but may on occasion be unavoidable in the case of people dealing with mundane affairs. Even the pious Buddhist deity Sakka, as a participant in mundane affairs, was no exception to this.

The points highlighted in the discussion should not be taken as implying that Buddhism places no moral restrictions on people who are concerned with mundane affairs in going to war. War involves violent behaviour on the part of those who directly participate in it, and violence proceeds from malice and hatred whether it is motivated by the desire to achieve what is conceived as a just cause or not. Therefore the canonical teachings often emphasize the importance of conciliatory methods of resolving conflicts before embarking on war.

The ethical teachings of the *Dhammapada* (v. 5) maintain that hatred can never be appeased by hatred and that it can only be appeased by non-hatred. Anger ought to be won over by non-anger, and miserliness by generosity (v. 223). Forbearance and non-injury are considered as cardinal virtues of rulers. The Buddha himself had intervened in situations where people had thought of resolving their problems through war, and persuaded them to resort to peaceful and conciliatory methods of resolving conflicts, drawing their attention to the intrinsic worth of human lives (J.V.412ff).

From the Buddhist point of view, most wars are a consequence of the collectivized emotions ruling over a sound sense of judgement. The teachings of the Buddha contain immensely valuable principles that can be applied for the purpose of educating people for peace. Attention has already been drawn to the role of unwholesome emotions, the various obsessions, prejudices, psychological complexes and pre-conceived notions that influence people's judgements. Collective delusion and ignorance often play havoc in society. A great deal of human suffering is produced as a consequence of improper reflection (P. *ayoniso manasikāra*). If some of the principles of proper reflection (P. *yoniso manasikāra*) introduced in the Buddhist teachings are clearly identified and really applied in social thinking and behaviour, it might be possible to reduce the tendency to seek to resolve disagreements through violence.

Before this discussion is concluded it seems appropriate to mention one last point about the Buddhist canonical accounts relating to war. Where one of the parties engaged in war is considered as righteous and the other as unrighteous, the Buddhist canonical accounts highlight the ethical qualities of the righteous party by showing that although they are compelled by circumstances to engage in war for the purpose of self-defence, they do not resort to unnecessary acts of cruelty even towards the defeated. The righteous party in war avoids harm to the innocent and is ready to pardon even the defeated enemy. Skilful methods are adopted in order to cause the least harm. Texts such as the *Ummagga Jātaka* (J.IV.329ff) illustrate well cases where the enemy could be defeated without injury to and destruction of life.

An example of the ethics of war, which takes measures to minimize the damage resulting from the war, is found in Buddhist mythology where the wars between the righteous *deva*s and the unrighteous *asura*s are mentioned. According to one story, on one occasion the *asura*s defeated the *deva*s and they had to flee from the battleground for the protection of their lives (S.I.224). As they were taking to flight for fear of the enemy they had to cross the Simbali forest. As the armies crossed the forest a large number of nests of Supannas (mythical birds) built on tree tops were in danger of being broken and falling into the ocean as the tree tops were getting crushed by the fleeing armies of the *deva*s. It is said that the armies headed by Sakka, turned back through fear of harming innocent beings not caring for the risk they were facing due to the pursuing armies of the *asura*s. In another mythical story, the *deva*s became victorious over the *asura*s and the king of the *asura*s, Vepacitti was taken prisoner and was brought to the territory of the *deva*s, driven in Sakka's chariot by his charioteer Mātalī, Vepacitti's limbs all bound with chains.

Vepacitti became extremely abusive using harsh words against Sakka, the king of the *deva*s. Sakka, however, did not retort, and the driver of Sakka's chariot was curious to know whether Sakka's behaviour was due to fear or weakness. Sakka responds saying that he is not so stupid as to retort to a foolish person like Vepacitti. Endurance of the abuses of a foolish person, according to Sakka, is a greater strength than retaliation. The last line of the verses where this canonical myth is introduced says 'the person who does not express anger in return for one who expresses anger wins a war which is difficult to win' (S.I.221–22). While mentioning instances in which even the righteous are compelled to fight wars, Buddhism shows the striking difference between the behaviour of the righteous and the unrighteous even when they are warring parties. The canonical teachings also draw attention to the fact that in war, victory brings forth hatred; the defeated lie in grief; the one who is calm or of pacified mind puts aside both victory and defeat and lies in comfort (S.I.83).

In summing up the inquiry into the question whether there can be any reasons in favour of a righteous war according to the canonical teachings of Buddhism, it should be reiterated that war, according to Buddhism is necessarily evil. Anyone who engages in it is compelled to commit acts of violence at least against the enemy who needs to be subdued. Participation in any kind of violence is absolutely out of the question for those who seriously pursue the goal of *nibbāna*. Their only option is to win over those who are cruel and violent through kindness and compassion.

Wars and conflicts are endemic in society, due to the strong tendency of people to protect their own possessions with miserliness (P. *macchariya*) and due to the jealousy that affects people who are deprived of certain possessions enjoyed by others. More often than not, attempts to justify violence could be mere rationalizations of self-interest. Buddhism grants that the large majority, who are engaged in mundane affairs, although they may be devout Buddhists, and may be to a high degree righteous people (as exemplified by the mythological stories of *deva*s headed by Sakka going to war with *asura*s), are sometimes compelled to fight wars. The Buddhist teachings, by means of mythological tales and story telling homilies attempt to introduce a sense of morality and a concern for justice and fair play even in situations where people are compelled to fight wars. Reflection on the Buddhist canonical teachings outlined in this chapter by all Sri Lankans who cherish Buddhist moral values could be useful and important in the context of the current conflict.

6

SEMANTIC TRANSFORMATIONS OF THE *DHAMMADĪPA*

Peter Schalk

The common and frequent translation of *dhammadīpa* is the 'island of the *dhamma*'.[1] *Dhammadīpa* is understood as a reference to the island Laṅkā / Īḷam. The *Mahāvaṃsa* maintains that Gotama Buddha visited Sri Lanka on three different occasions. Later Arhat Mahinda established the *dhamma* on the island. In using the word *dhammadīpa* as the island of the *dhamma*, three decisions have been made. First, the *implied* subject is stipulated to be the island, not the individual. Second, *dīpa* is used to mean the same 'island' and the alternative meaning of 'light' is excluded. Third, the compound is a *tatpuruṣa* and not a *bahuvrīhi*. I have my doubts with regard to the correctness of these three decisions. These interpretations have no support either in the canonical passages where the word *dhammadīpa* appears or in the post-canonical *Mahāvaṃsa* 1: 84. One has to examine critically these conventions because they cement Sinhalatva values. An examination of these semantic transformations of the concept of *dhammadīpa* will relativise the present Sinhalatva interpretation and will place it in its rightful position. There are at least three concepts of *dhammadīpa*: (i) the canonical one, (ii) the 'vaṃsic' one and (iii) the *Sinhalatva* interpretation. Historians can identify a shift of meaning from the canonical concept of *dhammadīpa* via the 'vaṃsic' tradition to modern *Sinhalatva* concepts.

The canonical concept of *dhammadīpa*

Let us look closer at the canonical concept of *dhammadīpa*. The reference to *dhammadīpa* in the *Mahāparinibbāna Sutta* (D.I.100), has to be translated as '(whoever) has the *dhamma* as (guiding) light'. The *implied* subject is 'whoever'. Depending on the maturity of one's mind, one can acquire the *dhamma* as light to guide one beyond rebirth. The subject is the individual and the *dīpa* is the guiding light. The compound *dhammadīpa* is *bahuvrīhi*. The translation above indicates a universal religious-soteriological concept of *dhammadīpa*. Here the word *dīpa* has generally nothing to do with an island. When the exceptionally ambivalent word *dīpa* means 'island' it is only a metaphor for *saraṇa* (refuge), but it does of course not refer to Tambapaṇṇi/Laṅkā/Īḷam.

In the *Mahāparinibbāna Sutta*, the dying Buddha is reported to have said that the disciples should not have any other *saraṇa* (refuge) other than the *dhamma* (D.II.100–101). He also uses the term *atta* (self), in connection with *dīpa: attadīpa* (having oneself as *dīpa*). It is implied by the context that the monks should have themselves as *dīpa* and not the dying or dead Buddha or anybody else. Furthermore, the Buddha introduces the concept of *dhammadīpa*, which here is not *tatpuruṣa* 'the *dīpa* of the *dhamma*', but which is *bahuvrīhi* 'having the *dhamma* as *dīpa*'. Therefore, we have four terms that are connected with each other in a semantic chain: *dhamma*, *dīpa*, *atta* and *saraṇa*. Connecting these, the Buddha is reported to have said to Ānanda: *Tasmāt ih' Ānanda atta-dīpa viharatha atta-saraṇā anañña-saraṇā, dhamma-dīpī dhamma-saraṇā anañña saraṇā* 'Therefore, Ānanda, dwell you (all), having yourselves as *dīpa*, having yourselves as refuge, having no other refuge, having the *dhamma* as *dīpa*, having the *dhamma* as refuge, having no other refuge' (*Tasmāt ih' Ānanda atta-dīpa viharatha atta-saraṇā anañña-saraṇā, dhamma-dīpī dhamma-saraṇā anañña saraṇā* D.II.100). *Atta* is of course here not 'the soul', but the logical counterpart of reference to somebody else than myself, to 'the other', who is made explicit in the text. The *atta* and the *dhamma* have common attributes, to be a *saraṇa* and to be a *dīpa*. It is implied that *dīpa* is a simile for *saraṇa*. The *dīpa* is not a physical island and is therefore of course not the island Laṅkā.

The monks themselves should seek no other refuge than the *dhamma*, that is their *dīpa* – *saraṇa*. If anything is a *saraṇa*, it is the *dhamma*. *Dhammadīpa* refers to a state of mind when a person has the *dhamma* as *dīpa*. The *Attadīpa Vagga* of the *Aṅgüttaranikāya* reproduces the Buddha's words to Ānanda including the word *dhammadīpa*. In a clearly soteriological context, it adds that those who have *dīpa*, the knowledge about original causation of suffering, know their births.

Different translators of the Pāli Text Society have chosen 'light' sometimes and 'island' sometimes for the same passage when they translate the Buddha's words to Ānanda (DB.II.108). If the Buddha refers to 'light', the distance and alienation of the Buddha's words to the modern political interpretation becomes evident.

Commenting on the Buddha's words to Ānanda, the *Sumaṅgalavilāsinī* (1971: 548) compares the *attadīpa* to *mahāsamuddagatan dīpaṃ* (island surrounded by the great ocean). Here the text identifies the *attadīpa* with an island, but not explicitly with the *dhammadīpa*. The *ṭīkā* confirms that the *dīpa* in *attadīpa* is an island in our association with the *dhammadīpa*.[2] These two texts compiled in Sri Lanka do not identify the island with the *dhammadīpa* mentioned in the Buddha's address to Ānanda. It is clear that the *dīpa* as physical island is again nothing but a simile for the concept of *saraṇa*. Even when the *dīpa* refers to an island, 'island' is not a physical entity, but a metaphor for *saraṇa*.

One can find the soteriological meaning again in the post-canonical *Milindapañha* (1962: 257). It mentions an ideal monk who purifies [from evil selfish thoughts] the *dakkhina* (gift) that he receives. He purifies the gift by making his final intention and *gati* (destiny), the acquisition of the *dhamma* as *dīpa*. Here also, *dhammadīpa* is a metaphor for *dhamma* as the ultimate refuge. In the *Milindaṭīkā* (1961: xii–xxiii) of the fourteenth century, the word *dhammadīpa* is not related to the island.[3]

In translating the Pāli text into Sinhala, the modern translators of the *Sinhala Milinda Praśnaya* (1970: 355) have also been faithful to the original without manipulating it with comments. One can, however, imagine a modern mind, heavily preformatted by Sinhalatva concepts, transforming this ultimate aim into a *tatpuruṣa*, making the *dīpa* into an island and the island into Laṅkā. This is exactly what happened with the passage from the *Mahāparinibbāna Sutta*.

In the *Saṃyuttanikāya*, the *attadīpa* is compared to 'mighty tree', and to a 'body'. Those who know what happens to a tree and the body – they are rotten away – will not be sad when facing death of Sāriputta and Moggallāna. The Buddha orders the monks to have the *atta* only as refuge (S.V.164–65). Here it is clear that the *atta* is not an unchanging and eternal soul, but is part of change. The *dhammadīpa* is not made explicit in this text, but it is implied by the fact of the paradigm and that it has been mentioned earlier in the same *Saṃyutta* (v.154). Having the *atta* as *dīpa* makes a person realise that he is part of change, and so, having the *dhamma* as *dīpa* makes a person by implication realise that he is part of this change.

To sum up, the canonical concept of *dhammadīpa* refers to a universal state of mind that is prepared to accept the *dhamma* as only refuge and goes from there towards liberation of the mind from bonds to the world. The concept has nothing to do with a physical island, with a specified territory whatsoever.

The concept of *dhammadīpa* in the *Mahāvaṃsa*

The concept of *dhammadīpa* in the *Mahāvaṃsa* can be analysed as '(the island) having the *dhamma* as (guiding) light'. In the *Mahāvaṃsa*, the *implied* subject is not 'whoever', but a thing, 'the island'. The universal subject has become parochialised. *Dhammadīpa* appears here in a special non-canonical context. The *Mahāvaṃsa* describes the establishment and institutionalisation of Buddhism in the island Laṅkā. The main theme in this description is 'the sealing theme'. It is no doubt an important paradigm in the *vaṃsa* literature. The theme is precisely formulated in 'the coming of the *sāsana* to the island' (Dv. 1: 1).

According to this *vaṃsa* tradition, Gotama himself has literally 'sealed' the island by putting his footprint on the Sumanakūṭa (Mv. 1: 77). As a result of his three visits, the island(ers) have finally got the *dhamma* as *dīpa*, which in the *Mahāvaṃsa* 1: 84 means and refers to 'light'. The compound is again *bahuvrīhi*. Here, one group of the island, the Buddhists, is highlighted and are distinguished by implication from other groups of islanders by their having the *dhamma* as light. In our modern, but also anachronistic, way of expressing this idea, we say that an ideal person, Sinhala or Tamil, is classified as Lankan Buddhist by the pious compiler of the *Mahāvaṃsa*. The *dhamma* here is not Buddhism in general, but Theravāda, more precisely the Mahāvihāra tradition from Anurādhapura at the exclusions of other forms of Buddhism and other religions. This sectarian concept of *dhammadīpa* is found in the *Mahāvaṃsa* 1: 84. Buddhist traditionalists, not Sinhalatva ideologues, retrieve it today. Here, the implied subject is the Lankan Buddhist, not the Sinhala Buddhist. The *Mahāvaṃsa*, compiled in and reflecting interests of the fifth century CE tries to drive home the point that the island cannot be represented but by Buddhist islanders, may they speak Prakrit or Tamil. The first part of the *Mahāvaṃsa* was not anti-Tamil, but it was against anti-Buddhists. When some Tamils were anti-Buddhists, they were rejected not because they were Tamils, but because they were anti-Buddhists.

Religious people in many parts of the world practise paradigmatic historical writing. The Torah's fundamental paradigm is the Covenant between Israel and God. This paradigm is repeated throughout history as parameter for evaluating the performance of Israel in terms of good and bad. One of the four paradigms found in the chronicles is the coming of the śāsana, which results in sealing the soil as Bauddha soil. This paradigm reappears throughout the history of pre-colonial Sri Lanka. It is also related to the *dhammadīpa* concept, but not in the way Sinhalatva ideologues and some scholars present it. The alleged third and the last visit by the Buddha as described in the *Mahāvaṃsa* 1: 84 resulted in a statement – not by the *Buddha*, but by the compiler of the text – that the island has the *dhamma* as *dīpa*. The text (1: 84) states: *dīpo tenāyam āsi sujanabahumato dhammdīpavabhāsīti* (Therefore this island shone with the light of the *dhamma* (and) came to high honour among devotees).[4]

Dīpa is used twice in 1: 84: first in the meaning of 'island' and second in the meaning of 'light' in connection with the *dhamma*. Earlier in the same verse the Buddha is identified with *lokadīpa* (light of the world). The compiler evidently liked to hammer into the mind of the reader that *dīpa* is light. It is evident here that *dhammadīpa* cannot mean 'island of the *dhamma*'. If we would insist on that meaning, the translation would be pure nonsense. It would mean that the island shone with the island of the *dhamma*.

Not only in Geiger's translation into English, but also in the translation into Sinhala such nonsense has found no place. In Sanskritising Sinhala it is possible to distinguish between *dvīpaya* and *dīpaya* and thereby avoid ambiguity. The translation also gives *pahana* (lamp, light), instead of the ambiguous *dīpa*. *Dhammadīpa* is given as *dharma pahana*. The *Sinhala Mahāvaṃsaya* makes clear, that *dīpa* in *dhammadīpa* is understood as light, and that the island is the explicit subject that possesses this light of the *dhamma*. Like the Pāli text, the *Sinhala Mahavaṃsaya* (1967: 6) refers to good men, not to Sinhalese, excluding Tamils: *ē karaṇa koṭa gena me dvīpaya dharma namäti pahanin bäbalum ätta vu sajjanayan visin buhuman karaṇa laddēya* (because of this (the three visits of the *Buddha*), this island, having been brought to shine through the light called *dharma*, has come to great honour among good men).

In the *Vaṃsatthappakāsinī* (1: 118), all explaining words belong to the category of religion, to the religions of the three jewels. The devotees are Buddhists. There is no allusion to any ethnic, communal or racial category.

From all these quotations, it becomes clear that it is not the island that is the *dhammadīpa*. Instead, the island through the visits of the Buddha has the light, which is the *dhamma*. The island has now the *dhamma* as light. The shining of the *dhamma* (as if it was a light) is again emphasised in connection with the prediction by the Buddha in *Mahāvaṃsa* 1: 20, where *Laṅkādīpa* is described as a place where the *śāsana* of the Buddha would shine (P. *sāsanujjotanaṭṭhānaṃ*). There is then a close connection between *Mahāvaṃsa* 1: 20 and 1: 84.

To sum up, the word *dhammadīpa* in the *Mahāvaṃsa* 1: 84 is a *bahuvrīhi* compound. *Dīpa* of the compound means light. The devotees are not defined as a linguistic or territorial ethnic group, but as a group of Buddhist devotees. The passage has to be seen in relation to the *Mahāvaṃsa* where we are told that the *dhamma* was spread not only to Tambapaṇṇi, but to many more regions and countries. Tambapaṇṇi is only one of many places that have the *dhamma* as light. The text says that the island shone with the light of *dhamma*. It does not say that this island is the *dhamma* as ultimate refuge. In spite of all this, some have advanced a Sinhalatva interpretation using the *Mahāparinibbāna Sutta* and *Mahāvaṃsa* 1: 84.

Sinhalatva interpretations of the concept of *dhammadīpa*

Sinhalatva is a recently invented term for an ideology known as *jātika cintanaya* (national thinking). In 2001, Nalin de Silva, former professor of Mathematics, who is well-known for his militant writings, coined the term *Sinhalatva*. For this ideology, earlier I used Sinhala-Bauddha ethno-nationalism.

Sinhalatva interpretations take the *dīpa* in the compound *dhammadīpa* as a *tatpuruṣa*, meaning 'island'. They do not take the Lankans as the implicit subject but as a reference to Sinhala *jātiya* (ethnic group) who rules the island of the *dhamma*. Here the subject is rather limited since it refers to Sinhala Buddhists. Buddhists who belong to the Tamil ethnic group are excluded. It is exclusively an ethnocentric interpretation.

In the beginning of the twentieth century, original soteriological concepts were transformed into political concepts. Anagārika Dharmapāla (1864–1933) used the concept of *dhammadīpa*. For Dharmapāla, *dīpa* had only one reference, physical island. He did not even consider the alternative meaning 'light' or that the island was a *metaphor* for refuge. He also considered the word to be a *tatpuruṣa* compound meaning 'the island of the *dhamma*'. He interpreted *Mahāvaṃsa* 1: 84 from that angle. He also interpreted Sinhala as a racial category and accordingly *sihaladīpa* as the island of the Sinhala race. Dharmapāla also reinterpreted the canonical text, the *Mahāparinibbāna Sutta*. His reinterpretation fits into his ideology of martial Sinhala-Bauddha Sinhalatva.

In 1928, writing to the Mahā Bodhi Society journal, Dharmapāla stated that Ceylon helped the world long before the birth of Christianity. The children of

Ceylon – Ceylon being the *dhammadīpa* – know best what is to be done: 'It is the European followers of the Semitic barbarism that destroyed the aesthetic civilisation of the land of the *dhamma*' (Bechert 1973: 120; Dharmapāla 1928: 70). Alluding to the *Mahāvaṃsa* 1: 84, Dharmapāla changes the meaning of 'having the *dhamma* as light' to 'the island of the *dhamma*'.

A precursor to this is found in a famous pamphlet *A Message to the Young Men of Ceylon* (1922) where Dharmapāla quoted *attadīpā viharatha* (D.II.100) passage and applies the *dīpa* concept to his island in the time of Duṭṭhagāmaṇī 'who rescued Buddhism and our nationalism from oblivion' (Dharmapala 1965: 510). It is implied that the time of Duṭṭhagāmaṇi is similar to our own time that demands a fight against the colonials and the ethnic minorities having been classified as foreigners. His *dīpa* is the (ultimate) refuge from where the resistance against Tamils and the British is mobilised. Further, in direct connection with his canonical quotation in the same speech Dharmapāla states:

> 'We must learn to stand on our legs and not depend on the alien...'
> 'We must work systematically having before us the goal of self-Government and Home Rule...'
> 'We have lost the spirit of patriotic independence...'
> 'With Buddhism Ceylon shall yet become the beacon light of Religion to the World...'
>
> (1965: 511–12)

It seems that the *attadīpa* mentioned by the Buddha is identified – not with human being himself looking for salvation – but with the Dharmapāla's Ceylon under colonial suppression. The *saraṇa* is here not the *dhamma*, but the *dīpa*. Dharmapāla evidently made a political interpretation of the island of the *dhamma*: the island is the place to which the Sinhalayo should seek their refuge and make it independent from destructive foreign influence.

Quoting the *Buddha*'s words, Dharmapāla wanted to encourage the young men of Ceylon to internalise the idea of *dhammadīpa*. His interpretation is a form of Sinhala-Bauddha nationalism in the spirit of Duṭṭhagāmaṇi. It is a communalisation of the Buddha's soteriological and universal concept of *dhammadīpa* as found in the *Mahāparinibbāna Sutta*.

For Dharmapāla, the island was not only the *dhammadīpa* but also the *sīhaladīpa*, in the ethonationalist meaning as the 'island of (or for) the Sinhalayo', excluding the Tamils and the colonials. In accordance with this concept, in 1908 Dharmapāla stated 'To these rulers nothing appeared more supreme than this religion...and was thus completely identified with the racial individuality of the people' (Dharmapala 1965: 509). This is probably one of the most conflict creating public statements made in the twentieth century. It is also a statement that is detrimental nationally and internationally to the reputation of Buddhism. Dharmapāla's interpretation of *dhammadīpa* with the meaning of *sīhaladīpa* made the physical island the ultimate refuge; it was the ultimate refuge for the

Sinhala-only, by excluding all 'foreign' elements. His exclusiveness focused on the welfare of the Sinhala Bauddhas only. He stated explicitly that Laṅkā belongs to the Sinhalese Buddhists.

The wrong interpretation of the concept of *dhammadīpa* facilitated its politicisation. Once the concept was wrongly conceived as *sīhaladīpa* (island of the Sinhalese), it was easy to connect the two words and use them interchangeably: *dhammadīpa* = *sīhaladīpa* and *sīhaladīpa* = *dhammadīpa*. We are now in the very centre of modern *Sinhalatva* thinking.

Final reflections

The present territorial conflict between Tamils and Sinhalese cannot be resolved through religious means, either by going back to the authentic teachings of the Buddha or by appealing to the *Dhammapada* which advocates to overcome hate by love. A territorial conflict has to be solved by distributing the territory for control and for use by both groups – Tamils and Sinhalese. It is through partnership and co-operation between equal parties that a peaceful situation can be created. This has nothing to do with Buddhism or with any other religion. It has to do with pragmatic considerations dealing with gains and losses. We cannot yet expect the two parties – Tamils and Sinhalese – to love or forgive each other. The use of metaphysical concepts of unity may only suspend conflict in short term but it cannot prevent worsening the natural crisis. The concept of a unitary/united state has been an obstacle for peace for decades. This territorial conflict cannot also be resolved by mere historical and critical analysis of the *Sinhalatva* interpretation of *dhammadīpa* as a historical anachronism of recent origin. It is a break with the tradition and is only of relative importance in the long history of Laṅkā. Such an analysis may, if not resolve conflict, discourage Sinhalatva interpretations.

Notes

1 Steven Collins (1998: 598–99) and I had worked independently on the same topic (Schalk 1999: 101–10). A short version of the present chapter entitled 'Inventing History: The Interpretation of the Concept of *Dhammadīpa* by Siṃhala-Bauddha Ethnonationalist' was read at *International Conference on Tamil Nationhood and Search for Peace in Sri Lanka* held at Carleton University and The University of Ottawa on 21–22 May 1999 and was subsequently published as conference proceedings.

2 *Dīghanikāyaṭṭhakathāṭīkālīnatthavaṇṇanā* II.188.

3 For a critical analysis of the *Milindaṭīkā* see von Hinüber (1996: 86).

4 Geiger translates: 'therefore this isle, radiant with the light of truth, came to high honour among faithful believers' (Mahānāma Thera 1950: 9). Turnour's translation is: 'From this circumstance this island became venerated by righteous men. Hence it shone forth the light itself of religion' (Turnour 1889: 2).

7

SINHALA FEARS OF TAMIL DEMANDS

Alvappillai Veluppillai

A common thread running throughout the history of the Sri Lankan ethnic conflict in the postindependence period is the Sinhala fear of the Tamil demand for sharing one nation with two states in which equal opportunity for individuals is guaranteed. Both Sinhalese and Tamils now have fears and there was probably some fear even at the time of independence. The Tamil perspective on this issue is that the majority of Sinhalese could have been magnanimous, accommodative, and reassuring. A peaceful solution to the conflict can be found only if this angle is understood.

The ethnic problem in Sri Lanka can be described as a conflict between Sinhalese and Tamils. Some foreign scholars and journalists describe it as a problem between Sinhala Buddhists and Tamil Hindus (Knipe 1991: 151). This equation is technically correct, but it could be misleading since the Hindus or Hinduism as such is not involved directly in the conflict. The majority ethnic community, Sinhalese, focuses its inflexible attitude for the sake of preserving Buddhism. Some Buddhist monks lead political processions, make inflammatory speeches and even burn national flags of countries, like Norway,[1] which facilitate the peace process in Sri Lanka. Some Theravāda Buddhist majorities seem to have a problem in adjusting to modern multicultural societies. Tambiah points out:

> These convergent attitudes which are common place in these three Theravāda Buddhist countries (Sri Lanka, Myanmar, Thailand) of Southeast Asia, should warn us about the militant and chauvinistic resonances that have constituted the dark underside of other terrifying face of Buddhism as a religio-complex . . . This other face presents itself in the twentieth century as a distorted "political Buddhism" emptied of its ethical content and inflated with the poison gas of communal identity. Under its banner populist leaders mobilize masses who are losing their traditional roots and their traditional Buddhist moral restraints, and

> whip them into a heady collective identity and a fury of displaced and misplaced anger against the alien others, the minorities, who are seen as a challenge to their chauvinistic manhood.
>
> (1986: 139)

Though there is a problem regarding the three Theravāda Buddhist countries, which maintain very close relations, the problem is more acute in Sri Lanka than in Thailand. In Thailand, the Buddhists constitute about 95% of the population and so the minorities manage to co-exist even though they have complaints. In Myanmar, civil war is going on against tribal peoples for decades. Of the three Theravāda Buddhist countries, Sri Lanka has the least the percentage of Buddhists. But some Sri Lankan Buddhist monks claim that politics is their heritage. Some of them have spearheaded the Sinhala nationalist movements; as a result Tamils have suffered in the process. However, there is no Hindu clergy counterpart in the Tamil national movement.

The Pāli chronicles speak about the Tamil invaders of the Buddhist kingdom, and they refer to the Buddhist kings, who defeated the Tamil Hindu kings, as heroes. The Pāli chronicles, written by Buddhist monks, contain myths, legends, and historical facts. One of the narratives in the *Mahāvaṃsa* maintains that the Buddha had specially instructed deities to protect the ancestors of the Sinhalese to enable the establishment and flourishing of Buddhism in Sri Lanka. The victorious Duṭṭhagāmaṇī, anxious about the karmic consequences of his violent activity, is assured by the monks that he need not worry because the thousands killed in the war were nonbelievers and nonhuman; killing them causes no retribution to the king. The chronicle also mentions some events where monks wielded power over their colleagues and over the political power.

There were Tamil Buddhists in Sri Lanka from ancient times. But there was never a Tamil Buddhist king either in Sri Lanka or in South India. Buddhism was a minority religion in South India for more than a millennium. Occasionally there were good relations between Buddhists in Sri Lanka and Buddhists in South India. From about the seventh century CE, some Brahmin poets and authors associated with the *bhakti* movement, were harsh in their condemnation of Buddhism. A recent work has well documented the history of Buddhist legacy among Tamils (Schalk and Veluppillai 2002).

Immediately before and after independence, the Buddhists appear to have talked about an inclusive nationalism, as it was directed mainly against foreign rule and English language. By 1956 an exclusive nationalism emerged directed against a perceived Tamil domination then and possible Tamil domination in the future. The 1972 Constitution went further and focused on Buddhism, obviously to please the Buddhist clergy. The Republic of Sri Lanka is to give Buddhism "the foremost place" and it became the duty of the State "to protect and foster the Buddha *Śāsana*" (Wilson 1974: 246). The 1978 Constitution tried to accommodate the claims of Tamil and English as official languages to some extent but the clause regarding Buddhism was retained. The proposed Constitution of the

People's Alliance (PA) government of 2000 tried to make the clause regarding Buddhism, an entrenched clause in the Constitution, requiring a two-third majority in parliament and the approval of the country at a referendum for amendment. This also spoke about the setting up of Supreme Council in consultation with the *Mahāsaṅgha* and consulting it in all matters pertaining to the protection and fostering of the Buddha *Śāsana*. If this clause were to become an entrenched clause, this could be interpreted in different ways to harm non-Buddhists, especially the Tamils. The government probably calculated that its proposals regarding devolution would not face opposition from the Buddhist clergy, if they found that the clause regarding Buddhism was entrenched in the Constitution.

If this clause were to continue, then the provisions, elsewhere in the proposed constitution, that assure equality of all religions would be incompatible with this, and would therefore become meaningless. Conferring a superior status to the religion of one group of citizens over that of others is of much greater consequence than even the question of what powers would be delegated to the regional councils. Here again, there seems to be a fear to accept the situation that the state should treat all citizens alike. The PA government brought forward an Equal Opportunities Bill a couple of years ago in the parliament and then withdrew it because there was much opposition to accepting equal opportunity for all citizens.

The clause giving Buddhism the foremost place among religions in the country and stipulating a duty of the State to foster and protect the *Śāsana* will make the Buddhists who form nearly 70% of the population of the country, practically a high caste ruling elite. The attempt to make it an entrenched clause signifies that a substantial section of the population is very unhappy about this position and they might try to overturn this position and this overturning has to be made very difficult. It is divisive clauses like this that lead to perpetual conflict in a multilingual and multireligious society. The Buddhists can have their organizations "to protect and foster the *Śāsana*" and contribute to them. It is unfair to force non-Buddhists who form about 30% of the population of the country to pay for the "pleasure" of the other 70% of the population. The Buddhist clergy should agree to let the State to treat all its citizens and ethnic groups alike.

The differences of opinion among the Sinhalese and the Tamils about the ethnic tensions are quite significant. The Sinhalese would suggest 1976 (if not 1983) as the year of ethnic tensions, when the Tamil United Liberation Front (TULF) opted for an independent state for the Tamils when militant movements originated among the Tamils. The Tamils will be suggesting 1948 (if not 1956) when tentative steps were taken for the restoration of a Sinhalese and Buddhist dominated state. According to a Tamil perspective, the Tamils were pushed to the limits of desperation to demand separation and to take up arms in the 1970s (Manogaran 1999). The Sinhalese started to fight against imaginary Tamil separatism in 1957 when the Regional Council/Councils, which S.W.R.D. Bandaranaike (1899–1959) agreed to set up in the Northeast (which was much less than Federalism), was blown up as a separate Tamil country by its Sinhalese opponents of the United National Party (UNP) and others. It was the Buddhist clergy, which forced the issue, marching to Bandaranaike's residence, threatening a sit-in, unless he abrogates the pact. The Sinhalese opponents belonging to the Sri Lanka Freedom Party (f. 1952) and others campaigned against imaginary Tamil separatism again in 1968 when Dudley Senanayake (1911–1973) tried to set up District Councils, "under the direction and control" of the central government in the Northeast. Some Buddhist monks participated actively in this campaign also.

During the late fifties and the sixties, some Tamil politicians put forward the claim for a separate state for the Tamils. C. Suntharalingam, the popular Member of Parliament for Vavuniya, was the first to campaign for a separate state in the late 1950s and early 1960s. The Tamil Federal Party (FP) campaigned against his demand, characterizing it as extremism, and soon he lost even his parliamentary seat. In 1968, when Dudley Senanayake abandoned the District Council bill, V. Navaratnam, MP for Kayts, defected from the FP and started the "Self-Rule Movement," to establish a separate state for the Tamils. In the 1970 elections, the FP put forward a loyal candidate against him and got him defeated in his electorate. These are instances to show that Tamil nationalism continued to be inclusive. The Tamils continued to have hopes of a fair settlement within a united country.

In the ethnic conflict of Sri Lanka, the issue of majority versus minority is very important. Little over one fifth of the population (including Muslim minority) use Tamil language. Nearly 18% of the Sri Lankan population is Tamils in origin and it includes 6% of Tamils of Indian origin who work in plantations in the upcountry. Regionally the Tamils are the majority in the North while the Sinhalese are the majority in the Southwest. It is the Tamil majority in the Northeast who have been fighting, trying to remain afloat, without getting lost and losing their identity. Tamils have been putting forward various demands to be able to share power and to have equal opportunity. The history of the ethnic problem during the last six decades could be described as the Tamils trying to share power and the Sinhalese trying to monopolize power. Even the demand for separation is an attempt to share the island, if the Sinhalese could not agree to share power and wanted to hold on to a virtual Sinhala Buddhist state.

In the Tamil perspective, which has become hardened after half a century of oppression and two decades of civil war, the Tamils, who could have settled down for compromise solutions in the fifties and the sixties, have begun to feel that they constitute a people or a nation. They have their own language, culture, and habitat within Sri Lanka. They are loyal to their motherland and that is why they have been fighting for the last two decades. If Sinhalese nationalism continues to be exclusive, it is doubtful whether unity will ever return to the island. If Sinhalese nationalism can be inclusive, a genuine attempt must be made to make possible real power sharing. As a people, the Tamils want to be treated as equals of the Sinhalese. Independence implies equality before the law and equal opportunity in the country.

The Tamils believe in the sovereignty of the people. State comes into being by the free will of the people. If the present state caters to one people exclusively, the other people should have a right to establish a state of their own and share the island. The unity of the country as well as its territorial integrity can be preserved if constitutional arrangements are so made and governments are so carried on as to enable the Tamils to have equality and equal opportunity.

In the Tamil perspective, the Sinhala talk about the unity and territorial integrity of the country appears hypocritical, because the proper course for establishing the unity of the country is to win over all sections of the people of the country. If all sections of the people of the country can be made to feel that they have a stake in the unity of the country, then, there will be unity and territorial integrity. My personal feeling is that the Sinhalese want to have the land of the Northeast, but not its people. They do not care for the misery of the people under the long civil war and the prolonged military occupation, if land can be brought under the control of the State and ultimately under their control. Some Buddhist monks perform *bodhipūjā*s and bless the armed forces to bring unity by conquest and military occupation. Tambiah, who has written widely on the ethnic issue, points out the irony of the situation:

> I find it necessary to pose the question of how the "sons of the Buddha" – ideally dedicated to nonviolence and required by disciplinary rules to abstain from killing and to be no-where near marching armies and the traffic in arms – have taken on the more compelling identity of "sons of the soil", which entails militant and violent politics.... If in previous times prime ministers and ministers of state did this, now military commanders too worship at the Temple of the Tooth Relic in Kandy upon appointment and obtain blessings from the head monks of the Asgiriya and Malvatta chapters.
>
> (1992: 95–96)

The Tamils have been at the receiving end of all this; they have been treated as foreign enemies. The Tamils have been so demonized that any atrocity against Tamil civilians is glossed over or ignored under the plea that actions against "terrorists" or "terrorist supporters" should not be prosecuted. Military atrocities against the Tamil civilians very rarely received any attention from the State or from the media controlled by the Sinhalese because it was considered "unpatriotic" to condemn them or to take action against them. The agony of the Tamil people in what the Buddhists consider the island of *dharma* has not touched the heart of the vast majority.

During the last 60 years, the Tamils have put forward several demands: (i) fifty-fifty, (ii) parity of status, (iii) federalism, (iv) separation, and (v) self-determination. It is ironic that the Sinhalese are always for unity while the Tamils are always for separation. The Tamils began gradually to demand federalism. What they wanted was power sharing and equal opportunity. At the time of the Soulbury Commission in the mid 1940s, the Tamils demanded fifty-fifty – 50% representatives for the Sinhalese (though Sinhalese population was proportionately larger than that percentage) and 50% representatives for the non-Sinhalese – a form of balanced representation in a unitary constitution so that the Sinhalese cannot dominate all the others combined.

The Buddhist revival under Anagārika Dharmapāla (1964–1933) has given the Sinhalese the ideology of a Sinhala Buddhist state. Dharmapāla's revivalism had a dark side, too. He was a champion of Sinhalese nationalism and had attacked vehemently Tamil and Muslim minorities in his writings. For the glorification of Sinhalese Buddhist identity, he was reinterpreting the ancient Pāli chronicles.[2] The Tamils feared that the Sinhalese would use their political power to oppress other sections of the people of the country. They had a bad experience in 1936 when the Executive Committee system was manipulated to establish a Pan-Sinhalese Ministry.

To form a government, the Sinhalese should be able to get the cooperation of at least one or two members from the other communities so that the government will not ride rough-sod over the other communities. The Tamils were thinking primarily of equal opportunity for all individuals and trying to secure that position within the unitary constitution. It is ironic that in 1920s S.W.R.D. Bandaranaike put forward for the first time the idea of a federal constitution for the island, with three units, one of which was for the Tamils. The Kandyan Sinhalese chiefs were demanding the same from the Donoughmore Commissioners in 1930s. No Tamil of consequence showed any interest in this idea for almost a quarter century after Bandaranaike. It was in 1949 that a splinter group of the Tamil Congress formed the Federal Party, demanding autonomy for the Tamil-speaking peoples of the Northeast. After independence, the Tamil demand became parity of status for Sinhala and Tamil languages under a unitary constitution. The Tamils felt that parity of status would ensure equality of the speakers of the two main languages of the country as well as equal opportunity for individuals. The Sinhalese argued that parity of status would lead to the disappearance of Sinhalese language, as it did not have enough resources to compete with Tamil language and as a consequence, of Buddhism itself from the island. This irrational argument swept through the Sinhalese electorate. The major parties opted for Sinhalese only and then the Marxist parties also followed suit about a decade later.

The Tamils began to vote for the Federal Party (f. 1949) in large numbers from 1956 and continued to do so till 1970. Federalism can provide "one country, two states, and equal opportunity." In the Tamil perspective, the demand for federalism was a Tamil realization that the Sinhalese wanted a restoration of the Sinhalese Buddhist state and in that set-up there could not be equality of different nationalities and equality of opportunity for all individuals. The demand for a Tamil state was for equality as a nationality. The word "state" can mean either a country or a unit in a federation. To avoid confusion, "country" is used for an independent country and "state" is used for a unit in a federation in this chapter. Even after the establishment of a federation, where states will provide for some form of power-sharing, equal opportunity for individuals in the central or federal government has to be worked out. The unity of a country can be preserved under a federal constitution. Federalism is a strategy to promote unity and prevent separation.

Even though there are many countries with federal constitutions and they remain united, this demand was portrayed by unscrupulous politicians and some Buddhist monks in an irrational way to the Sinhalese electorate as a demand for dismemberment of their country. The question of unitary constitution versus federal constitution is really a question of monopoly of power for the Buddhists or the Buddhists sharing power with the other groups. The Sinhalese leaders and the Buddhist clergy vehemently opposed the federal demand, equating it to separation or as a step towards separation. Any gain to the Tamils is portrayed as a loss to the Sinhalese.

Wilson (1988: 229) rightly points out throughout his book how the ideology of "the land, the race and the faith" have become so interwoven in Sinhalese Buddhist nationalism. In this ideology, the entire island belongs to the Sinhalese Buddhists; the most important thing is land, the intermediate important thing is Sinhalese people, and the least important thing is Buddhism. As the Tamils were demanding federalism, claiming the creation of a state in territories, which were their habitat, it was perceived as an evil to which the Sinhalese should never agree. The Sinhalese have never made an attempt to understand federalism or to explain the concept of federalism to the electorate. But the Tamil leaders were not at all intransigent. They were ready to settle for much less, when the relationship between the two peoples had not yet been embittered by a long drawn-out conflict.

The Federal Party tried to be pragmatic and tried to make compromises. In 1958, it came to an agreement with Bandaranaike known as the Bandaranaike-Chelvanayagam Pact. A form of regional autonomy for the Northeast with Tamil as the administrative language was found to be agreeable for both leaders. Though it was far short of federalism, the Federal Party was willing to compromise in the interests of peace and asked the Tamil people to accept it as an interim measure. This provincial autonomy could have been established under a unitary constitution. The compromise solution was portrayed by the UNP as a betrayal of the Sinhalese to the Tamils and as giving away of one-third of the country to the Tamils. Several Buddhist monks marched to Bandaranaike's residence and demanded that Bandaranaike abrogate the Pact. Bandaranaike obliged them and an opportunity for peace was lost. The Tamil leadership climbed down to be pragmatic. But nothing worked out.

The Federal Party tried to be "kingmaker" twice in the 1960s to find justice for the Tamils. In the1960 March elections, neither of the two main parties obtained an absolute majority. The UNP with the largest number of seats formed the government. The Sri Lanka Freedom Party (SLFP) obtained the support of the Federal Party (FP) to defeat the government, promising to redress the Tamil grievances. In the 1960 July elections, the SLFP came to power with an absolute majority and formed the government. There were talks between the government and the FP but the government, which already had an absolute majority in the parliament, refused to honor its former pledge. This effort of the Tamil leadership resulted in "nothing" again.

In the 1965 elections there was a stalemate in the parliament again and this time the UNP with the largest number of seats came to an agreement with the FP, known as the Dudley Senanayake-Chelvanayagam Pact (1965). In return for giving full support to the government, Dudley Senanayake (1911–1973) agreed to District level autonomy with Tamil as the administrative language in the Northeast. The FP agreed to have much less than even what Bandaranaike offered in 1957. Instead of provincial council/some provincial councils in the Northeast with administration in Tamil, the new scheme envisaged the already existing districts in the Northeast to have local assemblies, with elected representatives, conducting their affairs in Tamil. This arrangement could have worked under a unitary set-up.

Though there were serious misgivings among a section of the Tamil Federal Party (f. 1949) that it was too little, the party leaders argued that the Tamils should accept it and try to build on it in the future. When the District Councils bill came up for debate in 1968, the opposition and a section of the government opposed it strongly, using the arguments, which the UNP used in 1957. Some members of the Buddhist clergy were at the forefront, demanding the rejection of the bill. They were not willing to betray the Sinhalese to the Tamils and they should not hand over one-third of the country to the Tamils. Dudley Senanayake could not stand up to the pressure from the extremists and withdrew the bill. Some foreigners, who understand very little about the situation in Sri Lanka, advise the Tamils to solve the problem through parliamentary politics. Wilson has clearly brought out the impossibility:

> Can an ethnic majority political grouping have a decisive say in the making and unmaking of the government of an ethnic majority political party? The answer is "no," both in this instance and, as I shall indicate later, even when the ethnic majority actively supports the winning candidate in a presidential election. The evidence is relevant especially in the island of "the land, the race and the faith," where the ethnic minority does not count politically; even if it does count temporarily, as happened in the case of the Tamil Federal Party, it is of little consequence.
>
> (1988: 21)

About the use of Tamil as an administrative language, which Bandaranaike introduced in 1958, some provisions were made for its implementation during this period. Some Buddhist monks were in the forefront opposing this, one Buddhist monk losing life in police firing to preserve order. The opportunistic opposition honored the monk as a hero and built a monument for him. Another important opportunity to redress the Tamil grievances had been missed. Disillusionment with the parliamentary method of redressing Tamil grievances grew among the Tamils.

Sri Lanka is sometimes described as a democracy, and the Tamils have been advised to choose the democratic way to solve their problems. It is true that

Sri Lanka has periodic elections and frequent changes of government between the two major parties. There is very little democracy, however, except for periodic elections. Election campaigns and elections are generally violent and corrupt, especially since the infamous referendum of 1982. Except for short periods, the country had been under emergency rule for the past three decades when all normal individual human rights are suspended. The draconian Prevention of Terrorism Act of 1979, which targets the Tamils in practice, overrides all individual freedoms. The principle of majority rule in a democratic society has been abused to justify ethnic majority rule. Tambiah has pinpointed the situation:

> For it has become the accepted thesis among numerous Sinhalese – including many elements of the educated middle classes – that the principle of majority politics entitled their government to insist on "affirmative action on behalf of that majority...." The same majority claim has stimulated populist politicians and monks to press for the granting of Sinhala "nationalism," with its potent mix of race, religion, and language, its "rightful place" in the island's political culture.... And most of the Sinhalese majority, and the most important Sinhalese dominated political parties – the UNP, SLFP, and JVP (Janatha Vimukti Peramuna) – by and large take for granted that discriminatory legislation and the imposition of quotas in favour of the majority as justified and justifiable action. There are no serious moral qualms or conflicts in this regard.
>
> (1986: 76–77)

Ethnic majoritarianism has been so well entrenched among the major parties from 1956 that there is no scope for minorities to get justice through parliamentary methods. More than half a century of so-called democracy in Sri Lanka give the Tamils no hope. The Sri Lanka Muslim Congress has emerged recently as a very important political party. It is almost "the king-maker" in Sri Lanka politics during the last decade. There is some resentment about their influence and power, especially among some Buddhist nationalist elements of the affected parties. The solution they suggest is that the two major parties should form a coalition government to thwart the minorities' wielding power. What they do not seem to visualize is that it will lead to perpetual conflict and may open a third front of war, in addition to the present Tamil front.

There is a point in the argument that a minority party should not be allowed to dictate terms and unfair demands when it becomes the "king-maker." The problem arises from the fact that the major parties become in effect primarily Sinhala Buddhist parties, looking after the interests of the majority community only. The three major Sinhalese dominated political parties in current politics do not carry the ethnic label in their names, but all of them champion Sinhalese chauvinism when it suits them. Of these three, the JVP, which now plays the extremist anti-Tamil and anti-LTTE card, was flying the balloon of self-determination for the Tamils for a short period in the late seventies. There were two Sinhalese dominated Marxist parties – the Laṅkā Sama Samāja Party (f. 1935) and Communist Party (f. 1943) – who were prominent during the first quarter century after independence. They were advocating multiculturalism strongly in the fifties, only to succumb to chauvinist forces in the sixties and seventies, so that they could share political power (see De Silva 1981: 510–30). There are many countries with multiparty democracy. But there are very few multilingual and multireligious countries where compartmentalization of political forces on ethnic lines is so deep as in Sri Lanka. This situation indicates a serious malady in the political structure. The major political parties should formulate their policies and programs that at least large sections of the other ethnic groups can feel satisfied.

When the country became independent, the UNP government took certain steps, which made a section of the Tamils suspicious. D.S. Senanayake (1881–1952) started many colonization schemes in the Eastern Province, starting the process of settling a large number of Sinhalese, changing the demographic nature of the province (Manogaran 1999). Patrick Peebles has documented the transformation of the Dry Zone from a sparsely populated and unhealthy, but ethnically diverse, region to a rapidly growing, and almost exclusively Sinhalese and Buddhist, one. Tamil protests against this transformation have been followed by intensification rather than moderation. What is especially provocative is "insistence that such colonization is a Sinhalese entitlement on historical grounds, in which the resources of the state are dedicated to one community with no comparable benefits to others is intolerable" (Peebles 1990: 35). Senanayake also disfranchised the entire Tamil community of Indian origin, who had voting rights before Sri Lanka became independent.

There is a general view that of the two major political parties, the UNP is more moderate than the SLFP, even though the former also has played the communal extremist card when it suits them politically. This view traces the development of the ethnic conflict from 1956, when the SLFP swept the polls with the Sinhala-only slogan. But the roots of the conflict goes to 1948, the very first year of independence, when the UNP took the earliest opportunity to disfranchise the Indian origin predominantly Indian Tamils, who then formed more than 10% of the total population of the island (Nissan and Stirrat 1990: 34). It appeared a betrayal in a sense as the representatives of that community stood with D.S. Senanayake in voting in the State Council. But in the 1947 elections, they had Ceylon Indian Congress, a party of their own, and they also helped in the election of left-wing anti-UNP Marxist politicians. There was controversy over the question of the national flag for Sri Lanka. The minorities feared that the restoration of a flag with lion having a sword in its paw symbolized the restoration of the Sinhalese kingdom, ready to use force to subjugate the Tamils. A Parliamentary Committee went into this question and the present national flag was adopted by a majority vote, with one of the two Tamil representatives, dissenting. Legitimacy is sometimes sought in Sri Lanka that one or more Tamil person has supported most of the measures, which the Tamils list as their grievances.

Many governments since independence have been able to buy up or hire some Tamils to support them. Of the two Tamil members in that committee, the one, who joined the government then as a cabinet minister, gave his assent, to satisfy his cabinet colleagues in the committee. What the governments should do is getting mainstream Tamil support. Throughout the last century there were many Tamil politicians who co-operated with the Sinhalese for pragmatic reasons and then ended up utterly frustrated and hopelessly betrayed.[3] Why I mention this is to show that on matters like this, something could have been done to arrive at a consensus to adopt a flag, other than a terrorizing lion with a raised sword, ready to attack. The number of independent countries in the world is nearing 200 mark. No other country has a flag with a ferocious animal in an attacking posture. The armed forces of Sri Lanka have been using this flag in fighting the Tamils, bringing them death and destruction during the last two decades. It is better to devise a flag to indicate that Sri Lankans are not uncultured. If the Sinhalese cannot give up this emblem, the tiger emblem also should be incorporated in the national flag as a mark of co-existence of two peoples within the island.

Some members of the Tamil Congress defected from their party which was then supporting the government, saw dangerous signals in these trends, and formed the Federal Party in 1949 to press for a Tamil State in the Tamil dominated Northeast within a federal set-up and to press for citizenship for the Indian origin Tamil community. It is interesting to see how the Tamil community voted in the 1952 elections. Even though sections of the Tamil community had misgivings, the FP had only two members elected and the vast majority of the voters in the Northeast voted for Tamil Congress, UNP, and independents. The election result was an indication that in the immediate post-independence era, the Tamil people were willing to be pragmatic, to settle for "one country and equal opportunity" in a unitary constitution. The Tamil voters were willing to be accommodative in some important issues and hoped that they might be able to benefit in some other issues.

Solomon West Ridgeway Dias Bandaranaike (1899–1959), who was formerly the leader of the Sinhala Mahāsabhā, broke away from the UNP in 1951 and formed the SLFP. The party had a nationalist agenda, but at the beginning his nationalism was inclusive. His declared aim was to replace English with Sinhala and Tamil as official languages of the country. The title of his party is intriguing. The frequently used name of the country was Laṅkā or Laṅkāva. Even though the name Sri Lanka was recorded in medieval times, it was not a popular name. The epithet *Śrī* has many meanings; it could mean holy or sacred Laṅkā as well. The question arises as to whom it is sacred or holy. It is quite possible that Bandaranaike wanted to make the country holy or sacred to the Buddhists. New converts are always overenthusiastic to establish their credentials. Bandaranaike, who was a convert from Anglican Christianity (his family enjoying all privileges by being close to the British rulers) to Buddhism, probably wanted to make this country sacred to the Buddhists.

In the Sinhalese nationalist discourse it is often argued that the Tamils gained an unfair advantage over the Sinhalese as the British rulers and Christian missionaries favored them. But it is ironic that Sinhalese Buddhist nationalism was cleverly manipulated by some Sinhalese leaders like Bandaranaike and Jayewardane (whose father was a Christian) who gave up their religion and culture to gain maximum favors from the British and Christian missionaries and reconverted to Buddhism opportunistically to manipulate the preponderant Sinhalese Buddhist electorate. The Bandaranaike family, which appears to have gained the maximum from the Dutch and British rulers, now functions like a royal family in Sri Lankan politics. Even the significance of the word "Freedom" in the title of his party is not clear because Sri Lanka was already an independent country when he formed his party. The nationalist rhetoric of the party soon lapsed into exclusivism, excluding not only English but also Tamil. Sinhala as the only official language, with reasonable use of Tamil became the policy of his party. There was a popular wave of support for this party among the Sinhalese.

The UNP, which had already promised parity of status for Sinhalese and Tamil, was in jitters. It thought that it could come to power only by taking a stand even more extreme than the SLFP. The UNP adopted the Sinhalese-only slogan, omitting mention of any place for Tamil. Tamil ministers and members of parliament resigned en bloc from the UNP. From this time onward both major parties gravitated to a Sinhalese Buddhist center. In the 1956 elections, the UNP was routed because the Sinhalese electorate distrusted its last minute change of policy. D.S. Senanayake's disfranchisement of Indian Tamil voters helped Bandaranaike's political line in a big way because Sinhalese in electorates with a majority or with a substantial Indian Tamil "stateless" disfranchised population, elected Bandaranaike's Sinhala-only nationalists.

In order to defeat the UNP, the Sinhalese electorate elected some Laṅkā Samasamāja Party (LSSP) and Communist Party of Sri Lanka (CP) members who had some electoral understanding with Bandaranaike, even though these parties continued to stand for parity of status for both languages. All the sixteen members of parliament from the Northeast, who were either Tamil or Muslim, plus the representatives of the two left parties, opposed the Sinhala only Bill. It is important to notice here that Sinhala voters and settlers in the Northeast were so few in 1956 that they had no chance of winning any seat at that time. But all postindependent governments were carrying on state-aided Sinhalese colonization so rapidly that at present, the Eastern Province is claimed to have almost equal number of Tamil, Muslim, and Sinhalese people.

The UNP was with the government on this legislation. N.M. Perera (1905–1979) and Colvin Reginald de Silva (1907–1989), the leftist leaders, made eloquent speeches that the adoption of this language policy would destroy national unity. The former also asked the rhetorical question how the Tamils could place trust on the words of Sinhalese politicians, if such injustice could be done to them within a decade of promises of fair treatment after independence.

The Sinhala-only Act divided the country into two distinct regions, the Northeast and the Southwest. Tambiah ponders at the tragic situation thus:

> Nevertheless, a disturbing and sobering fact about the Bandaranaike era was that this charismatic politician, who voiced many of the political sentiments and aspirations of the Sinhalese masses, proved unable to direct or control them, and was extinguished by the very forces he had helped to attain dignity and power. ... Perhaps the greatest tragedy suffered by Sri Lanka since independence is that such a gifted politician, who might have presided over a radical reordering of a "colonial society," had not the statesman's stamina, guts, and greatness to implement solutions to the country's ailments, including the spiraling Sinhalese–Tamil ethnic conflict, whose outlines he saw clearly.
>
> (1986: 134)

This division of the country manifested itself dramatically in 1958 when there were massive anti-Tamil riots in the Southwest. Tamils in the Northeast, except in recent colonies, were safe. Tamils from the Southwest had to be transported to the Northeast for their safety till the return of normalcy. The concept of the need for a Tamil state received much boost from this experience. B.H. Farmer (1963), who was studying the developments in the island, wrote *Ceylon: A Divided Nation*. The *de facto* division of the country had taken place in 1956. A refusal to face realities has been going on for nearly half a century.

The FP emerged as the Tamil nationalist party, winning 10 seats out of 16 from the Northeast. Since the member of FP felt they were not strong enough to block the Sinhala-only Bill in the parliament, they opted for some extra-parliamentary forms of passive resistance. They wanted to use Mahatma Gandhi's *satyagraha*, a method of passive resistance, a kind of sit-in and fasting at Galle Face Green in front of the parliament building. Thugs manhandled the peaceful protest of Tamil leaders and their supporters. The thugs were not identified, but they must have been Sinhala nationalists.

Having realized that passive resistance was not understood in the Southwest, the FP and some other Tamil leaders adopted passive resistance in 1961 in the Northeast. *Satyagraha* was organized in front of government offices. They declared that these offices could work only if administration was carried on in Tamil. As thugs could not go all the way to disrupt the *satyagraha*, the Sirimāvō Bandaranaike government sent the armed forces to put down the movement violently and to arrest the Tamil leaders. The government thus succeeded in crushing passive resistance. What happened in 1956 and in 1961 indicated that passive resistance on the model of Mahatma Gandhi could not work when Sinhalese were the opponents.

The 1970 elections brought the United Front (UF) government, led by SLFP to power with a two-third majority. The government took two big steps, which led to a crisis situation. The government introduced media wise standardization of marks for the university entrance examination, with the clear aim of disadvantaging the Tamils. The government also convened a constituent assembly to draw up a suitable constitution. The FP was invited to participate and to present proposals for the new constitution. The FP proposed various measures to redress the Tamil grievances. Their proposals were rejected in *toto* and a constitution, acceptable only to the UF government, was promulgated in 1972. The Tamils felt that they were pushed beyond the margin. In 1978 when the UNP government had five-sixth majority in the parliament, it overhauled the constitution.

The UNP which promised to redress the Tamil grievances in its election manifesto of 1977, made no effort at all to accommodate the Tamil demands in the new constitution. Incidentally it is pertinent here to remark that the 1978 Constitution was acceptable to the UNP alone. The TULF proposed various amendments to accommodate Tamil grievances but they were summarily rejected, as in 1972. The government started talks with the TULF, which received a mandate for a separate state from the Tamil electorates, and introduced District Development Councils (DDC) bill. This appeared too little to many Tamils and the Liberation Tigers of Tamil Eelam (LTTE). Even then the SLFP, as is customary for the main opposition in Sri Lankan ethnic politics, opposed it as giving too much to the Tamils. Preserving the unity of the country became the slogan of the opposition and large number of Buddhist monks were in the forefront of the campaign to oppose any concessions to the Tamils. Elections were held in 1981 and in the Northeast, the TULF won all the districts except Amparai. The UNP expected to make inroads in the TULF strongholds and failed. High expectactions of the Tamils turned into huge disappointments as the government neither voted sufficient money for them nor allowed them the power to tax on their own. So the DDC as a solution to the ethnic problem turned out to be a practical joke, perpetrated on a long-suffering Tamil people. The UNP wanted to discredit the TULF, which committed itself to the DDCs, trusting J.R. Jayewardane (1906–1996), but ended up strengthening the Tamil militants, especially the LTTE, which actively campaigned against the DDC "farce."

As there seems to be no way out for the Tamils to have power-sharing and equal opportunity in a united country, the Tamil demand has become "leave us alone in our land." If the Tamils could not share power and if they could not have equality, they wanted to establish a country in the land where they were in a majority so that they could enjoy freedom. The Tamils have been influenced by modern political ideas. This is a step in desperation, from a people who felt profound alienation. The situation of the Tamils then, and the demand for a separate country, can be understood in the following preamble of the American Declaration of Independence of July 4, 1776:

> We hold these truths to be self evident, that all men . . . are endowed . . . with certain inalienable Rights that among these are Life, Liberty and the pursuit of Happiness. That to secure these rights, Governments are instituted among Men, deriving their just powers from

> the consent of the governed, that whenever any Form of Government becomes destructive of these ends, it is the Right of the People to alter or abolish it, and to institute a new Government, laying its foundation on such principles and organizing its powers in such form, as to them shall seem most likely to effect their Safety and Happiness.

The French Revolution of 1789 has emphasized the importance of Liberty, Equality, and Fraternity. Many Marxist thinkers also argue that nationalities cannot be subjugated permanently by force.

The Tamil demand to "leave them alone," was a way of giving notice that if the centralized unitary Sinhala-Buddhist framework could not be dismantled, the Tamil people would use their sovereignty to establish a separate country. The Sinhalese could not be expected to agree to share the island with the Tamils in two independent countries. In fact they started fighting against an imaginary Tamil country in 1957 even before any Tamil thought of demanding a separate country. They say that peace in the island is possible only if the Tamils give up the demand for a separate country. The Tamils, including the LTTE, have been proclaiming again and again that the demand for a separate country is negotiable if a just and proper alternative constitutional arrangement was proposed. The Sinhalese groups, which demand the Tamils to give up separation, are not at all willing to go half the way. No Sinhalese leader of consequence has said till now that he is prepared to accept federalism, even though it is well-known that federalism preserves unity, integrity, and sovereignty of many countries. There is a clear attempt among Sinhalese politicians to confuse and mislead what political structure they could accept. They tell the international community and the Tamils that anything short of a separate country could be discussed during negotiations. They tell the Sinhalese electorate that they would settle for any solution within a unitary constitution. It is a calculated attempt at deception, which could lead to trouble soon.

Devolution within a unitary constitution cannot provide real power-sharing. The equal opportunity for individuals is possible in a unitary set-up but such a set-up has been so abused for more than half a century that Tamils will not trust it again. When India intervened in the ethnic conflict in 1987, Indian lawyers came to Colombo and helped the Sri Lanka government to draft devolution proposals. When these proposals were submitted to parliament, the Supreme Court deleted some provisions because they were inconsistent with the unitary nature and the entrenched clauses of the constitution. The National State Assembly passed the other provisions as the thirteenth amendment to the constitution. Sri Lanka now has many elected provincial councils and administrations, but they have very little power and authority, except concurrent powers with the central government.

Some of the Sinhalese-Buddhist liberals who stand for the solution of more devolution under a unitary constitution, want to continue a set-up similar to this. It is an extended version of the 1981 DDC scheme. It is an irony that the provincial council scheme, which came into being through Indo-Sri Lanka Accord of

1987 and subsequent collaboration between the two countries, to give some autonomy to the Northeast, functions everywhere in the island except in the Northeast, where a former army general, appointed as governor by the Colombo government, carries on the administration.

In 1995, the PA government introduced devolution proposals, which tried to bypass the shortcoming of the unitary set-up. The government omitted provisions referring to unitary nature. G.L. Pieris, then a minister in the PA government, explained that it was done purposely so as to enable devolution to work. The LTTE, the Tamil militant organization fighting against the state, rejected it as too little, while the TULF welcomed it and suggested that some improvements be made to meet Tamil aspirations. There was a hue and cry among the Sinhalese, and the government started the process of strengthening the unitary character of the constitutional arrangements and continued to do so in its subsequent reformulations (Ponnampalam 1999). The PA government introduced its latest proposals in the National State Assembly in 2000. The TULF and other Tamil political parties were thoroughly disillusioned with the new proposals while there was opposition from some Buddhists, even a Buddhist monk threatening to fast and die, that so much of devolution should not be given to the Tamils. This indicates a continuing example of the modern transformation of Buddhism which Tambiah identifies from political Buddhism of the late 1980s in the following words:

> The phenomenon of the late eighties may be seen by some observers as the final shift of "political Buddhism" from a localized religiosity of earlier times primarily enacted among monk-laity circles in villages and towns in terms of ethical teachings, moral concerns, and gift-giving (*dana*) to a vocal and sloganized "religious-mindedness," which has objectified and fetishized the religion and espoused a "Buddhist nationalism," even as regards the monks themselves, so that important tenets of their religion regarding detachment, compassion, tranquility, and non-violence and the overcoming of mental impurities are subordinated and made relevant to Sinhala religio-nationalist and social reform goals. In this changed context, Buddhism in its militant, populist, fetishized form as espoused by certain groups, seems to some observers to have been emptied of much of its normative and humane ethic, denuded of its story-telling homilies through the Jataka stories, and to function as a marker of crowd and mob identity, as a rhetorical mobilizer of volatile masses, and as an instigator of spurts of violence.
>
> (1992: 92)

The "divide" between what the governments have been offering till now and what the Tamils demand seems to be so big. It is necessary to agree on some basics before any meaningful negotiations. In the India-sponsored peace talks in Thimpu in 1986, the Tamil parties, including all important militant groups like the LTTE, came out with the Thimpu principles, specifying the acceptance of the concepts of Tamil homeland, Tamil nationality, and self-determination for the Tamils as basics on which a political solution acceptable to the Tamils could be worked out. In the Tamil perception, these are all essentials if the Tamils were to feel free and secure in Sri Lanka.

A frequently asked question is why do the Tamils ask for self-determination when the government is prepared to give devolution. One of the arguments advanced against self-determination is that it could lead to separation or something unacceptable to the other peoples of the island. It is correct that the ethnic problem could be solved only if there is consensus among major sections of the other peoples. There is no point in going for a solution if that solution could be overturned in the foreseeable future. Many attempts have already been made to evolve a solution acceptable to all the parties. To forestall Indian attempts to impose a settlement, J.R. Jayawardene convened an all-party conference in 1985. In addition to political parties, the Buddhist clergy was also invited. Ponnampalam queries this point and points out the tragedy:

> President Jayewardane gave them a place in the 1984 All Parties Conference. No one knows on what basis they were brought in. But they have come to stay and they have become high profile political beings. With the role they play in politics today, it is unlikely there will ever be a political solution to the Tamil issue.
>
> (1999: 270)

S. Sathananthan, who is very skeptical of the future of the peace process, highlights the Tamil fear of the political Buddhist monks:

> The prospects for creating the indispensable condition of political symmetry between the Sinhalese and Tamil nations are virtually extinguished by the obdurate hostility of the Buddhist clergy, whose political power is amply demonstrated by the additional provision conceded in article 7 of the alleged PSC report (Parliamentary Select Committee Report of the PA government). They have resisted, and will resist, any dilution of theocracy and the consequent diminution of their power.
>
> (1999: 227)

The Sinhalese Buddhists adopted a totally noncooperative attitude about devolving power to the Tamils, and nothing came out of this effort. R. Premadasa (1924–1993) appointed a Select Committee of Parliament. This committee made some proposals but they were not at all satisfying to the Tamils. Again, nothing came out of this effort also. As already noted, the PA government's proposals for reform of the constitution to accommodate Tamil aspirations floundered between 1995 and 2000 in the same way. It should be now clear that no solution acceptable to the Tamils could be found in this way. The only sensible approach seems to be for the Tamils to decide what they want and then for the other parties to put in place some safeguards to preserve the unity of the country. Another reason for Tamil demand for self-determination is that what one Sri Lankan government offers another successive government could take away. The Tamils want to feel that they are equal partners in the constitution-making and that they form part of the country on their free will and not because they could not throw off the military occupation. The Tamils look forward for the recognition of their rights; they do not beg for alms, gifts, or grants.

What worries the Tamils most is that up till now no Sinhala leader of consequence has come out with the statement that Tamil aspirations are just. Some appear to believe that modern independent Sri Lanka is the restoration of medieval Sinhalese kingdom, which should be governed as it was then. Many of them may be ignorant but at least some others are mischievous in that they do not realize that the structure of an ancient or medieval kingdom is very different from a modern centralized unitary state. At the time of independence in 1948, about 90% of the people of the Northeast were Tamil speakers consisting of both Tamil and Muslim communities. At every election from 1956, it is clear that Sri Lanka is divided, Tamils in the Northeast expressing aspirations different from the rest of the island. As the number of Tamil representatives is small, their aspirations are ignored consistently.

The Sinhalese are settled in large numbers to change the demographic pattern and to elect representatives who will help to keep the Tamils in check. The Tamils are not simply a minority but a people or a nationality having a contiguous territory as their habitat. There are many independent countries in the world today, with a territory smaller than the Northeast and with a population smaller than the Northeast. The Tamils have been able to carry on the war so long because they have a contiguous territory and the militants have mass support in that territory. Some Sinhala leaders do not care for the misery of the Tamil people when the latter's territory became the war zone. They wax eloquently on the unity of the country but not on the unity of the peoples of the country. In *Only the Man is Vile*, William McGowan seems to pinpoint the underlying factor in the whole Sri Lankan ethnic problem. The title of McGowan's book is taken from Reginald Herber's *From Greenland's Icy Mountains: Missionary Hymn* (1811):

> What though the spicy breezes
> Blow soft o'er Ceylon's isle
> Though every prospect pleases
> And only man is vile.

McGowan has recorded some profound thoughts on the Buddhist factor in the Sri Lankan tragedy:

> I found it hard to accept that such awful political and ethnic violence could happen in a country... so outwardly suffused with Buddhist piety and passivity... Sri Lanka, the Resplendent Isle as it was known in

> ancient Buddhist scriptures, had an underside.... And what passed for equanimity was often an illusion beneath which raged emotions deeply repressed by Buddhist prohibitions...there was the legacy of its own Buddhist spiritual tradition that it had betrayed.... But despite considerable government patronage and ostentatious displays of public devotion like the monumental displays of public devotion like the monumental Buddha statues scattered all over the country, Sri Lanka hardly became the island of the dharma celebrating the ideals of non-violence and compassion. Instead, it had become a country of routine massacres, rampant human rights abuses, and moral obduracy where the implacable hatreds of race, class, and culture had created a nightmare world of viciousness, opportunism, and envy.
>
> (1992: 6–7)

The Tamil representatives, through their long experience in parliament, realize that they cannot deliver anything to the Tamils. Extra-parliamentary passive resistance can be crushed by brute force, as seen in 1956 and 1961.

The "peace process" is on and the government is trying to negotiate a peaceful settlement. There is some sort of military stalemate in the war front and the country is in serious financial difficulties. The international community appears to be pushing both sides to negotiate a peaceful solution. Some Buddhist leaders urged the government to use proscription of the LTTE and normalization of life in the Northeast as bargaining points so that Tamil aspirations would not become the focus of negotiations. The question is frequently asked how you could trust the LTTE. Those, who question thus, do not care that for the Tamils, it is a question of how could any Sinhalese leader of consequence be trusted. Speaking on the Sinhala-only Bill in parliament in 1956, N.M. Perera (1905–1979) asked how the Tamils could trust any Sinhalese leader as they had betrayed their trust many times. Periodically, many Sinhala leaders have raised the hopes of the Tamils; everybody has backed out in the face of extremist threats or the lure of cabinet portfolios. Perceptive Tamils are still skeptical of the future because so many hindrances are still possible in the three stages of the process.

The 2001 elections as well as what is happening among the Tamils recently clearly indicate that a vast majority of Tamils pin their hopes on the LTTE to negotiate on their behalf. Normalcy to the Northeast must return; this also should not be a bargaining point. A radical political solution has to be worked out. It has to be incorporated into the constitution. The constitution has to be implemented. The second and the third stages of the process cannot be accomplished if the two major parties do not adopt a bipartisan attitude. There could be a big gap between incorporation in the constitution and implementation at the ground level. Though the present constitution provides for the use of Tamil language, complaints continue that the provision relating to Tamil is not properly implemented. Tamils who do not know Sinhalese are forced to transact business in Sinhala and even forced to sign Sinhala legal documents. Many Tamil civilians, even Tamil elites, continue to have experience of humiliation for not being able to transact business in Sinhala language. What has been accomplished so far in the peace process is the preliminary step of signing a memorandum of understanding for a permanent ceasefire. The Janatha Vimukti Peramuṇa (JVP) and a section of the Buddhist clergy make so much noise against it that it is clear that extraordinary statesmanship and courage among political leaders will be needed at every stage of the long "peace process."

The Tamils remain skeptical even now because of the retention of the Prevention of Terrorism Act (PTA) of 1979. This draconian act, which suspends all individual rights for anybody suspected of being a terrorist or aiding a terrorist, has been used by the government for indefinite detention of suspects in prisons, where some of them are beaten up, tortured, and killed. Cases have not been instituted against many of them even after many years because there are no cases, but only suspicions. After suffering so long, they sometimes start hunger strikes, demanding that they should either be released or tried in courts. This Act brings untold sufferings to the Tamil civilians but very ineffective in preventing Tamil militancy which it characterizes as terrorism. When this Act was passed, there were only two militant movements – the LTTE and the People's Liberation Organization of Tamil Eelam (PLOTE) – with their membership, not even reaching a 100. Militant movements mushroomed after 1983. The LTTE continues to thrive till today. So it is clear that the PTA is worthless in controlling militancy. It has only served to inflict inhuman and degrading punishments on Tamil civilians who are "suspects." The Tamils find it difficult to understand the merits in having an excellent constitution with a wonderful chapter on fundamental rights, if the PTA can override all the rights. The LTTE has released many times, its prisoners, who had been fighting against it. The government still cannot make up its mind on releasing long suffering prisoner suspects, against whom it has no cases, because they are detained under the PTA.

One of the arguments used by some persons from the ethnic majority for opposing regional autonomy for the Tamils is that in that case the Muslims and the Upcountry Tamils could also ask for it and the majority Sinhalese could not give away so much of the country to the minorities. In addition to many other factors, in the Tamil perception, some persons from the ethnic majority have encouraged the other two communities to raise their demands so that they could be used as a counterweight to weaken the demands of the Tamils. The Tamil speaking Muslims of the East, who form about a third of the population there, want to secure their position. The Muslims in the East are not concentrated in a contiguous territory; their villages and towns intermingle with Tamil villages and towns. So it may not be possible to have separate territorial units for the Tamils and the Tamil speaking Muslims. Some adequate safeguards for them should be worked out during negotiations on substantive issues when their representatives should also take part.

The principle guiding the future constitution of the country should be equal opportunity for all individuals. This should try to establish equality for all individuals and groups. This aim could have been achieved easily under a unitary constitution. But the opportunity was sadly missed. The distrust that has grown among the Tamils for almost half a century by the oppressive use of the unitary constitution will not allow them to accept empty verbose promises and platitudes. There should be checks and balances to see that an ethnic majority does not take over everything into its hands once more and try to consolidate its power by military conquest and occupation in the name of "unity, sovereignty, and territorial integrity of the country."

The process of negotiation with the LTTE could be difficult. The sweeping victory of the Tamil National Alliance (TNA), an alliance of traditional Tamil political parties and some erstwhile Tamil militant groups, in the 2001 elections in the Tamil electorates of the Northeast is an endorsement of their election manifesto that the LTTE should be the sole representative of the Tamils during the peace process. Half a century of political experience has convinced many Tamil political groups – most of whom suffered at the hands of the LTTE at one time or another – that there was no other way to come to a just settlement of the ethnic problem. The LTTE reason for the failure of previous negotiations is that the previous governments treated them as just another group or party of the minority community and evaded discussion of important issues as equals. But the government, the Buddhists, and the Sinhalese have one big advantage in negotiating with the LTTE. If an agreeable political solution could be worked out and implemented and the LTTE made to have a stake in the administration of the country, one can be sure that the settlement will hold, at least as far as the Tamils are concerned.

Notes

1 The burning of the Norwegian flag was carried out by a group of monks belonging to Jathika Bhikṣu Peramuṇa (National Bhikṣu Front) affiliated with the JVP.
2 Schalk (1999) challenges the basis of one of Dharmapāla's misinterpretations.
3 Wilson (1988: 229) documents a long story where there were so many tales of betrayal or treachery during the last century. In this context, it is very strange to hear the argument that the LTTE has proved to be untrustworthy from 1987 to 1995. The reality seems to be that the LTTE refuses to be the latest addition to the list of betrayed Tamil leaders.

8

HISTORIOGRAPHY IN CONFLICT AND VIOLENCE

Ananda Wickremeratne

> "You promised to tell me your history, you know" said Alice…"Mine is a long and sad tale" said the mouse.
>
> (Carrol Lewis 1992: 37)

There is no history. There is only historiography. The reflection, trite though it was, struck me with force as I surveyed the prolific outpourings of writing on the ethnic conflict in Sri Lanka especially after the benchmark events of 1983, in the process of putting my thoughts together for this article. Cumulatively what scholars have written has virtually determined the parameters of the problem as well as how particular issues should be viewed. Given their prestige and standing in the academic world it would be rash to suggest that there might well be alternative views and perspectives leading to conclusions and judgments of a different order. A hundred years from now, someone seeking to understand the troubled times we are going through could be overwhelmed by what they read seeing in the academic pronouncements, evidence of almost scriptural verisimilitude. Few would have the will, the inclination, or a fierce sense of independence to insist on coming to their own conclusions by patiently working through masses of archival material and primary sources, in the best tradition of the historian's craft, if only to avoid Voltaire's celebrated riposte that history was no more than a pack of tricks we play on the dead (and one might add) to suit the agendas of the living. This article, which addresses these and other issues, seeks to come to grips with a clutch of extraordinarily complex ideological issues.

It took only a single spark to set off the conflagration which would devour the over dry expanse of jungle, too long denied the invigorating monsoon rains. In a strange way it seemed as though the great forest was watching and waiting for just this catastrophic moment. In Sri Lanka, the *ignis fatalis* was sparked off on the night of July 23, 1983 when an army patrol was ambushed by the Liberation Tigers of Tamil Eelam (LTTE) on the Kopay–Urumpirai Road in the Jaffna Peninsula, a region which sadly continues to remain both psychologically and spatially *terra incognita* to the Sinhalese mind. Thirteen Sinhala soldiers were killed. A few days later, in a state-sponsored funeral at the Kanatte cemetery in Colombo, no Sinhalese Pericles could dare to rise – occupying the moral high ground which would soon be forever lost – to declaim that after all the thirteen soldiers had died worthily and gloriously defending the values of a society which were worth dying for. Instead, recrimination and smouldering rage was in the air. The silence of an ever-increasing restive crowd was ominous.

Within hours, in Colombo, Kandy, Galle, and in smaller towns (as in India the urban centers becoming the predictable foci of activity), ethnic violence broke out. A large number of Tamils (identified cursorily and cynically by the mindless mob as physiological stereotypes, or by how the hapless victims accented Sinhala words) were killed regardless of age, gender, and condition of life. Properties, homes, and business establishments were gutted by fire and the sun arose on successive mornings to reveal scenes of numbing desolation, hopelessness, and above all the sense of hurt, and mistrust – the last the most enduring stigmata of an ongoing conflict.

The incidents which made up the infamous pogrom of 1983 in Sri Lanka have been documented by independent monitoring organizations obviating (particularly for researchers), the need to make do with official statistics and newspeak. The roving mobs of marauders were armed with government lists of streets and lanes carrying precise details of who lived where, an inestimable tool for swift retributive movement in the rabbit warrens of Dehiwala and Wellawatte where large concentrations of Tamils lived. There was no escape. Even the lone deer staying too long at the water hole at dusk in the African savannah, had a better chance of escaping the lion moving toward his prey with terrifying speed and near perfect symmetrical agility.

And yet for all its agony and undeniable pathos, 1983 like other kindred phenomena involving collective violence, is marked out for a short shelf life. Almost as a biological imperative, finally a sense of salutary oblivion takes over and we move on. Who these days – scholars included – would remember Armenia, Jedwabine, Warsaw, Algiers, Mai Lai, Babi Yar, the list goes on, Bosnia, Northern Ireland? Or, it may well be that younger generations far removed in time from the events would be congenitally incapable of relating to textbook descriptions. In the light of newer agendas, the legacies of terror – the dead tell no tales – might appear to be a saga of made-up stories. For older generations who can role up their shirt sleeves and show you their concentration camp I.D. number (as I was privileged to be shown after a talk in New York), the skepticism and denial would be painful. Or worse, there is, as Daniel Goldhagen (1996: 5–24) brilliantly showed, Hitler's willing executioners were not a small coterie of deranged individuals who surrounded him, but were the German people who supported him in all his anti-Jewish draconian policies. They would later disingenuously claim that they were unaware of what was happening.

Notwithstanding its momentous nature, 1983 with its reductive potential continues to be a mirror of distortion. Historical events are best viewed not as isolated phenomena but in an extended temporal linear perspective enabling us to better evaluate continuities and discontinuities. Facile moral judgments could be avoided as well as attempts – alas, a sad and increasing phenomenon these days – to dissemble prejudice, and even pique, in a mountain of scholarship.

From a strict historiographical perspective, it is evident that historical writings (avoiding the clumsy neologism, sociohistoric), largely the work of Sri Lankan scholars, have been strikingly reactive. The exception to the rule would be Volumes II and III of the University of Ceylon's *History of Ceylon* which were produced in the post 1970 era to complete a fascinating trilogy covering the island's history from ancient times till 1948. For example, the Che Guevara or Janatha Vimukti Peramuṇa (JVP) uprising in April 1971 produced a rash of academic writings which today in an aseptically decontextualized atmosphere make strange reading. With the dramatic collapse of the uprising and the gradual obsolescence of the JVP, academic focus shifted elsewhere. The second incarnation of the JVP in our own day and time, as an intra and not an extra parliamentary force, failed to produce ripples in the pool. The alluring mystique of a third force waiting in the wings in *avatāri*c fashion to step forth and intervene at a time of political instability and social malaise, seems to have been shattered – at least for the time being.

By contrast, it was no accident that the decade of the 1970s – when the disillusionment of the Sri Lankan Tamils saw the birth of the LTTE and the infant began to flex its muscles with remarkable vigor – there arose genres of academic writings which directly addressed the ethnic issue in scholarly impressive ways to psyche out its complex ideological roots.

In tandem there were other factors too which contributed to the widespread perception of malaise and disenchantment. The late 1970s saw radical constitutional changes which reduced parliament to a cipher and concentrated immense power in the hands of the executive: a single individual who though elected, enjoyed a tenure of office for seven years with the power to extend his term – accountable to neither God nor men and women who elected him. The judiciary was emasculated and all pretence at its presumed independence was abandoned. There was no Bill of Rights to safeguard the individual against arbitrary acts of the state, enforceable in a court of law. The appropriation of Buddhist trappings and symbols to give the state and those who wielded power in its name, the veneer of righteousness and legitimacy, created the impression of a Buddhist state when no such thing strictly existed.

Clearly, enough was happening in the 1970s to call for a revaluation not only of the ethnic problem but also more importantly of the larger matrix in which it was unraveling. The search coalesced with a mood of self-chastisement, guilt, and a desire to make amends for acts of commission and omission toward the aggrieved Tamils, where it was visible and mattered most – in the grand battlefield of ideology. This rather than the shifting battle scenes of the North East where the army fought the LTTE became the true Kurukṣetra (field of the Kurus).[1] It was wondrous to behold! A Sinhala *Rāma* rode forth to battle girt with valor, fortitude, compassion, and equanimity to confront a demonic Sinhala *Rāvaṇa*.

For example, in 1979 the Social Scientists' Association in Sri Lanka convened a seminar on the theme of nationality problems in Sri Lanka. Following the 1983 eruption, the organization decided to publish the papers most of which were evidently revised for the purpose (Social Scientists' Association 1985). The unnamed social scientist in his introduction observes that the relationships between the Sinhalese and Tamils have been "always charged more with fervour than with intellectual analysis." He goes on to say that emotional bias has clouded perceptions leading to judgment. The publication of the papers is clearly timed to prevent civilized people from becoming savages. The hope is expressed that as a result of the publication of *Ethnicity and Social Change in Sri Lanka*, "some of the exponents of Sinhala and Tamil nationalism" would "look more closely at the myths, misrepresentations and misunderstandings that have nourished their ideologies" (Social Scientists' Association 1985: vii).

Other writings in the 1970s almost exclusively from academia did not share the missionary fervor and were less emphatically didactic. There were however features common to all genres. First, it is an unmistakable penchant to regard Sinhala Buddhism as pathology and not as either a cultural phenomenon or simply a classificatory genre. Second, the identification of myths on which the Sinhala-Buddhist collective consciousness of an identity, was based. And lastly, the need – almost a moral imperative – to demolish the myths exposing their irrationality and absence of historical foundation.

The failure in this context to discuss the Sinhalese who have been Christians for generations is intriguing. At first sight it may seem to be an unintended omission. Indeed over time the percentage of Sinhalese who were Christians had by the 1970s fallen from 9–6%. These days, however, there is mounting evidence that their number could be steadily increasing thanks to the frenetic activities and legerdemain of Evangelical Christian missionaries who shamelessly exploit rural poverty – especially in remote areas which are inaccessible – to effect conversions very much in the spirit and manner of their predecessors in China and Japan centuries ago whose native converts were derisively known as "Rice Christians."

In 1983 when the ancient ethnic divide was furrowed afresh and probably deeper, the Sinhalese Christians (Catholic and Protestant) regarded themselves as Sinhalese and have continued to do so, as if by long and ancient habit. Indeed, as Michael Roberts (one of the few Sri Lankan scholars who has addressed this facet), reminds us in the critically formative years of nationalism (1910–1932), Sinhalese Christian leaders exulted in being Sinhalese and sought to create and emotively foster a collective Sinhalese consciousness by instituting a Sinhalese National Day as well as a Sinhalese National Anthem (Roberts 1979: 228–29).

The fact becomes awkward for more than one reason. First, it goes against the stereotypical and sacrosanct view, which establishes a rigid monocausal correlative between Sinhala Buddhism (especially its presumed exclusivism), and ethnic violence as well as a certain Buddhist intransigence, which stands in the way of the resolution of the ethnic conflict. Secondly, in a surreal sense the assumption is made that although the Sri Lankan Christians are Sinhalese, the fact of being

Christian would make the critical difference in their behavior, since a Christian would be of a superior and moral and ethical caliber. To buttress the point as it were, the claim has been made that in the JVP uprising in 1971 there were no Sinhalese Christians. They were also (it is claimed) conspicuous by their absence in the pogroms of 1983 (Roberts 1979: 1–61). Granted there is hard evidence to support the contentions (which is not the case), the preponderating Sinhala-Buddhist presence simply reflected the fact that the Sinhalese Christians numbered only 6% of the Sinhalese population. There was also the unpalatable probability that when the chips are down it was the visceral ethnic passions that had great weightage. By the same token it is ethnicity that divides the Roman Catholic clergy in the North and the East, from their Sinhalese brethren elsewhere in the island, imperiling the established Catholic policy of a single unified diocesan authority.[2]

In *Collective Identities: Nationalism and Protests in Modern Sri Lanka* (1979), Michael Roberts might well have pointed out that between 1900–1948, one would have to look really hard to discover Sinhala-Buddhist nationalism emerging as an independent political force with a distinctive template of its own. The coincidence that many of the nationalist leaders who successfully spearheaded the movement were Buddhist, did not of course amount to the same thing. Indeed the key figures widely regarded as the leaders of the movement, Don Stephen Sēnānāyake (1884–1952) and Sir Don Baron Jayathilaka (1868–1944) albeit prominent Buddhists, went out of their way to avoid giving the impression that the nationalist movement was a Buddhist platform or was espousing Buddhist sectarian causes. Such an admission coming in the wake of a decade and more of divisive communal representation would have shattered the fragile unity the leaders had cobbled together, encompassing individuals and interests who were neither Sinhalese nor Buddhist (De Silva 1993: 307).

It is not a little ironical that an increasingly strong collective Buddhist consciousness or nationalism as much nurtured by deep ontological roots as by a reactive response to the activities of Christian missionaries and the ambivalent policies of the British government, failed to transmute itself into a political force with a strong programmatic orientation. The failure or the unwillingness to create, say a *Bauddha Eksat Peramuṇa* (BEP) inevitably led to the marginalization of the Buddhists both in the pre-independence and post-independence eras and may also account for Anagārika Dharmapāla's (the one-man party) extraordinary and continuing popularity. It seemed and seems that here at any rate was a man of vision with a strong gerundival sense of what ought to be done. The long-term effects of the Buddhists to capitalize their power have been twofold. First, it has inculcated into the minds of post-independence Buddhists an irredentist mentality, a sense of unrealized blueprints. Secondly, it has made it possible (especially after 1956) for successive governments, obsessed with political survival, to adroitly woo or forestall Buddhist opposition by purely symbolic or emblematic gestures (carefully withholding anything of substance) reminiscent of the Greek hero in Hades who threw sops to the fierce dog Cerberus and successfully distracted him.

The demolition of myths – the third string to Rāma's bow as it were – became an academic passion more so in the absence of accountability given the intrinsically amorphous nature of the myths. The Aryan origins of the Sinhalese, the coming of Vijaya (a miscreant at best) with 700 followers from Bengal, his shameful treatment of Kuvēṇi who befriended him, the Buddha's visits to Laṅkā, the exhortation of the dying Buddha to the king of the gods to protect Vijaya the progenitor of a race, who would in time make the *dharma* flourish in resplendence in favored Laṅkā, the epic battle between Duṭugämuṇu, the hero king of Laṅkā, and the Tamil Elāra, and the tradition of Sinhalese kings being compelled to ward off Tamil invasions from south India, were all earmarked in a hit list of sorts for demolition to rid modern Sri Lanka of demonic myths (and the inane nonsensical prattle of Sinhala lullabies). The scene was reminiscent of the Buddha in his first visit to Lanka, expelling the demonic *yakkhas* to make the fair land of Laṅkā fit for habitation and the unfolding of the *dharma* (Mahānāma Thera 1950: 3–5). After the heavy demolition equipment had moved out, on the bare site, there was no Sinhala, no Buddhist, least of all a Sinhala Buddhist to be seen. The few that had survived, affrighted and shamed, had fled, like Kuvēṇi's children, to the jungles, to be seen no more. Such was (and continues to be) the power of Sri Lanka's scholar myth busters.

It may be objected that the recurrent use of the terms myth busters and demolitionists, is unwarranted. After all, the early history of Sri Lanka continues to cast its baleful shadows over our own day and time. Apart from issues of conflict and violence and a conniving mandate the past seems to provide for both, Sri Lankan history is undeniably remarkably cathectic. Consequently, restatement and fresh evaluation is called for, and in the eyes of many, becomes almost an ethical obligation especially when one considers its curative potential.

In the processes of restatement – to use an agreeable neutral term – we may see a variety of methodologies. First, the myth is never – at least in the academic writings we are talking about – dismissed outright. Parallel possibilities are suggested. Nonetheless the epigrammatic sting in the tail element is never absent.

In *Ethnicity and Social Change in Sri Lanka* (1985), the compiler echoes sentiments held by the individual contributors:

> This [Sinhala] consciousness – expressed today in the concept that Sri Lanka is the land of the Sinhala people of Aryan descent – does not really derive from the island's history, if one is to understand and analyse it correctly. It is a myth that has been developed to legitimize the claims of the Sinhalese to sole ownership of this country. It becomes evident however, that this sense of identity, this concept of a Sinhala-Buddhist hegemony to be protected from the inroads of a South-Indian derived Tamil group has been pervasive from around the 4th century AD and forms, even today, the basis of Sinhala Buddhist chauvinism and of ethnic conflict. That this concept arises from a distorted view of the island's history needs to be impressed on the minds of the Sinhala people.
>
> (Social Scientists' Association 1985: x)

In the war between the Sinhalese hero king Duṭugämuṇu and Elāra (which provides so much ammunition for fiery post 1983 polemics) we are told that in the Sinhala mind the war "magnified to epic proportions, is shown as a war to restore Sinhala Buddhist domination over the island from the usurpation of a Tamil Hindu." The writer adds that "the Dutugemunu legend is one very potent source used to nourish Sinhala chauvinism" (Social Scientists' Association 1985: x). Such worthy cogitations are more than a trifle eclipsed when the attention of scholars turns to the grand saga of the genesis of the Sinhala people marked by the advent of Vijaya. Care is taken to point out, no doubt reasonably, that the island that had been peopled by migrants who trickled in had already "laid the foundations of Sri Lankan society." Consequently, we are told: There is "no priority in chronological time that could be construed as conferring priority of 'ownership' on any particular group of migrants" (Social Scientists' Association 1985: viii).

With Gananath Obeyesekere, not surprisingly, we move into a more sophisticated interpretive level. Having narrated the Vijaya myth with clarity, Obeyesekere would have us understand that if the myth is to be accepted, ironically the origin of the Sinhalese comes to us in a dirty package, containing the ingredients of "bestiality, incest, and parricide." In the story, Siṅhabāhu flees with his sister Siṅhasīvalī from their father a marauding lion who had many years before abducted their mother, the daughter of the king of Kāliṅga. Recognized and restored to their princely status, the brother marries the sister. Obeyesekere observes that bestiality "was compounded with that of incest," adding that nothing good could be expected from such a union. Predictably, Vijaya, who was born of the union, turns out to be a good-for-nothing fellow causing great distress to the people at large. His father, mindful of his larger obligations as a ruler, banishes Vijaya and 700 of his followers consigning them to the vagaries of wind and wave. Vijaya, the founder of the Sinhala race, lands in Laṅkā, to begin the island's long and chequered history (Obeyesekere 1972: 60).

One may wonder, in passing, why Obeyesekere lays pointed emphasis on an incestuous union, which occurred presumably over 2,500 years ago. For one thing, the union takes place under the auspices of the grandfather of Siṅhabāhu leading us to conclude that such unions, especially at the level of royalty, were not uncommon. The abhorrence of incest in premodern traditional societies has been widely noted. Its very universality across cultures, however, would also suggest that incest was quite prevalent until for pragmatic, rather than for ethical or moral reasons, it gradually fell into obsolescence. Interestingly, elsewhere in the same article Obeyesekere makes the point that in contemporary Sri Lanka the sexual mores prevailing in rural areas is more lax than is generally assumed. By contrast, notions of sexual propriety among the anglicized Sri Lankan middle class tend to be more formal and conventional due to the fact that Christian (missionary) influences centered around the sanctity of monogamous unions. It may be another example of how in the nineteenth century Buddhism reflected, to use Obeyesekere's celebrated trope, "Protestant Buddhism" (Obeyesekere 1972: 62).

The somber gravity in which critics of Sinhala Buddhism regard such myths, contrast sharply with the attitudes of the Sinhala Buddhists themselves who are either apathetic to the myths or took them *cum grano salis*. This certainly was the writer's own experience and that of his friends all belonging to traditional conservative Buddhist backgrounds. The current obsession with Sinhala myths associated with Buddhism would at first sight seem baffling.

However, the constant regurgitation or resurrection of this or that myth by scholars ironically giving each myth a fresh lease on life was not fortuitous. It was sound methodology. Confronted with recurring spasms of violence in Sri Lanka or elsewhere, a scholar would be obliged to painstakingly analyze each episodic manifestation as well as seek to identify recurring patterns of a secular nature. All this involves hard, patient, and unglamorous work. An easier way would be to postulate a single centrally critical factor capable of explaining everything in terms of a portable reductionist formula. And consequently the anti-Tamil riots of 1958, 1977, 1981, and 1983 are attributed to Sinhala extremism or to use the more fancied term, Sinhala chauvinism, exculpating the user from the burden of deeper analysis. Indeed, in each of the years cited there was a veritable web of factors, which had little to do with the ethnic issue *per se*.

To James Manor, causality was a matter of pellucid clarity:

> The extremists believe, indeed, their identity has been grounded in the belief – that their Theravada Buddhism is the pure form of the faith . . . etc and that it is they, the *Sinhalese* who have preserved the Theravada tradition in its purest form. They derive these ideas in part from a chauvinistic interpretation of a text, the *Mahāvaṃsa*. They argue that the text provides evidence that the Buddha bestowed the island of Laṅkā on the *Sinhalese* and charged them with the mission of preserving it as a citadel of pure Buddhism . . . This mission is seen as the fundamental basis for their collective identity, indeed for their very existence as a collectivity.
> (1994: 772)

Manor clearly sees ideology providing continually a charter for violence. The extremism of Sinhala Buddhism, he points out, is at variance with the fundamental teachings of the Buddha. Apart from a strong implication that the Sinhalese Buddhists lack anything called a moral conscience, Manor does not tell in clear dialectical terms why the circumvention is taking place. In the absence of rational explanations for the gap between theory and actual practice, one must conclude with Manor that the Sinhala Buddhists are mindless "extremists" (Manor 1994: 774).

Myths are not inviolate. As in Greek mythology, myths are constantly examined and fascinatingly interpreted to suit what is considered deriguer. There is clearly no finality to the process. Proteus blends into the myth; and the myth is Proteus. By contrast, it is rare to study myths narrowly in terms of their factuality or how this or that myth is congruent with history and its presumed veracity as is the case in Sri Lanka. It is a dangerous occupation when a scholar, not allowing for his own subjectivity, sets himself up as an adjudicator sifting the good myths from the bad ones in a futile exercise watching all the sand he scoops up, repeatedly slipping through his fingers. Put in another way, the mismatch is plain: rationality is used to study what is in its very nature seemingly irrational and commonly thought not to exist at all. And yet, ironically, when history dies, myths will live on. Their longevity has little to do with Hegel, Vico, or Collingwood. It has everything to do with the *weltanschauung* (of which it is a critically integral part), with its promise to make all things mundane, ethereal, supermundane, and frankly inexplicable, plain thereby giving comfort to those within the tradition to see phenomena in a meaningful totality rather than in splintered visions. The Theravāda Sinhalese Buddhists in Sri Lanka, Burma, Thailand, and Cambodia, are nobody's fools – an unfailing impression one gets in reading western scholarly writings on the travails of Sri Lanka.

Is it possible that being born and exclusively nurtured in secular western societies (where secularism is both a shibboleth as well as a litmus test for a certain left-of-center species of politically correct liberalism) may have something to do with it? How else may we account for the all too evident united front in western scholarship with regards to India and Sri Lanka?

Meanwhile in unfailing mimetic fashion their aficionados in India (where a near savage epic battle of *Mahābhārata* proportions rages between secularists and their Hindu opponents) and in Sri Lanka, an anglicized déclassé intellectual elite, driven almost by a sense of comprador loyalty, are striving to distance themselves from traditional religion to mark out their own modernity and sense of cultural emancipation. This may account for a bizarre phenomenon: Sri Lankan social scientists (historians, sociologists, anthropologists, *et al.*) born and bred in Sri Lanka (then Ceylon) looking upon an all too familiar cultural landscape as if they were seeing it for the first time.

In the search for the roots of violence in Sri Lanka, one wonders whether we are making headway by focusing somewhat exclusively on myths and their symbolism. Going deeper into the Vijayan myth, Obeyesekere draws our attention to the lion that becomes ultimately the symbolic icon par excellence of the Sinhalese. It is the familiar predatory lion of the myth, this time holding a sword and suggesting in his demeanor a purposeful onward march, and clearly girded for battle. Given the axiom that myths have exponential growth potential with accretions of meaning, which the original object (in this case the lion) *per se* does not possess, innovative variations are not surprising. Obeyesekere recalls that in the early 1970s, displayed at a busy junction in Colombo were four large concrete slabs, each placed against a Bodhi tree. In the middle of the slab was displayed the prominent figure of the Sinhala lion. But superscribed above, each leonine figure with greater prominence and in bold lettering were the celebrated transcendent Buddhist virtues of *mettā* (loving-kindness), *karuṇā* (compassion), *muditā* (sympathetic joy), and *upekkhā* (equanimity). Although Obeyesekere draws our attention to a critical spatial shift of power in Buddhism in Sri Lanka which the artifacts in their totality symbolize, he emphasizes what at first sight seems to be a paradoxical incongruity, "the painting of the lion, a predatory, carnivorous creature grasping a sword, a symbol of violence, seems to contradict the lofty doctrinal sentiments" (Obeyesekere 1972: 60).

Indeed the problem of violence in Buddhism, to which Obeyesekere almost presciently drew attention as early as in 1972, became an unfailing motif in academic writings notably in the decades of the 1980s and 1990s. Over time, however, the very reiteration of the theme made it lose its topical appeal. Albeit like a cork floating in the water, the paradox – or what is widely construed as such – never left our sights. We have, for example, James Manor (1994) who points out that some Sinhalese Buddhists see violence as being "contrary to Buddhist principles." However, the voices of protest or conscience, made a category by Manor as "purists," are clearly a marginal force *vis-à-vis* the preponderating numbers of the "extremists." Throughout his article on "Organizational Weakness and the Rise of Sinhalese Buddhist Extremism," by consistently making the differentiation, Manor forestalls the objection that after all in fairness you cannot condemn an entire people in the lump as it were (Manor 1994: 771). Manor's categories are conceptual. They could only exist in the real world as genres either on the basis of ideology (improbably within a commonly shared Buddhist matrix), or, on class lines which in Sri Lanka for the past four decades continue to be in a state of change and flux, precluding easy judgment. Both categories, extremists, and purists, are unhelpfully faceless and amorphous.

Meanwhile, the recurring emphasis on the paradox of Buddhism and violence may arguably be inspired by a desire to create guilt and remorse in the minds of Sinhala Buddhists. In a curious way, too, it amounts to an oblique compliment to Buddhism given the lofty morality and ethics of Buddhism and its visible influence on societies that largely remained traditional until modern times, enabling the ethos to take deeper root, it was not unreasonable to expect a higher standard of accountability.

However, western scholars and the influential media pundits, who insistently make the point, somehow do not see a similar inconsistency between the excellent precepts of Christianity and what actually happened in European history, particularly in Germany, France, and England, from medieval to modern times. In our own time, too, in a less evident way, missteps between Christian precept and practice, leading to violence or its imminent possibility at all levels, are not subject to the same intense scrutiny, as would be the case when the focus is on Sri Lanka. Indeed, these days in the somber and more reflective world which emerged after September 11, we are reminded here in the USA that what is really at stake in the guise of the war on terrorism is – to use Samuel Huntington's lithic phrase – a clash of civilizations involving Islam and Western values scanned correctly to mean Judeo Christian values. Given the change in public mood, few would hear voices in the wilderness such as that of Edward Said who thinks otherwise: "As someone who has lived my life within the two cultures, I am appalled that the 'clash of civilizations,' that reductive and vulgar notion so much in vogue, has taken over thoughts and actions" (Said 2002: 23–25). Indeed, if current trends continue, the holy grail of secularism and secular values, so lovingly cherished, would be a trifle more obscured from the common view.

And yet, the presumed paradox may well be a chimera. In premodern Europe, particularly in England, the relations between church and state – competing for hegemony as historically coequal entities, were tense. The reigns of Henry II (1133–1189) and Henry VIII (1491–1547) saw the state making gains at the expense of the Church. The process culminated with the breakaway from Rome, the beginnings of a national church with its own Articles of Faith, and the massive confiscation of church properties, which passed into the hands of a new class of landowners who would be stoutly committed politically to perpetuate and reinforce the emerging status quo. All this was achieved in the searing crucible of violence but has not been rightly perceived as such. Indeed, as is well known, violence in history has been a surprisingly constructive force performing the midwifery functions to usher in a new order of things, which in time becomes entrenched and conservative and resolutely opposes violence directed at it. The dialectic surpasses politics and moral aphorisms which, lacking power, have about them a certain will-o'-the-wisp quality, but endows the user with a sense of moral superiority.

In Sri Lanka, the state and church (Buddhism) were not competing for power in the European sense. Nor was each anxious to whittle down or contain the other's power. Mutual relationships were subtly balanced on an understanding of common ends, which transcending the visible mundane world, clearly reached heavenwards. However, whether the relationship was that of a symbiotic kidney–liver affair (as is widely assumed) is a moot question. Strictly, the state could exist without the church because its core functions (distribution of political power, center peripheral relations, administration of justice, economic affairs, and foreign relations), *per se* had little to do with the Buddhist Church, which was by definition *lokuttara* (P. other-worldly), to use a venerable Weberian phrase. There is no record of eminent Buddhist monks holding high secular office comparable to Cardinals Richelieu (1585–1642), Mazarin (1602–1661) in France, or more famously Cardinal Wolsey (1475–1530) in England. No Buddhist monk – however eminent – had put himself in a position to finally bitterly exclaim to a Sinhalese king as Wolsey did, that had he served God with the same zeal that he served his king (Henry VIII), he would not be thrown naked unto his enemies.

In a sense the question would not arise. In strict theory kingship though by definition involving largely secular affairs, was ethicized according to Buddhist notions of morality. As part of his tutelage as a prince, the future ruler was aware of the *dasarājadhamma* (P. "ten norms of royal conduct") which would guide him. Equity and even-handed justice were key ingredients. Above all, power was to be tempered by compassion, lest its hard prickly thorny nature would have hurt the user (Wickremeratne 1995: 81–89).

At any rate there was the theory by and large which gave the ancient and medieval history of Sri Lanka, in spite of turbulence and instability, a remarkable coherence. However, variables could and did alter the picture, emanating not so much from the monkhood but from a ruler who could be unusually assertive and idiosyncratic, and who would have a mind of his own. Such a ruler was the great King Mahāsena (*c*.274–301 CE) who broke with tradition and switched royal patronage from the Mahāvihāra (the main Buddhist monastic fraternity and a bastion of orthodoxy) to support the rival Abhayagiri fraternity of monks who were regarded as heretics (Mahānāma Thera 1950: 267–70).

The emphasis on a presumed paradox of violence in Buddhist Sri Lanka could be attributed to an unwillingness to view violence in a wider and possibly more rewarding perspective. The penchant has given studies of violence a parochial almost incestuous stamp not unlike the treatment of violence in contemporary Indian historiography, mired along ancient acrimonious fault lines. When it comes to India and Sri Lanka, as if by ancient reflex, somehow everything becomes special, with cultural variables weighing in heavily.

In *Buddhism and Ethnicity in Sri Lanka: A Historical Analysis* (1995), I took pains to discuss what scholars were no doubt widely aware of. For example, that violence (brought about either by purely secular factors, or by seemingly religious ones) was a constructive force bringing resolution of long-standing issues which by sheer attrition would tear down the thin fabric that holds a nation together. The positive benefits would last until new forces of a contradictory nature begin to play out, to establish in turn a new order (Wickremeratne 1995: 1–21).

Indeed the redemptive quality of violence may account for the long period of stability, which England enjoyed after the "glorious revolution" of 1688. It brought closure to a century's turmoil, which began in 1603, marked by chronic disorder, regicide, bitter religious persecution, and the virtual disruption of the fledging tradition of parliamentary rule. The long peace may well have been a factor in enabling England to be the pioneer in the Industrial Revolution. By the same token, in France after the convulsive events of 1789, the rise of Napoleon and his constructive work, together with the peace settlements of 1815, ushered in a period of stability which neither the will-oer-the-wisp revolutions of 1848 nor the self inflicted wounds of Louis Napoleon could undermine.

The Hegelian dialectic is no doubt reductive. However, one may commonsensically accept the likelihood that the state – born in the crucible of violence – would logically resort to unbridled force if need be to defend the status quo. Karl Marx (1818–1883), who saw the state essentially as the handmaid of the prevailing economic and political power structure, had no illusions about the potential of the bourgeoisie state to resort to violence. Both Georges Sorel (1847–1922) – who disagreed with Marx on a variety of issues – and Jean-Paul Sartre (1905–1980), went further. Sorel, who sagaciously pointed out that we do not ordinarily perceive the state in the light of violence, associating it instead with the abstractions of legality, morality, and law and order, advocated the importance of counter violence against the state almost as a moral and ethical imperative. For his part, Sartre viewed violence as a spiritually purifying force. Franz Fanon's uniquely idiosyncratic perceptions of the colonial state poignantly expressed in *The Wretched of the Earth* (1963), and in the remarkable *Black Skin, White Masks*

(1967) added subtle dimensions to our collective realization of the power of the state. Indeed in classical studies of violence, such examples could be multiplied (Wickremeratne 1995: 1–21).

It may even be possible to accept that violence is endogenous in us, a reliquary of our long evolution as a biological species, preserved still intact for potential future contingencies. Such a conclusion might well be distasteful to those who on religious grounds make a sharp distinction between animals and ourselves, in spite of scientific evaluations continually suggesting remarkable affinities. However, a Buddhist who is aware of the view of theory of the constitutive aggregates, would not think it improbable or fanciful that in the genre of the *Jātaka*s – the previous birth stories of the Buddha – that animals should be talking or carrying on very much like human beings.

Given therefore the ideological universality of violence and its ubiquitous presence, it would be wrong to view violence in Sri Lanka in the last three decades as some sort of aberration, or as a uniquely Sri Lankan phenomenon. The view nonetheless has led to characterizations, which excuse the user of the obligation to reflect on the problem. One such characterization is the coinage of Sinhala chauvinism or more pejoratively Sinhala-Buddhist chauvinism. In a study of three decades of historiography, it becomes almost impossible to identify a scholar – Sri Lankan or from the West – who has not virtually exulted in its usage, taking care with almost ritual finesse to distance themselves from the contamination of chauvinism. By the same token, the focus at the other end of the spectrum has been on the LTTE, the terrorism of the Tigers, rather than on the Sri Lankan Tamil problem. In the process the genuine fears and anxieties of the one in a situation of chronic uncertainty and peril defensively and defiantly reiterating a sense of Sinhala identity, and the just and legitimate expectations of the other (Tamil) are all too easily forgotten.

Judgment is no substitute for understanding. Logically the second would make the first redundant. For numerous Sri Lankan Buddhists, it has been possible to understand the terrorist fringe (LTTE) of the Tamil cause, applying a simple but an all too easily overlooked Buddhist perspective: namely that one rightly focuses on the action and not the actor. The focus shifts to the roots of human action whose arising and eradication in the stream of consciousness, and its depersonalized understanding, becomes an ethical necessity. In this way, Buddhist tolerance goes beyond the homiletic and platitudinous to be what it was intended – a sustainable viable ethic of action, for oneself and for others.

In this context, the writings of P.D. Premasiri (1985), a Sinhala-Buddhist scholar of erudition, who wants us all for the last two decades to focus on the roots of violence, have not received the recognition they deserve. One reason may be Premasiri's penchant (inevitable in a primarily text-biased analysis) for focusing on the Ganges Valley of sixth century BCE rather than on the more credible and accessible contexts of our own times. More pertinently Premasiri's reasoning would not easily fit into what is very much in vogue in academic colloquia, prefabricated modular paradigms with their own Procrustean insistence on conformity.

How would such abstractions play out in the real world of politics? In many developing countries, in the aftermath of colonial rule, volatility in politics (brought about largely by rising popular expectations), was matched by the tendency of the state to augment its power by far reaching constitutional reforms, which invariably emasculated the power of popularly elected legislatures. The beneficiary was the executive and its incumbent. In 1972, following a dramatic electoral victory, Sirimāvō Bandaranaike (1916–2000) became the president of the Republic of Sri Lanka concentrating in her hands (theoretically and in fact) a pulchritude of power which none of her predecessors, as heads of state, had ever enjoyed. In 1978, however, following a massive electoral defect, Sirimāvō Bandaranaike fell from power, to begin a long period of political exile.

Shortly afterwards, quite by chance, I met her in Welimaḍa (at the residence of a close kinsman of hers) in the highlands of Sri Lanka, while I was on my way to Ella and broke journey at Welimaḍa knowing as I did her genial host quite well. I was surprised to see Sirimāvō Bandaranaike who greeted me warmly for no more reason than that I was "H.A.C.'s (my father) son." During a leisurely lunch and well into the late afternoon, I was able to interview Mrs Bandaranaike, anxious to make the best of an opportunity the gods had thrown in my lap. At journey's end in Ella that night, while it was still fresh in my mind I made notes of my conversations, which I now reproduce verbatim. When I had thanked her for giving me so much of her time and she in turn asked me how my father was coping with his health, she asked me:

> "Have I answered all your questions? Why do I have the feeling that you want to ask me something besides what we have talked about but you are reluctant to do so?"
>
> "Yes, but it can wait."
>
> "Why not now? After all they have kicked me out of power. So, I have all the time in the world!"
>
> "It has been said both in Sri Lanka and of course abroad that you suppressed the JVP uprising in 1971 with unparalleled use of state power and ferocity. Foreign correspondents claimed that many people were killed, their deaths unaccounted for. Looking back, what do you think of all that, especially as a Buddhist?"
>
> "Of course I am a Buddhist, and as you know, very much so. But Buddhism had nothing to do with it. I was the head of state. I was very much aware of that. In fact, when we realized the danger we were in – and yet we were not in the early days able to fathom its full extent – I remember I had to boost the sagging morale of our service chiefs – all these Sandhurst returned people! My first duty was to protect the state. The approaches to Colombo had to be secured. I told Sēpāla (Attygalle) to start with that. I had no doubt in my mind that the JVP had to be crushed."

"I understand. We could not know – all that we had to go by was what the radio would tell us. But I remember everybody was tense."

"You see, because of my non-aligned policies, I was able to get help from all countries. You see, those policies paid off."

"Since you asked this question, let me tell you I was the head of state, but I was also a woman. When the beauty queen was molested in Kataragama and then shamefully killed, I reacted as a woman. We punished all the guilty officers. Lots of people put pressure on me to show leniency. There was no question of that happening."

"I agree. Even the newspaper, I remember, did not give the whole affair the attention that it deserved."

"Now, here's where your Buddhism comes in. Even at the height of the JVP uprising, I felt sad. These were after all young men and women who had been clearly misled, and manipulated. After we arrested the bulk of them we began a scheme of rehabilitation so that finally they would be useful members of society. In setting it up, I consulted the *Mahāsaṅgha*. Because we are a Buddhist country, we relied on compassion. In other countries all these people would have been killed. You know how that is. I think we won international respect putting our Buddhism into practice."

The encounter – a moment in Sri Lankan serendipity – may provide vestigial clues to our understanding of the dilemmas of Sinhala kings and the conscience of rulers, be they Duṭugämuṇu or Sirimāvō Bandaranaike. It is, I would argue, a legitimate comparison given the concentration of power in a single individual, and of course, the common element of Buddhism, though, widely separated in time. It was with a certain aseptic detachment that the *Mahāvaṃsa* recorded the stewardship of kings who resorted to violence either driven by greed, vaulting ambition, the lust for power, or by considerations of *raison d'etat,* to repulse foreign invaders. In either event, the venerable author illustrated the thesis – which required no end of reiteration – which men were, after all, a mixture of good and evil, and yet had the potential for accomplishing enormous redemptive good, for the well being of the many. The didactic exemplification par excellence was not Duṭugämuṇu, but Mahāsena, the last king in the great chronicle. Driven by sectarian passion Mahāsena had effectively undermined the Mahavihāra, the center of the Orthodox Buddhist fraternity to which Mahānāma belonged. Yet, with impeccable evaluatory judgment and poise, the chronicler declares with epitaphic brevity, "[t]hus did he gather to himself much merit and made guilt" (Mahānāma Thera 1950: 271). A fitting conclusion to the *Mahāvaṃsa*.

Never participants, but always as observers on the sidelines, the monks saw how politics compounded the frailties of the human condition already tainted by the defilement (P. *kilesa*). They looked with unwearying compassion on the kings who, the pomp and circumstance notwithstanding, in their lives had made a poorer choice, namely that of regulating the affairs of men as the herdsman would tend his cattle. Indeed then as now the clerical advice proffered to a head of state was no more than an exercise in damage control. The monks were consulted but there is no record that they dictated national policy. In this respect, they followed the example of their master, the Buddha.

Modern monks followed tradition. Baddēgama Sumana Thera, the chief incumbent of Pūjārāmaya, a well-known Buddhist temple in Kalutara District, knew President Junius Richard Jayewardene (1906–1996) and Prime Minister Ranasinghe Premadāsa (1924–1993) quite well, practically in terms of intimacy. He would often be summoned to the presidential residence, which the monk in his conversations with me invariably referred to quaintly as the *Rajavāsala*, the traditional term for a king's residence. He told me that Jayewardene was really a lonely man who would speak his mind only with close associates. India's involvement with the ethnic issues in Sri Lanka troubled him deeply, all the more so out of a realization of his (Sri Lanka's) helplessness. Delhi had crossed a timeless divide to make common cause with Tamil Nadu to jointly accomplish the destabilization of Sri Lanka. The truth was galling to the president who, like other Sri Lankan politicians of an older generation had found lyrical inspiration in the India of Jawaharlal Nehru (1889–1964) and Indira Gandhi (1917–1984). Illusions were being shattered one by one, while old political foes that he personally cherished and admired, were disappearing, plucked by the hand of death. This aging hero, unlike Tennyson's Ulysses could hardly contemplate the labor of smiting the sounding furrows, one more time. Everything was closing in. One day, in a conversation marked by long spells of silence, the president startled the monk by suddenly exclaiming, "sometimes I feel like a frog tossed into a well... Try as I might, I cannot get out." I took some moments to react to what Sumana Thera was telling me. My mind wandered off to a spectacularly trenchant passage in the *Upanishads* wherein a great sage bitterly disillusioned with the world and its ways, and longing to achieve the transcendence which would release him, but ever eluded him, exclaims, "Sir, I feel like a frog in a waterless well." I recall being irritated with myself, unable to precisely determine whether the marvelous piece came from the *Chandogya* or the *Maitrī Upanishads*. I snapped out of my reverie to ask the monk whether it was not true that men weep most at self-inflicted wounds. Sumana Thera, who was pleased with my observation, said that Buddhism was all about self-inflicted wounds.

At the other end of the political spectrum, as it were, Māduḷuvāvē Sōbhita Thera, who ideologically was clearly left of center, was friend, philosopher, and guide to the Bandaranaike family, and through thick and thin shared their triumphs, tribulations, and reversals of fortune. He evidently tried – a role expected of a monk – to bring some resolution to the sibling rivalries that bedeviled the family, and were clearly a source of pain to its great matriarchal head. Like the best of narrators in the Buddhist traditions, Sōbhita Thera would invariably conclude some incident he related with the sapient comment that after all such was the nature of the world.

Sōbhita Thera saw most things in a Buddhist idiom. He believed, for example, that of all Sri Lankan leaders Sirimāvō Bandaranaike had consciously striven to make the Buddhist ideal of *upekkha* (equanimity) her guiding principle. This then was the source of her charisma and the deep loyalty she inspired in many of her followers. Then again, one evening in the course of a long official visit to the United States (during which I was deputized by the State Department to serve as his traveling companion) when we were sitting on the step of the Lincoln Memorial looking across the Washington Mall, Sōbhita Thera, apropos of nothing, remarked that power was a terrifying thing. Sōbhita Thera made this observation with his customary *gravitas*. Yet as I half listened to him, my mind went back to the very first afternoon we had met. He warned me that he was a poor sleeper as he suffered from severe intermittent pains at the back of his head as a result of repeated blows he had received from an irate police officer who, like his colleagues, were wielding batons to disrupt a protest meeting in which Sōbhita Thera took part. One of J.R. Jayewardene's senior ministers, himself a professing Buddhist had orchestrated the violence. As if to forestall skepticism on my part, Sōbhita Thera hastened to add that all one had to do was to look at Buddhist literature, especially the *Jātaka* stories.

In Sri Lanka the present easily coalesces with the past. In all too visible iconographic representations, carefully choreographed rituals, in tropes taking the form of metaphor, *syne doche*, in collective acts of anamnesis, and in discourse, the past is reborn to keep its tryst with the present. Ordinarily all this would pass muster as no more than harmless, innocent cultural expressions of Sinhalese Buddhism. But then culture belies its looks. It is often a statement of power and hegemony. If the actors on the stage, the purveyors of the culture may not (other than in a surreal sense) be aware, others who are outside of the culture, certainly perceive it in exactly those terms, and understandably continue to do so.

Indeed, in the post-1983 historiography critical characterizations of the use of the past, are evident, namely that Sinhala Buddhists in their modalities of thinking live in the past, they make the past an integral element in the agendas of action, refuse to see contemporary strictly on their merits sans the dimensions of the past, the past is an imagined construct, if history it is "mythico history" at best, and above all the use of the past is exclusive, and not integrative. The clamorous refrain continues.

The question may be deeper than the characterizations would suggest. However, a perceptive and balanced analysis could be found in Steven Kemper's *The Presence of the Past* (1991). Kemper concedes that the idea of a past has the potential for manipulation especially in the overly politicized ethos, which marked the issues of power from 1972 onward. J.R. Jayewardene, in spite of a long tutelage in democratic liberal traditions going back to the Donoughmore Constitution in 1932, as head of state, single handedly derailed a genuine system of parliamentary democracy, which had begun to take root. Although it is clearly *passé* for an analyst to indulge in speculation, it is possible to think that but for the constitutional changes of 1978, which clearly precluded consensus, we might have been spared the terrifying twin perils we confront today: a formidable ethnic problem which defies resolution, and worse, a system of governance, sans any credible accountability, breeding cynicism in the public mind. In a manipulative use of the past, not without a touch of megalomania, Jayewardene saw himself as a king, in a long lineage of Sri Lankan kings extending over 2,500 years. He would share this reflection with a head of state whose own country was born in a violent and successful repudiation of monarchy, an event annually celebrated with uninhibited eclat and panache in July, in the United States (Kemper 1991: 129).

All the same, it would be a mistake to go reactively in the opposite direction, to contend that the past is a spurious artifact of the Sinhala-Buddhist mind, as spurious as its derivative – a self-conscious collective Sinhala identity, easily crossing timelines and having the potential to continue to do so. In recent years, this trend has gained a certain legitimacy in Sri Lankan scholarship following the works of Ernest Gellner (1983) and Benedict Anderson (1983), especially the latter. In Sri Lankan historiography Benedict Andersen's celebrated phrase "imagined" communities has been taken to mean that such entities never existed but were as it were cooked up.

Kemper puts the point well:

> I think that part of the scholarly inability to take nationalism on its own terms derive from portraying nationalism as absolutely discontinuous with the past. Nationalism is an invented political community, yet to describe it as "invented" as Anderson remarks of Gellner, is to link it not to "falsity" and "fabrication" but to "imagination" and "creation"... The modern imagination can hardly overlook the traditional, especially in places such as Sri Lanka, where the "national" imagination has both 2,500 years of history to invoke and a chronicle tradition reliable enough in many of its representations to win the credence of professional historians... Nationalism, in Sri Lanka and elsewhere, is simply the most recent stage in the ongoing construction of a "past."
>
> (1991: 15)

The unwillingness to resist sloganizing and soberly evaluate issues as Steven Kemper has done, has sometimes led to painful academic *faux pas*, as when it is suggested that Anagārika Dharmapāla (1864–1933) invented Sinhala-Buddhist nationalism. May we not extend a scintilla of compassion to this much-maligned man to concede that even he was not fool enough to reinvent the wheel? Nor can we credit him with single handedly inventing nationalism given all the character flaws attributed to him.

The problem may lie in perception, using the word in its purely secular and not in a philosophical or religious sense. Both in European ideology and history, nationalism meant the successful fusion of discrete elements in a given territory to achieve an overarching unity or identity. We may take as an illustration Great Britain and British nationalism, before (to be a trifle facetious), the days of Tom Nairn (2002) and Scottish devolution. By contrast, in the developing countries, (notably Sri Lanka) the constituent elements like the Sinhalese and Tamils – each rightly conscious of its identity – have been reluctant to subsume their identities for the sake of a common Sri Lankan (or Ceylonese) identity, especially when the latter has failed (not because of the ethnic crisis: an easy scapegoat) to create a credible basis for doing so. Such as, for example, ethnicities on both sides of the divide having a powerful vested interest in the perpetuation of the status quo from which there is visible and continuing gain.

One learns, and learns best by looking away from the page, as it were, to see a wider spectrum. I understood the depths of Sinhala nationalism and Tamil nationalism (unfairly dismissed as merely a reactive response to the heavy history laden nationalism of the Sinhalese), better than I previously did when I read two books on Russia. Their very titles were uncannily appropriate. The first, Ronald Grigor Suny's *The Revenge of the Past: Nationalism, Revolution, and the Collapse of the Soviet Union*, and the second, Andrew Baruch Wachtel's *An Obsession with History: Russian Writers Confront the Past* (1994). It would appear that after all, Sinhala Buddhism, alias chauvinism, has friends in places where you are least likely to find them. Both serve as a pointed rebuke to Marxist and bourgeoisie ideologues who in their constructions underestimated the power of emotion, irrationality, and vision in the name of structure.

Catharsis lies in confronting the past, infusing creative elements of resilience and adaptability, rather than in a Canute like denial of its legitimacy. "Not in the sky, nor in the sea, nor in a cave in the mountains" (to adapt the *Dhammapada*, v. 127) could a people escape from their past.

Historians are not prophets. History confounds those who rashly seek to see the unrevealed other half of its face. Nonetheless, taking a page from an unrelated field involving the study of probabilities, one may reasonably indulge in prognostications, and if need be (to use the archaism), raise alarums. The Historian would very much be like the watchman on a tower in a Greek drama, scanning the dark brooding sea of the night for some stirring movement. What would those alarums be?

First, that the present moment when a seemingly interminable peace process is unfolding, is metaphorically the best time of the day, the lingering morning when each of the contending sides entertains sanguine hopes of lasting peace. This is the season of illusion, of innocence. Second, that if at any rate in the erroneous perceptions of this writer the peace processes are completed, paradoxically, they would give rise to new fears and anxieties, not existing previously, given that whereas one side would see peace in the retention of the status quo, the other visualizes lasting resolution in its radical alteration.

Third, after all, in the opening scenes of *Orestes*, the weary watchman who finally sees the great Agamemnon returning to the caress of home and hearth, could hardly have foreseen the terrible tragedies that would follow the king's return, even as his ship, cleaving the waters, came closer to the shore. The comparable beginning point, the fatal *casus belli* would be the projected amalgamation of the northern and eastern provinces in Sri Lanka, triggering off processes leading slowly but surely to the Balkanization of the island. One more time in Sri Lanka, the dragon's teeth are being sown. At the risk of mixing metaphors and images, we are like the man in Kafka's *Penal Settlement,* who with a mixture of unbelievable *naiveté,* curiosity, and fascination, watches workmen putting together the scaffold where on the following day he is marked to die.

The historian – ever the voice in the wilderness – is only too aware that political settlements imposed by negotiation, under the seemingly benign aegis of altruistic third parties – are pregnant with the seeds of its future dissolution. Would the Sinhalese, confronted by a fiat *accompli* created by the peace process develop the mentality of waiting for Godot? Indeed, more than once in recent visits to Sri Lanka, I would hear perfectly down to earth and rational Sinhalese say (without orchestration), that someday there will arise a Sinhala Prabhakaran, to spin the wheel of violence one more time.

Fourth, looking back from the beginning of the 1970s to our own day and time, it becomes abundantly clear – however distasteful the conclusion – that if the Tamil cause made spectacular progress, it was not because of table talk, but is attributable to the masterfully discriminating way in which the LTTE used violence. It is difficult to think that in the name of peace and vacuous moralistic pieties, the Tiger would change its spots, and abandon a clearly viable *modus operandi.*

One may add to the litany of things that should give us pause, our penchant for naively excluding India from the calculus – an India determined to play Krisṇa in the Kurukṣetra of Sri Lanka. Would then the good people of Sri Lanka, so manifestly yearning for peace on both sides of the divide, be in the tragic position of Ashwattama in the *Mahābhārata* to whom – such was Krisṇa's grim decree – the night brought no repose, nor the rising day, hope.

Notes

1 Kurukṣetra is the name of an extensive plain near Delhi, the scene of the great battles between the Kurus and Pāṇḍus (*Manu* 7: 193).

2 Personal Communication with Father John Gaomes.

9

BUDDHISM, ETHNICITY, AND IDENTITY

A problem in Buddhist history

Gananath Obeyesekere

This chapter examines the precolonial formations of "nationhood" and "identity" in Buddhist Sri Lanka, prior to the radical changes associated with modernity and the reforms of both Colonel Henry Steel Olcott (1832–1907) and Anagārika Dharmapāla (1864–1933) as a reaction to both colonialism and imperial conquest. This is a difficult task and because it spans over 2,000 years it is an awesome one and I cannot claim to make any authoritative statement. Yet, I believe that one must be able to sketch even in a tentative manner premodern ideas of nationhood and identity in order to understand the rapid changes in both Buddhism and identity formation since colonial rule. I do not know how far such an account helps us to understand the current ethnic crisis. Nor do I have answers or solutions to that pressing issue. However, before presenting my main argument I want to briefly indicate the complexity of the current situation in an admittedly impressionistic manner and pose the moral difficulties Buddhists face in the wake of the current peace initiative.

One of the questions often asked of us scholars from educated Westerners is why Buddhism, a religion that is given to an ethic of radical nonviolence, has produced a nation like Sri Lanka that has, over the last two decades, produced a culture of extreme violence. In my view this is a wrong question to ask even although it is an obvious question. Buddhism can no more than any other World Religion remain immune to the larger social and economic woes that beset a nation. However, one can ask a related question: what can concerned Buddhist lay-folk and monks do to bring about a critique of contemporary life that might in turn have some effect in creating a new vision of society, one better geared to Buddhist doctrinal values, rather than one oriented toward a destructive Sinhala nationalism. The latter is too complicated an issue for me to deal with here but I do not think that one can overcome the crisis facing Buddhists in Sri Lanka unless there is an ethical reform of the scale that occurred in the end of the late nineteenth and early twentieth centuries with the work of Colonel Olcott and Anagārika Dharmapāla (even though I do not approve of much of the content of that reform).

Instead I shall briefly comment on the current scene of violence and despair in Buddhist Sri Lanka and only then try to understand in more scholarly fashion the issues of ethnicity and identity in precolonial sociopolitical formations.

Though a so-called Buddhist nation, Sri Lanka has over the last twenty years produced an extremely high murder rate and perhaps one of the largest rates of suicide for the whole world. Sri Lankan Buddhists are all familiar with the five precepts; yet over the same period Sri Lankan Buddhist males have become one of the largest consumers of alcohol in the world. Politicians who have issued liquor licenses for party donors who can give Rs 1,000,000 for election funds have fostered this. The result is that even in small towns there are more liquor stores than rural banks. Youth and unemployed men are often incited to join party parades on the promise of huge quantities of booze. Sri Lankan Buddhists have become huge consumers of meat; vegetarianism is touted but it is the rare exception than the rule. In a famous temple in Kandy one of the monks in charge of coordinating almsgiving for monks, insists that the lay devotees supply chicken. The laity in turn can no longer supply vegetarian food to monks (fish maybe if meat is considered not kosher by lay-folk). While the laity is often critical of monk behavior, especially political behavior, they pile monks with luxuries, especially food during almsgiving rituals, which then reinforce monk worldliness. And excess robes, towels, and other items donated by them to wealthy temples are rechanneled (quite sensibly) back to the market.

Given this context it shouldn't surprise us if forests and grasslands in the hill country are burned periodically to suffocate animals that are then eaten. In some forested areas there are no four-legged wild animals to be seen. In my youth it was unthinkable for Buddhists to plunder temples and archeological reserves for artifacts; but now, spurred by the international antique market, such activities have become a minor industry and periodic newspaper accounts suggest monk complicity in plundering their own temples. Monks proudly affirm they are the ones who kept the Buddhist tradition intact yet ancient palm leaf manuscripts in the temple libraries I have visited are either rotting away or sold as artifacts and sometimes torn and sold to foreign tourists as examples of the "Buddha writing." Very few monks can read Pāli. In one major pilgrimage center hallowed by tradition, the chief monk who has consistently switched political allegiances, according to village gossip, carries a handgun. Buddhism is a religion of silence no longer. Loudspeakers pollute the environment around them every morning as monks conduct "noise warfare" with the *mullas* in their midst. In one instance in Kandy so much loudspeaker noise was created on a full moon day in a powerful Buddhist temple frequented by a minister that someone phoned the monk to protest. Soon a party of about fifty laymen lead by the chief incumbent monk, drunk and armed with clubs, entered my friend's house threatening him with death and challenging him to report him (the monk) to the police, if he dares. And my friend dared not. Monks can with impunity encroach on government land and build temples; they can take over archeological sites for the same purpose and though there are laws against such actions I have not heard of one instance where a monk had been taken to court for them.

Newspapers constantly report of extraordinary violence toward women; and underworld gangsters are committing acts of highway robbery virtually everyday and now, not surprisingly, high school kids who have been taught "Buddhism" as a subject for public exams and have come to be bored with it imitate these acts. Underworld drug barons and thugs are part of the teams of all political parties; they are recruited sometimes as security personnel for senior politicians. Underlying all of this are the problems of a stagnant economy, rendered nearly bankrupt by years of ethnic warfare, huge population increases with poor prospects of employment or underemployment for vast masses of people. These conditions in turn led to the devastating brutalization of the society in the late 1980s with the Sinhala nationalist Janatha Vimukti Peramuṇa (JVP) youth insurrection; appropriately it has been designated as the *bhīsana kālaya* or period of dread. Not only were the most fearsome and degrading crimes committed by the JVP but also the Government's counteraction in suppressing the movement was as brutal. I believe it is the JVP era and government counterterror that resulted in the degradation of life in Sri Lanka and a major cause of the current culture of violence.

Let me get back to the disorder in the Saṅgha. Monks are almost overwhelmingly recruited as children from rural areas, initially as little child novices. It is not surprising therefore that monks share some of the psychic characteristics of the lay-folk around them, though I think that the majority of monks, like the majority of ordinary folk, are decent persons, even though not very learned in the scriptures. Village monks continue to perform an indispensable role in Buddhist society but they simply lack self-criticism and the leadership potential to lead a new Buddhist reform movement. On the contrary many of the articulate monks and lay-folk carry on the self-delusion that everything seems fine with Buddhism and expect the government alone to solve "the grievances of Buddhists." Scapegoatism is rampant in the population: not only is the LTTE blamed for the ills of the nation but Christians also bear that burden and sometimes expatriate scholars. Such widespread self-delusion is not surprising in times of social malaise and anomie.

Given the fact that there are no real character differences between monk and laity and the fact that increasingly the gap in styles of life are also being blurred, one would expect monks also to engage in radical, even violent politics. And because monks belong to all major political parties (and this includes the JVP) one would expect them to respond to the political message of secular parties which is hardly the message of the Buddha. But in comparative perspective Buddhism does not do too badly: though nationalist monks and lay-folk remain politically vociferous, they are not as violent as those warrior ascetics in India today and murderous Hindu mobs in Gujarat; and the ones who have been influenced by Muslim ideas of *jihad* are very few in number. Though the chauvinist sentiments of monks have been partially responsible for radicalization of the Tamils and also to the continuity of the present ethnic war, one must see their current responses not in isolation, but in relation to the violence and atrocities committed by the LTTE, especially their (the LTTE) killing of Buddhist monks and novices going on pilgrimage, the attacks on civilian populations, and the more recent attack on the Temple of the Tooth in Kandy – to name a few of the provocations. However, one would think that if monks and laity were sensitive to human suffering (as they ought to as "Buddhists") they would not be opposed to a negotiated settlement with the Tamil minority. Fortunately, many leading monks have approved of the peace process and are willing to give it a chance though not the youthful monks from the JVP and the fledgling *Sihala Urumaya* (Sinhala Heritage) party and those representing all sorts of "Buddhist" organizations. Having vented my spleen I can now get to my main theme of nationhood and identity in the precolonial Sri Lanka!

Imagining a Buddhist "whatever"

I will deliberately refrain from employing terms like "nation," "nation state," or even "state" to describe the situation in precolonial Sri Lanka. For the moment I want to bracket these words from the Western lexicon and tentatively substitute "whatever" instead, till I have presented the empirical material. Let me begin by saying that whatever "whatever" meant the idea of sovereignty was clearly recognized in Sri Lankan kingship. It was an ideological construct, a fiction, though a very significant one. Even minor kings who had effective control over only a miniscule area (such as the Tamil kings of Jaffna after the fifteenth century) claimed sovereignty for all of Sri Lanka. In reality the provinces could have often asserted their autonomy though they paid ideological homage to the "seat" of sovereignty wherever it was located. For most of ancient and medieval history the province of Ruhuṇa in the south was a virtually independent kingdom, an ideological replica of Anurādhapura (and later Polonnaruva) of the *rajaraṭa*, "the royal province," so named because the seat of sovereignty was located there. In the Kandyan period – after the fifteenth century – Buddhist kingdoms approximated what Tambiah (1976) has called "galactic polities," but, as far as the Kandyan kingdom was concerned, kings had considerable control over the provinces, especially through land grants combined with the frequent transfers or dismissals of provincial governors. Hence the characteristic of all these Buddhist polities: structurally disparate, yet ideologically imagined as a unified Buddhist "whatever."

For the most part the center was politically unstable: yet the ideology of a Buddhist "whatever" was fairly constant, and implied that the legitimate goal of sovereignty entailed the union of the whole island under the aegis of a single ruler. Hence the three texts of the *Mahāvaṃsa* give prominent place to the sovereigns who effected the ideal in the practical polity – Duṭṭhagāmaṇī (161–137 BCE), Vijayabāhu I (1070–1110 CE), Parākramabāhu I (1153–1186 CE), and the last king to unify the island, Parākramabāhu VI (1411–1461).

Ideological unity in the popular Buddhist imagination

Let me now give some content to the "whatever" that I started with. There is some notion of ideological unity that transcends the fragmented and multiple notion of the "state." How then is this ideological unity conceived and expressed in the popular Buddhist imagination?

1 According to the first book of the *Mahāvaṃsa* written in the sixth century CE, the Buddha, flying through the air by virtue of his supernormal powers, landed in Sri Lanka three times, chasing demons to a distant isle known as *giri dīpa* (rocky isle or island city) and settling a dispute among contending *nāga* (snake beings) kings living in the north and converting them. He visited places that later became sacred sites: Kälaṇiya near Colombo and Mahiyaṅgana in the northeast where his collarbone relic was later enshrined.[1] In his third visit he placed his foot on the top of the spectacular peak known as Samantakūṭa, named after the guardian of the peak, Sumana, later to become one of the guardian deities of Buddhist Sri Lanka. The myth of the Buddha's visits is rarely contested. Its significance is also clear: the island has been cleared of malevolent demons while the benevolent *nāgas* are converted to the true religion. Major religious centers have been sanctified by his presence and his foot is indelibly inscribed on Samantakūṭa, later to become *the* most important pilgrimage site and exemplary center for Buddhists. It is as if the land is consecrated as a place where Buddhism will flourish, as virtually all historical texts recognize (Mahānāma Thera 1950: 1–13); it is made ready for the coming of the founding ancestor of the Sinhalas, Vijaya.

2 Vijaya ("victory") was the son of Sinhabāhu, a parricidal king who killed his father, a lion, and then married his own sister, and lived in Sinhapura ("lion city") in northern India. Owing to his violent and unlawful behavior, Sinhabāhu banished his son by putting him in a boat with 700 of his followers. Vijaya landed in Sri Lanka on the very day the Buddha passed into final *nirvāṇa*; thus Vijaya, the "victor," is the secular counterpart of the other victor (*jina*), the Buddha himself. What the Buddha is to the spiritual realm (*sāsana*), Vijaya is to the "secular" realm. This is one reason why the founder of the first Buddhist kingdom is named Vijaya (in the *Mahāvaṃsa* and the earlier *Dīpavaṃsa* history), and not "Sinhala," the name by which he is known in virtually all non-Sri Lankan texts.

The Buddha entrusted Sakra (Indra) to protect Vijaya, and Sakra delegated this task to Viṣṇu, who blessed Vijaya when he landed by tying a Buddhist protective charm on his person. Viṣṇu (Upulvan), like Saman before him, became one of the guardian deities of the land and a future *bodhisattva*. Vijaya married a demoness named Kuvēni whom he subsequently betrayed; from this union sprang the Väddas the "aboriginal" hunters of Sri Lanka (many of whom to this day claim Vijaya as their ancestor). Subsequently, in a formal ceremonial, he married a princess from South Madurapura (in the Tamil country, distinguished from North Madurapura, the land of Kṛṣṇa). There were no heirs from this marriage, and Vijaya's brother's son was brought from Sinhapura to take over the kingship (Mahānāma Thera 1950: 51–61).

This is the foundational myth for Sri Lankan history and it is an inescapable part of the historical consciousness of the Sinhalas. Modern scholars have scarcely noted the fact that it is a myth of ethnic separation and integration.

The land is consecrated and cleansed of evil spirits by the Buddha for Vijaya to land; the hunters are descended from Vijaya but by an illegitimate union, and hence outside the pale of legitimate kingship and Buddhist history and civilization. The Tamils have no affinities; they do not inherit the dynasty; it goes back to Paṇḍu Vāsudēva, whose name resonates with that of the protagonists of the *Kṛṣṇa*. Yet, unlike the Väddas, the Tamils are not only kinfolk but also cofounders of the nation. This aspect of the myth has been almost completely forgotten or ignored in recent times. The rest of the Vijaya myth appears everywhere and is so powerful that virtually everyone treats it as an empirically "true" beginning of Sri Lankan history.

These foundational myths provide political legitimation for the dominant group, justifying the essentially Buddhist nature of the place, Sri Lanka. These founding myths have proliferated Sinhala culture from the sixth century onwards, in popular myth, ritual dramas on the village level, in ballad literature, and right into modern theater. Even modern empiricist historians treat them as at least a symbolically correct account of the migration and colonization of the country by those funny people, the Aryans, introduced into our local histories by nineteenth century European historians, archaeologists, and other mythmakers. These kinds of charter myths are found all over the world, in almost every culture, but here they are given Buddhist validation.

3 Village rituals, whether for gods or demons, virtually everywhere, often start with a standard phrase: "*sasiri bara, me siri laka* (heavy with prosperity, this blessed Sri Lanka). Take the implication of this phrase: it does not express a geographic conception at all, but an imagination of a place. While people had little knowledge of anything like modern physical geography, there is little doubt that for many an ocean surrounded this place. This fixity of the land mass had important implications that I shall deal with later. Within this imagined space there is an internal geography recorded in *Kaḍaimpot* or boundary books that parallels the cosmic geography of Buddhist texts.[2] In addition there were even more fluid territorial domains of the various gods of the pantheon.

4 Following the preliminary incantation quoted earlier the Buddhist hierarchy in this place of Sri Lanka is recounted in ritual texts, as in the following stanza:

> The noble refuge of the Buddha
> The refuge of the Dhamma the taught
> And the jewel of the Saṅgha
> With piety we worship these Three Refuges.[3]

Then the great guardian gods are named, followed by a list of minor local deities who exhibit considerable regional variation. Thus, though the rituals might vary in content and form from region to region there is a recognized pan-island hierarchy of named deities, specifically the Buddha and the guardian gods who act as protectors of Buddhism, the state and the place, Sri Lanka. These stanzas occur in village *bali* and *tovil* (planetary and exorcistic) rituals all over the

Buddhist and Sinhala-speaking parts of the nation. They cannot be historically dated with any accuracy but from the Neville catalogue of ritual texts in the British Museum it seems that they emerged in their present forms around the sixteenth century and were written in what one might call "modern Sinhala." But it is likely that similar ritual formulas existed much earlier. The imagined place has a cosmography, if not a geography, in which an overlapping hierarchy of Buddhist deities were allocated territories and propitiated at their ritual centers.

When one moves from these village rituals for gods and demons into Buddhist temples there is a strong standardization of rituals and prayers for the Buddha, in spite of different types of monk orders and fraternities. The Buddha figure is also internalized in the conscience of believers as a benevolent figure, an almost maternal one, though he is formally recognized as a male. This standardization is made possible because Buddhist temples and monks (and other kinds of Buddhist religious virtuosos) are everywhere present and accessible to all. Buddhist temple frescoes also indicate a strong tendency toward the standardization of popular Buddhist stories. This is not surprising given the fact that Buddhism has been for a long time, a kind of fetishized "book religion." Even when people did not go on distant pilgrimages they often did move outside their villages into other areas when visiting kinfolk, or during military service or for trade purposes. Once out there one might visit a temple or shrine for the gods (the two often located in the same place). At the Buddhist temple there are few boundary problems, except sometimes for few of the lowest castes. Most people perform standardized prayers and ritual acts because there is a sense in which they share a common "salvation idiom" derived from Buddhism. In my view a common "salvation idiom" takes the place of Western-print capitalism in the formation of a trans-local communal consciousness.

5 One of the fascinating problems to emerge from the imagination of place is the two fundamental ways of designating it – as Lanka or Sri Lanka and as Sinhaladīpa, "the island of the Sinhalas." In my reading of literally hundreds of ritual texts I have not come across one instance of the country being called other than Lanka or Sri Lanka (Siri Laka), except when foreign gods or traders come to these shores and hail it as the country of the Sinhala (*sinhaladēsa*). With few exceptions Sri Lanka also seems to be the almost exclusive form of self-designation in Sri Lankan historical texts like the *Mahāvaṃsa*, except for "Tambapaṇṇi," which coexists with Sri Lanka in the earlier portions of these narratives.[4] In the foundational myth, when Vijaya lands in Sri Lanka and asks Viṣṇu for the name of the island Viṣṇu tells him: "The island of Sri Lanka" (Mahānāma Thera 1950: 55).[5] By contrast outsiders often, if not always, designated the island as Sinhaladīpa from which is derived the European term Ceylon or Ceilao (or any one of its variations), in turn derived from the Chinese rendering of Sinhaladīpa. So is it with Serendib, the Arabic rendering; and Ilam, which the Tamil guerillas nowadays identify as their homeland ironically means "Sinkalam," "the country of the Sinhalas," according to the Madras Lexicon.[6]

A tenth century Nepalese painting refers to a hospital known as the Siṃhaladvīpa Arogyācala Lokeśvara (Holt 1991: 79). A very important outside reference comes from the Mahāyāna text, the *Saddharmapuṇḍarīka Sūtra*. In this text the Buddha Gautama himself was born as Sinhala, a merchant of Sinhakalpa and the son of Sinha (the lion). Sinha and his 500 followers go in search of precious stones when they were shipwrecked off the coast of the island of Tāmradvīpa (Tambapaṇṇi). Celestial nymphs, who were in fact demonesses, rescued them planning to devour the crew. Sinhala married one of them but he was warned by a magic light about his imminent danger; and then informed him that a white winged horse named Balāha will take him and his comrades to safety but no one should open his eyes until they have landed on the further shore. They did as they were bid but all the merchants except Sinhala, smitten by desire and longing, opened their eyes only to drop into the ocean and consumed by the demonesses. Sinhala's demoness-wife appeared in Sinhakalpa and complained to the father about Sinhala's betrayal of her. The father would not listen to the son's admonishing and instead married her. The demoness brought her companions from Tāmradvīpa and soon devoured the king and other members of this family. The people then proclaimed Sinhala as their king. Sinhala succeeded in banishing the demonesses into the forest; in commemoration of this event Tāmradvīpa was named Sinhaladvīpa.[7]

According to Har Dayal (1932: 382), the major sections of the *Saddharmapuṇḍarīka Sūtra* was composed before the third century CE; but the section in which the Sinhala episode is mentioned – the *Kāraṇḍa-vyūha* – was probably composed around the fourth century CE, that is, before the *Mahāvaṃsa*. Though one cannot be certain of the chronology in the above instance, one can be confident that the naming of the island as Sinhaladīpa was an old convention by outsiders. Yet, how does one interpret this differential naming procedure? In my interpretation, the divergent terminology indicated that the people living in this place were sensitive to internal ethnic differentiations whereas outsiders adopted a more simplistic naming procedure after the dominant ethnic group. Take the foundational myth of Vijaya: in it the primary outsider ethnic group is the Väddas even though later the Tamils seem to consume the Sinhala historical imagination. It therefore seems to me impossible for the Sinhalas in ancient times (perhaps at any point in the precolonial period) to maintain that their nation was Sinhaladīpa or the land of the Sinhalas, when it was obvious to them from their own ongoing origin myth that the land also belonged to the Väddas. And if we ignore the foundation myth, which only has self-referential significance and go into prehistoric archaeology, it is clear that various groups, including hunters and gatherers ("Väddas"), existed here long before the Sinhalas.[8]

The propensity for a group to see itself as internally differentiated is nothing unusual. This is also the case with traditional kin groups like clans (and modern corporations like universities); outsiders see it as a single entity whereas the insiders are sensitive to the complexities of internal differentiation and, as far as clans and lineages are concerned, the differences between the perceptions of insiders and outsiders are given terminological recognition.[9]

6 All these cultural expressions permit the plurality of Sinhalas to imagine themselves as "Buddhists." Yet is imagining a community all that is necessary to

create a sense of *belonging* to a community that transcends local boundaries and allegiances? Contrary to Benedict Anderson (1983: 74) I think there are no "concrete communities": all communities are imagined but imagined in different ways. The ethnographic or historical task is to describe the manner in which communities are imagined. But this is not sufficient: the imagined community even that of a modern nation must be "concretized" in a variety of ways – in parades, national events, collective gatherings ranging from football to political meetings and so forth. These concretized gatherings of modern nations permit mass vicarious participation through their refractions in the media; and these media presentations in turn bring into question the very distinction between imagined and concrete. These diverse representations are intrinsic to the imagining of modern nationhood and they nourish it. The question I pose in respect of Buddhism is this: how is this sense of belonging concretized in the Buddhist case in precolonial times prior to the development of mass communications? I suggest that, in addition to the participation in common rituals (a "salvation idiom") in village temples, there is the crucial mechanism of the "obligatory pilgrimage" which I will now describe with an example from Rambadeṇiya, an isolated village in the northeastern hills of Sri Lanka where Stanley Tambiah and I did fieldwork in 1958–1960.[10]

In Rambadeṇiya, after each harvest, villagers will gather together in a collective thanksgiving ritual for the gods known as the *aḍukku* ("food offering"). During this festival the priest (*kapurāla*) of the *deva* or deity cults (never the Buddhist monk) pays formal homage to the Buddha and the great guardian deities and then actively propitiates the local gods, especially their main deity known as Banḍāra Deviyo (Banḍāra means "chief" rather than "king," the term reserved for the guardian gods). These rituals help define the village as a "moral community" under the benevolent care of Banḍāra Deviyo. Once every year, however, some of the villagers go to the great pilgrimage center of Mahiyaṅgana, about 35 miles away, which the Buddha himself consecrated by his presence. As we proceed through the forest we hang branches or twigs on trees sacred to local deities, implicitly acknowledging that we are no longer under the care of our local deity but under the aegis of another whose *sīma* (boundary) we are now crossing. In a matter of a few hours other villagers taking different pilgrim routes join us and there is a literal and dramatic expansion of the moral community, which ultimately becomes a vast sea of heads as we reach Mahiyaṅgana. Right along we sing religious songs mostly in praise of the Buddha, since this is the shared idiom that makes sense in the context of an expanded community. At the pilgrimage site we bathe in the river and purify ourselves and pray to the two guardian gods represented there – Saman and Skanda – and then worship the Buddha and perform exclusively Buddhist rituals. An important shift in allegiances has occurred: villagers have temporarily renounced their parochial local deities and are united under the common worship of the Buddha and the guardian gods. The once separate and discrete moral communities now lose their identities in the larger moral community of Sinhala Buddhists.

A powerful act of concretization has occurred fostering the imagination in a special way, reinforcing and nourishing ideas of being Sinhala and Buddhist that a person has learned by simply living in his village community and participating in its round of activities. The trip to Mahiyaṅgana is but one station in an ideal pilgrimage round of sixteen, a number that comes to us from at least the eighteenth century (Geiger 1960: 207). Rambadeṇiya folk rarely made it beyond Mahiyaṅgana in 1968, but all did make it to Mahiyaṅgana some of the time.[11] The "obligatory pilgrimage" makes it possible for us to identify the "whatever" that eluded thus far: it is *sāsana*, a term that could be loosely translated as the Buddhist "church." By contrast "nation" is an alien word that has no parallel in the Sinhala lexicon. It is *sāsana* that takes its place. In the doctrinal tradition *sāsana* refers to the universal Buddhist community or church that transcends ethnic and other boundaries. This meaning coexists with another meaning that is found in post-canonical historical texts: *sāsana* is the Buddhist "church" that is particularized in the physical bounds of the land consecrated by the Buddha – in the present instance, Sri Lanka. Here then is the word we were looking for: it is the *sāsana* of Sri Lanka or, for most purposes, simply, the *sāsana*. *Sāsana* in this particularistic sense is locked into what one might call "Buddhist history;" *sāsana* in a universalistic sense is locked into the Buddhist doctrinal tradition. This tension between the two meanings of *sāsana* is intrinsic to Buddhism. Thus King Duṭugämuṇu, the hero-king who has been resurrected in contemporary Buddhist religious nationalism, fights the Tamil unbelievers not for the glory of sovereignty but for the glory of the *sāsana* – in its entirely particularistic sense. Sinhalas had no term that could be translated as "nation;" they had a term that belonged to the same polythetic class as nation, namely *sāsana*.

Taming otherness: the collective representations at Mahiyaṅgana

The Buddhist *sāsana* in Sri Lanka is not what we imagine it today. I have shown its transformations in colonial times particularly in the nineteenth century in what I have labeled Protestant Buddhism (or Buddhist modernism, if you prefer that term). In contemporary discourse in Sri Lanka the main dialectical opposition is between Sinhala and Tamil; most Sinhalas are Buddhist and most Tamils are Hindu. Sinhala Buddhists self-consciously feel that the nation has been historically a Buddhist one and that the main oppositional conflict was between Tamil-Hindus and Sinhala-Buddhists. I have myself made a case for such a dialectical opposition but now I want to introduce what I believe is the more fundamental structural opposition in Sri Lanka that has had a long historical run, namely, between the Vädda hunters and Sinhala Buddhist agriculturalists, in effect a distinction between Buddhists and non-Buddhists that has profound implications for our understanding of Buddhist history up to at least the eighteenth century.

Väddas are today a remnant of a few thousand "aborigines" scattered in the area around Maha Oya near Mahiyaṅgana. My current research shows however that Väddas were a ubiquitous presence and that groups labeled "hunters" were everywhere in the island. While I cannot detail that research here let me present some accounts that suggest their pervasive presence before the eighteenth century. The first is an invocation known as *Väddan anḍagähīma* or "the roll-call of the Väddas," the idea being to ask them to participate in that part of the *kohombā kankāriya* (a Sinhala post-harvest ritual) known as the *Vädi dāne*, "the alms giving of the Väddas." The text starts with asking the god of Santāna to bring blessings on the audience; *santāna* is of course the mountain of Hantāna in Kandy and the god is known to the Sinhalas as Hantāne Deviyo and to the Väddas as Hantāne Mahā Vädi Unnähä, "the venerable great Vädda of Hantāna." However, contemporary Väddas no longer associate him with the mountain of Hantāna; his domain at the beginning of this century is Mavaragala in what is now known as the Vädda country or Bintänne. The Vädda god of Hantāna has retreated from Kandy and his shrunken abode is now in what is considered Vädda territory proper. Yet, the text of *Väddan anḍagähīma* suggests that the Vädda country proper was practically coterminous with the Sinhala country of the Kandyan kingdom. In two texts of *Väddan anḍagähīma*, one edited by Charles Godakumbura and the other by Mudiyanse Dissanayake, over ninety Vädda villages are mentioned; no reference is made to Väddas living in the province of Sabaragamuva (lit. "the villages of hunters") either. Some of the areas where Väddas lived are familiar to those living in and around Kandy: the text mentions Väddas from Asgiriya, Bogambara, Hantāna, Batalagala, Gomiriya, Maturata, Hunnasgiriya, Lower Dumbara, Kotmale, Nuvara Eliya, Kehelgamuva, and Uragala. Needless to say, these are all Sinhala (and estate Tamil) areas today. These lists are by no means exclusive: but they are almost always from the area around Kandy, the North Central Province, the Dumbara, and Kotmale valleys and Uva. For us Mātalē would be unthinkable as a habitat for Väddas because its present inhabitants are mostly Sinhala, followed by later immigrants into the region, Muslims and estate Tamils. Yet the *Mātalē Kaḍaimpota* ("the book of boundaries of the Mātalē district") written around the mid-seventeenth century presents an entirely different picture. In this account the king of Mātalē, Vijayapāla, the older brother of Rajasinha II, summoned a leading chief and asked him to name the denizens (lit. men and animals) of Mātalē and the reply was: "Lord, there are only three [noble] houses in the district of Mātalē" and when the king asked what these houses were, "Lord, there is Kulatunga Mudiyanse of Uḍupihilla, Vanigasekere Mudiyanse of Aluvihāra, Candrasekere Mudiyanse of Dumbukola [Dambulla], [and then also] Gamage Vädda and Hampat Vädda of Hulangamuva." And when the king asked who are there in the lands beyond (*epiṭaraṭa*):

> Lord on the other side of the steep waters (*hela kandura*) of Biridevela, there is Kannila Vädda guarding (*hira kara hiṭiya*) at Kanangamuva, and Herat Banda guarding at Nikakotuva, and Maha Tampala Vädda guarding at Palapatvala, Domba Vädda guarding at Dombavela gama, Valli Vädda guarding at Vallivela, Mahakavudalla Vädda guarding at Kavudupalalla,

> Naiyiran Vädda [some texts Nayida] guarding at Narangamuva, Imiya Vädda guarding at Nālandā, Dippiṭiya Mahage [a female] guarding an area of nine gavuvas in length and breath in the district known as Nāgapattalama, and Makara Vädda and Konduruva employed in the watch of the boundary (*kaḍaima*), Mahakanda Vädda guarding the Kandapalla [today's Kandapalla korale], Hempiti Mahage guarding Galevela, Baju Mahage guarding the Udasiya Pattuva of Udugoḍa Korale, Minimutu Mahage guarding the [same] Pallesiya Pattuva, Devakīrti Mahage guarding Melpitiya. . . .[12]

A.C. Lawrie's *Gazetteer of the Central Province* compiled at the end of the nineteenth century has references to over thirty Sinhala villages that were once Vädda according to local histories.

Consider the implications of this information. The Väddas mentioned earlier have names, which suggest a variety of social backgrounds: you have Väddas that have lineage names like Gamage associated with members of the ordinary farmer (*goyigama*) caste. There are names that might well be unique to Väddas of this region because they are not recognizably Sinhala ones, for example, Imiya Vädda, Makara, Hampat, and Konduruva. One Vädda, Herat Banda, has a straightforward Sinhala name; and in Lawrie's list there are two Väddas named Herat Banḍāra, which normally one would think were simply Sinhalas of "good families." Three Väddas have the word "Maha" or chief or a similar term attached to their names suggesting persons of great importance, such as Huwan Kumaraya, "Noble Prince." Then there is Kadukara ("sword-wielding Vädda") of Bibile whose name suggests expertise in swordsmanship. Most fascinating are the five Vädda "Mahage" of the Mātalē boundary book, that is, women who are heads of presumably Vädda villages and also engaged like their male counterparts as guards at watch posts, contradicting all of the latter day information of Vädda women as shy creatures kept under strict protection by their menfolk. Lawrie who mentions a Vädda woman Ambi as the founder of Ambitiyava village indirectly confirms the tradition of female Vädda chiefs. Now for the final thrust: Lawrie refers to a Vädda King of Opalgala who married the daughter of a Sinhala king, Vira Parākramabāhu, a strategic alliance between two kings. His son was significantly named Herat Banḍāra in Sinhala aristocratic style and he founded the village of Uḍugama and was perhaps the ancestor of distinguished Kandyan aristocrats now living there. It therefore seems, that as far as the Väddas of Mātalē are concerned, they were as internally differentiated as the Sinhalas though they probably did not have anything approximating the latter's caste system; and some were clearly already adopting high status Sinhala names.[13] I have recently been collecting unpublished popular palm leaf manuscripts from the seventeenth to the nineteenth centuries and some of these texts indicate that Väddas were everywhere in the nation though no estimate of numbers is possible.

In the minds of the Sinhalas contemporary Väddas are associated with the desolate region of Bintänne, north and east of Mātalē. Yet historical sources indicate that Bintänne-Alutnuvara (the "new city of Bintänne") was a crucial stopping point for the king and for foreign visitors and local officials on their way to the east coast and back. Alutnuvara, as the term implies, was one of the alternative capitals of the king when he moved out of Kandy, known then and now, as Mahanuvara, "the great city."[14] A Dutch account of 1602 gives a fascinating description of the great temple of Alutnuvara (Mahiyaṅgana) and the ceremonies and bustle associated with it.[15]

Väddas were fiercely loyal to the King and not only had easy access to the Palace (addressing him in familiar terms as "cousin") but also were part of the palace guard (and the guard of important royal officials). During the revolt against the British in 1818 the Väddas were steadfastly loyal to Dorai Swamy, the Tamil claimant to throne (while Sinhala aristocrats were betraying their country). It was a Vädda aristocrat, Kivulegedera Mohoṭṭāla, later deified, who was the major resistance fighter against the British. After the two rebellions of 1818 and 1848 were brutally squashed by the British the once impressive Alutnuvara simply became another "ruined city" and the larger region of Bintänne was designated as the region of "primitive" hunters and gatherers.

Let me now get back to the foundation myth according to which Vijaya married Kuvēni and later banished her and his two children by that marriage. We noted that out of this union of brother and sister sprang the Pulindas ("hunters," i.e., Väddas). The myth implies that the Väddas are kin of the Sinhalas through Vijaya, yet are separate from them, having been banished into the forest and living by hunting, a very un-Buddhist profession. The charter myth for the opposition between hunting and Buddhism is known to most Buddhists and is first presented in the *Mahāvaṃsa*, which describes the Buddhist *arahant* ("Saint") Mahinda flying through the air and landing in the mountain of Mihintale where the king (Devanampiyatissa, 250–210 BCE) was out hunting. Not only was the king converted but also the place of this archetypal wrong act became a meditation site for the first monks and a center of Buddhist worship and pilgrimage. These myths have no literal truth value but they illustrate the manner in which Väddas were perceived by the dominant group as an alien community in their midst, even though linked to them by historic and economic ties. This notion of likeness and difference is beautifully expressed in the dramatic ritual known as the *Vädi perahära* ("procession of the Väddas") performed during the annual festival at Mahiyangana, the Bintänne-Alutnuvara already mentioned. Like the footprint of the Buddha in Sumanakūṭa Peak in the wilderness of hunters or Sabaragamuva, the Buddhist shrine indicated the hegemony of the Buddhists over the Vädda hunting population. Today, alongside this Buddhist stūpa (relic chamber) and temple, there are also shrines for Saman and Skanda, major gods common to both Sinhalas and Väddas. My description of the Vädda procession is based on the rituals I witnessed in the late 1950s and early 1960s.

In one of these rituals I counted seventy-one Väddas carrying poles representing spears that line up near the shrines of the god Saman and Skanda, led by a "chief" carrying a bow and arrow. After circumambulating the shrine three times in a graceful dance, the Väddas suddenly increase the tempo and, at a signal from the chief, start hooting, yelling, and brandishing their spears and terrifying the assembled Sinhala spectators. They stage several battles in front of the shrine by "assaulting" it, striking their spears on its steps. They then run toward the Buddhist temple and try to enter the premises of the *stūpa*, where the Buddha relics are enshrined. Here their path is blocked by two gatekeepers (*murakārayō*) who shout, "You can't approach this place. Go back to the royal altar" (*rajavīdiya*, the altar of the guardian deity). These mock battles are repeated several times and end with the Väddas placing their "spears" gently against the *stūpa* and worshipping it. They then run toward the monks' residence (*pansala*), stage a battle there, and as at the *stūpa* end up by worshiping the assembled monks'. Then, from the monks' residence back to the shrine where they again perform a "battle" beating their spears against its stone steps until the spears break into small pieces; and finally they fall prostrate on the ground to worship the gods housed in their shrine (*devāle*). After this they run toward the nearby river ("the ferry crossing of the gods") and bathe and purify themselves. Returning to the shrine, calm and self-possessed, they are now permitted to enter the inner sanctum where the Sinhala priest (*kapurāla*) chants an incantation for the gods Saman and Skanda and other major deities, and blesses the Väddas by lustrating them with "sandal water." The ritual ends with the Väddas all shouting *harō-harā*, which in Sri Lanka is the paean of praise for the god Skanda, the great guardian deity of Sri Lanka and formal overlord of both the Vädda and the Sinhala pantheon.

The difference in the social functions of the rituals performed by the Sinhalas and the Väddas at Mahiyaṅgana are impressive. In the case of the Sinhalas there are no rituals that separate one group from the other: all the assembled Sinhalas form one moral community participating in common worship at Mahiyaṅgana. In the case of the Väddas, the rituals define their status in relation to the dominant religion in that they are prevented from entering the temple and *stūpa*. Though they are made to formally acknowledge the Buddha, they are clearly outside the community of Sinhala Buddhists. Yet they are not total strangers either; after initially resisting the gods Skanda and Saman, they finally acknowledge the fact that these deities also head their own pantheon. Further, it must be recognized that the guardian deities, are not only protectors of the Buddhist religion: they are also protectors of the secular realm. The Väddas are incorporated into the "state" structure; not into the Buddhist "nation" or *sāsana* symbolically represented in the *stūpa*. Their incorporation into the political order of the Kandyan state is recognized in another part of the *Vädi perahära*; the Väddas rub their bodies with honey and then cover themselves with cotton wool. Honey is the substance they used to collect as the king's due or *rājakāriya*; it is likely that some Väddas were also the suppliers of cotton cultivated in forest clearings or small garden plots. We know both from Robert Knox (1641–1720) and from early Dutch accounts that cotton was a crucial local industry, later destroyed by British colonialism. Supplying cotton must have been an important historical role for some Väddas and this is recognized in the foundation myth itself which says that when Kuvēni first met Vijaya she was spinning cotton.[16]

The level in which the Väddas are incorporated into the larger symbolic order shared by both communities is not on the level of Buddha worship but that of the guardian deities. In the present time the great guardian god that unites Vädda and Sinhala (and both with Tamils) is Skanda who is the overlord of the Vädda pantheon (the *Mahāvaṃsa* evidence suggests that in ancient times it was the god Saman). This integration is given further symbolic validation in the mythology of Valli Amma, who was adopted by the Väddas as a child and became Skanda's illegitimate spouse or second wife. Rituals and practices at Kataragama recognize the Vädda connection in many ways. For example, prior to the present enbourgeoisment of Kataragama it was permitted to sell venison (the "pure" meat for the Väddas) near the shrine premises and venison was also offered as part of the *aḍukku* or meal given to the god. Similar techniques of articulating Vädda with Sinhala were practiced in village rituals. Thus, in Sinhala communal post-harvest thanksgiving rituals, including the *kohombā kankāriya* mentioned earlier, there is a sequence called the *Vädi dāne* (Vädda almsgiving) or *Vädi Pūjāva* (the Vädda offering); it is likely that this too was an attempt to bring in Väddas into the Sinhala-Buddhist ritual scheme of things on the village level. In some rituals there are actors who represent Väddas and they are permitted to eat meat substances, not in reality but in mimesis. Whereas no meat, cooked or otherwise, was ever brought into the ritual arena by Buddhists. As I interpret it, the *Vädi Pūjāva*, like the previous rituals, is a mechanism for incorporating Väddas into the religious and social structure of adjacent agricultural communities while at the same time recognizing their separateness. For Buddhists these rituals like the procession of the Väddas at Mahiyaṅgana was a way of recognizing their own separate identity as members of the *sāsana* in opposition to those who are not.

The creation of axiomatic identities

In our previous discussion I made the point that Buddhists had a conception of a trans-local cultural consciousness that was conceptualized in the notion of *sāsana*. When we talk of *sāsana* as a "form of nationhood" one must bear in mind that it is constructed by the ethnographer on the basis of a phenomenological reality existing in Sri Lankan culture and consciousness. *Not so with "identity" which a conceptual invention of the analyst.* There is no word that resembles "identity" in the Sinhala lexicon. So with the concept "axiomatic identity" which in my usage refers to those statuses and social positions that one takes for granted and which carry an important though varying emotional investment, the root of which is "birth." Thus "son" is a "status" or "position" in the conventional sociological sense of a bundle of rights and duties; as an *identity* however it is associated with "birth" together with emotional investments of various kinds, such as feelings of filial piety as well as all sorts of ambivalences. As a status it is taken for granted; but this taken-for-granted-ness can get a jolt if, for example, I begin to question whether my father deserves my love or whether fatherhood is not a bourgeois institution that ought to be abolished, and so forth. The questioning of axiomatic identities, precisely because of their taken-for-granted quality, can be profoundly troubling and agonizing. Axiomatic identities are woven into one's sense of worth, wholeness, and well-being. When one talks of an axiomatic identity one can also examine the processes whereby an identity is created, reproduced, broken, changed, and reconstituted. Thus the Freudian Oedipal crisis is, among other things, a process whereby an identity crisis pertaining to the axiomatic identity of son-ship takes place. The processes or mechanisms that help create identity formation can also be depicted, such as the "introjections" of paternal values and "identification" with the father.

I do not want to make a sharp distinction between individual and group identities because the individual does not stand alone but is related as brother, sister, father, spouse and so forth to a larger entity, the family, and, I might add, to even larger structures like lineages and clans.[17] While recognizing the fuzziness of these boundaries let me nevertheless, for heuristic purposes, refer to group identities that also have an axiomatic quality, as, for example, caste identities; or lineage identities; or that of ranks such as aristocracies; or, in the largest sense, that of modern nations; or even the emerging forms of transnational identities like that of an universalizing Islamic cultural consciousness; or that recent formation struggling to emerge, namely, European-ness. In all of these cases axiomatic identity is an end product or consciously or unconsciously sought as one. Yet this end product did not emerge out of the blue; there had to be a lot of work to create it. Even when the axiomatic identity is one that is already in place it must be reproduced or recreated or refashioned according to changing sociohistorical circumstances. Axiomatic identities need not necessarily produce intolerance, though that possibility always exists for some identities. To say one is French is certainly to say one is not Dutch or English; it need not be a statement about enmity. However in times of crises such as wars or football games, the axiomatic identity gets an infusion of passion and commitment; and it gets sharpened in opposition to an equally simplistically defined and opposed Other. Thus strengthening – weakening is a dialectical process inextricably associated with axiomatic identities. Naturally these processes depend on historical circumstances that must be contextualized for each case.

I noted that the critical feature of axiomatic identity is *birth*: it is the one incontestable feature of any kin relation or membership of a lineage, caste, or nation and so forth. Thus the popular word for caste in many South Asian languages is *jāti*, which means, "birth." The modern word for "race" is *jāti*; when Sinhalas think of themselves as a nation they also use the term *jāti*. The etymology of the European word "nation" is also birth. What modern nationhood has brought about, as Eugen Weber (1976) shows for France, is to refigure the idea of "birth" associated with axiomatic identities by transfusing it into a larger domain, namely, nation – an enormously difficult and complicated work. Being born into a group identity is in fact the critical mechanism that renders an identity axiomatic. In European thought an identity associated with birth is "natural," a *cultural* idea that has resonances in other traditions. In Europe the outsider who adopts an axiomatic identity of a citizen of a nation state has therefore to be "naturalized."

Parallel with this is another notion in modern nationhood: birth is not in any place but in a particular "land." Yet such metaphors are also found in the pre-colonial Sri Lankan case: this blessed isle, this Sri Lanka – blessed by the Buddha himself as a place where the *sāsana* will flourish. In modern times even more powerful familial metaphors are invoked in both nationalistic and ethnic discourses everywhere: patria, fatherland, and motherland. In the latter instance the violation of the land is associated with sexual violation and rape of the mother. Patria is associated with juridical rights that have to be defended in the name of the father, often associated with duty. Both can lead to an extraordinary level of violence, as we can see in modern ethnic and nationalist conflicts.

The precursor to violence is the passion that one associates with nationalist cultural identity. This is why I find Anderson's attempt to divorce nationalism from racism and patriotism misleading; you can have racism without nationalism but as a special kind of axiomatic identity sharing family resemblances to nationalism, it can easily spill over to the latter. Let me phrase the issue in another way. Some scholars, following Edward Shils, have dealt with the resurgence of "primordial loyalties" in the non-Western discourses on nationalism and fundamentalism, replacing or coexisting with, the earlier equally pejorative term "tribalism." In the West, we are told, these primordial loyalties have been replaced by the more rational discourses of nationalism. The position I take is very different: "primordiality" is a *sine qua non* of nationalism, and, as the work of scholars like Linda Colley and Eugen Weber have demonstrated, it was an essential condition in French and English nationalism, both based on opposing identities, rooted in two religions, Protestantism and Catholicism. By contrast, primordiality in the sociological imagination is the idea that a particular identity comes from a long past, evoking passionate (xenophobic) responses, which are almost innate (primordial). But in my view, this is not something confined to "the rest" by the West: whether it be tribes threatened by other tribes, or religious sects warring with each other, or nations in a similar situation, make not the slightest difference because primordiality has to be culturally constructed and fostered through wars and other mechanisms and hooked into the historical consciousness of a group through the myths and literary products of an age ranging from serious literature to jingoistic national anthems such as "La Marseillaise." Primordiality might be submerged under certain conditions, let us say in times of peace or prosperity, but it is reawakened when an axiomatic identity is threatened – be it an oedipal, tribal, or national or even a transnational one. And often enough a negative view of primordiality is projected on to the Other as we can witness once again today, for example in the notion of an "evil empire" or "axis of evil," or the demonization of ethnic groups by the majority community and vice-versa.

As far as Buddhists are concerned the tension between the two meanings of *sāsana* resurface in the historically constructed and then essentialized and primordialized axiomatic identity. Buddhist soteriology denies any enduring reality to the body or the self: the doctrine emphasizes the fluctuating and senseless nature of all structures of existence. Therefore an axiomatic identity in Buddhist soteriological terms is a kind of "false consciousness." Nevertheless, such an identity (or rather what it substantively stands for) is the self-perceived "true consciousness" of Buddhist history and lived existence in different periods of its history, particularly when the *sāsana* cum nation is under threat. It is therefore to be expected that in Buddhist history there will occur a continual Buddhicization (i.e., a *sasanization*) of South Indian groups, including their gods, magical practices, language and texts, which if translated into the European language game is a form of life that is akin to "naturalization." Viewed in long-term historical perspective Sinhalas have been for the most part South Indian migrants who have been *sāsanized*. It is interesting to note that *sāsanization* embraced most but not all the castes in the Sinhala system. *Sāsanization* has been facilitated by the relative absence of contestation by immigrant groups in areas dominated by Sinhala speech communities. A parallel process perhaps took place in the northern peninsula which, after the fifteenth century at least, was controlled by Kerala and Tamil peoples who in their own way assimilated previous Sinhala speakers.[18]

Because an axiomatic identity is often given at birth it may seem to us ready made, as it were. Yet, this initial birth assigned nature of an axiomatic identity, while intrinsic to its character, is only a formal feature. Axiomatic identities have to be learned and this can be a complicated process. Take even a simple case. I am born as a son, but this is not sufficient to create an axiomatic identity because I have to learn the rights and duties and the affective ingredients that go to constitute son-ship in my culture. Again: the puberty rites that we know from many preliterate societies give content, meaning, and affective valence to the idea of belonging to a particular kinship and social group, helping to create an axiomatic identity or identities through special kinds of learning experiences, some none too pleasant. Thus, an axiomatic identity is an end product and an ideal condition, whether we are talking about a kinship or "tribal" status or the cultural identity of being a member of a nation. If the cultural identity Sinhala-Buddhist is an ideal condition that can be realized as the end-product of a variety of socializing strategies and cultural practices, then one can legitimately speak of this identity as existing in a variety of imperfect conditions in situations where such strategies did not exist. Let me give an example. Rambadeṇiya from where I embarked on my pilgrimage is Sinhala; there is no question of it because that is the language they speak and it is their self-conscious identity. Yet there was no Buddhist temple there in the late fifties; neither was there any in Gangāhēnwela, a nearby hamlet; nor in some of the other villages in the area. On important occasions Rambadeṇiya folk invited the monk from the nearby village of Aṭanvala to perform religious ceremonies like *pirit (paritta*, special text recitals) and they had a sermon hall or *baṇa maḍuva* for this purpose. It struck us that Rambadeṇiya folk, though Sinhala, were not fully incorporated within the frame of Buddhist culture at that time. For example, all of them used to hunt and this was considered a noble activity. On one occasion, on the commemoration of the Buddha's birthday (Vesak), the headman of the village used poisonous herbs to kill the fish in the local river, something unthinkable in most Buddhist villages. The memory was still strong of a time when, the night prior to the holding of a Buddhist ceremony or *pinkama*, they had to have a ritual to ask the "forgiveness" of the *yakku* (nowadays meaning "demon").[19] I felt that this society was once culturally close to those of the Väddas in whose proximity they now live. And it is Väddas who use the term *yakku* without any pejorative connotation, as for example when they call their dead ancestors *nä yakku* ("kinfolk deities"). Thus, it was likely that Rambadeṇiya was a Sinhala speaking non-Buddhist village, or a purely formal Buddhist village, which now has become, imperfectly even at the time of our field work, a Sinhala-Buddhist one.[20] Here then is a situation where *sāsanization* had been going on for some time. I think this is no isolated example and one must therefore see *sāsanization* as an ongoing cultural process. I think it is necessary to apply now this insight to the texts that we considered previously and show them as cultural products that assisted this ongoing process, the topic of our next discussion.

Restoring history and indeterminacy in cultural identity

Because axiomatic identities have a paradoxical character of being seen by people living in a society as essentialized or primordial and seen by the analyst or a detached outsider as something culturally constructed, it is time to put this notion back into the vortex of history from which it was abstracted earlier by considering Richard Helgerson's *Forms of Nationhood* which shows how the emerging sense of national consciousness in England was supported and given literary expression by several Elizabethan writers – poets, historians, dramatists, philosophers, travel writers, and compilers of Apocalyptic texts. Helgerson (1992: 3) says: "To men born in the 1550s and 1560s, things English came to matter with a special intensity both because England itself mattered more than it had and because other sources of identity and cultural authority mattered less." To rephrase what I think Helgerson is saying: these Elizabethan texts might give you an account of the cultural identity of "Englishness"; but more importantly they are diverse and sometimes opposed ways of constructing such an identity. For example, in John Foxe's *Acts and Monuments* (popularly known as the "Book of Martyrs" and running into 2314 pages), the church is both universal and particularistic, very much like the Sinhala concept of *sāsana*. Foxe and other apocalyptic thinkers, argues Helgerson (1992: 263), created an imagined community of Protestant martyrs who in a sense existed outside the state. Yet, Foxe also supplies the evidence and arguments for later thinkers for whom Protestantism and Englishness are inextricably linked. If Foxe is the apocalyptic thinker, the legalistic Richard Hooker is the "apologetic historicist" in his *Laws of Ecclesiastical Polity*. But Hooker, like other Elizabethan writers, also tried in his own way to create the idea of an English nation, which, in his case, should not conflict with the state.

> We hold that... there is not any man of the Church of England but the same man is also a member of the commonwealth; nor any man a member of the commonwealth which is also not of the Church of England.
> (1992: 277)

Thus different visions of the English national and cultural identity were being created by a variety of writers. The end product of these activities is to foster or to begin to create an axiomatic identity of being English. After the union of the England, Scotland, and Wales in 1707, it was additionally being *British* that were being created as Linda Colley shows in her book, *Britons: Forging the Nation*. The subtitle of the book has a double significance; it is creating nationhood as in a forge and also practicing a kind of forgery or a fabrication of the nation.

Now we can, I think, get a better insight into the historical "texts" written by monks. The *Mahāvaṃsa* is not just a text that gives us information on Sinhala-Buddhist identity; much more importantly *it is a text that helps to create such an identity* in a way that the previous chronicle, the *Dīpavaṃsa*, did not. And central to that process of identity creation is the hero, Duṭṭhagāmaṇī Abhaya (161–137 BCE), the man who conjoins the land or the place, Sri Lanka, with the *sāsana*, already blessed by the Buddha as a place where the *dhamma* will flourish. And when the anguished king asks the monks what consequences will befall him for having killed millions of people, the monks reply, that no real sin has been committed by him because he has only killed Tamil unbelievers, no better than beasts. And, fitting one notion of *sāsana* but violating the other, the *Mahāvaṃsa* monks assign Duṭṭhagāmiṇī a place in heaven in the proximity of the next Buddha, Maitreya.

The *Mahāvaṃsa* then attempts to forge the nation in the double sense of that term. The historical period in which this forging took place is not the time of Duṭṭhagāmaṇī but the time in which the *Mahāvaṃsa* was composed, namely the sixth century CE. From that time on, it seems to me, the process of forging went on with its ups and downs, as in other nations. It seems futile to construct an omnipresent Sinhala-Buddhist identity on the basis of the *Mahāvaṃsa*, as it is to deny its nonreality. We will never know how widespread this identity was during that period. However, the evidence from the Grafitti scribbled on the Mirror Wall of the mountain fortress of Sīgiriya suggests that Sinhala people from distant places were meeting each other in pilgrimage centers between the eighth and twelfth centuries and this communion was spurred by a common language and script.[21] By the time the popular literature of the thirteenth century was written, there seemed to have developed a language and script, which is remarkably close to modern Sinhala. One of these texts is the *Pūjāvaliya* which has an extraordinary account of the Sinhala-Buddhist identity in its thirty-second chapter entitled *uddesika pūjā kathā* which is a synoptic history of Sri Lanka from its very founding. Let me render this text into reasonable English.

Sri Lanka in non-Buddhist times (*abauddhakālaya*) was entirely the home of demons (*yaksa*s) but during the dispensation of the Buddhas (*bauddhōt-pādakālaya*, lit. when Buddhas arise or are born) by humans. Several previous Buddhas at their very enlightenment controlled (or destroyed) the *yaksa*s and the country became home to humans; other Buddhas actually visited this country, defeated the *yaksa*s, and established the *sāsana*. Since during the enlightenment of countless Buddhas, the right branch of the Bodhi tree and the *dhammadhātu*s ("essence-teaching") will no doubt be preserved, this island of Laṅkā is like a treasury of the Triple Gem [that is, the Buddha, the Dhamma, and the Saṅgha].[22] Just as the demons could not find permanence here, neither can this land become a place of residence for nonbelievers (*mityādṛṣṭi gatavunge vāsaya*). If any non-believer becomes a king of Sri Lanka by force, at any time, that dynasty will not last owing to the special influence of the Buddha. Because this Lanka is rightfully those of kings who have right views [Buddhists], their rightful dynastic tenure (*kula praveniya*) will absolutely prevail. For these various reasons the kings of Sri Laṅkā are drawn by a natural love of mind to the Buddha, and will establish the *sāsana* without delay or neglect and protect the wheel of the law and the wheel of the doctrine and reign so that the rightful dynastic tenure will be preserved (Buddhaputra Thera 1965: 746).

The text adds that in the time of the very first Buddha of our *kalpa*, Kakusanda, this land was called *ōjadvīpa*, that is, the land that contains the creative life force or *ōjas*. At that time Anurādhapura was called Abhayapura and the king was Abhaya.... The Buddha Kakusanda, knowing the great meritoriousness of its citizens and spurred by great kindness (*karuṇā*), accompanied by a retinue of 40,000 noble monks flew through the air and landed at the mountain named *devakūṭa*, that is, Mihintalē. The text describes the citizens who gathered there making offerings to the Buddha; the Buddha Kakusanda consecrated the various sacred spots in Anurādhapura during that visit. These visits were repeated by the other Buddhas of the age (*kalpa*), namely, Konāgamana, Kāśyapa, and finally our own Buddha, Gautama (Buddhaputra Thera 1965: 746–47).[23]

I cannot analyze this extraordinary text here in any detail except to suggest that it outdoes the *Mahāvaṃsa* in its myth of an eternal return, namely, that this land is a Buddhist one consecrated by the four Buddhas of our age (*kalpa*) and some Buddhas of previous ages. There is no question that nonbelievers can last here; only Buddhist kings have just tenure. In doctrinal Buddhism only a Buddha can establish the *sāsana* in the soteriological sense of that term; here Buddhist kings establish the *sāsana* defined as Buddhist history. In my view this statement is more important than the *Mahāvaṃsa* one because it is written in Sinhala and accessible to ordinary laypersons either through direct reading or through public recitals or monk sermons. Yet, it too has to be seen in historical context. The *Pūjāvaliya* was written soon after the devastating invasion in 1214 of Māgha of Kāliṅga (in Orissa). These invasions combined with historical forces that made coastal trade lucrative resulted in the movement of Sinhala civilization to the south-west. There is a desperation in the tone of the text; hence its preoccupation with the eternal return of Buddhas to Sri Lanka. Anurādhapura has already been abandoned as the capital; hence the nostalgia for it and the idealization of that city.

Now let me deal with an interesting problem that arises from our reading of both the *Pūjāvaliya* and the *Mahāvaṃsa*. It is indeed the case that to be Sinhala is *ipso facto* to be Buddhist: they are twin facets of the same identity. Yet, on the other hand, to be Buddhist is not necessarily to be Sinhala because some people knew, particularly the monks who wrote these texts, that there were Buddhists who were not Sinhala. The question is: which facet of the twin identity is the dominant one? The *Mahāvaṃsa*, and most certainly the *Pūjāvaliya*, are clear that it is the Buddhist side of the identity that is dominant. I think the reason is not too far to seek: the emphasis on the Buddhist aspect of the identity would make a lot of sense to monks because they had continual historical contact with South Indian Buddhists; the Tamil country itself contained urban centers of Buddhism during this period. It is hard to believe that there were no Tamil-Buddhist communities in Sri Lanka among those who invaded the island and were being assimilated into the social structure of their neighbors. And we know that as late as the mid-fifteenth century there were Tamil monks studying in Śrī Rāhula's Buddhist College (*pirivena*) at Toṭagamuva and Tamil itself was part of curriculum there.

Let me now move from historic texts back into the folk traditions and focus on contemporary ritual dramas, versions of which I think must have occurred right through the nation's history. The basic scenario common to all these ritual dramas is as follows. In the ritual arena two performers take the role of the Buddhist guardian deities of the island. They hold a stick that acts as a barrier, a *kaḍavata* (literally an entrance to a "city gate"). An alien deity or magician or merchant (or groups of them) try to break through the barrier and enter Sri Lanka but the gods prevent them. These aliens speak a funny kind of Sinhala with a strong Tamil accent and they constantly utter malapropisms, unintended puns, and spoonerisms. In their ignorance they make insulting remarks about the gods at the barrier; they know not Sinhala and Buddhist customs and the audience has a lot of fun at their expense. Gradually the alien visitors recognize their errors of speech and custom; they learn to speak properly; they begin to properly worship the deities and acknowledge the superiority of the Buddha. Then the gods open the barrier and these aliens enter Sri Lanka.

I think these rituals give symbolic expression to an important historical process: the foreign visitors are "naturalized" as Sri Lankan Buddhists; and only then can they be "citizens" and permitted to perform *rājakāriya* or "work for the king," the legitimate right of citizenship. These ritual performances parallel what I have previously described and dubbed as "colonization myths" – myths that describe the arrival and incorporation of South Indian people into Sri Lanka and their subsequent Sinhalization and Buddhicization (or better still their *sāsanization*).[24] In my work on the goddess Pattini I have shown how the ritual texts of these migrants were soon translated into Sinhala (Obeyesekere 1984: 521–28).

The *Pūjāvaliya* then is in sharp contrast to these ritual dramas found in large areas of the Western, Sabaragamuva, and Southern provinces. In the latter we see foreigners with Tamil accents and alien gods being converted into Sinhala Buddhists. The emphasis in these village rituals is on both aspects of the identity; it is ordinary people in these areas who had to contend with immigrants of all sorts from South India; for them it would make sense that the identity Buddhist also implied Sinhala. The universalizing of the unconditional identity, Sinhala=Buddhist, with the primary emphasis on the first part of that duality, namely being Sinhala, is the product of the colonial period.

Unfreezing Tamil-Hindu otherness

In today's ethnic conflict the Tamils, at least in the abstract, are the primary Other for many Sinhalas; the feeling is mutual as far as the Tamils are concerned except that for the latter there also exists the Muslims in their own midst. It is a mistake to think that this is a primordial conflict rooted in the nation's history. The fact that history imagines a Buddhist *sāsana* in the island of Sri Lanka does not mean that the Tamils were exclusively depicted as enemies. So was it in other nations where national or ethnic identities surface in history. One must therefore avoid two kinds of "prejudices." First, one must avoid the European language game, which often defines "Otherness" as a radically exclusive conception. One can be an "other" in respect of some specific defining feature or attribute but not in respect of another. Second, the contemporary Sri Lankan prejudice which, in recreating the past from the present, have read the *Mahāvaṃsa* simply as a text that represented the Tamils as enemies who should be destroyed.

Yet a critical reading of the *Mahāvaṃsa* itself and, more generally, a broader look at the Sinhala-Buddhist imagination, suggest that Tamils (the generic Sinhala terms for South Indians) appear in history in a variety of ways that I have discussed in an earlier article (Obeyesekere 1995: 231–56) and which I shall now briefly summarize.

During periods of invasions from South India many Sinhala Buddhists viewed Tamils as the "Other". The colonization myths and ritual dramas that I have mentioned bring both invaders and the many peaceful immigrants who do not appear in history into the frame of a larger Buddhist culture and social order. But Tamils were also historically allies of the Sinhalas; Sinhala kings sought the aid of Tamil kings in their local conflicts. Some kings fled to India to seek the aid of their Tamil allies while others cemented alliances by marrying Tamil queens. But there was no consistency in this latter project either. In some periods in history the popular imagination records that the offspring of Tamil queens were illegitimate or inferior to Sinhala ones; this is reversed at other times. These marriage alliances were not only a historical reality for both commoners and kings but they also refract back into the foundational myth giving legitimacy to intermarriages for, according to that myth's proclamation, the union of Vijaya and his followers with the Tamils from Madurapura produced the Sinhalas. Thus Sinhalas have Tamil blood, since "blood" is bilaterally inherited in Sinhala genetic theory.

Tamils can be kings, though subsequently Sinhalized and brought within the frame of the Buddhist *sāsana*. Some of the greatest Sinhala kings had South Indian origins, though not necessarily from the Tamil country: for example, Nissanka Malla (1187–1196), Kīrti Śrī Rājasiṅha (1741–1780), and Bhuveneka Bāhu VI (1469–1477) who, as Sapumal Kumāraya, was one of the great heroes of the Sinhalas and, ironically, the conqueror of the Tamil kingdom of Jaffna![25] One of the most persistent historical images of "Tamils" (from Kerala, Tamil Nadu, and Orissa) is as sorcerers and ritual specialists. Even today in spite of the enormous hostility to them some of the most popular shrines for Buddhists are the Kāli temples at Munnesvaram, near Chilaw north of Colombo, and in the city of Colombo itself, both controlled by Tamil priests. In Colombo there are Tamil priests who have set up an institution for reading *nāḍi vakyam*s, astrological sheets written in Tamil, supposed to have been compiled by *rishi*s thousands of years ago containing the horoscopes of most human beings of the past, present, and future. These are enormously popular with Buddhist middle classes and even monks patronize these priests for horoscopic readings. It is also well known that past presidents and prime ministers have consulted astrologers from South India for the timing of most state events and the solution of personal crises and anxieties.

I am not suggesting that these images of Tamils were consistently operative, but some were operative all the time in the pre-colonial period. Some images, such as Tamils as enemies to be vanquished, must have surfaced during invasions from South India while at other times marriage and affinal connections must surely have been important. One also cannot assume that these diverse images did not imply that Tamils were not seen as "others," because their language and customs were in fact not Sinhala and also often not Buddhist. "Otherness" was not a total exclusion but rather a series of identity boundaries that tended to be fuzzier in some periods of history than in others. This can be illustrated during the period of European invasions beginning with the Portuguese in 1505 till the capitulation of the last Sinhala kingdom of Kandy to the British in 1815. During much of this long period the "Otherness" of the Tamils hardly surfaced (with one important exception to be discussed later); instead the new enemies of the *sāsana* were the Europeans.

Let me illustrate this with one vignette from around 1558 when the Sinhala king Māyādunne of Sītāvaka waged war against his nephew Dharmapāla of Kōṭṭe (near Colombo). Dharmapāla himself was sympathetic to Catholicism and was baptized in 1557 and ceded his kingdom to the Portuguese king in 1580. The Franciscans were busy proselytizing in the coastal areas and in 1556 about 70,000 persons of the *karāva* (fisher) caste, along with their leaders, became Catholics in a mass conversion organized by the Franciscans:

> Even more disastrous was the donation of all the lands belonging to the hallowed temples of the Buddhist faith to the Franciscan order with all their revenue to be expended to the colleges and seminaries established

> by them in the Island. The temple complex at Kälaṇiya [one of the holiest places for Buddhists] on one side of the river and the Dalada Maligawa [the temple containing the tooth relic] on the other side of the river at Kotte were to be transferred to the Franciscans.
>
> (Da Silva Cosme 1990: 78)

In this historical situation, Da Silva Cosme pointed out, it was possible for Māyādunne to "pose as a champion of Buddhism."

> An eminent Buddhist monk took up Mayadunne's cause and so did a renegade Portuguese Buddhist... [and] it was argued and harangued in public that Dharmapala had forfeited his right to the throne the moment he embraced Christianity just as Christian princes of the Catholic faith did the moment they became heretics.... Some of the monks stepped into Kotte and fomented trouble at bana [sermon] preaching at night. Dharmapala and Diogo de Mello and the bodyguards stepped out of the palace to investigate and met a surging crowd led by Buddhist monks. A hail of stones injured the royal face.
>
> (1990: 79–80)

Da Silva Cosme's information is derived from Father Queyroz's voluminous history and is rare in the published historical literature.[26] But it surely must have been more general. It also meant that the Portuguese (and later by the Dutch and the British) replaced Tamil Otherness. There was one exception though: from the reign of Rājasiṅha II (1635–1687) Sinhala kings of the Kandyan kingdom obtained queens from Madurai and eventually these Telegu and Tamil speaking Nāyakkars became such a powerful force in the court that they eventually took over the kingship with the accession of Śrī Vijaya Rājasiṅha in 1739 and stayed on till the fall of Kandy to the British in 1815 during the reign of the last Nāyakkar, Śrī Vikrama Rājasiṅha. Yet, the Nāyakkar kings not only learnt Sinhala but they also embraced Buddhism. One of the greatest kings was Kīrti Śrī Rājasiṅha (1747–1782), a patron of Buddhism who was instrumental in sending a mission to Thailand to bring monks to revive the Buddhist ordination that had lapsed during the period of conflict with the European powers. In spite of his contribution to the Buddhist cause, Saraṇaṅkara, the Buddhist patriarch (*saṅgharāja*), in conjunction with some members of the aristocracy, planned his assassination (which failed). There is much historical evidence to show that some monks and laity were opposed to the Nāyakkar on the grounds of Tamil alien-ness symbolized by their daubing themselves with holy ash, an action that indicated a commitment to Śaivism than Buddhism. I am certain that the Nāyakkar period produced debates regarding the moral legitimacy of the Nāyakkars, some emphasizing their Tamilness and others their lack of genuine commitment to Buddhism.[27] But it is as likely that the vast majority of the Sinhala simply viewed them as Buddhist monarchs and was loyal to them. It is doubtful whether there was anything like popular discontent against them, except in the case of the last king, Śrī Vikrama Rājasiṅha. Śrī Vikrama was installed as king by the first minister Piḷimatalāva who had royal ambitions himself and tried to negotiate with the British (who had control over the maritime provinces they had seized from the Dutch) to usurp the kingdom. This did not work. The historian Paul E. Pieris has a detailed account of the intrigues of the Kandyan chiefs with the British and the British manipulation of the weaknesses of these chiefs.[28] Further, the British had an astute spy in John D'Oyly (1774–1824) who learned Sinhala and fomented the discontent in the kingdom, explicitly exploiting the foreign-ness of the Nāyakkars and their lack of political and moral legitimacy. At the very most the historical evidence reveals that the last king of Kandy was unpopular with some segments of the population but this did not imply a resurrection of a primordial Sinhala–Tamil enmity.

Conclusion

In this chapter I try to make a case for the idea of a Buddhist "nation" in precolonial political formations in Sri Lanka. For the most part Sinhalas took for granted that they belonged to the *sāsana* of the Buddha; such a stance implied an identity "Buddhist" even though there was no indigenous term designating such an identity. Being Buddhist constituted an "axiomatic" identity which takes its bearing from a fundamental structural opposition between "hunters" or Väddas who were not Buddhist and Sinhala who were Buddhists for the most part. Nowadays the Väddas exist as small dispossessed groups labeled as "aborigines" by scholars as well as ordinary people. Though I did not deal with it here, my general argument would be that Väddas gradually became Sinhala-Buddhist when the vast area of the Western, Sabaragamuva, Uva, and Kandyan regions were converted into rice cultivation after the fifteenth century consequent to the emergence of Buddhist states in those areas. Additionally, I demonstrate the further structural opposition between Tamils and Sinhalas that was exacerbated during periods of wars. This oppositional structure was frozen in written historical texts like the *Mahāvaṃsa* and *Pūjāvaliya* and unfrozen in other ways that I mention in this work. On the popular level people had to contend with immigrants of all sorts from South India and I describe briefly the ways they were *sāsanized* and incorporated into the larger cultural order. After the arrival of the European powers it was the Portuguese, the Dutch, and the British who were the enemies of the *sāsana* for most Sinhalas. But while many Sinhalas became Christians we have only glimpses of Europeans, especially Portuguese, who intermarried with Sinhalas and eventually became Buddhist.

How the preceding argument is linked to the current ethnic conflict cannot be elucidated here. My main argument would be that after the British colonization of the Island, particularly after the late nineteenth century, the identity Sinhala began to take precedence over the Buddhist. This is not surprising because after the colonial periods there were many Sinhalas who were not Buddhists. But while the Sinhala identity was primordialized, even for some Buddhist monks, one must not assume that it was necessarily an instigator of violence. For example, the violence against the Tamils in 1983 that in turn led to the escalation of the ethnic conflict was the work of the Jayewardene government of the time and was entirely politically motivated. In spite of my preface one can see some hopeful signs: after the 1983 riots there has been a progressive decline of violence against Tamil civilian populations by the Sinhalas, even when the provocations by the LTTE have been acute. Yet on the minus side the intransigence of extremists on both sides of the divide will surely make the current peace moves a complicated and vulnerable process. And part of the problem lies with those who claim to be Buddhists and this includes monks who seem to have forgotten or ignored the teachings of the founder.

Notes

1 The *Mahāvaṃsa* states that during his first visit the Buddha, on the urging of the god Sumana (now known as Saman), gave some of his hair for enshrinement at this *stūpa*; after the death of the Buddha the collar bone relic (according to Wilhelm Geiger) or the Adam's apple (according to G.C. Mendis) was enshrined (Mahānāma Thera 1950: 5, 303).

2 *Kaḍaimpot* literally means the "books that deal with the limits or borders of a *kaḍavata*," the latter meaning an entrance to a city or a specified domain.

3 *Utum budu* *ruvanē*
Lova desu daham *saraṇē*
Samaga saṅga *saraṇē*
Sadā vandimuva metun *saraṇē.*

4 *The Dīpavaṃsa* (Oldenberg 1982: 160) has it thus: "The island of Laṅkā was called Sīhala, after the Lion (sīha).

5 According to the foundation myth, the Buddha entrusted the king of the gods, Sakka to protect his *sāsana* in Sri Lanka; and Sakka in turn entrusted this task to Viṣṇu. Sakka is known in Sinhala as Sakra, a transformation of Indra of Hindu mythology.

6 It is one of the ironies of ethnicity that the Tamils want a separate state of Eelam, which means "Sinhala country"; while the Sinhalas want to hang on to Laṅkā which is derived from "ilankai" the Tamil word for "island."

7 A detailed account is available in Holt (1991: 48–51). For another fascinating account of this myth and a related one, see mid-seventh century text, *The Great Tang Dynasty Record of the Western Regions* (Ronxi 1996).

8 For information on the prehistory of Sri Lanka, see Deraniyagala (1992).

9 Apropos of Sinhaladvīpa – it must also be remembered that in the colonial period people in the maritime provinces referred to the remote parts of Uva and Sabaragamuva, as Sinhalē. Thus: "I am going to Sinhalē" was a familiar expression even in my childhood. I think this too is a variation of the old theme. By this time the resistance to the foreigner was by the people of these areas, and they were thus appropriately designated as Sinhalē. In the twentieth century, the term Sinhalē had connotations of "old fashioned," "remote," not unlike the European term "primitive."

10 I draw heavily upon my article (Obeyesekere 1966). In using the term "obligatory pilgrimage" I was influenced by Gustave E. von Grunebaum (1951: 15–51).

11 The "obligatory pilgrimage" also has an important political function in fostering a sense of a larger consciousness in Buddhist societies as it did in the poet Geoffrey Chaucer's (1342–1400) England:

> And specially from every shires ende
> Of Engelond to Caunterbury they wende,
> The hooly blisful martir for to seke,
> That hem hath holpen whan that they were seeke.
> (Introduction, line 15–18 in *The Canterbury Tales* (1476), http://www.librarius.com/canttran/genpro/genpro001-042.htm (accessed 5 October 2005))

It is very likely that these obligatory pilgrimages set the stage for the later development of a more powerful sense of nationhood in Elizabethan England.

12 Abeyawardana (1978: 223–31), my translation.

13 A neat example of this shift comes from the *Mātalē Kaḍaimpota* which refers to Kulatunga Mudiyanse of Uḍupihilla. Uḍupihilla, now practically a suburb of the town of Mātalē, was founded by Väddas and the present farmer castes are their descendants, according to Lawrie's *Gazetteer of the Central Province*, vol. 2, p. 858). It seems likely that Kulatunga Mudiyanse of Uḍupihilla, a Sinhala aristocrat, is a descendant of Väddas.

14 Others were Mädamahanuvara, Hanguranketa (Jayatilaka pura), and Nīlambe. In times of war Kandyan kings moved into these alternative capitals.

15 This account says that

> the old Emperors used to hold court as it is a beautiful city where there are many large streets, beautiful buildings and wonderful pagodas or heathen temples and among others there is one whose base is 130 paces round, extraordinarily beautiful, very tall... In it is also a beautiful and large palace of the Emperor full of beautiful buildings within. Here the best galleys and *sampans* of the Emperors are made. Here are also many shops but no market, stone monasteries and a great many bamboo [bark?] houses which stretch for a mile or two in distance along the river.
> (Valentijn 1978: 152–53)

16 I am not sure how far one can go in interpreting the theme of Kuvēni spinning cotton. It is obviously derived from an Indo-European one circulating in a vast region because the same theme is found in *The Odyssey* in the episode of the goddess Calypso. However many women in this epic are presented at the looms whereas this representation of women is unusual in Sinhala history.

17 Freud (1981: 69).

18 Given our discussion of axiomatic identities and modes of representing the Tamils, it is difficult to accept the positions taken by several leading scholars regarding the attitude to ward Tamils in Sri Lankan texts. Thus Tambiah (1992), following an important paper by Gunawardana (1985), thinks that the relations between Sinhalas and Tamils were traditionally harmonious until the changes brought about by colonialism and the imperial conquest. By contrast K.N.O. Dharmadasa (1992) looks at another set of historical sources to prove the very contrary. Thus each protagonist brings forward historical evidence to advance the hypothesis he favors against the one he opposes. My position is that "evidence" of this sort is indicative of debates that were going on in the society at large and these debates could easily have co-existed at any particular time span. Stated in another way, people could have had *both* views of Tamils at any particular time; or in some periods of history one set of views may have dominated

over the other. The debates between these scholars provide evidence of debates in the society at large; they cannot be used as "facts" to vindicate one scholarly hypothesis over another. Even today in spite of the virulence of the ethnic conflict, there are a variety of views about Tamils, though the predominant view is that of the hostile other. I do think, however, that Gunawardana is basically correct in arguing against fixing a specific date for the development of a Sinhala-Buddhist identity or giving it a historical fixity.

19 In many low-country exorcistic rituals, it is necessary to offer a chicken as a *billa* or offering to the demons. In reality this is only a token offering because the chicken is never killed; instead a little bit of blood is taken from it as a substitutive *billa*. In the neighboring village of Gangāhēnvela, the exorcist consistently killed the chicken as a *billa*, by cutting its neck off and drinking its blood. These practices are not unusual in rituals known as *nīca kula tīnduva*, roughly translatable as "low caste sorcery."

20 Such situations can easily be multiplied. There are cultural zones where Tamils and Sinhalas met and where intermarriage often took place. One such "intermediate zone" is Pānama in the extreme end of the Eastern Province, today sandwiched in the North by Tamil speaking communities and further West by Sinhalas. It is not unusual to see a member of the same family called Hīn Baṇḍa (Sinhala) and Subramaniam (Tamil), as a consequence of either Tamil–Sinhala intermarriage or a Sinhala woman marrying a Tamil man on the death of her Sinhala husband.

21 Scribbles on the "Mirror Wall" of the great mountain fortress, Sīgiri, built by the parricide king, Kāśyapa (*c*.473–491 CE) are called Sīgiri Graffiti. For an account of these graffiti see Paranavitana (1956). For accounts and translations of Graffiti missed by Paranavitana see Gooneratne *et al.* (1984: 196–98).

22 I have translated *dhammadhātu* as "essence-teaching" which is not the conventional meaning of that term. In general *dhammadhātu* is an important technical term that has several meanings, the primary one being "element." Nyanatiloka Thera (1980: 56) translates *dhammadhātu* as "Mind-object-Element." I think the *Pūjāvaliya* does not use the term in its technical sense but in a more literal sense as "essence teaching."

23 This part of the *Pūjāvaliya* is derived from the *Dīpavaṃsa*, written at least a 100 years before the *Mahāvaṃsa*. Unlike the *Mahāvaṃsa* and *Pūjāvaliya*, the *Dīpavaṃsa* has very little anti-Tamil feeling in it. The heroes of this text are those associated with the founding of Buddhism, the Buddha, the Buddhist king Aśoka, and his Sri Lankan contemporary Dēvānampiyatissa.

24 Obeyesekere (1984: 306–12).

25 The Kandyan rulers from the time of Śrī Vijaya Rājasiṅha till the reign of the last king, Śrī Vikrama Rājasiṅha (1798–1815), were South Indian Nāyakkars. See Dewaraja (1988).

26 De Queyroz (1930: 327–37).

27 For details of this debate see Tambiah (1992), Gunawardana (1990), and Dharmadasa (1992).

28 See especially his two remarkable books (Pieris 1995, 1939).

10

IDENTITY ISSUES OF SINHALAS AND TAMILS

Bardwell Smith

The political and social stalemate in Sri Lanka is composed of ethnic, class, religious, and other indicators of the elusive quality called "identity," in particular the differing interpretations of past and present grievances.[1] The narrowness and animosity with which social identity keeps being defined and defended impairs efforts to imagine new possibilities. The Sinhalas have been portrayed as a "majority with a minority complex," seeing themselves as being threatened by the huge Tamil presence in the south of India. These fears are not completely irrational if one recalls past periods of history and takes into account the extent of current economic and military assistance from supporters of the Liberation Tigers of Tamil Eelam (LTTE) from Tamil Nadu and around the world.

From an opposite perspective, militant Sri Lankan Tamils see themselves as victims of Sinhala self-aggrandizement and, in response, have as their goal becoming a plurality within an independent "nation" or homeland of Eelam in the northern and eastern provinces of the country. Experiencing what they interpret as communal violence, discriminatory legislation, and aggressive forms of state-aided colonization in the Tamil areas, the LTTE's emergence as a guerrilla movement in 1972 was to fight for political rights and to counter what they view as state-promoted violence. The failure to establish a politically inclusive vision of identity, acceptable to both sides and made credible through legislative enactment and equitable social policy, has generated social impoverishment, a culture of disarray, profound mistrust, and a neglect of the country's economic needs for decades.

To gain further perspective on how each side of this ethnic conflict depicts the other, I spent several days a few years ago exploring a number of pro-Tamil and pro-Sinhala websites that existed on the Internet.[2] By linking one website to another the variety of topics and points of reference were almost without limit. The initial impression derived from these materials was of self-justification, oversimplification, condemnatory language, and unconvincing rhetoric. Searching beyond form and style to substance, one found a familiar chorus of grievances which, when endlessly repeated, distracted from more important issues.

At times, dealing with ethnic conflict in Sri Lanka, one discovers thoughtful statements and wonders why more analyses of that sort could not be placed on the Internet. The value of websites that goes beyond ideology would be clear, particularly for those who have no access to some of the better journals and magazines published in Sri Lanka or by Tamils and Sinhalas in other parts of the world. In trying to assess the relationship between militant Tamils and Sinhalas, I make use here of two approaches. The first deals with issues that are directly political; the second focuses on questions of a religious nature. When discussions are about "identity" these two areas overlap.

Beyond rhetoric to inclusive democracy

In circumstances of ethnic communalism around the world, and certainly in Sri Lanka, the grounds for sustained enmity include factors beyond those of ethnic background. Typically, divisions are worsened by economic and class issues, educational inequities, long-held historical grievances, a climate of confrontational politics, persistent recourses to violent engagement on both sides, and the relative absence of effective conflict resolution. In the 1990s, military operations in Sri Lanka had been waged with a new intensity of violence. As the virus of separatism flourishes and as some see the necessity of the decimation of the enemy, the ability of persons to envision an alternative reality beyond the confines of ethnocentrism is siphoned away.

For outsiders trying to understand a complex political climate without taking sides it is difficult to find an objective stance. For one thing, the picture never stands still. If there is any certainty, it is that recriminations provoke counter charges with extreme actions fueling counterattack. I would like to highlight three among a number of recurring themes that appear on the websites sponsored by Tamils and Sinhalas alike. The partisan manner in which these three themes are discussed is not surprising. On the other hand, when dwelled upon they become a major distraction from fresh conceptualization of the real problems, serving only to harden the already entrenched antagonism.

1 An initial theme is the barrage of accusations about the campaign of terrorist tactics waged by the "other side," that is, the indiscriminate terrorism promoted by the LTTE against ordinary citizens in the "struggle for freedom" and of the Sri Lankan army and police in their efforts to contain and defeat the LTTE. No one would minimize such activity, for it inflicts enormous suffering upon the entire country.[3] Whatever each side charges and however much these charges may be inflated, the actual reality is senseless and tragic. The fact that each side carries its own share of blame does not mean that these accusations cancel each other out or that protests across partisan lines or by *impartial* human rights groups have no significance. Only that accusation has no lasting impact except to fan the flames higher.

2 A second recurring theme appears in militant Tamil claims about their right to a homeland in the northern and eastern provinces of the country and the reciprocal denial of these claims by the Sinhalas.[4] To question the historical validity of these claims, as has been done by many scholars, is not to deny the very diverse Tamil population its right to full participation in the democratic process, not just in the north and along the east coast but in the country as a whole. The importance of honoring minority voices is crucial to the democratization process, as we will shortly discuss.

The matter of historic claims to a Tamil homeland arose in part out of British confusion about what they thought were two kingdoms when they first assumed their colonial prerogatives.

> Since the decade of 1970 the Sri Lankan State has been waging a protracted war against dissent and centrifugal tendencies. While the state in Sri Lanka, under successive regimes, is projecting itself as the defender of Buddhism and chief patron of Sinhala culture, the LTTE on the other hand has unleashed a similar process of hegemonic control over primarily Tamil-speaking areas and has imposed an ideological control from above.
>
> (Seneviratne 1999)[5]

The issue is one of great interest but is not one, which can be decided on the fields of battle. The ultimate test will be Sri Lanka's ability to respect and utilize the extraordinary pluralism within its society.

3 A final example is displayed in the zeal shown by each side in courting international opinion for moral support and in discounting the qualifications of the other side's defenders.[6] This appeal to a wider public is natural, but it is rhetorically charged. And, because the world's media devotes so little attention to what goes on in Sri Lanka, in contrast to similar situations in Northern Ireland, the Balkans, and the Middle East, there is little sustained nonpartisan analysis of Sri Lankan internal affairs available through the world's media. This phenomenon of being relatively ignored means that important issues are rarely given adequate scrutiny. The result of this neglect makes it less likely that significant impact might be made by the outside world. These efforts to influence international opinion are more than just another distraction. Instead, they contribute to the world's confusion about the actual situation in this country. Such an outcome is ironic, for it deprives Sri Lanka of informed nonpartisan judgment, which could be of great assistance.

These three examples suggest how partisan exchanges get snarled in issues, which, while important, can distract from understanding the deeper sources of grievance. A newspaper article by Sumanasiri Liyanage (1996), an economist at the University of Peradeniya, provides a useful way of understanding the role of ethnic identity in the political context.[7] Since this piece appeared in a government newspaper *Daily News*, one may assume that in some sense it represents a government-backed position. At any rate, while locating his main topic within the national conversation about "devolution," his principal argument deals with the process of democratization, which, he argues, has never been fully implemented in the country. Though skeptical about the adequacy of devolution as it is normally articulated and even more about how it might be administered, I see value in Liyanage's central thesis, which is the importance of minority representation. According to Arther Lewis the word "democracy" has two meanings:

> Its primary meaning is that *all who are affected by a decision should have the chance to participate in making that decision*, either directly or through chosen representatives. Its secondary meaning is that the will of the majority shall prevail. ("Beyond African Dictatorship: The Crisis of the One-Party State," *Encounter*, vol. 25, no. 2)... In countries where civil society is strong, well-knit and inclusive, the system based on majoritarian democracy may not produce adverse results on an excessive scale... *However, in multi-ethnic, pluralist societies with the state playing a dominant role, majoritarian democracy may not be democratic at all... So* in pluralist societies like India, Malaysia and Sri Lanka, democracy in its primary meaning cannot be established through developing a system ensuring majoritarian rule. *What is necessary is to create political institutions and to restructure the state ensuring that those who are affected by a decision get a fair chance to participate in the decision-making process...*
>
> The democratization of the state as one of the national democratic tasks in the post-colonial societies thus includes the development of mechanisms to politically integrate minority ethnic groups living in the territorial space of the country. These attempts have not been successful in many post-colonial societies... *In the last fifty years, the Sri Lankan state has gone through a process of Sinhalization, which resulted in the political exclusion of Tamils in the legislative and executive process. So the so-called ethnic question is none other than a problem emanating from the political exclusion of one group comprising the population.*
>
> (1965)

In short, unless the process of democratization is extended to the entire citizenry and unless citizenship itself is extended to those who are presently excluded, there is no prospect of establishing a climate of trust within which controversial issues can be negotiated.

While Liyanage's essay is an important statement, in my opinion he does not go far enough. For his theoretical position to have greater credibility there must be a serious effort not only to get the more or less official minority groups involved in the process of democratization but also to embrace those groups which rarely get included, which have no influential advocates, and whose long-term welfare is therefore ignored.[8] True expansions of democratic representation take into account how marginalized groups of various kinds are bypassed by the normal workings of representative government.

Among seriously marginalized groups in Sri Lanka the Plantation Tamils stand out. They constitute a sizeable community whose needs receive little attention by mainstream political parties, and who are among the casualties of an economically shaky society, and who are also mistreated by the militant Tamils, their ethnic kinsmen with whom they have little in common. Liyanage's main point represents a *prelude* to the possibility of negotiation not just between the two principal factions but between them and the fundamentally unrepresented minorities. And yet, by what it omits, his essay seems to reinforce the tendency of governments and political parties to heed the powerful and to ignore the rest. Concern for those who lack power is the supreme test of an accountable democratic society.[9]

I am suggesting that behind twenty years of military carnage, decades of communal tensions, often exploding into deadly rioting, and fifty years of separatism there has been a failure by both Tamils and the majority Sinhalas to look across caste lines as well as ethnic, class, and religious divides in a manner which acknowledges and affirms the specificity of the various "others."[10] Instead, there has been but a semblance of representation in which the condition of those who are politically and economically disempowered is not a high priority. The consequence is deepening alienation throughout the society.

Liyanage hints at but does not expand the sorts of social, political, and economic structures, which enable a society to take seriously the well-being of its entire people. The difficulty of this process is self-evident, and Liyanage's reflections do lend a quality of *gravitas*, which is healthy. While not a recipe for resolving ethnic strife, his perspective has *begun* to articulate the problem of why and how one takes seriously a process of democratization, namely, how to comprehend the concerns of all its citizens, especially the disenfranchised, and to enable their voices to be heard. This task has gained increasing importance throughout the modern world. Paradoxically, when groups become sensitive to the true self-interest of their adversaries, they begin to learn more about their own.

Beyond fundamentalism to a larger identity

Through discussing some of the main points in a collection of essays edited by Tessa Bartholomeusz and Chandra R. de Silva titled *Buddhist Fundamentalism and Minority Identities in Sri Lanka* (1998), this section seeks to identify other elements in the complex mix of ethnic identity alongside traditional portrayals of Sri Lanka as a Sinhala-Buddhist society.[11] The volume's subtext is that the constructed images of Sri Lanka have been shaped and promoted over the past hundred years by a form of Buddhist fundamentalism which sees itself as the "curator" of true Buddhism but which has been and is still influenced by ethnically driven forms of historical, social, and cultural forces. The political policies emerging from this constructed image of identity have led to distorted representations of what constitutes the actual pluralistic nature of Sri Lankan identity and have thus fomented divisions among the many segments of this society.

From various angles the contributors to the *Buddhist Fundamentalism* (1998) volume describe what they mean by "fundamentalism" and, in the process, identify a range of attitudes and positions in and among the minority groups in their relationship to the Sinhala majority. John Holt questions using such a term as "fundamentalism" but acknowledges that its use serves to underscore the evolving self-identification among Sinhala Buddhists over the past century. In the process he shows in what ways this evolution inspired similar quests for identity by other religious and ethnic communities, and how it has issued in numerous forms of communalism. While the larger social movements of the late nineteenth century in Ceylon bound many religious and ethnic groups together in anticolonial and anti-Christian sentiments, the driving force, especially since the mid-1950s, has been nationalistic form of Buddhism. These were "consciously invoked by politically motivated Sinhalas to advance their own empowerment (usually to the exclusion of other communities) or to rationalize their agendas for action taken against other communities in *post hoc* fashion" (Holt 1998: 189).

Holt asserts that the aim of modern Sinhala-Buddhist fundamentalism is to achieve and maintain political power, though factors such as language, race, and ethnicity have also been potent "in generating social identity and alienation between communities" in contemporary Sri Lanka (Holt 1998: 189). As a way of understanding the confluence of religion and political power as the core of Sinhala-Buddhist fundamentalism the tendency of many scholars, perhaps especially in the West, has been to locate the inception of this belief in the *Mahāvaṃsa*, a fifth century post-canonical text. Critics of Sinhala ideology saw the Mahāvihāra position as represented by the *Mahāvaṃsa* and rearticulated in the late nineteenth century as a kind of apotheosis of Sinhala-Buddhism. In the process, there were those who oversimplified the nature of the *Mahāvaṃsa* and tended to demonize it as the root and source of modern ethnocentrism. In my opinion, both apotheosis and demonization go too far.

In any case, the mythohistorical past represented by this ancient work does reveal the interweaving of sacred and political power known as the two wheels of *dhamma*. Behind images of reciprocity between these fundamental powers was an idealized vision of a precolonial, agrarian society, with its village life and temple at the symbolic center. It is precisely this envisioned past which became paradigmatic, however deeply the externals have changed, for contemporary politicians seeking religious endorsement of their policies and for monks who look to the state for protection of the *dhamma* and support of the *saṅgha*. The reemergence of belief in Sri Lanka as the *dhammadīpa* (the unique island of the *dhamma*) was intrinsic to the early stirrings of nationalism and became a political issue of great importance beginning with the 1956 elections. And, at the present time, it continues to be a unifying element among Sinhala people in the state's definition of Sri Lanka as a Buddhist nation and in its war of attrition against the LTTE. By the same token, it triggers animosity from the militant Tamils who regard this as coercive hegemony.

As Chandra de Silva and Tessa Bartholomeusz indicate in their separate essays, the religious justification of violence in the twenty-year war against the militant Tamils has created a major ethical dilemma which many Sinhala Buddhists, monks especially, continue to wrestle with. The issue of how to reconcile canonically specific Buddhist teachings against the use of violence with the active endorsement of violence, even if seen as a defensive posture, is taken seriously by many monks in high position. Bartholomeusz (1999) writes on the just-war ideology in Buddhism:

> It must be stressed, however, that those who make arguments for war – based on their interpretation of Buddhism – also maintain that Buddhism demands compassion and non-violence. How to balance the demands of non-violence with the protection of the entire island of Sri Lanka as a Buddhist territory has remained a constant feature of political and religious rhetoric in Sri Lanka since at least the 1890s, when archival resources allow for a comprehensive view.[12]

This conflicting obligation presents a critical dilemma to many, though to others the path is clearer. A small though vocal minority see "quashing" the Tamils as an imperative if the country and Buddhism are to survive, while others believe that the way of non-violence is the only one to be followed. Those who take this second path underscore the moral and spiritual danger for Buddhism itself when monks are "dragged into partisan politics," as some of de Silva's monk-informants put it.

The positions represented by these informants reveal the complexity of how the *saṅgha*'s relationship to social problems is viewed by monks and lay people and, specifically, how more sensitive Buddhists react to ethnically narrow Sinhala attitudes about the Tamils, even toward the LTTE. While there are strident forms of Sinhala-Buddhist fundamentalism, one also finds moderate positions, as may be seen in the following comment by a respected *bhikkhu*. In response to President Kumaratunga's vow to provide special protection to Buddhism this monk believes that giving "foremost place" to any one religion is "wrong because it is against Buddhist philosophy, it has no moral justification, and it is an infringement of the basic rights of other religions" (De Silva 1998: 61).

As we shall see at the end of this essay, this *bhikkhu*'s reply is in accord with Aśoka's expression of tolerance toward other religious sects, in contrast to the views of some monks and lay people who see no alternative but total elimination of militant Tamils. It is in contrast, however, to the infamous "arahants" featured in the *Mahāvaṃsa* (25: 104–11) who counseled the discomfited King Duṭugämuṇu, who had just slaughtered the *damila* (Tamil) King Elāra and his 60,000 men, that there was no need to feel remorse for these "[u]nbelievers and men of evil life were the rest, not more to be esteemed than beasts" (Mahānāma

Thera 1950: 178). While such justification of violence is not directed at the enemy's religion, nonetheless religious leadership espouses it. Again, the contrast in spirit to Aśoka is striking and reveals how fierce the ideology of Sinhala-Buddhist fundamentalism can be at its worst. And, in response to such chauvinism one finds similar strains within militant Tamil ethnocentrism, though they are rarely endorsed or legitimated by religious precepts.

An extended quote from John Holt's essay approaches the complexity of these issues in a balanced fashion. Wondering if his words might seem overly optimistic "in a South Asian political climate which continues to be fragmented or totalized by appeals to religion and ethnicity," Holt underscores the necessity of seeing the "otherness" of people who come from different communities not as aliens but as those whose participation is essential to the meaning of an inclusive society. He notes, however, how difficult this is:

> The dilemma is this: How to construct an inclusive nationalist discourse which recognizes the importance of a Buddhist *historical* past yet transcends its fundamentalistic myth-and-ritual function as a blueprint for the present and future. That is: How is it possible to transcend the sacred canopy of Buddhist nationalist discourse so that a new more inclusive discourse can recognize the diversity of Sri Lanka's various communities? What's at stake is the discovery of a new political vision for Sri Lanka's future, one that is not simply dependent upon a pandering to ethnicity, language, and religion. This new vision may . . . be one that celebrates the recognition of difference and the history of Sri Lanka's ethnic and religious diversity. For centuries, as I have argued elsewhere, the genius of Sinhala-Buddhist culture was expressed through its remarkable inclusivity and assimilations . . . An inclusive discourse that celebrates recognition of difference has the potential power to marginalize fundamentalistic and totalistic persuasions on the one hand, and militant separatists on the other. An apparent obstacle to unity (i.e., religious diversity) could become, potentially, a powerful *raison d'être* for an inclusive political dynamic. What Sri Lanka might discover is not so much its image as the *dhammadīpa*, but its lost and more recent "image" as a model multiethnic and multireligious society.
>
> (1998: 194)

This vision of an inclusive society is not the brainchild of the modern world, any more than Sinhala-Buddhist fundamentalism is a new entry within the past century. There are strong precedents for both of these conflicting visions. For the latter one finds threaded throughout the Pāli chronicles, which after all represent the world view of the powerful Mahāvihāra fraternity, a continuing inclination to reinforce the privileged position of this most influential of all religious groups in the society over a long period of time. This is not to make light of their contribution to Buddhist culture – its literature, its magnificent art forms, its understanding of Buddhist philosophy, its influence on political decision-making and social policy, and at many points in time its ability to coexist harmoniously with other religious sects. This is what John Holt means when he talks of the "remarkable inclusivity and assimilations" which have been a part of Sinhala-Buddhist history.

The problem has been this same group's temptation, as is often the case with long-empowered groups (in the religious as in the political order), to allocate to themselves power, authority, and privilege. This did not mean that countervailing powers were nonexistent in the *saṅgha* as a whole in Sri Lanka over these long centuries. What it did mean was that the dominant ideology of Sinhala Buddhism, clearly a Mahāvihāra vision, tended to prevail and when fortified by political power it brooked no competition, especially in times when the Buddhist Order and the sociopolitical fabric were threatened. It is no accident that this ideology surfaced anew in the mid-period of British colonial rule and that one of its main grievances was the proselytizing of the Sinhala people by Christians. What the Bartholomeusz and de Silva book (1998) makes clear is not only that Sinhala-Buddhist fundamentalism, which emerged in the late nineteenth century, is very much alive but that its resurgence stimulated sectarian movements within other religions and that this sectarian spirit indirectly and sometimes directly exacerbated the tensions which have thrived in recent decades.

What is also evident is that the voices of "fundamentalism" in Sinhala Buddhism, as in other religious communities, are not the only voices. Indeed, it is clear that some groups in Sri Lanka are strongly advocating a multiethnic society. Chandra de Silva's conversations with many *bhikkhu*s provide evidence of that. At this point I shall attempt, in a provisional way, to identify some of the main points of Tamil and Sinhala concern and conclude this essay with a quotation from Aśoka's 12th Rock Edict, which is a model of Buddhist insight and compassion. Far be it for an outsider to delineate any group's central concerns and the challenges it faces, but sometimes an outside vantage point sheds light on what is difficult to recognize when one is in the midst of turmoil. Starting with the Sinhala concerns, I would suggest the following:

1 *The first and overriding one would be the preservation of national identity and the achievement of viable unity*. To be successful, such a vision cannot be couched in monolithic terms or one, which excludes or minimizes the importance of other religious or ethnic groups. In other words, it would need to embrace the actual pluralism which constitutes Sri Lankan society and which has been fundamental to its long history. "Identity" is a protean concept and experience. Individuals, communities, and nations are continually reconstructing the shifting borders within which they define themselves.
2 *Of equal importance would be the restoration of Sri Lanka's erstwhile ability to engage in and promote harmonious relationships between various ethnic groups*. While many models of this capacity exist in Sri Lankan history, as

well as instances to the contrary, central to the process of deconstructing history and reconstructing it is the ability to understand how some forces have engendered inclusivity and why others have fought against it. For this reason it is imperative that Sri Lankan history, as found in the chronicles, the commentaries, the inscriptions, and especially some of the newly unearthed archeological evidence, be studied with dispassion and impartiality.

3 *There is an equal need for clearer discernment of the fundamental essence of Buddhism as a teaching and practice of the path of wisdom and compassion.* This would not be to homogenize Buddhism but to contrast it to using Buddhist influence to promote an ideologically driven vision and a social structure that safeguards and promotes positions of privilege and self-interest. This is a touchy subject in Sri Lanka, as the levels of defensiveness are close to the surface, but the resources within Buddhist teaching and practice are infinitely more impressive, and many models of these resources in the past and the present day are available.

4 *The possibility for Sri Lanka to become once more a model of pluralism that fosters harmony and wellbeing, not divisiveness.* Such a challenge would need to recognize that there is no conceivable health in separatist or narrow sectarian positions. While this vision may seem impossibly remote to all of the religious communities and to each of the political parties, it is nevertheless required if Sri Lanka is to emerge from the rancor which suffocates it today.

Among fundamental Tamil concerns and challenges, one could mention the following:

1 *The right to and the possibility of self-determination and self-empowerment within a larger Sri Lankan nation and body politic.* Such a scenario would be one in which not only Tamils but other ethnic groups are given voice, recognition, and adequate political representation. While this would mean the preponderance of Tamil influence in the northern and eastern regions, the same rights and opportunities for minority groups in these areas would be required for minorities throughout the country. As a work in progress, the intent would be to foster strong unity among the many parts and to realize the actual interdependence that is both a fact and a goal.

2 *Guaranteeing the importance of human rights by means of adequate structures and an open and responsive process.* It seems clear that Sri Lanka could learn a good deal from the struggles to achieve and protect such rights in other societies. The difficulty of approximating this goal is exceeded only by the necessity of aspiring to it. There is perhaps no more crucial task in the modern world than this, though it is naturally interconnected with other issues, such as the problems of overpopulation, threats to the environment, nuclear proliferation, ethnic communalism, to mention but a few.

3 *The continuing recognition and the strong encouragement of the best in Tamil cultural and religious traditions as a way of adding to the richness of Sri Lankan society*. This would be alongside similar forms of appreciating and encouraging Muslim, Christian, and Buddhist contributions to the social and cultural fabric of the society. There are increasing models of this around the world, though the counter examples of religious prejudice and self-righteousness continue to abound.

4 *The value of maintaining kinship with Tamils in South India in religion, culture, and history at the same time as the effort to play a constructive role within the larger Sri Lanka mixes*. The fact that this sense of a larger identity has existed in the past is crucial to its being renewed in the future, though it can only occur as an ethos of trust develops. In the meantime, for understandable reasons, the lot of militant Tamils is cast primarily with their racial and historical ties with South India and with Tamils in Diaspora. While models for a healthy sense of dual or multiple identity may be found elsewhere, for example, among the huge numbers of immigrants to the United States over two centuries, and while expanding the limits of one's self-identity is hardly free of tension, the process of stretching these boundaries helps to create within individuals and communities a greater capacity for openness and appreciation of diversity.

In conclusion, among the world's remarkable examples of generosity of spirit and open-mindedness, combined with pragmatic good sense, may be found in the 12th Rock Edict of the Emperor Aśoka in the mid-third century BCE. The words in that proclamation provide a deeply humane and Buddhist perspective and are in contrast to the sectarian position of Sinhala-Buddhist fundamentalism. As Romila Thapar suggests, Aśoka's statement may have been inspired or prompted as a result of criticism from leaders of other schools, but this is only speculation. Even if this were the case, the nature of Aśoka's response is itself impressive. As Thapar (1961: 165) says, it is "a direct and emphatic plea for toleration amongst the various sects . . . [it is not to be viewed as] a passive co-existence but an active frame of mind." She is perceptive in seeing Aśoka's view of *dhamma* as a "policy of social responsibility," not as an attempt to impose Buddhism upon others in his empire, and his motives as essentially "a plea for the recognition of the dignity of man, and for a humanistic spirit in the activities of society" (Thapar 1961: 3).

Because Sinhala Buddhism recognizes Aśoka as the supreme paradigm of political wisdom and compassion, his words have often been taken with great seriousness. The fact that they are in contrast to the distrust with which many Buddhists in Sri Lanka have regarded people of other religious or ethnic traditions represents a significant departure from the best in Buddhist tradition. The harshness in which Sinhala fundamentalist judgment is sometimes couched has been justified by the claim that it is not Tamil religion or even Tamils as a people who are the problem but the terrorists among the Tamils, specifically the LTTE. While this kind of distinction is important, it reveals how sectarian views and a lack of self-criticism on both sides contribute to the politicizing of ethnic identity, a circumstance that Aśoka observed and warned against centuries ago.

> This progress of the essential doctrine takes many forms, but its basis is the control of one's speech, so as not to extoll one's own sect or disparage another's on unsuitable occasions, or at least to do so only mildly on certain occasions. On each occasion one should honour another man's sect, for by doing so one increases the influence of one's own sect and benefits that of the other man; while by doing otherwise one diminishes the influence of one's own sect and harms that of another man. Again, whosoever honours his own sect or disparages that of another man, wholly out of devotion to his own, with a view to showing it in a favorable light, harms his own sect even more seriously. Therefore, concord is to be commended, so that men may hear one another's principles and obey them. This is the desire of the Beloved of the Gods [Piyadassi], that all sects should be well-informed, and should teach that which is good, and that everywhere their adherents should be told, "The Beloved of the Gods does not consider gifts or honour to be as important as the progress of the essential doctrine of all sects."
>
> (Thapar 1961: 255)[13]

Clearly, these are words of aspiration; they are not descriptive of how religious communities normally relate to each other. They are the words of Aśoka the political realist who understood how decimation of an enemy wreaks havoc upon one's own people. This was not only a turning point in his life; it was a vision which, however rarely followed, remains a counterpoint to cynicism and despair.

I began writing this essay after learning that Neelan Tiruchelvam (1944–1999) had been assassinated. Wherever someone of his intelligence, good will, and extensive contribution to the understanding of ethnic strife, the defense of human rights, and the path of political moderation have been murdered, it is singularly tragic. Because his adult life had been an advocacy of pluralism and diversity, as intrinsic to healthy political structures and process, the loss is incalculable. That is precisely why he was such a threat to extremists: his efforts toward justice and peace were based upon the vision of an inclusive society. Ideologues never held such a vision, let alone terrorists, on either side. In a world consumed by repeated outbreaks of hostility men and women yearn for peace but find it agonizingly elusive. Ideological divides are a common feature, with people arrayed in tightfisted camps. Even the possibility of compromise recedes, and discouragement easily takes over. In the words of a Sri Lankan friend, the uncommon tragedy of Sri Lanka is that it is "the hatemongers and evil-minded among our polarized society who seem to determine the current course of our nation. The sober, mature and thoughtful among us are marginalized" or, as in the case of Neelan, assassinated. The calculus of terrorism's breeding terrorism is well understood. As with the choruses in ancient Greek tragedy, one hears the familiar cry of "when will it ever end?" Apart from deeply affirmed visions of inclusivity there is no hope. This is why exclusive forms of ethnic identity are so virulent.

Notes

1 An early version of this chapter was published in *Excursions and Explorations: Cultural Encounters Between Sri Lanka and the United States*, edited by Tissa Jayatilaka (Colombo, Sri Lanka: The United States – Sri Lanka Fulbright Commission, 2002), pp. 133–67.

2 Within both Tamil and Sinhala websites (http://sangam.org and http://www.sinhaya.com (accessed on October 1, 2005)), respectively, there are many which are chauvinistic and disputatious and others which are carefully reasoned and moderate in tone. The most ambitious statement in terms of topics covered is the 103-page analysis by S.L.Gunasekara titled "Tigers, 'Moderates' and Pandora's Package," found on this website: http://www.sinhaya.com/tigers moderates-1.html (accessed on October 1, 2005). Gunasekara is an attorney who articulates a Sinhala position without being uncritical of Sinhala leadership, especially in its attempts to promote the implementation of devolution, which he regards as the abandonment of sovereignty. Gunasekara is known for his defense of human rights, especially those of minority groups, and for his advocacy of a pluralistic society.

3 In Gunasekara's essay, cited in footnote 1, there is the tendency to attribute the sources of terrorist activity and riots to

> thugs, criminals and perverts taking advantage of situations created largely by the overtly chauvinistic Tamil political leadership which has, from the time of independence and even before, strained... to drive a wedge between the Sinhalas and the Tamils to satisfy their lust for power.
>
> (p. 6)

Gunasekara's inattention to the deep-seated self-interest that exists within all human communities (Sinhala as much as Tamil) is evident in words which ignore how Sinhala forms of communalism for over a century has contributed to a climate of separatism, and acutely so since 1956. While characterizing as thugs and criminals those who may have been the direct agents of destruction and pillage, he fails to acknowledge that these kinds of fury have been stimulated by persistent expressions of Sinhala chauvinism even at the highest political and religious levels.

4 Gunasekara's rejoinder to the Tamil position that there should be a separate Tamil state because there has always been one, as some would maintain, since "the dawn of history" or, as others would claim, since the tenth century draws upon the writings of prominent historians such as Karthigesu Indrapala, K.M. de Silva, and C.R. de Silva, who argue that there were no permanent settlements of any size anywhere in the country until the tenth century. In K.M. de Silva's words,

> A Tamil Kingdom did exist from the thirteenth century to the early part of the seventeenth, but except during the brief heyday of its power it seldom controlled anything more than the Jaffna peninsula, and some adjacent regions on the coast and some parts of the interior... [revealing that there] is little or no evidence to support [claims about]... either an unbroken national consciousness or a continuing tradition of independent statehood.
>
> (See Gunasekara 1900: 29)

5 For over twenty-five years Sudharshan Seneviratne has questioned the constructions of Sinhala-Buddhist identity. He also questions a similar kind of phemonenon among

proponents of a Tamil identity. For a thoughtful questioning of how the constructing of Tamil identity makes "extensive use of culture-related sources in drawing symbols from the past in legitimating identities, consequently providing access to power, resources and territory," see Seneviratne (1999).

6 One of the more capable Tamil statements found on the internet is the relatively short publication, put out by the Political Committee of the Liberation Tigers of Tamil Eelam, titled *A Struggle for Justice*. See the website: http://www.eelam.com/freedom_struggle/ltte_publ/strug_for_just/(accessed on October 1, 2005). The search for international approval is complicated, of course, by the immense economic and military support that each side derives from outside the country. This is another issue which deserves to be analyzed at length.

7 To emphasize what I consider the core of Liyanage's remarks, beyond those on "devolution," and to represent the basis for serious negotiation I have italicized a few of his words. I also have taken the liberty of changing the spelling of "Thamil" to "Tamil."

8 While Liyanage makes a plausible case for the rights of minorities, with specific reference to the Tamil population, he might also have included mention of the Janatha Vimukti Peramuṇa (JVP), whose rampages of violence against Tamil communities are not to be justified but whose economic and educational needs and whose class-based resentments were not taken seriously. This is an instance of a segment of the society whose overall economic and educational needs were ignored even within the Sinhala community and who struck out in forms of ethnic retaliation. My own country's record with the Native Americans is a glaring example, as is the case with a large segment of the black community who remain caught in the cycles of poverty four decades after voting rights legislation and despite the much touted economic programs known as the Great Society in the mid-1960s.

9 For a well-documented discussion of the plight of the Veddas, whose entire way of life and culture is being "bulldozed" out of existence by the forces of "economic development," see Seneviratne (1983: 9–11).

10 See Sudharshan Seneviratne (1996: 264–75) who provides a fresh examination, based on archeological materials in tension with historical documents, about "the significance of ethno-historical history as a powerful undercurrent within the contemporary political structure" in Sri Lanka.

11 The collection of essays produced by Tessa Bartholomeusz and Chandra R. de Silva (1998) is a constructively critical contribution to understanding the causes of ethnic tension in this country, beginning in the late nineteenth century and becoming increasingly explosive in the past two decades. The essays are scholarly, non-partisan, and informative. This publication looks at less explored areas with a common theme in mind, namely, how the phenomenon termed Sinhala-Buddhist fundamentalism has stimulated and shaped the identities of non-Buddhist ethnic and religious minorities in Sri Lanka over the past century.

12 The subject of Sinhala-Buddhist attitudes, whether expressed by members of the *saṅgha* or by influential laypersons, toward the use of violence is obviously a complex one which requires extensive study.

13 An apt parallel in the modern world is the XIVth Dalai Lama's approach to political tensions in the social order. See Dalai Lama (1999: 161–237).

11

ROOTS OF THE CONFLICT AND THE PEACE PROCESS

R.A.L.H. Gunawardana

> Peace is more than a simple absence of war. It entails the active engagement in a battle for reconstruction, for identifying and rectifying the root causes of war and conflict. All this is true, very true of our own situation in Sri Lanka.
>
> (President Chandrika Kumaratunga)[1]

One of the most significant developments in the more recent history of Sri Lanka was the beginning in 2002 of a new process of negotiations between the Government and the Liberation Tigers of Tamil Eelam (LTTE) to resolve the problems basic to the tragic and protracted war in the island. This welcome development was to the credit of the leaderships of the Government of Sri Lanka and the LTTE as well as the Government of Norway whose participation as the facilitator has been a noteworthy aspect of the process. The ceasefire has held since December 2001 despite incidents fraught with tensions that both sides have in general carefully sought to defuse. The signing of the Memorandum of Understanding (MOU) at the end of February 2002, even though associated with some noteworthy lapses, has contributed toward ushering in a fragile state of cessation of hostilities. Though there have been many instances of violations of the MOU, some of them of quite serious nature, all parties have striven hard to ensure that the peace talks did continue till April 2003 when the LTTE announced what they termed a temporary withdrawal from talks. The ceasefire had provided an opening for reducing violence and the opportunity to develop a dialogue on the issues basic to the conflict as well as to commence the formidable task of repairing the massive damage caused by the long war. Despite protests and misgivings voiced and obstacles placed by extremist elements on both sides as well as reservations and criticisms expressed by varied concerned groups, hopes in the continuation of the peace process continues to be shared by the overwhelming majority of Sri Lankans and concerned observers outside the country. The leaders of all parties involved have to be cognizant of these expectations in guiding the process beyond the present crisis.

Previous failures at negotiations had led to fresh cycles of the conflict at high levels of intensity. This places a special responsibility on the shoulders of the entire political leadership in the island, whether directly involved in the negotiations or not, to ensure that the latest effort does succeed. In order to accomplish this, it is necessary to carefully understand the reasons for the previous failures as well as the factors behind the pattern of intensified reproduction of the conflict. Such an understanding would be most helpful in overcoming the current problems and guiding the peace process firmly forward, without haste and avoiding pitfalls.

Prominent among the factors behind the failure to achieve a lasting peace in Sri Lanka has been the absence of a broad national consensus on issues central to the ethnic problem. Good preliminary work toward achieving this objective had been done under the previous Government by the Ministry of Ethnic Affairs and the Sudu Nelum (White Lotus) Movement. However, much more remains to be done. Such a consensus has to be based on continuing dialogue and development of understanding not only among the political parties represented in Parliament but also forces outside, bringing in the leadership of civil society. The tasks before the peace process cannot be achieved merely by the ability to command sufficient numbers in Parliament. A patient strategy of building a broad nation-wide consensus is called for to meet the needs of the formidable tasks ahead. If such an approach were to be adopted, regular consultation and coordination of action among the national political leadership cutting across Party lines, and especially at the highest levels of state, would be of utmost importance. Unfortunately, this is an aspect that has not been yet accorded the priority it deserves.

The radically changing international scene of contemporary times has been characterized by certain trends sharply antithetical to terrorism and transnational mobilization of financial resources by terrorist organizations. This has been paralleled by the rise of international opinion opposed to employment of minors in military activity and to utilization of land mines. In recent years international opinion has been moving gradually but decisively against separatism in Sri Lanka and in favor of the preservation of a united Sri Lanka. This is reflected in the strongly worded statement issued by the Government of the United States on March 11, 2002, advising the LTTE to recognize that an independent Eelam is both unattainable and unnecessary (US Government 2002). Concurrently, for quite some time there has been very strong international opinion against the continuation of the war by both the Government and the LTTE, and in favor of a settlement based on a negotiated agreement on the issues basic to the conflict. In an era when there is emphasis being placed very correctly on the need for a dialogue across civilizations in international fora (Pico 2001), dialogue rather than war and mutual slaughter has to be necessarily recognized as the means for the solution of problems confronted by ethnic groups destined to share the island of moderate proportions that Sri Lanka is.

Continuing developments within the internal political arena in Sri Lanka, too, have been favorable, with the major political forces in both Government and Opposition moving, even though slowly, to positions supportive of the search for a negotiated, peaceful, political solution to the ethnic problem. This has been a gradual, long-term development, and it has to be understood that it is yet evolving.

In the period 1999–2001, it appeared that dramatic developments were imminent. Unfortunately, the trends did not fully mature at the time due to varied factors, including at least partly the elections pending at the time, first the Presidential election and then the Parliamentary elections. The Local Government elections of 2002 and the tensions between the Executive Presidency and the majority grouping in the legislature have seriously limited opportunities for adequate collaboration in the peace process. Since the overwhelming majority among all ethnic groups appears to be opposed to the continuation of the war and to desire peace, it is hoped that this would help to develop closer cooperation among the national leadership in the building of peace.

The agenda of the peace talks

The Agenda of the actual negotiations is undoubtedly a crucial element in the peace process, and the manner in which the Agenda is structured could decisively help or hamper the process of negotiations. The Agenda, therefore, was naturally expected to form a primary focus in the preliminary talks about talks. Initially, statements made available on the broad envisaged structure of the talks came mostly from LTTE sources. These statements suggested that there would be two broad stages in the talks. It was stated that at the first stage the focus would be on the formation of an interim administration in the Northern and Eastern Provinces. It was envisaged that the LTTE would participate in the administration of this territory. It was only at the second stage that the core issues were to be discussed and a permanent settlement negotiated. The LTTE gave the impression of believing that there would be a time gap between the two stages, and emphasized that the time was not ripe for the second stage of the talks: We do not think Ranil Wickremasinghe is capable of addressing the core issues and offer us a permanent solution at this stage because you know executive powers are vested with the President and his powers are limited to Parliament, the LTTE leadership stated at the press conference held at Kilinochchi on April 10, 2002. It was further added, somewhat indelicately, if not also bluntly: "we wish to insist that Ranil's government is not politically stable or authoritative or powerful enough to take up the core demands of the Tamils and offer us a permanent solution" (Pirapaharan 2002b). It may be noted that the actual resolution of the conflict, according to this perspective, was evidently being relegated to a somewhat distant and indeterminate future.

Even though the LTTE seemed to play down the significance of the first stage of the talks, it demanded that the proscription imposed on it be lifted before the talks began, insisting that this was a necessary condition (Pirapaharan 2002b). Another precondition had been incorporated in the MOU: the armed political groups opposed to the LTTE and operating in the North and the East were to be disarmed by the Government (MOU 2002). The Government accepted these two demands and took action to have them implemented. There has been, however, no mention by the LTTE of the laying down of its own arms. It would thus seem that the scheme of things, as envisaged by the LTTE, was loaded up front in its favor. The removal of the proscription, the right to administer territory some of which it had not been able to gain and retain through military activities up to the present, the withdrawal of Government forces from this territory, and the disarming of rival groups, thereby making its own armed cadre the only armed group in the North and the East, raising it to the *de facto* as well as legally recognized dominant force in the area, would indeed be prominent among the most valued and desired strategic objectives of the LTTE. In the originally suggested scheme for negotiations, all this would be gained *not through the process of give and take in formal negotiations* but at the commencement of the peace process as preconditions. The same approach surfaced yet again after the suspension of negotiations in April 2003 when the establishment of an interim administration for the North East was put forward as the precondition for the resumption of the talks. Although, as we shall see, there are several positive developments in the present stance of the LTTE, what is missing in its approach is *reciprocity* on its part that many observers in Sri Lanka as well as the outside world would be trying to identify. There is clearly a need to introduce a degree of balance and reciprocity, a reassuring sense of fairness and convincing signs of commitment to the peaceful path if the process were to win popular support as would be necessary in order to ensure a realistic possibility of an agreed settlement being implemented. It may also be noted that the two envisaged phases of the negotiations are not distinct or compartmentalized. In fact, the necessary conditions required to be implemented before the talks did impinge clearly on some of the principal core issues.

However, it has to be recognized that the actual path of the negotiations has diverged from the course the LTTE had unilaterally mapped out for it. Progress in the negotiations process has been painfully slow, but there have been markers indicating some gains of mutual benefit, the most noteworthy of which is the cessation of hostilities that has prevailed under acutely difficult circumstances. The agreement announced at the Oslo round of talks to find a solution to the ethnic problem "based on a federal structure within a united Sri Lanka" (Norwegian Communique 2002) appeared to point to an important break-through. It also evidently marked a divergence on the part of the LTTE from its earlier insistence on separation. The commitment to a federal solution was renewed at the subsequent round of talks at Hakone in Japan. For in a document released in April 2003 it was observed that "notably at the Hakone talks the parties to the negotiations reiterated their commitment to develop a federal system based on internal self-determination within a united Sri Lanka and have begun to discuss the essential elements of fiscal federalism" (Armitage 2003; Balasingham 2003; Basic Principles 2003).[2] This could prove to be a way out of the morass, but the difficulties involved in working out mutually acceptable details cannot be underestimated. The reopening of the A9 highway linking the Jaffna peninsula with the southern parts of the island facilitating two-way movement of people and goods is another mutually beneficial gain achieved through talks. It was an important step toward normalization and improvement of living conditions in the Northern

Province. A concurrent benefit, deeply appreciated by Sri Lankan Buddhists has been the opening up of opportunities, denied to them for too long, to go on pilgrimage to Buddhist shrines located in the North East.

On the other hand, some of the criticisms of the shortcomings of the peace process deserve careful attention. The LTTE has been strongly critical of what it has called the failure of the peace process to make an impact on the dismal living conditions of the people of the war-ravaged North East. The claim does have a basis in fact. Meanwhile the complaint from the residents of the North East has been that the nature of domination wielded by the LTTE has changed little despite some of the provisions in the MOU. The armed cadres of the LTTE constitute an Infantry in more than one sense: minors of both sexes abducted through sheer force figure prominently among their ranks, this in direct violation of the undertakings that have been given often. The taxes and contributions extracted by the LTTE from the residents of the North East, often through threat and compulsion, have been operative in an oppressive manner. Among the worst affected by this situation has been the Muslim community in the eastern region living under conditions of insecurity and tension as a result of frequent outbreaks of violence. The task of ensuring the basic human rights of the inhabitants of the North East including their right to exercise their vote should receive the highest priority. In this connection, the agreement that was reached during the Hakone talks to hold elections in this region (Basic Principles 2003) was particularly welcome, but the failure so far to implement it has caused concern. In the Sinhala-speaking area of the island criticisms have emphasized the failure to focus on the core issues resulting in growing apprehensions on its implications on the assurance of the territorial integrity of the island. The incidents rousing perhaps the most intense reactions have been the long series of political assassinations of leaders of rival Tamil political groups and of Government intelligence operatives. They have in fact raised serious questions about the commitment of the LTTE to the peace process and the renunciation of terrorism.

Nationalism and democracy: crucial issues basic to the ethnic conflict

The multifarious issues associated with the intensification of the ethnic problem in Sri Lanka may be grouped to a considerable extent within the broad themes of nationalism and democracy. Issues concerning human rights may also be placed within the theme of democracy. The specific characteristics of the development of nationalism within the island and the failures in evolving state structures providing democratic space to accommodate and subsume these developments lie at the very roots of the crisis. In trying to understand the nature of the nationalism(s) that developed in Sri Lanka one convenient point of departure would be to focus on the failure to generate a nationalist movement that could play a unifying role island-wide, bringing together all the peoples of the island, or in other words an overarching Sri Lankan nationalism. The formation of the Ceylon National

Congress in 1918, based on the model of the Indian National Congress, represented an attempt to nurture such a territory-based, rather than an ethnicity-based, nationalist movement. The differences which arose in 1920–1921 on the interrelated issues of territorial representation and representation for ethnic groups[3] led to a split in the Ceylon National Congress on ethnic lines less than three years after its formation. In the context of the failure of the National Congress project what emerged in place of a broad national movement were ethnonationalist movements of the Sinhala and Tamil varieties which in their ideologies drew freely on Aryan and Dravidian theories produced and being propagated by intellectuals of the Orientalist tradition at the time. The increasing emphasis on the Aryan/Dravidian dichotomy of the Sri Lankan population associated with these theories played a prominent role as an obstacle to the growth of a broad national movement.

Two remarkably retrograde political acts in the modern history of Sri Lanka, one prior to independence and the other in the initial years after independence, were to prove disastrous in sowing suspicion and estranging minority ethnic opinion. The first, which took place in 1936, is represented by the formation of the Pan-Sinhala Board of Ministers in the second State Council established under the Donoughmore Constitution.[4] The exclusion of non-Sinhala members from the Board of Ministers through manipulation of the Executive Committee system was to make cooperation among the Sinhala and Tamil elites even more difficult than previously. This particular incident should even today serve to caution us that "Donoughmore-type constitutional reforms" replacing the present Party-based representation, would not by themselves provide for equitable representation and sharing of power.

The second measure, undemocratic and socially unjust as it was politically most unwise, was the disfranchisement of labor of more recent Indian origin. This was the outcome of a series of legislation in 1948–1949 (i.e., the Citizenship Act No.18 of 1948, the Indian and Pakistani Residents (Citizenship) Act No. 3 of 1949, and the Ceylon Parliamentary Elections (Amendment) Act No. 48 of 1949). The three Acts in effect withdrew the voting rights of a large proportion of Indian Tamil estate labor more than 72,230 of whom had voted at the elections of 1947.[5] The series of legislation adopted by the newly independent state in Sri Lanka in 1948–1949 represented serious dents affecting the quality of democracy and a significant point in the shift toward limitation of space available to minority ethnic groups within the state. The retrograde measures of 1936 and 1948–1949 intensified the differences that had arisen in 1920–1921. Together these events contributed to creating a chasm between the Sinhala and Tamil communities that proved to be formidable and difficult to heal. However, it would be inaccurate to argue that it was merely intransigence on the part of only the Sinhala leadership that led to the deterioration of the situation. The offer of a scheme whereby 57 representatives in the legislature would be drawn from the Sinhala community while 47 would represent minorities, made by a group of liberal Sinhala leaders in the mid-1940s was a noteworthy attempt to arrive at a fair solution. This time intransigence was on the part of the Tamil leaders at the time: they insisted on their 50:50 formula, that is, 50% of the representation for the Sinhala electors and 50% for the minorities (Wilson 2001).

The success achieved by the astute labor leader S. Thondaman in persuading President J.R. Jayewardene (1906–1996) to take steps in the 1980s toward restoring in substantial manner the voting rights of the "Indian" estate labor population was a noteworthy development. The achievement was particularly remarkable since it had been accomplished without antagonizing the Sinhala population of the central highlands. The need to establish the principle of equity on a firm basis and to extend the democratic rights of all the peoples in the island still remain to be essential tasks today. The recent decision to extend citizenship rights to categories of estate labor who had been left out in the 1980s, and the resultant legislative act of 2003 that received unanimous approval in Parliament was a significant move in this direction.

Basic rights of the Tamil people: language

Perhaps more than any other grievance, problems relating to language rights of the Tamil-speaking population were responsible for alienating Tamil opinion. It was but to be expected that the clash of interests between the Sinhala and Tamil ethnonationalist forces would be sharpest on matters relating to language. Language was a crucial, perhaps the most crucial, factor behind both movements. Beginnings made in the post-1956 period in giving primacy to the Sinhala language in place of English had been stoutly resisted by sections of the numerically small but highly influential group among both Sinhala and Tamil people who had been educated in English. However, it was a move conducive to the extension of democracy and did clearly benefit the overwhelming majority of residents in the island. Unfortunately, this emphasis on only one language and the resultant failure to provide parallel facilities for the use of the Tamil language and to elevate it to the position of equal status as an official language was, on the other hand, a major lapse which in its effects turned out to be severely discriminatory. This placed the Tamil-speaking population at a serious disadvantage. The continued implementation of the use of the Sinhala language in official business meant that, while the use of English did continue, Tamil citizens began to receive responses in Sinhala to their letters to Government Departments. Very few among the Tamil recipients of such Government letters could understand Sinhala. This trend was the cause for acute anxiety and a growing feeling among the Tamil-speakers that they were being treated like foreigners in their own land. Acquaintances from Jaffna have told the present writer how, every time they received a letter from a Government Department, they had to sometimes go far looking for a person who could translate it from Sinhala into Tamil.

Curiously enough, in the long history of negotiations between the leaders of the Sinhala and Tamil peoples, there has been recognition of the problem and of the need to take steps in this regard. There was even some important legislation enacted with this objective in view. In the lamentably abrogated Bandaranaike-Chelvanayakam agreement of 1957 it was stated that Tamil would be recognized as the language of the national minority and made the language of administration in the northern and eastern provinces. Even though the agreement was abrogated, the Tamil Language (Special Provisions) Act was adopted by the Bandaranaike Government and approved in Parliament in 1958. In 1965 Dudley Senanayake (1911–1973) agreed to provide for Tamil as a language of administration together with Sinhala in the Northern and Eastern provinces as also to amend the Languages of the Courts Act in order to provide for the use of Tamil in judicial procedure (Sivarajah 1996: 202–05; Wilson 1974: 166–67). These provisions were incorporated in legislation. The recognition of Tamil as a national language came in the 1980s. However, in the implementation of the use of Tamil in official business in actual practice there was indefensible tardiness. The shortcomings in implementation meant that the actual ameliorative effects of the legislation on the disadvantages faced by the Tamil people were only marginal. Some of the reasons adduced to explain the shortcomings, such as the inadequacy of the number of available translators/interpreters for work in the two languages, even if genuine, appeared to be flimsy excuses. Such problems, if concentrated upon with seriousness, could have been overcome perhaps even in the short or medium term. It is not difficult to understand the depth of frustration among the Tamil population that led to the disaffection and to increasing alienation from the state.

The revitalization of what has been found to be a medieval Sri Lankan ideal, that of multilingualism, is an urgent need for our own times, and should certainly form an important part in a long-term strategy to develop greater mutual understanding among the peoples living in the island. In its application multilingualism would mean trilingualism, for instance, the cultivation of linguistic skills in Sinhala, Tamil, and English. The schools system in the country, especially since the changes introduced in the 1960s when the importance of English came to be de-emphasized, has failed in increasing measure to produce men and women who can effectively communicate with members of ethnic communities other than their own. It has to be recognized that, even before the 1960s, the knowledge of English was limited to a small minority of the population. This group performed an important link function in governmental and administrative work, helped to keep channels of communication open and permitted easy flow of information across ethnic lines. However, this was at the level of the elite. Even before the 1960s, there was hardly any significant and effective interaction at mass level among the linguistically compartmentalized ethnic communities in the island. With the de-emphasis of English in the education system, and the continuous diminution of the number of English-speakers in the country, the essential task of keeping channels of communication open, even among the elites of the ethnic communities, came under severe strain.

The basis for a policy of promoting trilingualism in education and society has already been laid in the recognition accorded to Sinhala, Tamil, and English as official languages. However, further clarity and specificity in policy are most essential, particularly because there has been in the islands history a tendency to opt for the politically expedient and easier option, often with dire consequences in the long term. In this case, the politically easy solution would be the return to the old model, that is, mere re-emphasis on English rather than aim at trilingualism. It is important to keep in mind that *both local languages* have to be encouraged and nurtured. In fact, it was the neglect of the two local languages, accompanied by failure to treat both languages equally that contributed to the intensification of the ethnic problem since the 1950s. Further, it is through being qualified in the two local languages that the future generations would find it possible to communicate with any person encountered in any place within the island. Some initial steps were taken in the late 1990s to introduce the teaching of Tamil to Sinhala-medium students. Similarly, the University of Peradeniya had initiated a program to give trilingual training to its students. The vigorous implementation of a national policy promoting trilingualism has become urgently necessary today. Facilitated by a well-planned and systematic implementation of such a policy, trilingualism may take about 20–30 years to achieve, but the facilities of communication it would ensure at mass level, and the effects that such a transformation would bring to bear in broadening and energizing activity in civil society are bound to be vitally significant in lessening the tensions currently evident in society. It may be relevant to note here that the majority of the Tamil-speaking population resides outside the Northern and Eastern provinces: hence, whatever the exact future status of this area might be, there would certainly be a need for trilingualism.

Reinventing the State: enshrining diversity

The present crisis has made perceptive Sri Lankans aware of, perhaps more acutely than at any previous time in their recent history, the inadequacies of the structure of the state in Sri Lanka, and the dire need to radically restructure it, in fact to reinvent it, firmly and pervasively based on democratic ideals, and in a manner that would make it more responsive to the aspirations of the diverse peoples inhabiting the island. Diversity[6] adds richness and luster to life in contemporary Sri Lanka as it did in the precolonial civilization of the island that had some striking achievements to its credit. Throughout a good part of the long history of Sri Lanka, diversity has been a striking feature attracting attention. Damsels depicted in the ancient rock paintings of Sīgiri, dated to about the fifth century CE, are suggestive of the presence in even the upper social strata of diverse physical types. Some were of lighter complexion described by ancient poets as golden while others were of a dark hue, referred to by those poets synonymously as black or blue (Paranavitana 1956). By about the twelfth to thirteenth centuries, both the golden and the darker physical types receive recognition in the ideals of physical beauty of the times: in order to be considered a beauty, it is said, a damsel should be either golden or black in complexion

(Gunawardana 1990). It would thus appear that in this civilization diversity was not only recognized but also accommodated in aesthetic theory.

This recognition of diversity extended to language. The mastering more than one language was considered a desirable accomplishment is another aspect deserving our close attention. This approach is but to be expected in an island located in the middle of the Indian Ocean and well known as a meeting point for transoceanic trade routes. Mastery of several languages would have been accorded high priority particularly among the merchant classes and the cosmopolitan *saṅgha*. The Sri Lankan Buddhist monk was expected to learn Pāli, the language of Theravāda Buddhism, and it is clear beyond doubt that quite a few were conversant with Sanskrit as well. This enabled them to keep tract of developments in Buddhist schools of opinion other than the Theravāda, as also to be able to pursue their scholarly interests in fields of learning beyond the needs of their religious training. Literature, grammar, astronomy, astrology, and medicine were among subjects that attracted their attention. Multilingualism facilitated the work of those monks and nuns who were involved in the propagation of Buddhism in other lands. The cultivation of linguistic skills in multiple languages appears to have been an aspiration, and those who had mastered 6 languages provided the ideal, as is clear from literary texts from the thirteenth century onwards. The idea of mastering six languages remained the ideal for several centuries (Gunawardana 1990). The six languages were not always listed in an identical manner, but Sinhala, Pāli, Sanskrit, and Tamil figure in almost all the lists.

Despite such a rich tradition of appreciative recognition accorded to diversity for a long time in the past, in the postcolonial state there has been a marked proclivity antithetical to the promotion of multiple traditions. Basic to the accomplishment of current tasks is the recognition of the principle of diversity, particularly in terms of ethnicity and culture, not only as representative of realities but also as a general principle to be actively fostered and encouraged. A Constitution that places significance and high value on the principle of diversity, transcending the dictates and tyranny of mere numbers, should contribute very positively to alleviating the present predicament.

Sharing of power

Absence of adequate opportunities for sharing of power among the ethnic groups in the island has been one of the primary factors behind the intensification of the conflict. Attempts at fostering sharing of power with special emphasis on devolution have been made, especially during the last decade, and the last attempt at a radical restructuring made under the Kumaratunga administration could not be implemented due to the lack of support from the Opposition in Parliament. It is becoming increasingly evident that power-sharing arrangements would have to go beyond devolution. It should also encompass meaningful sharing of power *especially at the center*. The concept may be given expression through such symbolically significant devices as representation for ethnic groups at the level of

Vice Presidents of the land as the present writer suggested in 1996.[7] The idea, which was incorporated in Article 57 of the draft Constitution presented to Parliament in 2000, now seems to find general support at the national level. Obviously, such symbolic devices, by themselves, would not be adequate. Radical steps are called for to bring about a transformation of the nature of the state so that a new state more clearly representative of the diversity of the population of the island is brought into being. Obviously, this task has to be based on the recognition and acceptance of the ethnic, religious, and cultural diversity of the island in its history as well as in contemporary times.

The confidence among the minority ethnic groups in the state as an institution that would impartially afford protection to all its citizens, ensuring security of life and property, has been badly shaken by their tragic experience. The riots of 1958 and 1977, the pogrom of 1983 and the burning of the Jaffna Library, one of the finest libraries in the entire country, have left too painful memories among the Tamils as well as the sensitive and concerned individuals among other communities. The dismal failure in the provision of security for the citizens, a basic function associated with the state throughout history, has not been overcome yet, and the gravity of the crisis of confidence in this fundamental respect cannot be overemphasized. The lost confidence can be restored only by a new type of state that is dedicated to invariably assuring security for all citizens, irrespective of ethnicity, language, religion, or class and is also manifestly constituted in such manner that it inspires confidence in its ability to perform this crucial task. To ignore this grave problem and the essential tasks it entails would be to ensure the continuation of the strife and conflict that tragically engulfs Sri Lankan society today. Hence the generation of constitutional provisions to enable genuine sharing of power at the center constitutes a primary focus calling for immediate and serious attention. Wider and fuller public discussion on mechanisms suitable for the practical implementation of the concept, than what has been achieved so far, constitutes an urgent and essential need.

The quest for Eelam

The establishment of Tamil Eelam has been for a considerable number of years the declared objective of the LTTE. In its long campaign of military and political activity aimed at this objective, the LTTE has not flinched from resorting to terrorism on the most violent scale. Even though Eelam has been accorded the central place in the political thinking of the LTTE, the task of comprehending in conceptual or geographical terms the meanings that are being inscribed in the term presents a formidable challenge. It is generally associated with the twin concepts of homeland and self-determination, and its connotation as a separate and independent political entity has been given emphasis.

The homeland theory

The demand that the Northern and Eastern Provinces be recognized as constituting the Tamil homeland represents one of the most contentious core issues.

The agreement in 1987 that the two provinces were areas of historical habitation of Sri Lankan Tamil-speaking peoples (Sivarajah 1996: 205–09) has not settled the issue. The cartographic representation of the homeland in LTTE publicity materials has been variable. Similarly, the answers to the question "Whose homeland?" have not been consistent. One answer has been that it is the homeland of Tamil-speaking peoples. This definition would include the estate labor of Indian origin currently known as Upcountry Tamils and also the Muslim ethnic group. The formulation did raise some problems. The Upcountry Tamils are located outside the Northern and Eastern provinces. While a substantial section of the Muslims are from the Northern and Eastern provinces, the dominant majority, including some of the largest concentrations, lives outside these two provinces and is widely dispersed over the island. The early 1990s witnessed what was evidently a shift in the definition from Tamil-speaking peoples to ethnic Tamils thereby excluding the Muslims, resulting in the tragic episodes of the expulsion of Muslims in extensive numbers from Jaffna, Vavuniya, Mannar, and Mullaitivu. The nature of these expulsions, the numbers and the scale involved as well as the brusque manner of their execution, gave the impression of ethnic cleansing. It has been reported that Muslim homes in such parts of Jaffna as Ottumadam, Sonakateru, and Bommaiveli have been allocated to Tamil refugees (Jeyaraj 2002). Sinhala people who had been present in moderate numbers in the Jaffna region had left earlier.[8] In the 1990s the LTTE thinking on the homeland appeared to be in terms of an ethnically pure territory reserved for the ethnic Tamils. Not long ago, it was reported that Karikalan, the LTTE leader in the Eastern Province at that time, had made a statement implying that Muslims have no rights to land in the Eastern Province as well. The statement raised a furor, and later Karikalan denied having made the statement. The LTTE subsequently moved him from the position he occupied in the Eastern Province.

As it may have been noted from the preceding discussion, access to land is an issue fundamental to the homeland theory. The allocation by the Government of newly developed agricultural land has given rise to contentious debate. The debate does raise certain crucial questions. One such question before the decision-makers would be whether land should be considered as vested with an ethnic quality, as Sinhala, Tamil, or Muslim land, and should be reserved as *lebensraum* for that particular ethnic group. Or is land to be considered from a developmental point of view as a factor of production and its allocation determined by social need, technological abilities, and commitment of applicants, as well as perhaps their capabilities at ensuring the requisite capital inflow? Relevant to the choice between the options is the fact that most areas within the island are multiethnic in character. Further, under prevalent conditions of migrations of labor from the rural areas to the towns and even overseas on a significant scale, labor settled today in an area suitable for agriculture may not be there tomorrow.

At the same time, it is very important to recognize that the argument adduced by both the Tamil United Liberation Front (TULF) and the LTTE that land policy could be, and has been, used as an instrument to change the ethnic character of the population in an area pertains to a matter of very serious nature. The criterion found generally acceptable already that, in the allocation of land, priority should be assigned to landless residents of that particular area, might prove to be useful in this context. General acceptance of the principle that policies which would alter the ethnic character of the population in any particular area would not be followed should help to meet the objections and allay the fears expressed by Tamil leaders on land policy as well as the general concerns among other ethnic groups as regards ethnic cleansing. This would also strongly support the case for vesting the authority for allocating land in committees of multiethnic composition.

It is not possible to ignore or forget the reality that ideas generated in the Sri Lankan context do carry implications, intended or unintended, for the neighboring subcontinent. A radical shift away from the definition of the concept homeland that guided the actions of the LTTE since the 1990s would significantly contribute to speedy progress and the success of the peace process. This is a matter that cannot be overemphasized.

Signals encouraging hopes that such a change may be a possibility came from some developments in 2002. At Pirapaharan's interview with the international press on April 10, 2002, it was announced that the LTTE considered Muslim participation in the peace process to be crucial and that this has to be provided for. Further, the LTTE apologized to the Muslims for its mistakes and stated: "(Report of Commissioners Appointed to Inquire into the Administration of the Buddhist Temporalities) The Tamil homeland belonged (Barber) to the Muslim people and we believe that there is no dispute that Muslims have a right to own land." At this interview the LTTE stopped short of inviting Muslims ejected from the north to come back, stating only that such an invitation would be extended in the future when the conditions are right (Pirapaharan 2002b). At a subsequent meeting between leaders of the LTTE and the Sri Lanka Muslim Congress (SLMC) led respectively by Pirapaharan and Minister Rauf Hakeem, and held at Kilinochchi on April 13, 2002, Pirapaharan invited Muslim refugees displaced from Jaffna and the Vanni to return to their homes. It was further agreed to stop levying imposts so far held to be payable by Muslims in the Eastern Province and to encourage Muslim farmers to cultivate their lands which had fallen into disuse. Pirapaharan further agreed to the inclusion of SLMC representation in the negotiations with the Government (Martinesz 2002). Implementation of these agreements has been fraught with serious problems. Minister Hakeem has since then participated in the negotiations as a member of the Government team, but acceptance of separate representation to the Muslim community has not been resolved so far. It may also be noted that there has been no invitation to the Sinhala people displaced from Jaffna to return. It is hoped that the positive changes that were implicit in the LTTE statements cited earlier would gather greater strength and momentum in the period ahead leading ultimately to a clearly expressed policy stance that *all* displaced families would be welcome to return to the Northern and Eastern Provinces and that the area would not be reserved for any particular ethnic group(s). The earlier such a policy develops to the level of implementation the clearer would it demonstrate not only to the Muslim population but also to the entire country and the world that most encouraging and positive changes are actually taking place as regards the policy stances of the LTTE.

Self-determination: Eelam and separatism

The ideology of separatism and violence has been strongly entrenched in the entire LTTE movement and is among the foremost factors behind the unabated continuation of the conflict. Neither of the two major political parties in Government and Opposition would be in a position to seriously consider partition as a viable option in a democratic political setting. World opinion as expressed through such international fora as the UN has clearly moved to a position discouraging fissiparous trends that would lead to the disintegration of existing states. Within the South Asian region India has been among the first to take a position strongly supportive of the territorial integrity and sovereignty of Sri Lanka, and now there is general agreement on this issue in the region. In the post-September 11 scenario in which forces against terrorism are gathering strength, a challenging question before the LTTE is in what respects a change in stance has become inevitable and in what respects could its policies and activities continue in their old forms.

The demand for a separate state has turned out to be a double-edged sword. On the one hand, it has helped to focus attention on the gravity and urgency of the search for a political solution to problems of inequities confronting the Tamil people. On the other hand, it has contributed toward complicating this very search for a solution. It is incumbent on the LTTE to carefully reconsider whether the option of secession is viable, and indeed desirable, if the interests of the entire Tamil population within the country, not merely those who live in the North and the East, are taken into account. Actual patterns of demographic distribution have to be taken into consideration before deciding on long-term strategies to solve the ethnic problem. Partition and separation could hardly be considered the way out of the ethnic problems in a situation such as Sri Lanka where *a substantial section of the Tamil population lives outside the merged Northern and Eastern Provinces, in close association with Sinhala people and other ethnic groups*.

It would indeed be tragic if Sri Lankans fail to learn lessons from the immense human suffering that followed partition in the neighboring subcontinent. The creation of the new states of India and Pakistan let loose forces on the stage of history which neither the imperial administrators of that time nor the subcontinents leaders had envisaged or could control. Families were thrown out of houses they had occupied for generations. They were reduced to the status of refugees and compelled to move into territory within the boundaries of the other new state. It is now estimated that about 12 million people crossed the borders between India and Pakistan. Of these, about 2,800,000 crossed borders by train within the first month. Some of the refugees used sea and air transport, but the vast majority, the poor, traveled on foot in unwieldy, mass groupings, known as *kafilas*, each numbering up to 40,000 individuals. Suffering from lack of food and afflicted by disease, these masses of humanity on the move were often attacked by fanatical mobs. Women and children suffered the most, and the number of women abducted during the partition is estimated to be as high as 100,000 (Butalis 1998). The tragic episodes experienced in Sri Lanka, cited previously, would pale in significance, if a mega-scale tragedy of similar type were to be enacted in the island. The first priority should be to avoid such a tragedy.

For a very long period the LTTE has been citing secession and the formation of a separate state as its main objectives. This thinking has been linked with the positions adopted by the TULF in the 1970s and associated with the concept of self-determination in Marxist thought on the nation and the state. In the explanations put forward by the LTTE there has been a tendency to steer away from the variant possibilities open in the exercise of the right of self-determination and to focus prominently on the right to secede which it has sought to enforce through armed struggle. Against this background some of the statements made at its international press conference at Kilinochchi, held on April 10, 2002, deserve special emphasis. This is the reference made to the concept of internal self-determination. Though the concept of internal self-determination is not entirely new, especially to students of UN documentation, the passage where it was mentioned merits quoting in full:

> By self-determination we mean the right of our people to decide their own political destiny. It can also mean / apply to autonomy and self-government. If *autonomy and self-government* is given to our people, then we can say that the *internal self-determination is to some extent met.* But if the Sri Lankan government rejects our demands for autonomy and self-government and continues with repression, then *as a last resort* we could opt for cessation [secession?]. That also comes under self-determination. *So self-determination entails autonomy and self-government. In an extreme case, in the last resort, it means cessation [secession?]. Therefore, we say, if the Sri Lankan government offers the Tamil people the form of self-government and autonomy in recognition of our nationality and also the right to self-determination then we will recognize that offer. But if the government refuses to give us proper autonomy, proper self-government and continues with this repression, then we have no other alternative but to fight for political independence and statehood.* This is our perspective.
>
> (Pirapaharan 2002b, emphasis added)

This statement made at one of the largest international press conferences held in Sri Lanka or elsewhere amounts to a declaration to the world public of the LTTE stance on a number of issues relevant to the peace process. The LTTE made a clear effort to emphasize that it was committed to peace. It is particularly noteworthy that the statements at the press conference seem to mark a shift toward greater flexibility in comparison with the rather rigid positions previously adopted by the LTTE. Presumably for the first time in a public statement made by the LTTE in its history, it cites the concept of *internal* self-determination as one of the definitions of what it understands by self-determination. Obviously, this is highly significant. This and the specific mention of self-government and autonomy as constituting an acceptable offer are crucial elements in the statement. Secession is presented here as the extreme case and the last resort. The statement also carries the message that it is in the eventuality of an offer of self-government and autonomy *not* being made that the LTTE would continue its *fight for political independence and statehood*. Developments implicit in these statements augur well for the long negotiations ahead.

While it is essential to focus upon and take note of positive aspects of the LTTE statements, we may be guilty of inattention and in fact fail to obtain a balanced understanding if we do not focus upon less positive, and in effect negative, aspects and also pay attention to what is missing in the statements. It is to be noted that there is no clear renunciation of terrorism or the violent path. Secession, the last resort, is pushed into the background, but it is not renounced and remains in the background very much a possible alternative. The statements made at the press conference to the effect that the Prime Minister of Sri Lanka was not Prime Minister in the LTTE territory where Pirapaharan is both President and Prime Minister, highlights some of the underlying problems that may eventually come to the fore (Pirapaharan 2002a). There have also been several reports of the LTTE ferrying arms into territory it controls after the MOU was signed in February 2002. The US Government, too, noted in its statement of March 11, 2002, that there have been credible reports of LTTE resupply operations since the ceasefire (US Government 2002). Such operations have led to hostilities at sea between the Sri Lankan navy and LTTE vessels. The continuation of resupply operations reflect a situation falling short of full commitment to the peaceful path and has had an adverse effect on public confidence in the peace process.

The above comments do not seek to underestimate the problems confronting the conversion of a terrorist organization from the military to the democratic path. It is not necessary to emphasize that it could be an extremely risky undertaking for the leaders, presuming they are willing and ready to give it priority. It may also be noted that it was at the very same press conference that, while responding to a question on a statement he had allegedly made to the effect he could be shot by his followers if he were to give up the demand for Tamil Eelam, Pirapaharan confirmed the statement by saying: That statement stands (Pirapaharan 2002b). This may be understood either as suggestive of the working of contradictory trends within the LTTE, which would be natural and expected at a juncture such as the present, or more positively as indicating that the working definition of Eelam may be undergoing slow but noteworthy change.

Imagining the state: the unitary and federal models

Matters pertaining to the current Constitution and its inadequacies would be among the core issues in the resolution of the ethnic conflict. A problem which will certainly demand close attention from the experts who will sit down to frame a new Constitution for Sri Lanka will be the relevance of the *unitary* and the *federal* models. Questions have been already raised whether even the present Constitution can be accurately described as a unitary Constitution. Some of the earliest discussions on the characteristics of a future Constitution suitable for Sri Lanka had raised the relevance of a federal model. During the past eight decades several perceptive minds recognized the problems involved in working for national unity and equity in Sri Lanka within the confines of a unitary constitutional framework. Thinking of constitutional provisions suited to the specific needs of the island, they saw merits in adopting a federal type of arrangement. S.W.R.D. Bandaranaike (1899–1959) was one of the earliest among such thinkers. He wrote a series of six articles (Bandaranaike 1926) revealing his fascination for the federal idea as reflected by his claim that the only satisfactory solution yet discovered was the federal system. At that time he appears to have been highly concerned about, and seeking ways to overcome, problems prevalent at that time arising from disunity among the Low Country Sinhala, Kandyan, and Tamil communities.[9]

It is virtually forgotten today that some of the ardent federalists of the 1920s came from the central regions around Kandy.[10] Two years after its formation in 1925, the Kandyan National Assembly demanded regional autonomy for the Kandyans and proposed that a federal constitution be adopted for the island with the territories occupied by the Kandyans, the Low Country Sinhala, and the Tamils forming three federal units and a central Government uniting all these. The federal demand was voiced prominently in its meetings, including one significantly staged at the Daḷadā Māligāva.[11] This was a time when such leaders of the Kandyans as A.F. Molamure, later to be the Speaker of the national legislature, spoke of the Kandyan race and the need for separate representation in the legislature for this group (De Silva 1973, 1986). Even though some British administrators were encouraging in their attitudes toward Kandyan demands, since 1833 the colonial administration emphasized centralization and the colonial state was based on the unitary model. The Donoughmore and the Soulsbury Commissioners were not enthusiastic about incorporating the Kandyan federalist demands.

Federalist enthusiasm was on the wane among the Kandyans when the concept was taken up and revived by the Tamil leader S.J.V. Chelvanayakam (1898–1977), a dedicated campaigner who in 1949 founded the Federal Party, known among the Tamil population by a variant name as the *Tamil Arasu Katchi* or The Tamil State Party. The new Party mobilized and catered to the needs of Tamil ethnonationalism and was to acquire a popular mass base dominating the North and influential to a lesser extent in the Eastern Province. The response that these developments elicited among the Sinhala leadership was one of critique, often tainted with antipathy. The fundamental weakness of this response was the failure to moderate the critique with an understanding of the factors at work behind Tamil ethnonationalism and, more importantly, a mellowness springing from sympathy for inequities weighing on the Tamil masses. With the adoption in 1972 of a new Constitution which firmly entrenched the unitary model, a decisive turn was made, and the door brusquely closed without adequate and due regard to the significance of a strand of Sri Lankan political thinking, including that of Bandaranaike, which had urged consideration of a different model of state.

Perhaps what is needed today is not mere unitarism or federalism of the inflexible ideologue, but the wisdom and the strength of will to decide on the elements necessary to meet the requirements of a specific historical and political context. This would involve not just borrowing from and combining elements from both models, but also transcending the constraints imposed by each model. Further, the task cannot be accomplished by the simple restoration of a historical model from the past or elsewhere in the world; hence, our use of the term reinvention. Given the present position so close to the brink of partition, the preservation of the territorial integrity of the island would be possible only if success is achieved in such reinventing of a state to represent *all* peoples of Sri Lanka and to accommodate their aspirations.

The arduous and complex tasks involved in developing a new model of state are not likely to be accomplished or completed at the negotiating table. The tasks demand the attention of the widest possible spectrum of the national political leadership and civil society as is feasible in practice. Here it is important to keep in mind that there is also the need to shift focus beyond the two main ethnic groups and their demands. The present situation is best utilized for a deliberate attempt to also provide for the fullest safeguards and security for the interests of other ethnic groups such as Muslims, Up-Country Tamils, Burghers, Malays, and the Väddā people. Denied adequate numerical strength to attract national political attention in a manner their grievances merit, some of the smaller among these communities are placed at a serious disadvantage. The Väddā community, whose culture and identity are threatened with extinction in the context of the gradual but drastic changes affecting their ecological niches, provides a good example of this situation.

Obstacles confronting the peace process and the way forward

There has been a good deal of discussion on obstacles to peace obviating the need for a detailed analysis in this paper. In his very informative and interesting contribution Eric Meyer (1990) drew attention to the role of images of the past in modern Sri Lanka. The production of competing representations of the past, heavily influenced by currents of ethnonationalism, grew along paths parallel to the intensifying ethnic conflict (Dharmadasa 1979, 1992; Gunawardana 1985, 1995; Veluppillai 1981) and tends to color the approaches of contemporary actors.

A survey of obstacles to the peace process has to necessarily focus on what may be called stakeholders and vested interests, including particularly the purveyors of war material and supplies, but not be limited to them. Elements among the armed cadre on both sides could be potential sources of obstruction unless the peace process is accompanied by programs for retraining armed cadre for the civil sector, actual provision of alternative employment and housing, and care for those physically disabled by the war. Only under such conditions would they be in a position to clearly perceive the peace process as a benefit and gain.

The Tamil Diaspora is widely dispersed internationally and with noteworthy concentrations in India, Europe, and North America, and it has functioned as a political barometer responsive to the fluctuations of the intensity of the ethnic conflict in Sri Lanka. The Diaspora also served to direct the attention of the governments of the host countries to the need to resolve the conflict, and has been, in that context, a contributory factor toward peace. In addition to the obvious humanitarian considerations, interests in repatriation may have been among the motivating factors behind this interest shown by the host countries. Presumed fears of links with repatriation carry the potentiality of turning large numbers among the Diaspora, especially those still awaiting citizenship in their host countries, to opposing and obstructing the peace process either directly or indirectly. The issue needs to be handled deftly with understanding and great care. Priority has to be assigned to the massive effort needed in reconstruction in the areas destroyed by the war, to the provision of basic housing, schools, transport, and medical facilities, to employment opportunities before repatriation can be even considered. While the emphasis placed in many analyses on the links between economic interests and emigration may be largely accurate, the role of concern for human rights and democratic ideals cannot be ignored. Thus the areas affected by the war have to be rehabilitated economically as well as politically, and respect for democracy and human rights assured for repatriation to be a reality.

In his well-documented and detailed study of the modern Sri Lankan *saṅgha*, H.L. Seneviratne (1999) highlights the close links maintained by members of the Buddhist clergy with ultranationalism. Seneviratne also focuses on what he calls their narrow Sinhala-Buddhist exclusivist ideology and the role they played in opposing the Devolution Package presented by the Kumaratunga Government. Some of Seneviratne's observations are acutely noteworthy, and the opposition of some organizations of the *saṅgha* to rapprochement on the ethnic issue between leaders of the Sinhala and Tamil communities goes back to the time of Prime Minister S.W.R.D. Bandaranaike. Some monks figured among the accused in the Bandaranaike assassination case.

It would be at the same time necessary to note that Seneviratne does not pay adequate attention to complex and divergent trends currently found among the *saṅgha* on the ethnic issue. His study also tends to ignore the continuous changes that are taking place within the *saṅgha*. As is well known, there are many instances from the life of the Buddha himself as well as from the history of the Buddhist *saṅgha* in Sri Lanka of Buddhist religieux being active in times of war in the quest for peace.[12] There is evidence that some members of the *saṅgha* have recognized the relevance of this model for contemporary times and have indeed been actively involved in the peace movement. Such prominent personalities as Professor Kumburugamuvē Vajira of the Vidyālaṅkāra Pirivena and Professor Varakāve Dhammāloka of the Asgiriya fraternity are notable representatives and spokespersons of this trend. They have continuously publicized their sober views in the national media. Dhammāloka is currently occupying a senior position of high responsibility as Secretary of the Council of the Asgiriya Chapter, one of the most influential organizations of the *saṅgha*. Baddēgama Samita, another leading figure in the movement, was elected a member of the Parliament during the elections of December 2001. Samita is the first Buddhist monk to sit in Parliament, and he has utilized his new forum to voice his strong stance in favor of peace. Some of the leaders of the movement have been keen to work in collaboration with leading elements from other religious groupings favorable to peace, and as part of their joint work proceeded to the Tamil settlements in the North to promote peace and inter-ethnic harmony. It is particularly noteworthy that, since the beginning of the current peace initiative, even though some monks have been vociferous in their opposition, there has been no such response from the four Nikāyas that constitute the major groupings among the *saṅgha*. In fact, the leading monks of the Asgiriya Chapter and Rāmañña Nikāya have extended their support to some of the activities associated with the peace initiative, and have been advocates of restraint, desisting so far from publicly voicing any concerns or criticisms they may have on the peace process. These positive developments are yet fluid, tentative, and need time and encouragement to mature as in fact some leaders in the Government appear to have grasped.

A highly vocal section within the political spectrum takes stances opposed to the peace process for ideological and tactical reasons. Rivalries among the established larger political parties in Sri Lanka have generally posed the more formidable obstacle preventing cooperation in seeking solutions to the ethnic problem. Even agreement on basic issues has not necessarily led to voting or working together. The search for means for minimizing inter-Party rivalries and for encouraging collaboration on matters of primary national importance has prompted attempts at considering a return to the past. In the Donoughmore Constitution of 1931 members in the legislature were divided into Executive Committees, each vested with authority over policies pertaining to a distinct field, and the leader of each Committee elected by its members came to be appointed Minister. It has been argued that a similar Committee system could help to moderate inter-Party antagonism and facilitate collaboration than is possible at present. However, it cannot be forgotten it was the Executive Committee system of the Donoughmore Constitution that produced the Pan-Sinhala Board of Ministers from which all representatives of the minorities had been carefully and deliberately excluded.

Even without such constitutional change, possibilities of cooperation do exist. The idiosyncratic arrangements in the current Sri Lankan Constitution, somewhat reminiscent of the French model, have made it possible for the two leaders representing the two major rival political groupings in the country to be members of the same Cabinet, as President and Prime Minister. On the one hand, this could be a situation attendant with alarming possibilities of aggravating rivalry with calamitous implications for the peace process. On the other hand, the same situation could also be viewed more positively as one that places before the two leaders of rival political parties an opportunity never open before in such manner to work in close cooperation. It is hoped that this opportunity will be seized upon and utilized imaginatively so that joint guidance could be given to the peace process in order to ensure its success. Treading the difficult path to peace successfully demands an unprecedented spirit of cooperation in the political arena bringing together erstwhile adversaries in a united effort.

This is particularly so in the context of the current crisis affecting the peace process. The sea to the North East of Sri Lanka witnessed some of the events contributory to the current crisis. These included several attempts at smuggling arms for the LTTE and the sinking by the Sri Lankan Navy of one such ship suspected of smuggling arms. Attacks launched by the LTTE on a Sri Lanka Navy vessel, and allegedly also on a Chinese fishing trawler, intensified the tension (Athas 2003). There have been initiatives to improve relations between the LTTE and the Muslim community, and the LTTE has replaced some of their cadres whose behavior and statements had been offensive to the Muslims. However, relations have at times turned quite violent as in the case of the clashes in the Muttur area in mid-April, 2003. Abductions, including those of children, and political assassinations continued, contrary to the undertakings given to the international community and in the MOU. Throughout the period since the signing of the MOU there have been violations of this agreement, the overwhelming majority of those, 502 out of 556, being by the LTTE (Torkelsson 2003).

Sri Lankans who had placed hopes and expectations in the peace process received a seriously unsettling surprise with the communication from the LTTE received by Prime Minister Wickremasinghe on April 21, 2003 indicating that the LTTE had decided to suspend its participation in the negotiations for the time being while stating at the same time that it wished to reiterate its commitment to seek a negotiated political solution to the ethnic question (Balasingham 2003). Cited in connection with this decision were complaints about the strategies proposed by the Government for the rehabilitation and strengthening of the economy affected by the long war, the slow pace of the resettlement of internally displaced persons, and, more immediately, the exclusion of the LTTE from the Washington donor conference held on April 14, 2003. The last-mentioned matter directs attention in dramatic manner to the acute need to focus sharply on many attendant nuances before taking every single step in the peace process. An oft-repeated grievance of the LTTE relates to the High Security Zones (HSZ) established by the armed forces in the Jaffna District. Extensive allotments of land in these zones have been either occupied by the armed forces or reserved for security reasons. Since the HSZ scheme does hamper resettlement of displaced civilians the problem deserves very serious attention. The difficulties in the resolution of the problem stem from the fact that it is tied up with the implications any changes in the HSZ scheme would have on the relative balance of armed strength of GoSL and the LTTE. While access to land and property for the displaced persons is a genuine and serious problem, it is not difficult to see that the emphasis placed on it by the LTTE is also determined by the strategic objective of tilting the military balance in its favor. The way out from the present situation probably lies in mutually agreed and balanced reduction of military forces in the North by both parties. In this connection it is welcome that the Northern Commander of Government forces was reported recently as considering easing restrictions to allow civilians to settle within areas demarcated for HSZ (ColomboPage 2004). Unmentioned in the LTTE missive of April 21, nevertheless most significant, was another development which had taken place slightly earlier, that is, the proposal forwarded by the Sri Lanka Monitoring Mission (SLMM), after a meeting with the LTTE leadership, that the sea-going vessels of the LTTE should be recognized by the Government as constituting a distinct naval unit, and that a demarcated area should be reserved for its live-firing exercises (SLMM 20031a,b). The proposal, which was later abandoned, again raised doubts about the commitment of the LTTE to the peaceful path. It would have in effect provided for two navies within the territorial waters of Sri Lanka or, in other words, a noteworthy step in the direction of independent statehood for the LTTE.

Another precondition for resuming talks was the demand forwarded in May 2003 that an interim administration should be established in the North East (ColomboPage 2003), the implementation of which faces such serious hurdles within the constraints of the present Constitution. The Government submitted its proposals regarding an "Apex Body on North East Development" in May 2003, which the LTTE was quick to reject (Apex Body 2003; ColomboPage 2003). The LTTE also decided to refrain from participating in the "Aid Lanka" meeting held in June 2003 in Tokyo where donors pledged US $4.5 billion, albeit with the condition that the release of funds would be tied to progress in the peace process in strict conformity with conditions they laid down (Tokyo Declaration 2003). The withdrawal from negotiations by the LTTE has been seen by quite a few observers as a means of increasing pressure to gain their demands. On October 31, 2003 the LTTE responded with its ISGA proposal for the establishment of an interim self-governing authority (ISGA 2003). The proposal has been the subject of intense national debate (Sarvananthan 2003), and some commentators have suggested that it is the LTTE's long-range objective of independent statehood that resurfaces in this proposal. Richard Armitage, the Deputy Secretary of State of the United States, has observed that the ISGA proposal "does go outside the bounds of Oslo and that envisioned in Oslo and Tokyo, where we talked about a federation, a democratic society, respect for human rights and the territorial integrity of the entire island" (Armitage 2003). Following quickly on the heels of this development was the takeover by President Kumaratunga of three ministries, including the Ministry of Defense. While the motivation behind the move is bound to be complex, it may be understood also as a response to the long-drawn debate on the inadequacy of attention paid to crucial issues relating to national security.[13] Despite the resultant strains on relations between them, there is clearly a remarkable confluence in the approaches of the President and the Prime Minister on the need to continue the present peace process and to retain the role of Norway as facilitator. Even on the vexed question of the ISGA proposals, there is surprisingly little divergence between their approaches.

While the withdrawal of the LTTE from the talks and its intransigence in refusing to comply with rulings given by the SLMM, thereby in effect violating the MOU, are most regrettable, it has to be admitted at the same time that, in order to evoke a more committed involvement in the peace process, the GoSL has to take adequate steps to convince the LTTE that the agreements ensuing from the process of negotiations have a good chance of being accepted by a requisite two-thirds majority in Parliament and by the electorate at a referendum. The LTTE has, as we noted earlier, indicated in unmistakable manner at its first international press conference at Kilinochchi that it was not convinced that the Prime Minister with the Parliamentary group under his leadership would be able to implement agreements arrived during the current process of negotiations.

Overcoming the current impasse and facing the tortuous path lying ahead call for modifications and even radical changes of approach from the entire political leadership in the country. Recognition of the implications for India of the developments relating to the ethnic problem in the island would serve to emphasize the importance of active Indian participation in the peace process. The neighboring power has a major responsibility in ensuring the success of the peace process. This would necessarily mean that the leading circle of international partners which currently includes Norway, Japan, the United States, and the United Kingdom will have to be revised to provide for gaining Indian participation in due manner. It is essential that both the Government and the Government-in-waiting assign to the peace process the highest priority, above every other political task. It is also absolutely essential that they both realize that a solution to the ethnic problem can be achieved only if both groups work in unison and that a go-it-alone approach is bound to end in disaster. The prime need of the times is for an innovative political strategy that ensures selective collaboration on the building of peace in the midst of the inevitable and ongoing scramble for power and bitter debate on all other issues. Working toward such a policy would call for sharing credit, prestige, and at times even power, treating the other party with utmost cordiality, frankness, and openness, and certainly eschewing attempts to present the potential partner as the enemy of peace.

Ideally, the President and the Prime Minister should both play key active roles in the direction of the process of negotiations while all political parties and leading elements in civil society supportive of a negotiated solution to the conflict should be represented in a wider consultative grouping. Such an arrangement would be most helpful in the long run when the results of the negotiations are placed before the legislature and the electorate for ratification, since there would be a widely representative, multi-partisan leadership to be drawn upon to canvass in support. While it may be possible to argue that the pursuance of a policy of selective collaboration would strengthen the negotiating position of the state *vis-à-vis* the LTTE, the most valuable aspect would be its role in strengthening confidence in the peace process among the LTTE leadership as well as the wider masses in the entire country. In a context where the LTTE has more than hinted that the absence of the executive authority at the negotiating table is a disadvantage, and the Sri Lanka Freedom Party (SLFP) has, on the other hand, indicated that President Kumaratunga is willing to play a pivotal role in the peace process,[14] curiously enough, this opportunity, which should have been seized upon, has been largely ignored. There has been much emphasis recently on the agreement between the SLFP and the Janatha Vimukti Peramuṇa (JVP) to establish an alliance as a factor that could compromise the SLFP positions on the peace process. The dissonance between SLFP and JVP positions on solutions to the ethic problem, openly admitted in their Memorandum of Understanding (MOU 2004), does encourage such speculation. However, it is essential to note that the SLFP has not diverged from its commitment to a negotiated solution through devolution of power. It would also be prudent to understand the current JVP stances within the wider context of its more accommodative policy declarations on the ethnic problem made in the past as well as the persistent indications by some of its present leaders of their readiness to be flexible.

Notes

1 Address before the Oxford Union, October 29, 2001.

2 Following this, as reported in some local newspapers, some prominent LTTE leaders did begin announcing that they were ready "to give up and opt for self-rule within the Tamil homeland" (Divayina 2002).

3 See De Silva (1973: 399) on the withdrawal of Ponnambalam Arunachalam from the Ceylon National Congress.

4 See, for instance, the comments of A.J. Wilson (1974: 13).

5 This was the number that voted for the Ceylon Indian Congress (CIC). It was also widely recognized that the Indian estate labor votes had the effect of changing the balance in constituencies not contested by the CIC, generally in favor of the Left-oriented contestants and political parties. See Table 4.1 in Wilson (1974).

6 I prefer to use the term *diversity* with its emphasis on the quality of being different rather than *pluralism* with its emphasis on numbers and its associations with long theological debates against monism.

7 Two series of articles were published in the *Silumina* and *The Sunday Observer*, Colombo, in October–November 1996.

8 Exact figures about this group of displaced people are not available. A figure of about 60,000 has been suggested. See *Sunday Times*, Colombo, April 21, 2002.

9 Bandaranaike's six articles (1926: 6–7) focused mostly on what he termed external federation.

10 As far as I am aware, Lakshman Kiriella has been one of the few politicians who have sought to highlight this aspect of Kandyan politics in the pre-Independence era. For a transcript of his address before the Toastmasters Club of Sri Lanka delivered in September 1997, see *Daily News*, April 29, 2002.

11 *The Ceylon Independent*, November 17, 1927, p. 1. The demands of the Kandyan National Assembly were published in a booklet titled *Rights and Claims of the*

Kandyan People from which the newspaper quoted this relevant section. These demands were also mentioned at the second annual sessions of the Kandyan National Assembly held at the Daḷadā Māligāva in Kandy reported in *The Ceylon Independent*, January 31, 1927, pp. 1, 7, and 8. See also comments by De Silva (1973).

12 Thilak Marapana, the Minister of Defense before the takeover, admitted in Parliament that the LTTE strength had "nearly doubled since the ceasefire" (Marapana 2003).

13 Some of the instances of the intervention of the *saṅgha* to restore peace and amity recorded in the *Cūlavaṃsa* are from the reigns of Sēna II, Kassapa IV, Udaya III, and Parākramabāhu I. The role of the *saṅgha* in these instances included intervention to settle clashes between the king and rebels as well as conflicts among local kingdoms and war between the Sri Lankan and Myanmar kingdoms.

14 A report on the statement issued by the SLFP appeared in *The Sunday Times* of May 5, 2002.

12

BUDDHIST MONKS AND PEACE IN SRI LANKA

Chandra R. de Silva

In exploring the categories of conflict, identity and difference in the context of peace negotiations in Sri Lanka and against the background of the enhanced concern for global security in the wake of the incidents of 11 September 2001, we need to keep three fairly obvious considerations in mind. First, problems of violence and peace are, in some senses, perennial problems. Second, as postmodernists have correctly emphasized, the analyses we offer are not only context specific but emerge from, and are embedded in, our own respective social and cultural heritages. Finally, the solutions or palliatives we offer must be recognized as ephemeral because the social structures, identities and cleavages on which they are based are themselves constantly changing. As John Gray pointed out in relation to politics:

> No settlement is final, and only the provisional is permanent; so the legal framework in which any particular political settlement finds embodiment will be subject to recurrent revision, and eventual breakdown.
>
> (1995: 128)

Let me begin with the concept of difference. If one analyses this concept as a theoretical construct, it soon becomes evident that it is based on the assumption of the existence of categories that are defined as self-evident: Sinhala Buddhist, Sinhala Christian, Muslim, Hindu Tamil and so on. But we know that concepts of identity are fluid, multiple and contested. For instance, there were contentious debates in the 1980s as to whether the Jayewardene government (1977–1989) was 'Buddhist' and whether the monks who supported the opposition Janatha Vimukti Peramuṇa (JVP) were good monks or 'criminals' (Abeysekara 2002). It is therefore clear that we begin not with a single monolithic group of Sinhalas or even one group of Sinhala Buddhists or one unit of Buddhist monks but multiple groups in very different positions in the social and political hierarchy engaged in spirited contestations and sometimes slightly shifting positions to gain political or moral advantage (Abeysekara 2002; De Silva 1998).

This does not mean that we are debarred from using categories. Indeed, many of us use categories on a routine basis in the academic world and political and social leaders have shown us that such categories – ethnic and religious – can be effective mechanisms as individual leaders or groups use such concepts sometimes called 'strategic essentialisms' to make their way up the hierarchy (Briggs 1996). What I wish to emphasize is merely the malleability of the categories we use.

In the rest of this chapter I will try to examine how heritage, hierarchy, organization and educational background as well as changing perceptions about others, create and transform ideologies of difference. Due to constraints of space, I will confine my analyses to one group – the *saṅgha* or order of Buddhist monks. However, much of what I argue can be applied to a greater or lesser degree to all kinds of ethnic and social groups.

In much of the recent literature on contemporary Sri Lanka, including some of my own writings, there have been some critical remarks on the attitudes of many Buddhist monks in relation to the civil conflict in Sri Lanka (Bartholomeusz and De Silva 1998; Seneviratne 1999; Tambiah 1992). The emphasis in this chapter is different. I start with the assumption that in order to promote rational discourse we need to look at why people think the way they do or at least what promotes them to articulate the views they express. If this is true, examining how people get their ideas and ideals and what factors reinforce or modify them is not merely an academic exercise but a crucial part of the peace process itself.

I will begin with the concept of a unitary Sri Lanka. This is a policy that is often cited as one that most Buddhist monks (and indeed, most contemporary Sinhalas) support and it is viewed as a major obstacle to a political settlement with Tamil leaders. I will argue that there is much in the tradition and history of the *saṅgha* that inclines them to value unity (Sin. *eksatkama*) but that the equation of unity and a unitary state (Sin. *ēkīya rājya*) is a more recent phenomenon. I also argue that there is some leeway to affect opinion if we make distinctions between a single state in Sri Lanka and a unitary state in Sri Lanka.

Ideally, each Buddhist monk is a truth-seeker on an individual journey. Buddhist texts consistently urge individuals to deal with others as individuals deserving equal treatment, not as parts of religious or social collectivities. This ideal is not always achieved. For instance, contemporary Buddhist monks are known to have looked down on 'low-caste' drummers (Reed 2002) but the ideal is constantly reiterated. On the other hand, there is also the concept of the *saṅgha* as a single indivisible organization. There are canonical injunctions against causing a schism among *bhikkhu*s. Ideas on unity are underwritten by the Pāli Canon, particularly in the images of the ancient Buddhist community of the Lichchavis, who were known for a unified stance that had positive political consequences. This religious tradition is reinforced by perceptions of history. The Sinhala Buddhist chronicle, the *Mahāvaṃsa* extols Buddhist rulers who unified the *saṅgha* and enforced the decisions of ecclesiastical tribunals. Thus, appeals for unity (Sin. *eksatkama*) have great resonance with Buddhist monks. Notwithstanding the ideal of the monk as an individual sojourner on a quest for liberation, the ideal of unity creates suspicion regarding policies that are perceived as producing division and discord, both among the *saṅgha* and in the political system. The aversion to discord is heightened by a perception that 'disunity' or the 'disconnect' between the *saṅgha* and the people of Lanka was something that was deliberately fostered in colonial times. When we combine this with the acceptance by most Sinhala Buddhists that one of the roles of the Buddhist monk is to defend the Sinhala-Buddhist heritage (Bartholomeusz 2002) we can see why many Buddhist monks are cautious about plans for political devolution.

This caution (and fear) springs not only from history and tradition but also from lived experience. Whatever the perceptions of outsiders, monks often see themselves as very loosely organized, weak and prone to disunity. The number of Buddhist monks in Sri Lanka is relatively small, around 37,000, and organizationally they are divided into three major monastic orders: *Siyam Nikāya, Amarapura Nikāya* and *Rāmañña Nikāya*. Overall, the *Siyam Nikāya* has over 18,000 monks or about half of the Buddhist monks in Sri Lanka and has close ties with the *goyigama* (farmer) caste to which the majority of Sinhalas belong. The *Siyam Nikāya* has 2 major units (Malvatta and Asgiriya) and 5 others that are aligned to one or other of the major units. There are no major doctrinal divisions within the *Siyam Nikāya* and, on the whole, the leadership of the *Mahānāyaka*s (chief patriarchs) of Malvatta and Asgiriya is rarely challenged.

The second major order, the *Amarapura Nikāya* has about 12,000 monks. Founded in 1802 by Ambagahapiṭiyē Ñānavimlatissa as an effort to open the *saṅgha* to more individuals outside the *goyigama* caste, the fraternity grew swiftly, but later split into many divisions due to geography, caste identity and other disputes. The push for unity was perhaps strongest in this fraternity because in the 1940s, the *Amarapura Nikāya* comprised over thirty separate branches, each with its own *mahānāyaka*. An effort to unite these subgroups succeeded in 1969 and today the *Amarapura Nikāya* has a unified leadership (Paññāsīha Thera 1990). One of the chief patriarchs of the *Amarapura Nikāya*, Venerable Maḍihē Paññāsīha was a leading figure in the movement for unity.

The smallest of the three major *Nikāya*s is the *Rāmañña*. It is estimated to have between 6,000 and 8,000 monks. However, unlike the other two *Nikāyas*, the *Rāmañña Nikāya* is structurally unitary, with a single *mahānāyaka*, and is organized into regional units. It is particularly strong in the southwest, but has expanded into other regions during the last century. While it has no specific caste affiliations, many of its prominent lay supporters are drawn from the *karāva* (fisherman) caste.

While many of the distinctions between the *Nikāya*s have become muted in the second half of the twentieth century – for instance monks routinely live for periods in temples belonging to other orders other than their own for purposes like education – discomfort about possible dangers to disunity remain. There is extensive support among *bhikkhu*s for state support of religion (De Silva 2001: 186) but one of the major concerns within the *saṅgha* is an effort to avoid division through party politics (De Silva 2001: 191). Thus, the 1993 Constitution of the

Amarapura Nikāya specifically forbids the use of official titles in the organization when participating in political activity (Śrī Laṅkā Amarapura Mahāsaṅghasabhāva 1993: 24).

All of the above would throw some light on why the leadership of the *saṅgha* opposed President Kumaratunga's negotiation with the Liberation Tigers of Tamil Elam (LTTE) in the 1990s and refused to support her proposals for the devolution of power (Nanda Thera 2002). Up to early 2002, the *mahānāyaka*s had argued that there should not be any talks with the LTTE (which they viewed as a terrorist organization) and that the solution to the civil conflict was the eradication of terrorism. By mid 2002, however, the Wickremesinghe government seemed to have succeeded in persuading the *mahānāyaka*s that its negotiations with the LTTE were on the basis of a single country and thenceforth, the *mahānāyaka*s have remained united in support of the peace process (Mahānāyakas 2002). The concept of the unity of Lanka has been separated from that of a unitary state.

Let me now turn to a different consideration. It is not just that tradition and recent experience have provided a basis for a fear by Buddhist monks. One might also argue that change comes slowly in the *saṅgha* because *bhikkhu* organization is such that it encourages the primacy of more conservative elements through emphasis on seniority. It is true that there are some elements of democracy and decentralization within the *Nikāya*s. Temple properties are owned not by the *Nikāya*, but rather by the chief incumbents of temples. In many cases, the chief incumbents of temples choose a close relative as their 'senior' pupil so that pupilary succession ensures that a temple remains within the control of a single extended family. Thus, the chief incumbent of a temple has a great deal of autonomy.

Nevertheless, seniority and respect among peers is a key factor in advancement in the *Nikāya* hierarchies. The *Rāmañña Nikāya* is arguably the most democratic of the *Nikāya*s. It allows a monk with three months residence in an area to have a vote in the *Prādēśīya Saṅgha Sabhā* (Regional Council). However, the President and Vice President of the *Nikāya* have to be *mahāstavira*s or monks with at least ten years of experience after their *upasampadā* (higher) ordination. Traditionally, all other office bearers also come from such senior ranks. Almost half of the central Ruling Council (*Pālaka Saṅgha Sabhāva*) of the *Nikāya* is made up of *ex-officio* members (see article 44, 46, 55, 58 in Śrī Laṅkā Rāmañña Mahānikāya 1989). Thus, while all office bearers, including the *mahānāyaka*s, face elections before appointment, monks are usually socialized into the prevailing structure.

In the case of the *Amarapura Nikāya*, the Ruling Council of 43 is made up of the *mahānāyaka*s and the Secretaries-General of the 21 constituent units plus the Chief Secretary-General of the *Nikāya*. It is this body of senior *bhikkhu*s that elects the Supreme Chief Patriarch (*Uttarītara Mahānāyaka*) who has life tenure. The Executive Committee of 11 *bhikkhu*s that makes most decisions is equally tilted towards senior monks being made up of 6 office bearers and 5 other monks elected by the Ruling Council (Śrī Laṅkā Amarapura Mahāsaṅghasabhāva 1993). The chapters of the *Siyam Nikāya* do not have published constitutions though they have standard operating procedures known to senior monks. These as well as the regulations relating to adjudication of disputes within the *Siyam Nikāya* strengthen the position of senior *bhikkhu*s (Siyam Mahānikāya 1973: 32).

As Tessa Bartholomeusz (1958–2001) and I have explained elsewhere (2001: 17–18), developments in the 1990s led to an enhanced ability of the leaders of the *saṅgha* to work across *Nikāyas*. In 1990 President R. Premadasa formed the Supreme Advisory Council that advises him on all matters related to Buddhism (Buddhasāsana Amātyansaya 1990: 2). All monks in this Council were to be appointed on the recommendations of the four *mahānāyaka*s (of the Asgiriya and Malvatta chapters of the *Siyam Nikāya* and of the *Amarapura* and *Rāmañña Nikāya*s). The Supreme Advisory Council met many times between 1990 and 1997 and these meetings gave the leaders of the *saṅgha* more experience in working together on issues of common interest across *Nikāya* lines. Thus, when the leaders of the *saṅgha* resigned *en masse* in 1997 due to a disagreement with President Kumaratunga, they were able to continue to meet periodically and issue joint declarations on issues of national significance. It is thus more likely today than twenty years ago that despite divisions in the rank and file of the *saṅgha*, the *mahānāyaka*s will speak with one voice on issues that seem important to them.

It might appear that these developments have given rise to a more secure leadership within the Buddhist *saṅgha* but this is not necessarily the case. Social changes in Sri Lanka in the last few generations have contributed to increasing dissident voices within the *bhikkhu* order. Some of the divisions are doctrinal. For example there have been disputes about the ordination of women and the acceptance of Mahāyāna doctrines and practices. More important are social divisions. There are significant rifts between monks who have received university training and through that some exposure to left wing ideas and others who have had a more traditional education. Some temples are richly endowed and others are very poor. For a long time there has been an undercurrent of social criticism that was partly responsible for the involvement of many young monks in the JVP insurgency of the 1980s. There has also been the rapid rise of extra-*Nikāya* organizations. Some of them have an ephemeral existence but are often quite important for short periods.

A good example of the swift emergence of such an organization is the emergence of the *Jathika Saṅgha Sabhāva* (National Saṅgha Council) in 1996. One of the major objectives in creating this organization of monks was the desire to have a national organization of *bhikkhu*s who would become a factor in national policy-making while remaining independent of all political parties. In fact, monks belonging to political parties are specifically excluded from the *Jathika Saṅgha Sabhāva* (National Saṅgha Council (NSC)). The list of office bearers and active leaders of the NSC included some of the most influential monks in the country. Māduḷuvāvē Sōbhita, Itthāpāna Dhammālaṅkāra and Bellanvila Vimalaratana (*Siyam Nikāya*), Brāhmaṇavattē Sīvalī (*Amarapura Nikāya)* and Keppeṭiyavala Sirivimala (*Ramñña Nikāya*) were key members. Dharanãgama Kusaladhamma was the Assistant Secretary and Kithiyavela Pālita worked as

Treasurer. Muruttettuvē Ānanda and Athurāliyē Rathana were organizers for the NSC. The NSC has not only campaigned against the constitutional proposals of the Kumaratunga government (Edirisinghe 1999: 169–87), but it has also involved itself in other issues, such as opposition to the privatization and exploitation of the mineral deposits at Eppāwela.

Six years later when the Wickremasinghe government gained the support of the *mahānāyaka*s for negotiations with the LTTE, and some members of the NSC expressed tacit support for the policy, there arose the *Jathika Saṅgha Sammēlanaya* (National Saṅgha Assembly (NSA)). The NSA is led by a group of active educated monks including Ellāwela Medhānanda (President), Nāgoḍa Amarawansa, Dharanāgama Kusaladhamma, Akurāṭiyē Nanda and Athurāliyē Rathana. It organized a number of public meetings, rituals and processions to galvanize opposition to the de-proscription of the LTTE and the establishment of an interim council dominated by the LTTE to rule the northeast. For instance the NSA organized a public meeting at Colombo on 11 May 2002, a procession and a meeting in Colombo on 2 September of the same year and a motorcade from Kalutara on the coast to Kandy in the highlands with public meetings along the way on 15–19 September 2002 (De Silva 2003).

Thus, despite their new connections, the legitimacy of the traditional leadership and their very identity as 'true Buddhist leaders' is open to being challenged. I will present one example to illustrate this last point. In late April and early May 2002, there was intense debate in Sri Lanka as to whether the proscription of the LTTE should be lifted and indeed, whether the February Memorandum of Understanding between the Sri Lanka Government and the LTTE should be supported by the *saṅgha*. The statements made by LTTE leader Velupillai Pirapaharan (Prabhakaran) at his 11 April press conference convinced the *mahānāyaka*s that the LTTE had not given up the campaign for a separate state and they signed a statement signalling their opposition to the whole peace process and urging that the proscription should remain. However, the Wickremesinghe government (December 2001–March 2004) immediately took action to brief the *mahānāyaka*s on LTTE's readiness to work within a single state, and the statement (prematurely published in one paper) was withdrawn (Pathirana 2002). Subsequently, in June 2002, the *mahānāyaka*s issued a statement from Tokyo, Japan supporting the peace process (De Silva 2002).

It is the sequel to the process that is enlightening. In his criticism of the reversal of the *mahānāyaka*s' decision, Akurāṭiyē Nanda, former Vice-Chancellor of Buddhist and Pali University of Sri Lanka seemed to have linked the change of heart of the *mahānāyaka* of Malvatta to a gift of 53 million rupees given to the Temple of the Tooth and the *Siyam Nikāya* about this time. In a subsequent interview, Ven. Nanda, Co-President of NSA pointed out that even a lay Buddhist observing the eight precepts (let alone a chief monk) was prohibited from accepting gold and silver. The relevant precept means: 'I undertake the precept to refrain from accepting gold or silver.' Ven. Nanda also indicated his revulsion at the practice of *mahānāyaka*s accepting luxury cars bought with state funds, a practice that had prevailed under the previous government. What thus emerged was an open challenge to the 'Buddhist' identity of the traditional leaders of the *saṅgha*. In other words, the current negotiations for peace are being conducted while the legitimacy of leaders is being challenged.

In a previous publication, Tessa Bartholomeusz and I argued that 'we are what we know'; that knowledge defines and forms our identity (Bartholomeusz and De Silva 2001: 20). It is well known that the political culture of a group is fashioned by a variety of influences, including the media, but we also know that much of the information we receive is often processed and analyzed through conceptual frameworks that are developed early in life. Most of the *saṅgha* has been educated with a world view that has not only romanticized a mythical, ideal past (Kemper 1991) but one that has developed a perception of threats (from the Christian West as well as from non-Buddhist minorities, particularly Tamils) which has hardened attitudes against change. Thus, we do need to pay some attention to the organization of the education and training of Buddhist monks in Sri Lanka.

Whatever be the *Nikāya* affiliation of the Buddhist monk, they receive knowledge through a common system supported by the state. It is important to remember that the curriculum in these *pirivena*s was developed in the twentieth century and is somewhat different from the traditional training offered to Buddhist monks in pre-colonial times. The old sixteenth-century curriculum had concentrated on religious texts, languages and grammar but also included medicine, astrology, literature and statecraft (Adhikari 1991: 185–95). Today, most novice monks begin their instruction under a senior ordained monk but after a few years they often attend a state supported *pirivena*. I have discussed the limited nature of the *pirivena* curriculum elsewhere (De Silva 2001). We need to be aware that the contemporary *pirivena* curriculum does not include Science at all and that it excludes 'Social Studies' after the initial five years. There is virtually nothing about Islam or Christianity or about Tamil and Muslim culture or a western language in the curriculum. There are about 25,000 Buddhist monks receiving education through this system. Suffice it to say here that the education that monks receive gives them very limited knowledge about the culture and religious beliefs of the minorities in Sri Lanka.

The facilities afforded to them are among the poorest in the country. The teachers are badly paid and often lack training. This is happening at a time when the Buddhist laity is receiving a somewhat different exposure to modern education and when education in and through English is being fostered by mushrooming 'International Schools' (De Silva 1999: 118). Monks might be forgiven for feeling that they are becoming increasingly marginalized in a changing society.

In view of all that I have said what is indeed remarkable is that a number of *bhikkhu*s have spoken out in terms of their commitment to peace and their readiness to support a negotiated solution to the current civil war (Bartholomeusz and De Silva 2001: 10). Clearly there are other areas that need to be addressed in the peace process (Roberts 2001) and as I emphasized at the outset, the attitudes of the *bhikkhu*s towards the peace process are complex and varied. However, one clear message emerges from this analysis. If the Buddhist monks are to play a key role in sustaining the peace process we certainly need to pay much greater attention to broadening the training of young Buddhist monks. I suggest this not because I am aiming to change their worldview through a broader education but rather to ensure that whatever view they take is based firmly on the best information available. As David Scott argued:

> What we ought to be systematically exploring in Sri Lanka are ways and means of inventing, cultivating and institutionalising cultural–political spaces in which groups ('minorities' as well as the 'majority' – though in my view this entire language of number ought to be put aside as irrelevant) can formulate and articulate their moral–political concerns and their self-governing claims in the (natural and conceptual) languages of their respective historical traditions.
>
> (1999: 185)

In other words, what we need is a framework that enables continuous renegotiation of the claims of historical (ethnic) communities as well as of other economic and social groups. As Scott puts it:

> What this means, in effect, is the establishment of intersecting public spaces – spaces that practice different forms of belonging, in which different self-governing practices can be cultivated in the different languages of identity.
>
> (1999: 189)

Thus what we should be aiming at is not the exclusion or vilification of views we do not agree with, or the total exclusion of religious, historical and cultural concerns from the body politic. We should rather strive to build structures through which constantly changing 'differences' of all kinds might be constantly articulated, defined and mutually comprehended. This is a key task that we need to work on if we are to build on and preserve that elusive peace. This is probably what Ananda Abeysekara was aiming at when he suggested that we might:

> [E]xplore how particular debates can enable plural persons, discourses, and practices, standing within and speaking from their respective positions of secular/religious domains, to authorize themselves to come into central view and battle out questions of what constitutes religious identity, pluralism, and difference.
>
> (2001)

13

THE ROLE OF BUDDHIST MONKS IN RESOLVING THE CONFLICT

Asanga Tilakaratne

Scholars have discussed widely the involvement and the role of the Buddhist monks in the ethnic conflict in Sri Lanka. Most of them believe that the Sinhala-Buddhist ideology held by a large majority of Buddhist monks has been a key factor in the etiology of the Tamil separatist movement operating mainly in the North and East of the island. The most formidable political challenge that Sri Lanka faced in the recent past is the separatist problem and the ensuing violence. The issue of Tamil separatism is also the main test Sri Lankan Buddhism has been facing in the postindependent history of Sri Lanka. Therefore, it is very important, both politically and religiously, to understand rightly the current ethnic problem.

The criticism leveled at the *saṅgha* in connection with Tamil separatism contains two claims: one is that the *saṅgha* has, over time, developed an ideology of Sinhala-Buddhist nationalism in which that particular identity is given prominence over the identities of the minority ethnic groups of the country. The second is the resultant exclusivist attitude and behavior of the *saṅgha* toward the Tamil minority in particular and the other minorities in general. It is further stated, as following from the earlier two claims, that it is due to this attitude that some Tamil factions have decided to create a country of their own within Sri Lanka and that they have taken up arms as a way of realizing their objective. In this chapter, I shall examine two recent publications on the role of monks in Sri Lanka. Then, I will highlight some significant aspects of the *saṅgha*'s role in the conflict and develop some constructive suggestions in achieving a stable solution to the problem.

The Work of Kings

H.L. Seneviratne's *The Work of Kings* (Seneviratne 1999) is a major contribution to the study of the contemporary Sri Lankan *saṅgha*. Seneviratne's work is very much a continuation of S.J. Tambiah's *Buddhism Betrayed?* (1992). Seneviratne's work, however, differs very much from that of Tambiah being much wider in its perspective and much more far-reaching in its criticism. The main task of

Seneviratne's work is to "explore" how Buddhist modernism in Sri Lanka could not usher a civil society characterized by such universal values of tolerance, non-violence, and pluralism. Seneviratne begins his exploration with Anagārika Dharmapāla (1864–1933), the founder of Buddhist modernism, who defined the Buddhist monk's role as "a caretaker of the flock and a social worker" (Seneviratne 1999: 27). The new role attributed by Dharmapāla to the monk had two distinct aspects: (i) economic and pragmatic and (ii) ideological and political. The former was the need to uplift the living standards and the quality of life of the ordinary people in the country. The latter was to revive what Dharmapāla thought to be the ideal Sinhalese-Buddhist culture of ancient Sri Lanka. Of these two tasks, the first was taken up by a group of monks associated with Vidyōdaya Pirivena, one of the two prominent centers of Buddhist learning established in 1873, and the other being Vidyālaṅkāra Pirivena established after two years, the members of which undertook to materialize the second aspect of Dharmapāla's interpretation of the monk's role.

Under the category of those who took to village upliftment and rural development, Seneviratne examines in detail the work of three leading monks, namely, Kaḷukondayāvē Paññāsekhara, Hīnaṭiyana Dhammālōka, and Henḍiyagala Seelaratana. In Seneviratne's assessment, these monks "separated ideological from the pragmatic" and did their best for the course chosen by them although ultimately "they simply had neither the vision nor the qualifications to launch a meaningful activist project" (Seneviratne 1999: 127–28). Seneviratne sums up his conclusions regarding the activism of these monks in the following words:

> But these monks had their heart in the right place. Because they were convinced of the truth and feasibility of Dharmapāla's message, they tried to do what he told them to do to the best of their capacity. They represent a pragmatic nationalism as opposed to a nationalist ideology with built-in propensities for degeneration into narrow ethnic and religious chauvinism. Their education and socialization was traditional as was their "monkness" about which the Vidyālaṅkāra monks made a loud, self-conscious and futile defense, and which for these monks was unnecessary because they had nothing to hide. They did not explicitly talk about their monkness or have to define or defend it because their lifestyle conformed to accepted rules of monkness, and they had no personal or ideological reason to change that lifestyle. They were patriots without being narrow nationalists and they were able to conceptualize in principle a social order in which the economic was primary, with the potential for economic self-interest to triumph over ideology, sided by the inner-worldly asceticism they, after Dharmapāla, were able to fashion.
>
> (1999: 128)

These remarks of Seneviratne anticipate the critique he would develop in discussing the role of Vidyālaṅkāra faction of monks who, in 1940s, undertook to articulate the ideological vision of Dharmapāla which "by the mid 1950s (it) turned into a hegemonic Sinhala Buddhist chauvinism" (1999: 131). The turning point in the Vidyālaṅkāra ideology was Walpola Rahula's *The Heritage of the Bhikkhu* which, according to Seneviratne, is "a work that has influenced the monkhood more than any other in the recent history of Sri Lankan Theravada Buddhism" (1999: 135). The key characteristics of the project proposed by *The Heritage* are: advocating secular education for the monks; discouraging monks from participating in their traditional religious (ritualistic) functions; advocating social service, meaning thereby basically the involvement in politics, as the proper vocation for monks. This way of life was embraced by the monks who accepted the ideology of *The Heritage* and the result was the emergence of a monastic middle class with money and power who paid only a "lip service" (1999: 334) to proper Buddhist monastic ideals. "These new monks," Seneviratne says:

> [N]ever intended any such [social service] in the fist place. What they meant by social service was a license for them to have greater involvement with secular society beginning with politics.
>
> (1999: 338)

The general appearance of this genre of monks is something like the following:

> [G]oing overseas and establishing themselves in foreign lands, facilitated by both philanthropists of those lands and by expatriate communities of Buddhists. A few of these monks control vast revenues and live the life of busy executives, replete with symbols like Mercedes Benzes, BMWs, and cellular phones. These monks have a foothold both in the country of their adoption and in Sri Lanka, and some hold immigrant status in several countries. At the lower end of this financially comfortable class are the salary-earning monks, mostly graduates, who, especially if they also have support from the laity as well as productive land, are able to invest money in businesses like repair shops, taxi services, rental properties and tuition classes. A small minority also commercially practice astrology, medicine, and various occultisms, the "beastly arts" that are taboo for monks. Throughout history there were monks who practiced these, but now they do so with a new sense of legitimacy and commercialism. These come from the new definition of monk's role as social service.
>
> (1999: 336)

"Stated differently," the author says,

> [T]he Vidyālaṅkāra idea that the monk's vocation is social service has been revolutionary in that it has provided the monks with an excuse to seek profit and other secular goals and satisfaction in an unprecedented

> manner. It has opened the flood gates and given rise to a new monkhood that many thoughtful members of the culture view with alarm.
>
> (1999: 195)

The most serious defect in Rahula's new definition of the monk's role is that it replaces the ascetic ideal, which is the source of the sense of morality in the monkhood with social service that does not have any such inner obligation. Seneviratne says:

> The true and clear commitment of the monk is the other-worldly goal, and when that is taken away, the monkhood is freed of its basis and monks can engage in any activity... But when the floodgates are open, as when knowledge is elevated over practice, there is no inner way to control the activities of monks, whereas such control is the essence of the renouncer's commitment.
>
> (1999: 172)

> in *The Heritage* and in *The History [of Buddhism in Ceylon]* it suits Rahula to be an advocate of a Buddhism that glorifies social intercourse with lay society...the receipt of salaries and other forms of material remuneration; ethnic exclusivism and Sinhala Buddhist hegemony; militancy in politics; and violence, war and the spilling of blood in the name of "preserving the religion."
>
> (1999: 186)

In this connection, Seneviratne discusses several specimens of "social service" as performed by some of the leading monks representing this field (see his paper on: Social Service: The Anatomy of a Vacation). The main thrust of Seneviratne's argument is that there has not developed, nor is there any room for development of a civil society characterizing such virtues as tolerance, pluralism, universalism in the contemporary Buddhist monastic tradition, and hence the exclusivist, hegemonic Sinhala-Buddhist nationalism which does not allow anyone other than Sinhala and Buddhist to be the legitimate inhabitants of the island. The reason for this unsatisfactory state of affairs is the mistaken or skewed adoption by Vidyālaṅkāra monks headed by Rahula (and Yakkaḍuvē Paññārāma) of Dharmapāla's definition of the role of the Buddhist monk as socially active caretaker of the flock.

This brief sketch is never meant to be a comprehensive summary of Seneviratne's work pregnant with an invaluable mine of firsthand information upon which he develops his deep and incisive appraisal of the contemporary *saṅgha* in Sri Lanka. My main concern is to see how far Seneveratne's analysis is helpful in understanding the role of the *saṅgha* in the conflict in Sri Lanka.

There is no doubt that explaining the arising and the perpetuation of what Seneviratne considers to be the Sinhala-Buddhist hegemonic tendencies or chauvinism of the *saṅgha* and the resultant discrimination against the Tamil community of Sri Lanka is, if not the key objective, one of the key objectives of his essay. The argument is: Rahula's *The Heritage* gave a new secular twist to Dharmapalite definition of the Buddhist monk. As a result of the adoption of this definition the Sri Lankan *saṅgha* discarded the inner, otherworldly element, which is the most important element in its monastic life. This opened the floodgates of the traditional monastic life and there came to be a new monastic middle class hungry for money, power, and prestige. The final conclusion of the argument is that this development ultimately produced the Sinhala-Buddhist hegemonic exclusivist worldview which "ensured the preparation of the ground for the subversion of democratic institutions, adventure capitalism, terror, anomic and violent call for a separate state" (Seneviratne 1999: 204). I do not have a problem with the premises of this argument. But I do not see how the specific conclusion follows from these premises. This is not to deny that the people Seneviratne discusses do not have these tendencies; they may or they may not have them. But the rejection of traditional morality, damaging one's monkhood, being capitalist, cherishing Mercedes or BMWs, none of these things has any logical connection with some of the leading members of the Sri Lankan *saṅgha* being Sinhala-Buddhist chauvinist and inhuman, "so attracted to murder and murderers" (1999: 305) monsters, as Seneviratne wants us to believe. In other words, ethnic or religious exclusivism is not a necessary entailment of "worldly individualism" that, as Seneviratne reveals in a masterly manner, emerged within the Sri Lankan *saṅgha*.

There are several difficulties in the manner Seneviratne goes about in articulating his argument. In the first place, the depiction of Vidyālaṅkāra and Vidyōdaya as absolute black and white entities, to say the least, is unrealistic and naïve. In particular, I do not really know how far an anthropologist can legitimately go in making moral pronouncements on people, let alone making such pronouncements that are not easily substantiated. Seneviratne (1999: 196) does refer to a Vidyālaṅkāra monk who allegedly smuggled precious stones concealed inside statues. I can understand why, contrary to his usual method, he does not mention the name. But such information would not support his argument any more than "bath-well" gossip would. But given the situation I am going to describe next, this kind of behavior on the part of the *saṅgha* can well happen irrespective of place or time.

Emergence of capitalism and worldly individualism may well be explained as a natural evolution of events. It is well known that landlordism was very much there with the *saṅgha*. It is quite natural that from this feudalist state capitalism follows. Whether *The Heritage* was there or not this was taking place in the *saṅgha*. The present monastic order was started with the revival of Saraṇaṅkara Saṅgharāja (1698–1778) in the mid seventeenth century. Some of those who received *upasampadā* (higher-ordination) at this occasion were none other than these landlords. It is also recorded that some of these monks who received *upasampadā* gave it up and became *sāmaṇera*s (novices) in order to resume their more worldly activities. (At least this suggests that they were serious about their monkhood!). I see that this process continued without a break amidst the more enlightened members of the *saṅgha* who were busy with ideological issues. It is true that those who wanted an excuse were provided with one by Rahula. But whether it was there or not capitalism was bound to come up. Capitalism does not need excuses or explanations. Money itself is both. I contend that among the people that Seneviratne discusses in the fifth chapter of his book there are only a few who are interested in national or religious activities; most of the others are simply moneymakers who wouldn't give a damn about nation or religion, although some of them may have social organizations as camouflage. I think that Seneviratne should have made a distinction between these two groups. The group that is involved in the national problem in particular deserves to be put in a different category no matter whether or not one may agree with their ideological position. How they came to hold the kind of position attributed to them has to be explained on different grounds.

In making a distinction between Vidyōdaya (f. 1872) and Vidyālaṅkāra (f. 1876), it is true that Seneviratne is making a broad generalization in which there can be exceptions. Such exceptions usually would not affect the main thesis as such. There is, however, an exception that cannot be overlooked without damaging his main claim considerably. Seneviratne does not overlook Maḍihē Paññāsīha Nāyaka Thera (1913–2003) altogether. He refers to him mainly in two contexts, namely, his acceptance of the *Aggamahāpaṇḍita* (Most Supreme Pundit) title from Myanmar and the critique of him by an unnamed member of the *saṅgha*. Apart from these two negative contexts Seneviratne does not see in him any relevance to his study. The curious fact is that Maḍihē does not fit into either of the two categories of the *saṅgha* Seneviratne constructs. He cuts across Seneviratne's categories. Although his teacher, Pälānē Vajirañāṇa (1878–1955), was a student of Vidyōdaya, he was not. He was pretty much a domestic product of the Vajirārāmaya (f. 1901) as many others of Vajirārāmaya were. Contrary to the view of his teacher Maḍihē accepted social service as his mission. His social service has both village reconstruction and economic and pragmatic aspect of Vidyōdaya and the ideological and political aspect of Vidyālaṅkāra (in so far as these two centers represent these two trends). Now, from the point of view of monkness and seriousness of the monastic purpose none including his detractors would have any misgiving. Of all what we know and hear he is the very embodiment, the ideal of Buddhist monasticism.

Seneviratne says that Vidyōdaya activism suddenly came to an end in the 1940s. But Maḍihē proves that it did not. In some respects, there is evidence to show that Maḍihē went even farther than Vidyōdaya social workers. As a young monk, he studied the Tamil language and preached in Nuwaraeliya to estate Tamils. At a later stage he made contact with Tamils in the North, in particular, those Tamils who were considered as low-caste and helped them in their education. Seneviratne finds fault, I think rightly, with the *saṅgha* who has not seen the significance of propagating Buddhism among the Tamils, in particular, the low-caste Tamils:

> It [parochial identification of Buddhism with the Sinhala] also explains the failure, surprising for a missionary religion, to explore the proselytizing possibilities of neighboring non-Buddhist populations, in particular the low-caste Tamils subjected to religious discrimination by the upper-caste Jaffna Hindu Tamil establishment.
>
> (1999: 324)

At least in the case of Maḍihē Nāyaka Thera, one finds a quite weighty counter-example. As my own study on Maḍihē Nāyaka Thera (Tilakaratne 1998: 396) shows that he is a textbook example of a harmonious amalgamation of traditional morality or pristine monkhood with political and social activism.[1] If Maḍihē is a Sinhala-Buddhist chauvinist, and undoubtedly he is according to Seneviratne, the phenomenon has to be explained differently. Maḍihē cannot be considered an unimportant lonely exception for he has been probably the foremost political activist among the *saṅgha* during, in particular, the 1960s through 1980s.

Furthermore it is not easy to establish a direct influence of Anagārika Dharmapāla (1864–1933) on Maḍihē. But this is not very important for the influence can well be indirect. The point I wish to make, however, is that it is possible that Maḍihē chose social activism simply on the ground that it was a proper thing to do by a renouncer. It is a major claim of Seneviratne that social service by the *saṅgha* is not an integral aspect of the teaching of the Buddha and that it became the accepted goal of the Buddhist monk only as a result of Dharmapāla's efforts. Seneviratne states:

> The role in that task Dharmapāla attributed to the monk in traditional Sri Lankan society, and which he wanted the monks to regain, was more a need of his paradigm and project than a fact of history.
>
> (1999: 35)

> It is the essence of the Buddha's doctrine to lead men on the *vibhavagami* path. The doctrine has no essential link with or interest in the progress of society…This does not mean that Buddhism has no relevance for mundane society. As a middle path that avoids extremes, it obviously contains numerous teachings that are relevant for the welfare of society. However, if behaviour resulting from such teachings contributes to social welfare, that is a by-product that constitutes a benefit to society but not the achievement of the distinctively Buddhist goal.
>
> (1999: 163)

There are two claims here: one historical and the other doctrinal, both are open to debate. In my opinion, the very acceptance by the Buddha of men and women householders as making up the four components of the *saṅgha* (A.II.8) is strong proof that the Buddha cannot have considered their worldly upliftment as secondary or incidental. With regard to the historical claim: it is clear that

Dharmapāla made this attribution with passion; that, however, does not mean that he invented it based on his experience with Christianity.

Throughout the history of Buddhism there seems to have been two categories of monks, or rather, monks with two different slants. The best example for this kind of division is the two great elders of the time of the Buddha, namely, Mahākassapa and Ānanda. The former was the epitome of relentless ascetic practice and austerity characterized by living in the forest, dislike for women etc., clearly, even more austere than the Buddha himself. Ānanda was the total opposite, city-dwelling, active, busy, a perfect private secretary, coordinator and champion of the liberation of women, visiting and meeting people. The texts say that Ānanda could not attain the state of *arahant*, the perfection of the path, till the Buddha attained *parinibbāna* (complete cessation). But the ironical situation is that the person who lived closest to the Buddha and who kept the entire teaching in his memory was unable to realize the main goal of his monastic life. Had Ānanda not spent his time for things like preservation of the teaching he would have attained arahanthood much earlier but posterity would have been deprived of the opportunity of following the teaching of the Buddha after he was gone. As Seneviratne holds, the *dhamma* is to be practised and not to be protected. But it does not seem that we can easily escape the hard reality exemplified in the story of Ānanda. It is true that not all were like Ānanda or even followed him. But the modes of behavior exemplified in the lives of the two elders have persisted throughout the history of Buddhism. Such categories as *granthadhura* (Sin.) and *vidarśanādhura* (Sin.), *dhammakathika* (P.) and *pānsukūlika* (Sin.), and *gāmavāsi* (P.) and *araññavāsi* (P.) that became the vogue in the subsequent history of Buddhism may be traced back to the two elders.

The Role of the Saṅgha in the Reconciliation Process

In 2001, T. Bartholomeusz and C.R. de Silva published *The Role of the Saṅgha in the Reconciliation Process* (2001). The contribution it seeks to make to this already extensive scholarship is to underscore the possibility that the "*saṅgha* is situated to play a major role in the ongoing, though elusive, reconciliation process in Sri Lanka" (Bartholomeusz and De Silva 2001: 1). In the opinion of the authors, this point has not received due attention. A key point in their argument is that the education that Buddhist monks receive is largely responsible for the "negative perceptions of Sinhala–Tamil power sharing" (2001: 1). They hold that the appropriate changes in the monastic education system will make the *saṅgha* of Sri Lanka adopt a more inclusive attitude toward the other communities including, in particular, the Tamils. The paper ends with the suggestion that the education of the *saṅgha* and education about the *saṅgha* should receive the highest priority.

The authors begin their discussion by highlighting the distinction between "*buddhaputra*" and "*bhūmiputra*" and the tensions arising in ideology and practise of the *saṅgha* from simultaneous adoption of these two identities not compatible with each other. According to the authors, ideology-wise *bhūmiputra* attitude is in conflict with the ideal Buddhist virtues such as loving-kindness and nonviolence. Practise-wise it has made the *saṅgha* to believe that they, namely, the Sinhala, alone were "the legitimate inhabitants of the island" (Bartholomeusz and De Silva 2001: 6) and their language is "the language of the sons of the soil" (2001: 5). This ideology was also instrumental in treating the non-Sinhala as "foreign" communities (2001: 7). Owing to this *bhūmiputra* ideology, they say, the *saṅgha* can be described as fundamentalists. The ultimate result of this way of thinking and behaving is the arising of a "competing *bhūmiputra* ideology" among the Tamils.

Subsequently, the authors discuss the divisions within the *saṅgha* and its concern about the unity among its own members and the implications of this phenomenon for national reconciliation. The argument of this section is that the Sri Lankan *saṅgha* is divided and is very worried about its divided state and yearns for unity. It carries this mentality to the issue of national reconciliation, and consequently, is unable to see any possibility of reconciliation while existing as separate groups. The authors also refer to Seneviratne's suggestion that the *saṅgha* should draw inspiration from "the model of decentralized authority among the *saṅgha* (Bartholomeusz and De Silva 2001: 20). It may not be too inappropriate to mention at this juncture that how Seneviratne perceives the phenomenon of the split in the *saṅgha* is very different from the attitude of the two authors. For Seneviratne, the *saṅgha* is living under a highly decentralized system. Living in that manner, it is strange that they do not allow the rest of society to enjoy the benefits of such a devolved system. Seneviratne says: "It is therefore incomprehensible to say the least for the monks not to allow the same principle, which has worked so well for Buddhism ensuring its luxurious variety and longevity, to be applied to the secular social order" (Bartholomeusz and De Silva 2001: 271). Seneviratne's assessment on this matter seems right historically. The two authors, however, seem to me right in articulating the real sentiments of the Sri Lankan *saṅgha* on the phenomenon of plurality of the chapters of the *saṅgha* which is usually described with the highly charged expression of "*saṅghabheda*" (schism of the *saṅgha*) which is considered to be one of the most serious *akusala kamma*s (unskillful actions) that a monk is capable of committing. In other words, what this means is that the Sri Lankan *saṅgha*, in particular, cannot view the multiplicity of the chapters as a salutary phenomenon. In such a mental frame it is unrealistic to expect from them any support for devolution on that count. This is not an argument to the effect that therefore they must not support devolution of power. The real dislike for devolution of power on the part of the *saṅgha* lies elsewhere.

The authors come to the issue of monastic education as the last part of their argument. They discuss the history and the extent of the Pirivena (monastic) education for the young members of the *saṅgha*. According to the authors the problem with this education is that "they [members of the *saṅgha*] have limited knowledge of the culture and religious beliefs of the minorities in Sri Lanka and this has implications for shaping attitudes toward minority rights" (Bartholomeusz and De Silva 2001: 22). The authors conclude that "it is imperative that all those who wish for an enlightened *saṅgha* should pay much greater attention to the training of young Buddhist monks" (Bartholomeusz and De Silva 2001: 22). In concluding their essay the authors lay emphasis on the need to be conscious of the roots of the dominant ideology of the *saṅgha* and to attempt to forge links among all opinion groups in the *saṅgha* as means necessary for building peace and reconciliation in Sri Lanka.

The general atmosphere of the Silva/Bartholomeusz essay is positive and optimistic. A glance at the vast amount of literature devoted for discussing the role of the *saṅgha* in the conflict in Sri Lanka, however, would show that the main claim of the paper is nothing new. What is new, perhaps, is the positive articulation of it, namely, that, given a proper education, the *saṅgha* can play a decisive role in bringing about harmony between the two communities and that the involvement of the *saṅgha* is a must. This conclusion is more instructive than informative, particularly, in the context of the near loss of hope articulated by Seneviratne:

> It is one of the stark facts of the contemporary elite monastic scene in Sri Lanka that we do not have a single monk who would fit the basic requirements to qualify as an urbane, cosmopolitan, modern intellectual who alone would be qualified to play the role of "guardian deity."
> (1999: 339)

In spite of my agreement with the broad flavor of the paper certain basic claims made there are questionable. For instance, the authors agree with earlier writers like Sarath Amunugama in holding that the *saṅgha* in Sri Lanka has adopted a *bhūmiputra* ideology. Accordingly, as shown earlier, it is claimed that the *saṅgha* considers Sinhala people alone as the "legitimate" sons of the soil and the others as "illegitimate." Amunugama (1991) introduced these two terms in the context of Mavubima Surakīmē Viyāpāraya (Movement for Protecting the Motherland), an organization of Janatha Vimukti Peramuṇa (JVP) oriented young monks which was active in the late 1980s. Obviously these terms have limited relevance in Amunugama since there is no concrete evidence for the usage. In Sri Lanka, only a recent nationalist political party carries "*bhūmiputra*" as a part of its name to describe its self-identity (the support of the *saṅgha* for this political party is minimal). The closest to this view held by the *saṅgha* is that resources of the country should be shared among its people in proportion to the ratio of its population. A relevant example is Maḍihē Paññāsīha Nāyaka Thera who has held such a position as the right way of assuring social justice (Tilakaratne 1998: 180ff). May be this "majority" view is faulty. But it does not seem fair that the two authors attribute the *bhūmiputra* ideology to the Sri Lankan *saṅgha*. It is a known fact that the Tamil militants adopted a real *bhūmiputra* type ideology in the recent history of Sri Lanka. According to the authors, this Tamil ideology came as a reaction "asserting a competing *bhūmiputra* ideology" (Tilakaratne 1998: 6) to the similar ideology by the Sinhala. I do not see any explanatory potential of this assertion except, of course, that it lends legitimacy to the ethnic cleansing carried out by the Tamil militants in the North and Northeastern regions of the island. The fact of the matter, however, is that the so-called Sinhala *bhūmiputras*' response to Tamil *bhūmiputra* ideology was to assert that the entire island is the *bhūmi* of all communities living there.

The authors' reference to "Sinhala homeland or *dhammadīpa*" is equally problematic. In the first place, it is difficult to see how "*dhammadīpa*" means Sinhala homeland. Perhaps the authors may have taken "*dhammadīpa*" as the island of the *dhamma* = the *dhamma* of the Buddha (Buddha-*dhamma*). This latter usage – the *dhamma* of the Sinhala – the island of *dhamma* could mean the island of Sinhala. It is really doubtful whether or not the term was used in this sense; even if it was used in that sense it does not mean Sinhala *homeland*. What is meant by the term by those who use it is the righteous land or the land that adheres to the *dhamma*. If Sinhala "fundamentalists" are talking in terms of a homeland what the authors should have done is to quote them without taking pains to produce far-fetched interpretations.

In their essay, the authors refer to what they call "Sinhala-Buddhist fundamentalism" and define it as "the penchant" for drawing on mythical and legendary history "as a charter for the special position of Sinhala Buddhists in Sri Lanka and the justification of the belief in Sinhala linguistic, political, religious and economic hegemony" (Bartholomeusz and De Silva 2001: 20). The authors refer to their previous work *Buddhist Fundamentalism and Minority Identities in Sri Lanka* (Bartholomeusz and De Silva 1998) in which they discuss this category in detail and try to show in what sense these Buddhists are fundamentalist. According to them there are certain family resemblances between Buddhist fundamentalists and the others as well as important differences. The trouble with this definition is that it is too broad and too vague; hardly anyone who takes religion as a valid form of behavior will be spared by this definition. According to this definition, all the Buddhist activists past and present are fundamentalists except those whom they call "traditional Buddhists," a category not very clear. Equally fundamentalist are those Buddhists in the late nineteenth century and early twentieth centuries who saw Western culture and Christian mission as "the main alien force" (Bartholomeusz and De Silva 2001: 3). I fail to see how else they could have seen these phenomena. The question ultimately is: what is it that the authors are trying to achieve by invoking this name? Surely they have contributed to introducing a new category and new concept that could serve as an attractive label in academic discussions of Sri Lankan conflict. But it cannot bite too much.

When one reads the two works discussed in this section one cannot help getting the impression that the entire problem lies in the "hegemonic" attitudes of the *saṅgha* and once the *saṅgha* is reformed everything will be perfectly alright and everybody will be able to live happily ever after. This is, undoubtedly, a very high estimation of the role of the *saṅgha*, on the one hand. On the other hand, however, the two analyses suffer from being totally and absolutely one-sided. Such efforts, undertaken even with the loftiest of sentiments stop at being nothing more than political sloganeering serving one against another.

Reflective remarks

My account in the previous section does not mean that everything is perfectly alright with the *saṅgha* and that they should just keep on doing what they are doing right now exactly in the same manner. Before trying to articulate some of the measures that I feel that the *saṅgha* should take let me briefly look at how and why the *saṅgha* has come to identify itself with the Sinhala people and the role of protecting these institutions. It is a truism to say that one's self-identity and self-definition do not arise in a vacuum. The very need to define oneself arises as against the presence of "the other." In the context of ancient Sri Lanka, the invaders from South India became the other. The *Mahāvaṃsa* reports that a number of invasions and attacks of this sort took place from a very early period. The first recorded attack came from two merchants called Sēna and Guttika in 177 BCE (*Mahāvaṃsa* 21: 10). Ever since this incident, till the arrival of Europeans in the fifteenth century, these attacks continued periodically. The worst attack from which the country never fully recovered happened toward the end of the Poḷonnaruva period (*Cūlavaṃsa* 80: 54). Māgha (1215–1236) invaded and destroyed practically the entire power base, religion, and the culture of the country. The *Cūlavaṃsa* (80: 65–70) records the disaster as follows:

> They wrecked the image houses, destroyed many cetiyas, ravaged the vihāras and maltreated the lay brethren. They flogged the children, tormented the five (groups of the) comrades of the Order, made the people carry burdens and forced them to do heavy labour. Many books known and famous they tore from their code and strewed them hither and thither. The beautiful, vast, proud cetiyas like the Ratnāvalī (-cetiya) and others which embodied as it were, the glory of the former pious kings, they destroyed by overthrowing them and allowing alas! many of the bodily relics, their souls as it were, to disappear. Thus the Damiḷa warriors in imitation of the warriors of Mara, destroyed in the evil of their nature, the laity and the Order.
>
> (Geiger and Rickmers 1980: 133)

What is significant is not whether these things happened exactly in the manner described but the fact that the particular incident was perceived in that manner. The threat to the religion was always there. The extent of the invasion and the destruction of religion by the time of Duṭugämuṇu are elaborately described in the *Mahāvaṃsa*. There is no reason to believe that the Buddhist monks had to invent these incidents against Tamils. Given the possibility that the country was invaded and the religion was attacked it is quite natural that the *saṅgha* developed a mind-set in which the protection of religion and the country was paramount. On the other hand, the *saṅgha* depended on Sinhala people, who were the only Buddhists they had around, and the Sinhala kings for the protection of their religion. A mutual bond was gradually created in this manner.

The history of the island till today shows that the threats from abroad were a part of its life. Up to the fifteenth century the invaders came from South India. After that the invasion was from Europe. Again the religion was a main target. With the arrival of the Europeans there was an added threat, namely, the forced introduction of a new religion. I do not need to tread the familiar grounds of discriminations against the people and the religions (both Buddhism and Hinduism) of the island[2]. The threats were real and they continue to be present even today. At the moment there are several hundred new Christian missionary organizations operative in the country surreptitiously under the camouflage of business ventures. Earlier the conversions were done under muscle power; today they are taking place under the cover of freedom of expression and freedom of religion. In the political arena, it is true that the *saṅgha* has opposed any attempt at devolution of power beyond certain limits. The reason has been that separatism has been always there overtly or covertly. If this is an unrealistic fear on the part of the *saṅgha* Tamil politician have done nothing to remove it. Hegemonic views and attitudes are not created in an ideological vacuum. Things are dependently co-arisen and this is true for both sides of the controversy.

The deeper "philosophical" question arising from this situation is: What should a monk do when one's religion, the people, and the country associated with it are in danger? Following a religion and protecting a religion are obviously two different things in the sense they involve different sorts of actions. In particular, when one's religious tradition is physically in danger there is no doubt that one has to do something. But what is the limit of such action? Can he be aggressive or use violence in the process? What is the degree of such aggressiveness or violence?

The *saṅgha* in Sri Lanka, in addition to facing the threats of disappearance in experiencing natural disasters such as the Brāhmaṇatissa famine during the reign of Vaṭṭagāmaṇī Abhaya (103 BCE), also faced severe physical aggression when Buddhism in India was physically destroyed by the invading Islamic forces. There were not any specific Buddhist efforts to remedy the situation in India. As a result, until Anagārika Dharmapāla (1864–1933) revived Buddhism to India by establishing the Mahābodhi Society in 1891, the massive conversions of Ambedkar Buddhists led by Bhimrao Ambedkar (1891–1956) and the Dalai Lama's exile in India 1959, Buddhism in India remained to be a thing of the past. The *Mahāsīlava Jātaka* says that the Bodhisatva king waited, surrounded by his ministers, till the enemy came and got hold of his kingdom. In an aggressive context, what should a Buddhist monk do?

Seneviratne seems to think that *vibhavagāmi paṭipadā* is the only one proper thing for a monk to do. In addition to the various statements he makes to this effect, his view becomes clear in what he quotes at the beginning of his book.

His quotes from *The Questions of Milinda* and the *Majjhimanikāya* highlight this attitude to the *saṅgha* life. The kind of Buddhism Seneviratne has in his mind is what may be called early or ideal Buddhism in which the sole occupation of the monk is to strive to attain arahanthood. We know that this ideal of perfection got somewhat softened in Sri Lanka. It does not mean that the ideal was totally rejected. While there were always those who opted to follow the ideal, Buddhism for a larger majority of the *saṅgha* proper life was one of service to people while occupying a religious position a little higher than that of ordinary lay persons. Here we come across the age-old dilemma exemplified in Mahākassapa and Ānanda referred to earlier. If the Ānanda was very serious about his inner life there is a good possibility that Buddhism would not have lasted long and we might not have the so-called Sinhala-chauvinist Buddhist monks to kick around!

Contrary to what Seneviratne maintains, I propose that a larger majority of monks who hold a so-called Sinhala-Buddhist hegemonic ideology are not necessarily liberal individualists who have money and pleasure as their ultimate aim, but are serious people who are faced with a moral dilemma: dilemma of choosing between Mahākassapa and Ānanda; or choosing between dispassionate inaction and compassionate action. One thing they seem to know for sure is that, on the face of being destroyed by another, suicide, either active or passive, is not the answer. Seneviratne discusses the debate that occurred between "the preachers of the *dhamma*" and "those who followed ascetic practices" (*dhammakathika* and *pansukūlika*) during King Vaṭṭagāmaṇī Abhaya (89–77 BCE) on the status of learnedness and practice (*pariyatti* and *paṭipatti*). The fact that the section that represented learnedness won in the debate indicates that a significant group of the Sri Lankan *saṅgha* took a turn toward practicality at an early date of its history. Although "doers" are more important than "talkers," a distinction Seneviratne employs, the ironical situation is that the former cannot survive in the absence of the latter. Putting it more specifically, one cannot follow the *dhamma* if there is no one to teach him what the *dhamma* is. History has accommodated both groups and lay society has found a particular group more useful than the other depending on the occasion or need. Going back to what I would like to describe as the deeper philosophical problem, it is necessary to acknowledge the fact that the *saṅgha* operates with the assumption of the validity of such categories as religion, ethnicity, and culture. In its ideal constitution the *saṅgha* is universal; in its practical constitution, however, the Sri Lankan *saṅgha* is local. In balancing these two trends the *saṅgha* has to constantly evaluate the situations that arise anew. The task is not easy and requires, as Seneviratne rightly points out, lot of skills. I agree with all three authors I discuss here on the deficiencies of monastic education. By education I do not mean, as very often it seems to mean, that monks must be trained to think in a manner that categories such as religion and culture are not valid and should be done away with. As in everything else, the *saṅgha* must be trained to follow a middle path in such issues too as a part of their formal education. I do not think that the dilemmas and contradictions visible in the contemporary monastic life can be resolved by going back to the ideal Buddhism of ancient India. It is imperative, nevertheless, that the *saṅgha* should review its path from time to time and make necessary adjustments in a collective manner.

Seneviratne points out the lost possibility of propagating the *dhamma* among the Tamils. While it is true that the Sri Lankan *saṅgha* did not make use of this opportunity, I see this inaction as a result of historical suspicion carried down throughout without much contemplation. As I made clear earlier, it is perfectly understandable why the Buddhist *saṅgha* had to develop a special linkage with the Sinhala people. This should not mean, however, that Sinhala people alone could be the protectors of the religion. It is a historical event that Sinhala people built up a close association with Buddhism in Sri Lanka. There cannot be anything intrinsically against Buddhism in Tamil. As Seneviratne rightly points out many contemporary *saṅgha* does not know that the great Pāli commentators such as Buddhadatta and Dhammapāla, on whom traditional Theravada orthodoxy so much depends on for the right interpretation of the word of the Master, are from Southern India and could well be Tamil. Now the question is: should past perceptions be carried to the future without subjecting them to scrutiny? It is a shame that Buddhism, which existed in the country for more than twenty-three centuries, does not have a Tamil-Buddhist community. Although there were individual actors who thought differently and learnt Tamil and extended their service to them the outcome does not seem to have changed the main picture. Here I think that postindependent enlightened *saṅgha* has failed in its duty and as a result they have also lost the opportunity of being effective mediators in the ongoing conflict.

Finally, I would like to go back to Seneviratne's book *The Work of Kings*. While the academic critiques of the role of the *saṅgha* are not uncommon in recent history Seneviratne stands out as the most open, straight, and ruthless. Seneviratne's conclusions are mostly negative and do not leave much hope for this time-tested organization. His sentimental involvement can, however, be understood as resulting from the methodology of being an observer-participant instead of being the other way round. In this sense, Seneviratne's effort needs to be understood as resulting from a deep interest in human welfare that necessarily includes the welfare of the *saṅgha* in it. The Sri Lankan *saṅgha* needs to take Seneviratne in the same spirit as an eye-opener the glare of which cannot be toned down and as a wake-up call the bang of which will be heard by all but the deaf and by those who do not want to hear. I do not think anyone who is deeply concerned about the welfare of the *saṅgha* can overlook Seneviratne. If his warning of rising commercialism, capitalism, and individualism is not taken seriously and done something about it, perhaps re-establishing "*saṅghika*" (communal) system, the *saṅgha* will not be able to arrest the already decadent nature of some of its members and will ultimately be reduced to being a priestly class with wealth and power but devoid of moral authority. Although I still do not see how being a capitalist, liberal individualist entails being a chauvinist, if taken in a positive and constructive manner, *The Work of Kings* is the best recent critique of the contemporary Sri Lankan *saṅgha*.

Notes

1 On his ninetieth birthday (June 21, 2002), I interviewed him for ITN Television in Sri Lanka. My last question for him was what was his message to the younger generation of monks. He promptly responded: "Do social service without damaging your monkhood!"

2 On the alleged discrimination against Buddhist education by the colonial power, Tambiah states:

> With regard to the charge that the colonial government's policy favored the Christian missions' grant-aided schools, and placed obstacles to the founding of Buddhist (and Hindu) schools, it clearly seems that by and large the authors of *The Betrayal* of Buddhism were correct in their allegations.
> (1992: 183)

14

SARVŌDAYA'S PURSUIT OF PEACE

George Bond

The Sarvōdaya Śramadāna Movement has been one of the most active groups working for peace in Sri Lanka. Sarvōdaya's peace movement has represented a Gandhian–Buddhist response to Sri Lanka's ethnic conflict. Sarvōdaya's understanding of the twofold nature of the quest for peace has distinguished its approach from that of secular and political efforts to find peace. Sarvōdaya believes that peace is a social goal as well as a spiritual goal for each individual. These two forms of peace are inextricably linked in Sarvōdaya's Engaged Buddhist vision. Sarvōdaya's peace movement has focused on the need to restore the human spirit and to work for peace from the bottom up rather than attempting to impose it from above. Ahangamage Tudor Ariyaratne (b. 1931) has followed Mohandas Karamchand Gandhi (1869–1948) in seeking to build this spiritual infrastructure as the key to changing the social and political infrastructure. The kind of peace that Sarvōdaya has sought represents not merely a return to a form of *status quo*, but rather a total social revolution that reforms the values and the structures that created the conflict. By building a spiritual infrastructure, Sarvōdaya has attempted to "promote an alternative and parallel series of processes within the law leading to a social order which manifests Buddhist values and objectives" (Ariyaratne 1987: 6).

From the Gandhian side, Sarvōdaya's vision of peace drew on Gandhi's commitment to nonviolence (Skt. *ahiṃsā*) and self-realization (Skt. *swarāj*). Gandhi understood clearly that these values could not exist without changing the violent and oppressive structures of society. His "Constructive Programme" sought to address these structures and reestablish traditional values in society. As Kantowsky (1980: 10) has noted, Gandhi believed that "Only when an equal share has been given 'unto this last', is a non-violent social order possible; only in such a society can Truth (*satya*) and Self-Realization (*swarāj*) grow."

In the context of the 1980s, with the ethnic conflict erupting in the north and economic problems emerging in the south, Ariyaratne and the Sarvōdaya Movement protested against the government in much the same way and over many of the same issues as the most vocal critics of the government at that time, a group that included some right wing elements of the *saṅgha* and the Janatha

Vimukti Peramuṇa (JVP).[1] However, what distinguished Sarvōdaya's protests from those of the JVP and the other critics was that while the JVP and others called for a violent response to the "terrorism," Sarvōdaya was calling for peace and a nonviolent revolution. This represented Sarvōdaya's Gandhian heritage and should be seen as one of the distinctive contributions of Sarvōdaya to the discourse surrounding the conflict.

From the Buddhist side, Sarvōdaya's vision of peace has found a rich resource in the classical Theravāda Buddhist teachings, which Ariyaratne regards as cognates of the Gandhian ideals. For Buddhism, the central datum for peace is the mind, and the definitive statement about the centrality of the mind is found in the first two verses of the *Dhammapada*. These verses have been viewed as answers to the questions: "What is the source of violence or peace?" and "What is the source of suffering or happiness?"

> Mind is the foremost of all realities. Mind is the chief and all are mind made. Whoever speaks or acts with an impure mind, suffering follows him as the wheel of the cart follows the foot of the ox.
>
> Mind is the foremost of all realities . . . Whoever speaks or acts with a pure mind, contentment/peace (*sukha*) follows him as the wheel of the cart follows the foot of the ox.[2]
>
> (*Dhammapada* vv. 1–2)

According to Theravāda Buddhism, there can be no true happiness for the individual without this kind of inner peace and there can be no true harmony for society without individuals who teach and exemplify the qualities of peace. The Buddha taught that, "When the five hindrances have been put away . . . then a person is filled with a sense of peace and in that peace his heart is content" (D.I.73). By controlling the mind and attaining inner peace, an individual is able to control his/her reactions to the actions of others and thereby to live by nonviolence. For example, the Buddha taught his followers,

> If anyone should give you a blow with his hand, or with a rock, or with a stick or with a weapon, even so you should get rid of those desires and thoughts that are worldly and you should train yourself thus: "Neither will my mind become perverted nor will I utter any evil speech, but kindly and compassionate will I dwell with a mind filled with loving kindness and devoid of hatred.
>
> (M.I.123)

Buddhism clearly teaches that this kind of nonviolence represents the only path to peace: as the *Dhammapada* (v. 5) says, "Hatred never ceases by hatred; hatred ceases by love. This is the eternal dhamma."

All of these Buddhist values related to peace have found expression in the philosophy of the Sarvōdaya movement where they blend with the Gandhian ideals. Sarvōdaya has maintained that the process of awakening begins with the individual and then moves to the family, the community, and beyond because all of these levels are interconnected. In this process of personality awakening or spiritual awakening the individual strives to realize the truths of interdependence (P. *paṭiccasamuppāda*) and selflessness (P. *anatta*), insights that lead to living without attachment and enable one to affirm nonviolence and work for peace. Ariyaratne explains that being nonviolent does not mean being inactive. He says that, "We have demonstrated an active non-violence," and also explains that "To be active in a (violent) situation like that and to work in a non-violent and non-sectarian way you need great spiritual power" (Kantowsky 1987: 16f).

For Ariyaratne this kind of spiritual power represents the common denominator of Gandhian and Buddhist thought, as well as the essence of all religions. Ariyaratne, like Gandhi and Vinobā Bhāve (1895–1982) before him, has been guided by a basic belief that there is an underlying spiritual unity to all religions. This ecumenical spirituality, which also has both Victorian and new age sources, relates directly to the campaign for peace because Ariyaratne has maintained that the achievement of peace depends on being able to actualize this spiritual unity. Ariyaratne (1987: 14) also has described all religions as "intrinsically messages of peace and brotherhood." The goal of Sarvōdaya's peace marches and the meditations that Ariyaratne has led during them has always been, as he has said, "to create a critical mass of spiritual consciousness and then create conditions to sustain that level" (Weerawarne 1999: 31). In Ariyaratne's view, transforming the consciousness of individuals and communities toward compassion and peace represents an essential step toward building a just and peaceful world (Ariyaratne 1989: 120).

By creating this "critical mass of spiritual consciousness," Sarvōdaya has sought to "transfer power to the people" and challenge the structures and parties that have created the violence. Ariyaratne has contended that the context that has permitted violence arose as a result of the colonial period in Sri Lanka. After independence, Sri Lanka's postcolonial governments, for the most part, continued the same approach as their colonial mentors, pursuing centralized social, political, and economic programs that ran counter to the Buddhist spirituality that had traditionally guaranteed peace. Ariyaratne has written,

> When Sri Lanka was Buddhist, both in precept and practice, there was no need to talk of peace making because there was no fundamental value crisis in Sri Lankan society in spite of internally or externally caused strife and power struggles . . . Peace prevailed in the minds of the general public and their communities because the generally accepted value system remained unattacked by contending groups.
>
> (1987: 1)

He goes on to say that now, however, "legalized structural violence prevails and extra legal violent methods are used as well to resolve conflicts." Ariyaratne's image of an ideal Buddhist past and his appeal to the past have served both to critique the contemporary government and to empower liberation and reform. The peace movement represents an integral part of Sarvōdaya's Gandhian–Buddhist revolution. Sarvōdaya's peace movement has attempted to awaken the people's spiritual consciousness and restore what it regards as Buddhist/spiritual values in order to counter the dominant material values that have led to violent structures and the oppression of the people. Macy (1983: 31) has noted that Sarvōdaya's goal of awakening has implicit in it "the belief that a root problem of poverty is a sense of powerlessness." The same assumption can be said to underlie the peace movement for it has represented an extension of Sarvōdaya's basic quest to "Awaken people to their *swashakti* (personal power) and *janashakti* (collective or people's power)" (1983).

Operating with this vision of the need for peace and the possibility of peace Sarvōdaya has actively pursued a program designed to facilitate peace in the country. We can summarize some of these activities here.

Following the 1983 riots that marked the escalation of the current ethnic conflict, Sarvōdaya established camps for the Tamil refugees and was one of the main organizers of a national peace conference that adopted a "People's Declaration for National Peace and Harmony." After this conference, Sarvōdaya sought to implement the spirit of the conference by undertaking a peace march or "peace walk" from Kataragama in the south to Jaffna in the north. This march, however, was halted because of a request from President J.R. Jayewardene (1906–1996) who said that he feared for the safety of the marchers.

Since that first march, Sarvōdaya has organized numerous other peace marches including what it described as a People's Peace Offensive in 1987. Sarvōdaya has also operated a program of relief in the conflict areas. Sarvōdaya established a Peace Center, Viśva Nikētan, in 1987, to serve as a place of meditation and peace. Sarvōdaya has continued to have peace marches and peace meditations. In 1999, Sarvōdaya assembled 170,000 people to contemplate peace in Vihāra Mahā Dēvi Park in Colombo.

On March 15, 2002, Sarvōdaya organized an even larger gathering for peace when some 500,000 people assembled in Anurādhapura to meditate for peace.

When its Peace Center, Viśva Nikētan, was in the planning stages, the Sarvōdaya Movement took a decision in the mid 1990s to reenergize its quest for peace. In the earlier part of that decade, Sarvōdaya had focused more on relief work than peace activism while it waited to see what the government's negotiations would produce. Buoyed by international peace awards to Ariyaratne and confronted with the lingering ethnic conflict, however, the movement decided to address the problem that was destroying the country. Sarvōdaya acted to broaden its peace effort by developing a new programmatic emphasis that it labeled the People's Peace Initiative.[3] The two principles behind this new initiative were drawn from Sarvōdaya's Gandhian-Buddhist experience over forty years. First, that, as Sarvōdaya has traditionally held, the prerequisite for peace is the building of a spiritual infrastructure: inner peace before external peace. Second, that peace cannot be imposed from the top down but must be founded on the people's consent, from the bottom up. Ariyaratne stated the rationale for this new campaign in his Gandhi Peace Prize acceptance speech:

> We recognize that the resolution of our war cannot be left to either the politicians or to the military commanders alone. Making peace calls for a realistic assessment of ground realities. Increasing the awareness of people at the grassroots and generating in them a sympathetic feeling for the sufferings of others is one part of changing those ground realities.[4]

The incentive for Sarvōdaya's becoming proactive in the peace process was also expressed in the movement's Annual Report for 1992–1993: "Sarvōdaya believes that while politicians play "politics" and armies fight battles, the people may get together with people to make both armies and such politicians unnecessary" (p. 48).

Sarvōdaya began this campaign with the belief that the time was right and that it was uniquely positioned to achieve a lasting people's peace. As D.J. Mitchell has argued in a recent Sarvōdaya publication on the People's Peace Initiative, "Realistically, Sarvōdaya is the only existing organization in Sri Lanka that could mobilize the population across ethnic and religious lines." The Sarvōdaya leaders were probably correct in concluding that Sarvōdaya represented the best hope for working for peace from the grassroots. However, some other factors also contributed to opening a window of opportunity for a Sarvōdaya peace campaign at this time. One factor was the new leadership that had emerged in the Sarvōdaya movement itself and a second factor that provided encouragement for moves toward peace was the Sri Lankan parliamentary elections of 2001 in which the United National Party (UNP) regained a majority in the parliament after making campaign promises to reopen peace talks with the LTTE. On February 22, 2002, the new Prime Minister, Ranil Wickremesinghe, met Tamil leaders and signed a ceasefire document with the help of Norwegian negotiating team. In the acceptance speech of Gandhi Peace Prize, Ariyaratne noted that in "the three most recent elections held in the country, the people voted in large numbers for political parties with a peace platform. But the reality is that the people are without the power to convert their desires into reality." But in the Autumn 2002 the people's desire for peace received a boost when the government and the LTTE actually initiated peace negotiations. It could also be argued that the atmosphere for peace was also strengthened in 2001 by the international focus on ending violence and terrorism. Although Sarvōdaya's campaign began before this international focus started in September 2001, the international momentum may have encouraged Sarvōdaya.

To conduct its peace campaign, Sarvōdaya established a new department, the Peace Secretariat, and issued a position paper analyzing the situation and setting out a strategy for peace. The paper argued that either side could not win the war; it can only be continued. The paper also suggested that there are three "armies" in Sri Lanka: (i) the government forces, (ii) the LTTE, and (iii) "Sarvōdaya's staff and volunteers, numbering close to 100,000."[5] The paper set out a "Sarvōdaya People's Peace Plan" that would provide a new approach to the war: "The war cannot be won; it can only be transcended." The first step and the most immediate requirement for this peace process was that a ceasefire should occur so that all sides would stop fighting immediately. Then peace meditations should be employed to accomplish a number of objectives, including "eliminating violence from our own hearts" and envisioning a "peaceful, harmonious and sustainable Sri Lanka."

To implement this plan, Sarvōdaya mobilized its supporters to hold some major peace meditations. The People's Peace Initiative began with a peace march and meditation in August 1999 that saw some 170,000 people from across the island come together in Vihāra Mahā Dēvi Park in Colombo. At that march, Ariyaratne led the ecumenical group in a meditation on nonviolence and unity. Following that initial event, the Sarvōdaya Peace Secretariat organized eight other regional peace meditations, so that altogether over 215,000 people participated in this campaign for a people's peace. In January 2002, Sarvōdaya announced plans for an even larger gathering for peace to be held in Anurādhapura in March. Accordingly, on March 15, 2002, Sarvōdaya's "Peace Samādhi Day" in the sacred city of Anurādhapura attracted 650,000 people from 15,000 Sinhala, Tamil, and Muslim villages to meditate for peace. Joanna Macy, who participated in this event, described it in this way: "Sitting on the grass as far as I could see, 650,000 people made the biggest silence I have ever heard. As the silence deepened, I thought: This is the sound of bombs and landmines not exploding, of rockets not launched, and machine guns laid aside. With these demonstrations, Sarvōdaya gave the quest for peace a central place on its agenda. In this quest Sarvōdaya again emphasized the importance of transforming the consciousness of the people and building a spiritual infrastructure. Ariyaratne has stressed this theme throughout, for example in this statement from his Niwano Peace Prize address in 1992: "When enough people who share spiritual values and experience come together, they generate a critical mass of spiritual consciousness that becomes a tangible reality and empowers much larger numbers of people." Sarvōdaya has employed the peace meditations to move the hearts and minds of people toward nonviolence and compassion. Recognizing that two decades of conflict in the country have created a culture of war that allows people to accept the violence and view it as normal, Sarvōdaya has sought to create a culture of peace that makes the violence unacceptable and unthinkable. Their goal in the peace campaign has been to change the climate so that, for example, the adults are not focused on discussing the war and the children in the primary schools do not draw pictures that deal with war and violence. The peace meditations represent an important first step in a process of healing, reconciliation, and national unity. Sarvōdaya takes a long view of this process, describing it as the "500 year peace plan."[6] Because Sarvōdaya recognizes the Buddhist truth of the interdependence of all, it has tied its quest for peace very closely to its overall quest for a nonviolent, village-based people's revolution as ultimately the only way to establish true peace.

Notes

1 The JVP originated as a Sinhala nationalist and socialist movement and tried unsuccessfully to overthrow the government on two occasions, first in 1971 and most recently in 1989.

2 My translation.

3 For Sarvōdaya People's Peace Plan see http://www.commonway.org/SriLankapeaceplan01.htm (accessed on October 2, 2005).

4 Acceptance Speech of Gandhi Peace Prize in 1997.

5 www.Sarvōdaya.org (accessed on October 2, 2005).

6 http://www.commonway.org/SriLankapeaceplan01.htm (accessed on October 2, 2005).

15

JHU POLITICS FOR PEACE AND A RIGHTEOUS STATE

Mahinda Deegalle

Until the dawn of the twentieth century, Buddhist monks were passive agents in the political history of Sri Lanka.[1] In the middle of the twentieth century, however, monastic involvement in politics took a remarkable turn. With Walpola Rahula's (1907–1997) advocacy of politics for Buddhist monks in *The Heritage of the Bhikkhu* (1974), which was originally published in Sinhala in 1946 as *Bhikṣuvagē Urumaya*, a new political Buddhist tradition emerged in Sri Lanka encouraging and justifying political activism of Buddhist monastics. Since the publication of *The Heritage of the Bhikkhu*, the degree of involvement of Buddhist monks in Sri Lankan politics has gradually increased marking clear phases of radical developments.

When the social and political conditions weakened the economy of the country partly as a result of severe disruptions and destructions of the two-decades of ethnic turmoil (beginning from the 1983 July ethnic riots), the monastic involvement in extremist, nationalist politics has given birth to radical innovations. Some aspects of these political trends in contemporary Theravāda Buddhist monkhood in relation to the Sri Lankan ethnic problem have already been documented in the recent works of Sarath Amunugama (1991), Stanley J. Tambiah (1992), H.L. Seneviratne (1999), Tessa J. Bartholomeuz (2002), and Ananda Abeysekara (2002). While these scholarly works have generated a rethinking of Buddhist political activism, the works of Tambiah (1992) and Seneviratne (1999), in particular, have subsequently created a considerable debate and tension both within the Buddhist *saṅgha* and lay Buddhist communities in Sri Lanka resulting the banning of Tambiah's *Buddhism Betrayed?*[2]

The debate and protest against *Buddhism Betrayed?* focused more on the use of a provocative photograph of the popular Buddhist preacher monk, Venerable Māduḷuvāvē Sōbhita, on the front cover of Tambiah's book. As a result of the protest in Sri Lanka, The University of Chicago Press withdrew the front cover of *Buddhist Betrayed?* and reprinted the paperbacks with a neutral motif. This illustrates the degree of sensitivity related to representing politically active Buddhist monks and their ethno-politics. In the media, today, the Buddhist monk, whether political or non-political in the public realm, is often intrinsically associated with the turbulent ethno-politics.[3] The Jathika Hela Urumaya (JHU), in particular, has realized the importance of creating a balanced image of Buddhist monks involved in politics and highlighted the necessity of an 'independent' and 'free' mass media with 'ethical principles' in its twelve-point political manifesto (which will be examined in detail later).

This chapter examines in detail the most recent radical development that occurred in the Sri Lankan Theravāda monasticism in the year 2004: the historic event of nine Buddhist monks becoming professional politicians in the Sri Lankan Parliament. By any standard, the year 2004 is the watershed in the entire history of Theravāda Buddhist monastic world in South and Southeast Asia. For the first time, a newly formed Buddhist monk political party identified as the JHU (National Sinhala Heritage Party) fielded over 200 Buddhist monk candidates[4] for the parliamentary election held on 2 April 2004 to elect 225 Members of Parliament.[5] The JHU, the only political party consisted of all Buddhist monks who hold all the key posts, was formed just two months before the election held on 2 April 2004. It was formed to enable Buddhist monks to contest the election as one group. Earlier these monks had formal affiliations with the Jathika Saṅgha Sammēlanaya (National Saṅgha Assembly). This chapter analyzes the political and religious events that led a section of the Sri Lankan Buddhist *saṅgha* to engage in active politics. It contextualizes the history of the development of the JHU by identifying its predecessors. And most importantly, it examines their religious rhetoric of establishing a *dharmarājya* (righteous state) in Sri Lanka.

Buddhist monks' involvement in Sri Lankan electoral politics

Sri Lankan Buddhist monks' active involvement in politics began in the mid-twentieth century. The last five decades show a gradual increase in the degree of monastic involvement in Sri Lankan politics, in particular, with the young Buddhist monks who closely associated themselves with the leftwing JVP (Janatha Vimukti Peramuṇa) politics. Even though the young JVP monks[6] paraded in the May Day rally, their participation in active politics was rather limited. The JVP monks are now well organized under National Bhikṣu Front (Jathika Bhikṣu Peramuṇa). However, contesting in the elections was not an option that was available to all politically active monks. The participation in active politics was not the Theravāda Buddhist norm. However, as presented later, there are several occasions in which individual monks decided to contest in the parliamentary as well as local government elections.

The first account of a Buddhist monk contesting in the elections comes from as early as 1943. Venerable Migeṭṭuvattē Jinānanda contested for Colombo Municipal Council but he was defeated. A decade later, in 1957, Venerable Wälletoṭa Paññādassi contested for a village council in the Mātara District and became the first elected Buddhist monk. Eventually, he was appointed as the chairman of the council and became a Committee Member of village councils in the Mātara District. Following Paññādassi, several Buddhist monks became members of village councils, in other local authorities and in provincial councils. Though monks contested in local elections, none dared to contest in the parliamentary elections. Venerable Pinikahanē Saddhātissa became the first Buddhist monk to contest in the parliamentary election held for Karandeṇiya in 1977 but he was also defeated.

Another significant turning point in monks' involvement in ethno-politics in Sri Lanka occurs in December 2001. In 1992, Venerable Baddēgama Samitha, Incumbent of Duṭugämuṇu Vihāra, Baddēgama, contested in the village council elections and became an elected member of the Southern Provincial Council. In the parliamentary elections held in December 2001, Venerable Samitha contested successfully in the elections held for Galle District and became the first Buddhist monk elected for the Sri Lankan Parliament.[7] He contested the election under People's Alliance (PA) ticket, although he had been a monk member of the Lanka Samasamāja Party (f. 1935), a leftwing political party. Samitha has been known as a political activist since his student days at University of Kelaniya in the late 1970s.

In comparison to other Buddhist monks who have involved in politics, Samitha stands out because of his genuine political views combined with humanistic visions of the Buddha's teachings. In the contemporary politically and ethnically turbulent context, with regard to the peace negotiations that the Sri Lankan government undertook in the early part of 2002 with the Liberation Tigers of Tamil Eelam (LTTE) who had been waging a dangerous and destructive war for an independent Tamil state for Tamils over two decades, Samitha took a very positive stand as a Buddhist monk and a genuine politician. As an able politician, Samitha's positive contribution in creating peace in Sri Lanka, the editorial of the *Daily News* captured as follows:

> The Ven. Baddegama Samitha Thera's impassioned appeal in parliament on Tuesday for undivided backing for the Government's peace effort, points to the positive role the clergy of all faiths in this country could play in realizing national reconciliation, peace and unity.[8]

The editorial of the Tamil daily newspaper, *Vīrakēsari*, stated that though Venerable Samitha was a member of the opposition party, PA, he had spoken openly about the Ceasefire Agreement of the government while criticizing others 'who were trying to stoke communal feeling among the Sinhalese people.'[9]

In the 2004 New Year wishes, again Venerable Samitha reiterated the importance of peace for Sri Lanka and the significant contribution that religious traditions can make peace a reality:

> In the year 2004, we hope for a peaceful life in a developed Sri Lanka, with no fear of suspicion among people . . . [W]e have wasted enough time talking about this. The time has now come to activate all facilities

> to usher in such a period for the country. Goodwill, which is to be fostered among all people, should not only be at the topmost but also at the grass root levels. Those who obstruct the spreading of goodwill among grass roots are the politicians who make irresponsible statements and the priests who preach rash opinions. I am asking the preaching seats of the temples, churches, mosques and kovils not to preach what could create conflicts… We must awaken all our people who are still in slumber. From the very night of December 31, all the ethnic communities in Sri Lanka must put behind everything which hindered our progress and look towards a better future.[10]

Samitha's election campaign for the Parliament in 2001 and his success in winning the election generated a renewed debate[11] whether Samitha should go to the Parliament or should give up his parliamentary seat because it is not the traditional custom in Sri Lanka that Buddhist monks become professional politicians. Though there was significant ideological opposition to him, Samitha stuck to his principles and took oath in the Parliament. Unfortunately, partly due to the ethnic sentiments raised by the JVP politics in southern Sri Lanka, he lost his electorate in April 2004 election.

These events demonstrate scattered evidence for occasional political activities of a few Buddhist monks. Within the last six-decades, several Buddhist monks contested elections before the JHU fielded over 200 monk candidates for the election in February 2004.[12] However, the JHU's election campaign stands out from previous election campaigns since it fielded the entire party with Buddhist monk candidates and it is exclusively a monk-led political party. On this occasion, the novelty and radical development is that Buddhist monks as a large representative group have decided to enter into the Parliament. This political event may have significant impact on the affairs of the *saṅgha* in future.

In the election on 2 April 2004, the JHU won 9 parliamentary seats: 3 from Colombo District, 2 from Gampaha District, 1 from Kalutara District, 1 from Kandy District and 2 from the national list.[13] Altogether, it polled 552,724 votes, 5.97% of the total polled in the election.[14] Its most popular candidate, Venerable Uḍuwe Dhammālōka, had received 42,850 votes. At the moment of writing this chapter, the JHU monks have become a symbol of Sinhala-Buddhist strength within the Parliament[15] and occasionally, an object of controversy and ridicule within the parliament and outside.[16] Their anti-conversion bill[17] to stop 'unethical conversions' among the Buddhists and Hindus has drawn the attention of international human rights groups and produced severe protests from Christian churches around the world.

The Sihala Urumaya roots of the JHU

In the wake of the general election, as a new, unregistered political party, the JHU sought the legal validation of the Sihala Urumaya (SU) as a political party registered in Sri Lanka in order to contest in the April 2004 election. To that effect, the JHU signed a memorandum of understanding with the SU (Sinhala Heritage Party, f. 2000) so that only the monks of the JHU would contest the election as opposed to the lay leadership of the SU. This political connection between the two groups, less transparent to the public, created a considerable debate and speculation among both the Buddhist laity and voting public in Sri Lanka. Because of these unclear political links, it is extremely important here to understand and distinguish the foundational ideologies of both the SU and the JHU for a proper comprehension and evaluation of their religious, ethnic and cultural claims with regard to the politics and future survival of the Sri Lankan state and Buddhism.

The birth of the SU, a lay political party and the prototype of the JHU, can be contextualized in the contemporary political environment in Sri Lanka in relation to the ethnic turmoil and the Sri Lankan Government's proposals of devolution in the late 1990s. To unify like-minded nationalists, the SU was formed on 20 April 2000. S.L. Gunasekara (Chairman), Thilak Karunaratna (Secretary) and Champika Ranawaka (National Organizer) filled the three key posts of the SU. The Sri Lankan Government recognized the SU as a political party on 17 August 2000. In its first election, the SU was able to secure one seat in the Parliament (through national list) by polling 127,863 votes (1.47%).[18]

This quick victory was a mixed blessing for the SU, since it led to a dispute within the party resulting S.L. Gunasekara to resign from the party with some key members. The post-election dispute within the SU led Mr S.L. Gunasekara, Chairman of the SU, to step down because of accusations related to his personal religion: his unwillingness to offer flowers to the Tooth Relic in his maiden visit to Kandy was used against him.[19] Gunasekera was also accused of being a 'former Catholic,' an 'agnostic' and an 'atheist'.[20] The present JHU MP, Athuräliyē Rathana, then, told the press: 'a leader of a Sinhala party must be a Sinhala Buddhist'.[21] Ironically, invoking Buddhist sentiments is as an accepted custom of political life in Sri Lanka. This post-election dispute within the SU had significant impact on the public perception of the party and even today the party has not fully recovered from this initial setback. As a result of the initial setback and public misperception, at the December 2001 election, it got 50,000 votes. However, in the local government election held in March 2002, the SU was able to make some progress by gaining four seats.

As a political party eager to assert its power in Sri Lanka, the limitations of the SU are clearly visible in its goals. Its objective is to seek 'political power for the Sinhalese' and to 'rebuild the unique Sinhala civilization'.[22] This objective may be valuable for the Sinhalese but how does it stand in the context of ethnic and religious minorities who form an important segment of the Sri Lankan population. Because of the SU's preoccupation on the 'Sinhalese' nation and 'Sinhala civilization', the media often accuses and identifies the members of the SU as extremists and nationalists.[23] This negative perception of the SU as a 'racist' group created by their own political ideas and media portrayals may create significant hurdles to the Buddhist monks of the JHU who have close links with the SU.

The SU sees a threat to the very existence of the Sinhala nation posed by Tamil separatism and opportunistic Sinhala politicians. The JHU also shares this vision of potential threats and fears caused by ethnic and religious minorities who have significant foreign financial support base. In addition, the JHU like the SU make severe criticisms of Sinhala politicians and allegations of corruption. The SU maintains that the politicians are 'prepared to barter the sovereignty of the nation for the sake of power'. Similar accusations are also found in the JHU election campaign posters.[24] The criticism of contemporary politics and Sinhala politicians remain to be at the centre of political rhetoric of the JHU as well as of the SU. The members of the SU and the JHU come from a cross section of Sinhala population who are unhappy with the present political procedures in Sri Lanka. They see that as the majority Sinhala people are in a disadvantageous political condition in the peace negotiations with the LTTE.

The cultural, religious and national aspirations of the SU are well expressed in one of their poems:

> A Sihala nation and a just land
> Rich in flora and fauna
> Free of hunger and terror.[25]

The following objectives make clear the nationalist aspirations that the SU holds dear:

1 To safeguard the independence and Sovereignty of the Nation and Territorial integrity of the Country.
2 To safeguard the unitary form of the National Constitution.
3 To uphold Sinhala, the National Language as the only official Language and the Sinhala culture as the National culture while respecting the other non-Sinhala cultures.
4 To uphold, protect and propagate Buddhism, the official religion and to respect the principle of religious freedom of the non-Buddhists.
5 To protect and develop the National Economy focusing mainly on the upliftment of the Sinhalese and Sri Lankan people in general.
6 To protect the rich environment and bio diversity in Sri Lanka and traditional Eco friendly knowledge systems and technology.
7 To uphold the sovereignty of the people and social justice by practicing a democratic system of governance.
8 To establish ethnic cooperation and harmony in order to create a strong united Sri Lankan people based on human rights and the National Rights of the Sinhalese.[26]

To meet the cultural, social and religious needs of contemporary Sri Lanka, the SU presents itself more than a 'political party but a national movement as well'. It maintains that while seeking political power for the Sinhalese, it also has to rebuild 'the unique Sinhala civilization' in Sri Lanka 'independent of the political process'.

The SU had identified two key ideas that it should use for its growth as a political power in Sri Lanka. First, it aims to build Sri Lanka by following the ten virtuous deeds of the righteous king (P. *dasarājadhamma*) as found in the Pāli canon. The *Jātaka* (III.274) enumerates the ten royal virtues as follows: (i) charity, (ii) morality, (iii) liberality, (iv) honesty, (v) mildness, (vi) religious practice, (vii) non-anger, (viii) non-violence and (ix) patience and (x) non-offensiveness. Buddhist politicians and academics in South and Southeast Asia often allude to these ten virtues since they are perceived to be important aspects of Buddhist social and political philosophy. Second, the SU wants to celebrate the secrets of the past glory of the 'unique' Sinhala civilization flourished in Anurādhapura from the third century BCE to the tenth century CE. As a new culturally sensitive political party, the JHU also shares these two key ideas with the SU.

Repercussions of Venerable Sōma's death: the emergence of the JHU

The socio-religious context that led to the new political awareness and birth of the JHU is the controversial untimely death of the popular Buddhist preacher, Venerable Gangoḍavila Sōma (1948–2003). The *Daily News* characterized that '[t]he Sri Lankan nation was left numb, if not, absolutely petrified with shock and intense sorrow as the news about the untimely death... beamed through electronic media.'[27] The JHU has effectively exploited Sōma's death for its own advantage by using rumours surrounding his death. The untimely death of Venerable Sōma, who has been characterized by the newspapers as 'the embodiment of Buddhist morality and paragon of virtue' and 'the champion of Sinhala-Buddhist cause,'[28] has raised conspiracy theories and most importantly, triggered a new awareness on the state of Buddhism in Sri Lanka, which the JHU employed in its election campaign. Many of nationalist persuasion consider Sōma's death as a sacrifice to the nation and hold the opinion that there has been a conspiracy to take his life since Sōma himself has invoked the alleged conspiracy theories over his own death in his last speech in Kandy. Announcing his entrance to politics, Sōma stated:

> There is a conspiracy to murder me. If my murder can awake Sinhalaya, I am happy to die. After my death, there will be another team of monks to contest the elections. Please help them on my behalf.[29]

Because of this tenuous background, anti-Christian sentiments, which have grown over the years on the issue of unethical conversions, have been evoked at the site of Sōma's funeral. At Sōma's funeral, the leader of the JHU, the then President of the Jathika Saṅgha Sammēlanaya, Venerable Ellāwala Medhānanda accused very bluntly: 'Christian fundamentalist connection to Soma Thero's untimely death in

St. Petersburg, Russia was not an accident.’[30] The poster made in honour of Sōma under the name of ‘Rāvannakäla’ bearing the Sri Lankan flag at the background explicitly mentions these issues as follows:

The poster dedicated to Venerable Sōma

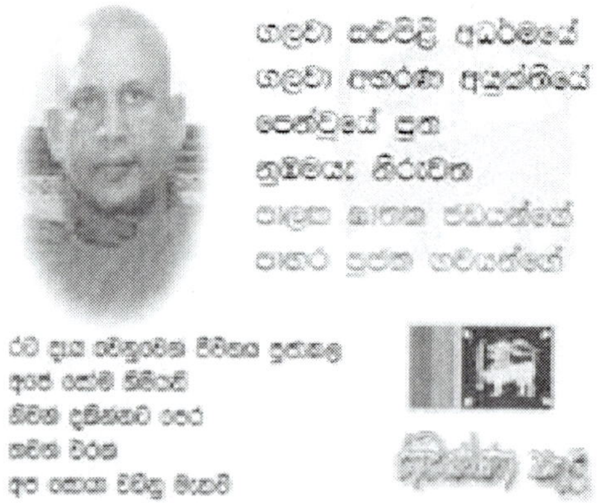

Galavā saḷupiḷi adharmayē	Stripping clothes of unrighteousness
Galavā abharaṇa ayuktiyē	Stripping ornaments of injustice
Penvūyē puta	Son, indeed,
Numbamaya niruvata	You unveiled nakedness
Pālaka ghātaka jaḍayangē	Of murderous ruling bastards
Pāhara pūjaka gavayangē	Of paltry clergy cows
Raṭa däya venuven jīvitaya pūjākala	Sacrificed your life for the sake of country and nation
Apē Sōma himiyani	Our Venerable Sōma!
Nivan dakinnaṭa pera	Before attaining nirvāṇa
Nävata varak	Once again
Apa soyā vaḍinu mänavi	Please come back seeking us![31]

Let me now introduce briefly Sōma’s life in order to show how he has earned public sympathy over the years. Sōma was often presented to the public as ‘the most outstanding and controversial religious leader’ because of his ‘outspokenness and straightforwardness’ in issues related to the Sinhalese and Buddhists.[32] Like the JHU,[33] Sri Lankan newspapers characterize Sōma as ‘[q]uite identical’ to the early twentieth-century Buddhist reformer, Anagārika Dharmapāla (1864–1933), ‘who inspired and aroused Sri Lankan Buddhists from apathy and led them towards socio-cultural awareness’.[34]

Sōma was born in Gangoḍavila, a suburb of Colombo, in 1948.[35] At the adult age of 26 years, in 1974 he received novice ordination and began monastic training at the Bhikkhu Training Centre, Maharagama, under the guidance of two prominent Buddhist monks – Venerable Maḍihē Paññasīha (1913–2003) and Venerable Ampiṭiyē Rāhula. Even before his ordination, Sōma had close links with Siri Vajiragnāṇa Dharmāyatanaya and functioned as a 'lay preacher' and student leader. In 1976, Sōma received the higher ordination. In 1986, for three months, he visited Australia. In his second visit in 1989, Sōma established Melbourne Sri Lankan Buddhist Vihāra. In 1993, he founded Buddhist Vihāra Victoria and served as the chief incumbent until his death on 12 December 2003. After seven years of *dhammadūta* activities in Australia, Sōma returned to Sri Lanka in 1996 in order to help the people of the country.

Sōma's strength lies in his preaching. As a popular preacher,[36] he was able to reach wider young audience. He was respected widely for his 'soothing and informative sermons' which reached 'the hearts and minds of not only the Buddhists but the non-Buddhists as well'.[37] Sōma's popular sermons and television discussions drew the attention of the young and the old and the Buddhists and the non-Buddhists since they discussed problems faced by ordinary people in day-to-day life. Sōma had two very popular TV programmes: *Anduren Eliyaṭa* (From Darkness to Light)[38] and *Näna Pahana* (Lamp of Wisdom).[39] In these public discussions, he expressed openly his ideas about the issues relating to Buddhism and culture of Sri Lanka and helped to get out of an impasse. His engagement in several national debates on the issues dealing with the rights of Sinhala people, made him more popular among the public. Due to his heavy criticism of politicians and their 'unrighteous' activities, it is widely believed that he was shut out from certain television stations. But in one of the collection of Sōma's articles, when this issue of political interference in media is discussed, it is mentioned that it was done under the recommendation of some Buddhist monks rather than on the basis of a decision taken by politicians (Sōma 2001: 78–79).

After Sōma's death, the JHU has systematically invoked Sōma for its own advantage.[40] The JHU's national campaign to win the parliamentary election for establishing a righteous state is presented as a continuation of Sōma's unfinished work:

> Ven. Soma Thera will continue to remain a guiding star as long as the much-cherished Buddhist civilization in the country survives.... The aching void left by his sudden departure is unbridgeable and will continue to be felt by millions of Sri Lankans... What his departure reminds us is the fact that time is ripe for Sri Lankan Buddhists to re-evaluate and re-think of our collective stand on national and religious issues of our motherland. You can be a part of his campaign by strongly supporting the Jathika Hela Urumaya. This will be the greatest respect you can bestow on this outstanding monk.[41]

The link between Venerable Sōma and the SU, the prototype of the JHU, was firmly established towards the end of year 2002. As *The Sunday Times* reported[42] Sōma with his Jana Vijaya Foundation joined the SU to 'unite the Sinhala nationalist movement in order to defeat the elements bent on separating the country'. This was seen by important members of the SU like Udaya Gammanpila, Assistant secretary of the SU, as a 'positive step towards Sinhala unity' in creating a 'powerful force' to 'defeat the separatist process in the country.' We may want to keep in sight that the Jathika Saṅgha Sammēlanaya, which is the heart of the JHU, is affiliated to the Sihala Urumaya.[43]

In the wake of April 2004 election, the JHU produced the following song in honour of Sōma. The song alludes to the fact that the three leading JHU election candidates – Kolonnāvē Sumaṅgala, Uḍuwe Dhammālōka and Ellāvala Medhānanda – are following the footsteps of Venerable Sōma. They are requested to lead the Sinhala public in this time of crisis in order to protect Buddhism from outside threats. It aptly illustrates the frustrations of the majority Buddhists at Sōma's death and raises religious concerns that they have in relation to potential threats to the survival of Buddhism in Sri Lanka.

The JHU song for Sōma

Desu Budu baṇa[44] *hāmuduruvane vairayak vunā*	Venerable Sir, Buddha's teaching that you preached became an animosity
Jivitayak bili aragena mulu raṭama händavuvā	Sacrificing a life, you made the entire country cry
Lova utumma dharmaya ape Śrī Saddharmaya mayi	Our *Śrī Saddharma* is, indeed, the most supreme teaching in the world
Misadiṭu adahas matuva vänasenne ēnisayi	Because of those teachings, in future, wrong beliefs disappear
Eya vindagannaṭa bäri ayagē *hadavata kuriruyi*	The heart of those, who cannot bear it, is cruel
Veḍi unḍaya ellava ättē budu dahamaṭa mayi	Indeed, the bullet is aimed at the Buddha's *dhamma*[45]
Śrī Sumaṅgala samindu Uḍuvē	Venerable Śrī Sumaṅgala with
samindu samagama	Venerable Uḍuvē
Ellāvala himiyan ätuluva maha sangaruvana	Venerable Ellāvala with the *mahāsaṅgha*
Avidin peraṭama bērāganu māna ape sasuna	Come forward. May you save our *sāsana*!
Budu himi desu dharmaya ma tamā lova utum dharmaya	The supreme teaching in the world is, indeed, what the Buddha preached
Pera budun vahansē väda siri patula pihiṭa vū	In the past, the Buddha visited and placed the footprint
Apē utum danta dhātun daḷadā karanḍū	Our sacred Tooth Relic and the relic caskets
Sat piyum piyā vända illamu raṭaṭa ahimi vū	We offer seven lotuses, prostrate and beg. The country lost him
Apē Sōma himiyanī yali ipadenna matu matū	Our Venerable Sōma! Please be reborn here again and again

A recent commentator who wants to support the JHU identifies Sōma as being a part of a Buddhist social reform movement.[46] As a socio-cultural reformer, Sōma was explicit in his criticism leveled at corrupt politicians. He believed that national and religious issues are interwoven with body politic of the country.[47] Sōma believed it was the bounden duty of the state to provide protection to Buddhism, as enshrined in the constitution. He asserted a state ruled in accordance with Buddhist principles of righteous living as the key for Sri Lanka's development as also insisted by the JHU.

A recent Internet publication in the pro-JHU website mentions several political, religious and economic reasons, including the death of Sōma, for the sudden birth of the JHU in the context of unstable political affairs in contemporary Sri Lanka. According to the writer, the JHU emerged as 'the end result of a long list of reasons' which he identifies as the result of political and democratic 'non-representation of Sinhalese Buddhists' in the Sri Lanka political system.[48] It goes on to state that the JHU is 'the manifestation of this collective will' in the political sphere. The author refuses the explanation that some put forward with regard to the birth of the JHU as a 'mere reactionary phenomenon' to Sōma's sudden death. Nevertheless, he himself acknowledges the importance of Sōma's death as one of the immediate reasons for the birth of the JHU by stating that the two major political parties, United National Party (UNP) and Sri Lanka Freedom Party (SLFP), failed to 'initiate an investigation into the suspicious death' and 'overt and covert attempt by the SLFP and JVP to make use of the nationwide sympathy and sorrow over' Sōma's death as a means 'to come to power'.

The long list of reasons that gives include economic factors related to past economic policies of Sri Lankan governments, the way politicians used the political process by using minority votes at the cost of Sinhala-Buddhist rights, the rulers' failure to recognize the Sihala-Buddhist cultural heritage and the use of the Buddhist *saṅgha* for political gains, the failure to establish a just and secure civil society and the extremist activities of some Tamils and some Muslim claims in the eastern province. This collective will, according to him, aims to see 'an alternative political organization that will openly, fearlessly and proudly represent Sinhalese Buddhists'.

Monks in the JHU election platform

Establishing a Buddhist state (Sin. *Bauddha rājya*) in Sri Lanka is the main objective of the monks of the JHU. In their political agenda, the highest priority is given to the determination for a Buddhist state. Devout Sinhala Buddhists are also keen to see this happen since they are fed up with moral decadence and chaos that has emerged in contemporary Sri Lanka.

On the whole, five reasons can be identified as motivating factors that led the Buddhist monks of the JHU to contest in the general election held in April 2004:

1 the perception of Venerable Sōma's untimely death as a systematic conspiracy to weaken Buddhist reformation and renewal,
2 increasing accusations of intensified 'unethical' Christian conversions of poor Buddhists and Hindus,

3 continuing fears of the LTTE's Eelam in the context of recent peace negotiations,
4 the unstable political situation in which the two main political parties – UNP and SLFP – are in power-struggle in the midst of resolving the current ethnic problem and
5 the political ambitions of some JHU monks.

Traditionally, the majority of Theravāda Buddhist monks have stayed away from politics. The monks of the JHU entering into Sri Lankan parliamentary politics is problematic both from cultural and religious perspectives. Due to the controversial nature of the issue and debates over monks' actions, the JHU monks themselves have tried to explain the current political and social circumstances that led them to take such an unconventional decision. Their entry into active politics, they consider as the last resort, 'a decision taken with much reluctance'.[49] Before handing over the nominations for April 2004 elections, Venerable Athurāliyē Rathana, media spokesman of the JHU remarked: 'the Sangha has entered the arena of politics to ensure the protection of Buddhist heritage and values which had been undermined for centuries'.[50]

Why did Buddhist monks decide to contest in the parliamentary elections? Their answer lies in the following justifications:

1 The first justification is concerned with possible political disadvantages that the Sinhala-Buddhist majority may face as a result of the current peace negotiations with the LTTE initiated by Norway facilitators. According to the JHU, popular consensus is that there is no more division within Sri Lankan society as pro-UNP and anti-UNP. The two prominent Sinhala dominated parties – the United People's Freedom Alliance and the United People's Front – stand for the same principles. To secure power within Sri Lankan politics, both parties are ready to negotiate with the LTTE on the ISGA (Interim Self-Governing Authority) proposals forwarded by the LTTE through Norway. From the point of view of the JHU, these negotiations may disadvantage the Sinhala-Buddhist majority.
2 The second justification is related to the current tense environment created by unethical conversions initiated by non-denominational, evangelical, Protestant Christian groups. A Buddhist group named 'Jayagrahaṇaya' (Success – Sri Lanka), founded in Kandy in 1991 and approved as a charity by the Sri Lankan government in 1995, has written extensively on 'unethical' conversions carried on among poor Buddhists and Hindus by various non-denominational Christian groups which the Success identifies as 'Christian fundamentalists'. To inform the public the threat that exists for Buddhism, the Success has also published a booklet: *Āgam Māruva* (Changing Religions) written by Venerable Mädagama Dhammānanda (Dhammānanda Thera 2001), Project Director of the Success. According to Success, there are over 150 NGOs registered in Sri Lanka under Company Registration Act who carry out conversions.[51]

Various Buddhist groups including the monks who formed the JHU have demanded from the Sri Lankan government to pass a bill in the parliament to ban unethical conversions carried out among poor Buddhists and Hindus. The current controversy with regard to unethical conversions is not purely a Buddhist concern. Before the current bills, former Hindu Affairs Minister T. Maheswaran had challenged the former Prime Minister Ranil Wickremasinghe that he would resign if 'the government did not bring in an act to prevent Hindus being converted to Christianity before the 31st of December' 2003.[52] Venerable Ōmalpē Sōbhita, JHU MP, and Rajawattee Wappa sat on a fast outside the Ministry of Buddhasāsana on 30 December 2003 demanding the government to take an action on unethical conversions.[53] Newspapers captured 'smiling minister W.J.M. Lokubandara walked up to them through the group of well-wishers and onlookers and sought their permission to sit beside them'. Though Mr W.J.M. Lokubandara, Minister of Justice and Buddhasāsana, promised to take an action, he could not do anything since President Chandrika Bandaranaike Kumaranatunga dissolved the parliament in early 2004.

In this uncertain and inactive political context, the JHU believed that both major Sinhala-dominated political 'parties are not willing to ban unethical religious conversions'.[54] This loss of hope and frustration had led the JHU monks to decide to enter into the legislature. As a result of the JHU's demands, by June 2004, there were two bills on 'unethical conversions' in the Sri Lankan Parliament for approval. Venerable Ō. Sōbhita published his bill on 28 May 2004 and the Sri Lankan Government also drafted a bill. These legislative measures show how religious concerns have become important in private and public lives of Sri Lankans. Two important factors – conspiracy theories surrounding Venerable Sōma's death and the potential threats of unethical conversion to Buddhists and Hindus – have motivated the JHU monks to enter into politics.

It is also possible to identify four key phases that mark significant mileposts in the gradual development of present political activism of Buddhist monks of the JHU by drawing support from a wide range of ideologies and a cross section of Sri Lankan population:

1. the founding of Jathika Saṅgha Sabhāva (National Saṅgha Council) in 1997 by drawing support from the monks of the three monastic fraternities,
2. the birth of SU (Sinhala Heritage) Party on 20 April 2000,
3. the birth of Jathika Saṅgha Sammēlanaya (National Saṅgha Assembly) and
4. subsequent formation of JHU in February 2004 as an all-monk political party to contest April 2004 election.

All these political movements, in one way or another, embraced an idealized notion of the *dharmarājya* (righteous state) concept thought be the underlying public policy of the ancient (Buddhist) polities of Sri Lanka. It was perceived that in the most authentic form, the *dharmarājya* concept was present in the government policies of Emperor Aśoka in the third century BCE. The Buddhist monk politicians of the JHU capitalize this idealized image of *dharmarājya* concept for their own political advantage in contemporary Sri Lanka.

The *dharmarājya* concept of the JHU

To attract a captivating audience, the JHU has introduced more fashionable religious terms for its political rhetoric. One of them is the *pratipatti pūjāva*, which literally means 'an offering of principles'. The Sinhala term *pūjāva* is strictly speaking liturgical in its connotations and exclusively used in religious contexts rather than in the political platform. However, the JHU has employed it self-consciously in the highly charged expression *pratipattipūjāva* in order to introduce its political manifesto in religious terms connoting their ambition of establishing a *dharmarājya* in Sri Lanka.

The election manifesto of the JHU is rather unique because of its interesting religious content and the way it was introduced to the Sri Lankan public by invoking religious sentiments. Unlike other political parties, the JHU offered its political manifesto (*pratipattipūjāva*) to the Tooth Relic of the Gotama Buddha in Kandy.[55] On 2 March 2004, the JHU monks and lay supporters marched to the Tooth Relic Temple, Kandy from Kelaniya Temple[56] in the midst of thousands of Buddhist monks and lay people who shared the noble mission of restoring Buddhasāsana (message of the Buddha) and promoting Buddhism in Sri Lanka.

The selection of 2 March as the date of launching the election manifesto and Kandy as the place for the launch are quite significant in historic terms. March 2 symbolizes an important historic event: the day that Sri Lanka lost her independence to the British under Kandyan Convention signed on 2 March 1815. Another event that happened on that day in Kandy still in the ears of the Sinhala nationalists: when the British raised the union jack before signing the memorandum, the monk Kuḍāpola protested against it and he was shot dead there. The JHU's unveiling of its programme at a gathering in Kandy deliberately invokes religious and national sentiments.

The JHU launched its political manifesto in the hope of restoring the weakening status of Buddhism in Sri Lanka. The monks of the JHU have a clear agenda and ambition of purifying the political process from corruption and abuses. The JHU manifesto includes twelve points as principles for constructing a righteous state (Sin. *dharmarājyayak udesā vū pratipatti pūjāva*). Each item in the manifesto includes more than one principle and the Sinhala version[57] is more comprehensive than the English rendering.

1 The first principle stresses that Sri Lanka should be ruled according to Buddhist principles as it was in the past and the protection of the Buddhasāsana should be the foremost duty of any government.[58] The state is, however, identified in the manifesto as a 'Sinhala state'.[59] The state also should safeguard the rights of other religions to practice their own religious traditions. Showing the urgency of addressing religious concerns of the

majority and achieving political ambitions of the JHU, the very first principle of the manifesto mentions the issue of unethical conversions. It asserts, 'all unethical conversions are illegal'. This is an indication that the JHU will take a legislative action on 'unethical conversions' once its members are elected to the parliament.

2 The second article stresses that Sri Lanka is a Buddhist unitary state that cannot be divided.[60] National safety is an essential condition. At times when there are threats to national security, without political interference, the Police and the Three Armed Forces should be given powers to act according to the constitution to safeguard the national interests of the country.

3 Emphasizing the JHU's stand as National Sinhala Heritage Party, the manifesto states that national heritage of a country belongs to the ethnic group who made the country into a habitable civilization. The hereditary rights of the Sinhalese should be granted while protecting the rights of other communities who inhabit the island.

4 The rulers of Sri Lanka should adopt the *dharmarāja* concept of Emperor Aśoka, which was influenced by Buddhist Philosophy, and should work for the welfare of all ethnic groups. Their exemplary attitude should reflect Dharmāśoka's idea of 'all citizens are my children' (*save munisā mama pajā*).

5 The Government should control and monitor all the activities and monetary transactions of the non-government organizations (NGOs) that are in operation in Sri Lanka. This is an indication of a religious concern that the JHU has raised with accusations to evangelical Christians that the majority of NGOs that are registered in Sri Lanka under the corporation law undertake evangelical activities of converting poor Buddhists and Hindus to Christianity in the guise of providing technical education.

6 Following the *grāma rājya* concept that Sri Lanka inherited, a decentralized administration should be adopted. This is the Buddhist option that the JHU plans to adopt instead of devolution proposals that the successive Sri Lankan governments plan to implement to resolve the ethnic conflict that has arisen with terrorist activities of the LTTE. The JHU sees negatively the devolution of power as a solution to continuing ethnic problem in Sri Lanka. They maintain that the notion of devolution of power is an imported concept imposed upon them with vested interests to break Sri Lanka.[61] Their negative attitude to devolution of power is based on two factors: their fear that it will lead to the creation of a separate state for Tamils and it will lead to the creation of fanatical religious beliefs and conflicts within Sri Lanka. Instead of the devolution of power, the JHU prefers a 'decentralization' within a unitary Buddhist state. They believe that effective 'decentralization' to village level communes will solve many of the issues related to defense, administration, education, health, trade, agriculture, water and transport. Their conception of 'decentralization', they identify as '*grāma rājya saṅkalpaya*'.

7 The development should centre on the natural habitat, animals and humanity. The development should be based on the principle 'by developing the

individual human being, country should be developed'.[62] The creation of a just, national economy based upon Buddhist economic philosophy and empowering local farmers and entrepreneurs.

8 An education system that fits into the Sri Lankan cultural context and that meets the needs of the modern world should be introduced. A society in which the lay–monastic, male–female, employer–employee, child–parent, teacher–student, ruler–ruled who are mutually bound by duty should be introduced. A righteous society in which the five precepts are observed should be built on the basis of Buddhism.

9 In the past, Sri Lanka was the land of *dhamma*, which spread Buddhism around the world. Therefore, international relationships should be established with sister Buddhist countries. Friendships should be built with other countries. Whilst maintaining close relationships with the neighbouring countries, we should consider that Sri Lanka is an independent state.

10 A Buddhist council should be held to reinforce Sinhala *bhikkhu* lineage and the recommendations of 1957 and 2002 Buddhist Commission Reports[63] should be appropriately adopted.

11 Female moral rights, which are destroyed by commercialization, should be safeguarded. Nobility and dignity of motherhood should be restored.

12 Independent, free and ethical principles should be adopted for mass media.

These twelve points demonstrate guiding principles of the JHU as a Buddhist political party in Sri Lanka. In engaging in politics and in presenting this twelve-point manifesto, the key visible political motive of the monks of the JHU is their desire in creating a 'Buddhist voice' within the Sri Lankan Parliament so that Buddhist and Sinhala interests can be secured and guaranteed within the legislature. Increasingly, they perceive that power-hungry-Sinhala-lay-politicians have betrayed the Sinhala and Buddhist rights of the majority population of the country.

Election victory, chaos and the JHU in the parliament

The JHU monks have faced several controversies within the JHU's short existence so far. The act of nominating over 200 monks to contest a parliamentary election was controversial in itself. The JHU's act of using monks to contest the election has been criticized both in abroad and Sri Lanka. In addition, the existing major political parties attempt to weaken them at every possible opportunity.

The election success of the JHU, however, was a shock for many who perceived their significance very lightly since none of the candidates were highly versatile politicians. In the election held on 2 April 2004, the United People's Freedom Alliance (UPFA) – a combination of SLFP and JVP – won 105 seats out of 225. The UNP, the Sri Lankan government from 2001–2004, was defeated in the election and secured only 82 seats. Tamil National Alliance (TNA) backed by the LTTE won 22 seats. The JHU and the Sri Lanka Muslim congress (SLMC) had 9 and 5 seats respectively.

As the newest political party, the JHU had a significant success in the election; though its candidates were novices to parliamentary politics, they were able to convince a considerable section of urban population in Colombo, Gampaha and Kalutara Districts for their national and religious causes. The success of both the JHU and the JVP in 2004 election suggests that 'national unity' has become an important concern for the majority Sinhala population.

The chaos generated in selecting the speaker at the thirteenth Parliament session on 22 April 2004 shows the significance of the JHU monks in determining political process in Sri Lanka.[64] While the JHU casted the critical two votes (out of 110 against 109) in electing the former Minister of Justice, Mr W.J.M. Lokubandara of the UNP (Opposition) as the new speaker, the monks of the JHU also faced abuse within the Parliament from the UPFA Government benches and outside the Parliament by unidentified persons often associated with the JVP. When the JHU Member of Parliament, Venerable Athurāliyē Rathana, began to speak in the Parliament congratulating the elected speaker, he was disturbed by the Government peers, particularly by JVP MPs by making noises, calling names as supporters of 'separatists, terrorists and Eelamists', and throwing books at him.[65] Outside the Parliament, an array of offensive posters was posted on walls and billboards accusing the JHU monks for casting votes against people's verdict. This post-election chaos made front-page headline news in the local media.

Post-election events that occurred in relation to the acts of two members of the JHU – Venerable Aparekkē Paññānanda elected from the Gampaha District and Venerable Kathaluwē Rathanaseeha from Colombo District – have created unpleasant reactions in political sphere. Even before the elections, though Venerable Paññānanda withdrew his nomination, in the election, he won a seat from Gampaha District. Paññānanda had publicly criticized the JHU charging his companions with bribery and corruption. During his campaign, he maintained that the JHU monks accepted black money to finance their pre-election campaign and eventually voiced more support for the UPFA than for the JHU. This event created chaos within the JHU; in the public eye, it made the JHU a divisive political party. The JHU wanted to nominate another candidate on behalf of the withdrawn candidacy of Paññānanda. However, Paññānanda did not want to submit to the JHU's political wish and became a rebellion within the party. Another rebel MP, Venerable Kathaluwē Rathanaseeha, joined the dissident monk Paññānanda to create further chaos within the JHU. Before the Parliament met on 22 April 2004, both of them disappeared mysteriously and UPFA[66] was accused of the abduction.[67] All that happened thereafter is now part of Sri Lanka's very fractured and divided political sphere. Some politicians have been accused of creating this chaos atmosphere within the JHU.

Because of popularity and potential political power of the JHU within the Parliament and chaotic and divisive atmosphere within the JHU, some opponent Members of the Parliament used the opportunity to harass some members of the JHU. The opponents were not even hesitant to abuse fellow parliamentarians of the JHU physically. On 8 June 2004, when Venerable Akmeemana Dayārathana was about to take the oaths going towards the speaker's chair, 'the Government

MPs engaged in a struggle to prevent' him doing so by 'grabbing his robe and holding him from his arms'.[68] In this incident two members of the JHU – Akmeemana Dayārathana and Kolonnāvē Sumaṅgala – were seriously injured due to physical assault and admitted to Śrī Jayawardhanapura General hospital.[69] Within a short time, the JHU has become a political party of internal disputes. External pressures also have aggravated this situation. First important key member to leave the party and parliament was Ven. Kolonnāvē Sumaṅgala. Soon after Tsunami, on 6 January 2005, Ven. Dhammālōka left the JHU revealing internal divisions. Afterwards, he decided to remain as an independent Member of Parliament. His decision was not well received by the JHU supports. Letters from disheartened Sri Lankans who had actively supported the JHUs success in the election were published in the Internet. Both Ven. Ō. Sōbhita, through his fast unto death in Kandy in June 2005 and Ven. A. Rathana through his political comments on important national issues remain in the public eye as important voices within the JHU. JHU monks were also immensely efficient in helping people who were affected during the Tsunami by providing food, sheltering the victims and building houses.

On 28 May 2004, the JHU MP, Venerable Ōmalpē Sōbhita, published in the *Gazette* a bill entitled *Prohibition of Forcible Conversion of Religion Act* as a Private Member's Bill.[70] The Sri Lankan Government also drafted a bill for the approval of the Cabinet. These two events are meant to fulfil a demand that Sinhala Buddhists made over the last few years with regard to 'unethical conversions' carried out by evangelical Christians in the poor Buddhist and Hindu communities. These bills on 'unethical' conversions bring another phase of religious tensions present in the ethno-religious politics in Sri Lanka. As the youngest and the first monk-led political party, the JHU has already created a significant discourse on its policies and how it will adapt its policies in implementing them in the Parliament and outside it. It has already upset the newly elected ruling party, the UPFA and continues to be an influential factor in Sri Lankan politics.

Conclusion

I began writing this paper with reservations about the JHU's political ambitions and real intentions of entering into the Sri Lankan Parliament. Once I read their literature and reflected upon the current political crisis in Sri Lanka, I can see their importance and value in democratic politics at a crucial juncture of Sri Lankan history. On the one hand, as a minority party, the JHU can raise issues dealing with religion in the Parliament to safeguard Buddhist and Sinhala interests; on the other, their activities in the legislature with vested interest on the Sinhala and Buddhist communities can be perceived by others in future as an inhibiting force for peace in Sri Lanka.

In determining the political role of the JHU as a political party of religious members, one has to pay attention to what the Buddhist public thinks of them. When I discuss the importance of the JHU in Sri Lankan politics with Buddhist monks and lay people, they are often convinced that in difficult times Buddhist monks have to take a stand. Though monks are not allowed to involve in politics actively, considering the contemporary Sri Lankan situation, which can be seen by Buddhists as a genuine threat to the future survival of Buddhism in the island, the JHU's agenda for parliamentary politics can find justifications. Though the members of the JHU are portrayed in overseas media as nationalists and extremists, their current standing as a nationalist voice has also to be interpreted in the current volatile ethno-politics in Sri Lanka.

Notes

1 This is a revised version of an early paper 'Politics of the Jathika Hela Urumaya Monks: Buddhism and Ethnicity in Contemporary Sri Lanka', *Contemporary Buddhism* 5 (2), 2004: 83–103.

2 A critique of Tambiah's three works (1986, 1992, 1996) related to Sri Lanka can be found in Goonatilake (2001: 165–219).

3 A recent academic attempt to study the role of Buddhism in the Sri Lankan ethnic problem is *Bath Conference on Buddhism and Conflict in Sri Lanka* (Deegalle 2003).

4 On 19 February 2004, *The Island* reported that Venerable U. Dhammālōka, Colombo District Leader of the JHU, announced that 286 Buddhist monk candidates from the Jathika Saṅgha Sammēlanaya (National Saṅgha Assembly) would contest in the general election of 2004. *Spotlight on Sri Lanka*, vol. 8, no. 25 (20 February 2004).

5 Newspapers reported a colorful pageant of traditional drummers who fetched the Buddhist monk candidates of the JHU to Colombo District Secretariat on 21 February 2004 to hand over the nominations for the general election. More than 5,000 people who gathered along the roads to see the pageant uttered the traditional Buddhist response 'Sādhu ! Sādhu' to express their solidarity and joy. *Spotlight on Sri Lanka*, vol. 8, no. 25 (20 February 2004).

6 In the past, the monks of the National Bhikṣu Front affiliated with the JVP have burned the Norwegian flag opposing Norwegian mediation in Sri Lanka. They are known for visible protests. On 16 February 2005, a group of monks of National Bhikṣu Front held black banners and demonstrated in front of the UN office in Colombo against the UN General Secretary Koffi Annan's expression of condolences on the assassination of a senior LTTE leader Kaushalyan on 7 February. http://www.bbc.co.uk/sinhala/news/story/2005/02/050216_bhikku_un_protest.shtml (accessed on 2 October 2005).

7 http://www.dailymirror.lk/archives/dmr181201/index.html (accessed on 2 October 2005).

8 *Daily News*, 7 March 2002: http://www.priu.gov.lk/news_update/EditorialReviews/erev200203/20020307editorialreview.html (accessed on 2 October 2005).

9 http://www.priu.gov.lk/news_update/EditorialReviews/erev200203/20020307editorialreview.html (accessed on 2 October 2005).

10 Jayanthi Liyanage, 'Which Way Year 2004?: Ven. Baddegama Samitha Thera, Member of Parliament, Galle District'. *Sunday Observer*, 4 January 2004, http://www.sunday-observer.lk/2004/01/04/fea19.html (accessed on 2 October 2005).

11 For example, see D.A. Weeraratne, 'Ven. Samita as Pioneer Bhikkhu MP: Whither Buddha Sasana?' *The Island*, 29 December 2001 and later with the case of the JHU monks, P.G.G. Palihapitiya, 'Buddhist Monks in Politics', *The Island*, 26 February 2004 and 'JHU Monks Have Become a Laughing Stock', *Lanka Web* News, 28 April 2004.

12 'Buddhist Monks at Election: Replies to Allegations', 15 March 2004, http://www.sinhala.net/View-Point/View-Point-1.htm (accessed on 2 October 2005).

13 *Newslanka*, 8 April 2004, p. 4.
14 'Final Election Results: A Hung Parliament,' SinhalaNet, 5 April 2004, http://sinhala.net
15 S.K. Hennayake, 'Sri Lankan Politics: 2004 Election and JHU', http://members.tripod.com/amarasara/jhu/jhu-slpolitics-skh.htm (accessed on 28 August 2004).
16 http://www.dailynews.lk/2004/04/23/pol01 (accessed on 2 October 2005).
17 Venerable Ō. Sōbhita published the bill entitled *Prohibition of Forcible Conversion of Religion (Private Member's Bill)* in The Gazette of The Democratic Socialist Republic of Sri Lanka, Part II of 28 May 2004–Supplement (Issued on 31 May 2004). There are several responses both in favour and against it. See 'Conversion Battle Reaches a Climax', *The Dhamma Times*, 1 August 2004, http://www.dhammathai.org/e/news/m08/bnews01_2.php (accessed on 28 August 2004).
18 http://sihalaurumaya.s5.com/beginning.htm (accessed on 2 October 2005).
19 http://www.lankaweb.com/news/items04/290604–1.html (accessed on 2 October 2005).
20 http://www.wsws.org/articles/2000/dec2000/sri-d04.shtml. (accessed on 2 October 2005).
21 See the following site for more details: http://www.priu.gov.lk/news_update/Current_Affairs/ca200010/20001016dispute_over_national_list.htm (accessed on 2 October 2005).
22 http://www.sihalaurumaya.org (accessed on 10 April 2004).
23 The World Socialist Web Site labels the SU as a 'fascist organisation': http://www.wsws.org/articles/2000/dec2000/sri-d04.shtml (accessed on 2 October 2005); see also Panini Wijesiriwardana and K. Ratnayake, 'New Sinhala Extremist Party Fields Buddhist Monks in Sri Lankan Elections', *World Socialist Web Site*, http://www.wsws.org/articles/2004/apr2004/jhu-a01.shtml (accessed on 2 October 2005).
24 See the JHU posters at http://www.shamika.50g.com/paramithaperahara/messages/messages.html (accessed on 2 October 2005).
25 http://www.sihalaurumaya.org (accessed on 10 April 2004).
26 http://www.sihalaurumaya.org (accessed on 10 April 2004).
27 *Daily News*, 20 December 2003, http://www.dailynews.lk/2003/12/20/fea01.html (accessed on 20 October 2005).
28 *Daily News*, 20 December 2003, http://www.dailynews.lk/2003/12/20/fea01.html (accessed on 2 October 2005).
29 'Buddhist Monks at Election: Replies to Allegations', 15 March 2004 http://members.tripod.com/amarasara/jhu/jhu-replies1.htm (accessed on 2 October 2005).
30 http://www.lankaweb.com/news/items04/290604–1.html (accessed on 2 October 2005).
31 Both the transliteration from Sinhalese and English translation are mine. The location of the poster: http://www.shamika.50g.com/paramithaperahara/somathero/forsomethero.html (accessed on 2 October 2005).
32 *Daily News*, 20 December 2003, http://www.dailynews.lk/2003/12/20/fea01.html (accessed on 2 October 2005).
33 See the front page of Amarasara Website in which the photos of Sōma and Dharmapāla are displayed side by side: http://www.amarasara.net (accessed on 18 April 2004). Also see http://www.shamika.50g.com/somathero/
34 *Daily News*, 20 December 2003, http://www.dailynews.lk/2003/12/20/fea01.html (accessed on 2 October 2005).
35 For Sōma's biography, see http://vihara.org.au/ (accessed on 2 October 2005).
36 For a discussion of popular Buddhist preaching and its development in contemporary Sri Lanka see Deegalle (1997, 2003).

37 Andrew Scott, 'Soma Thera – Dedicated Buddhist and Nationalist', *Daily News*, 25 December 2003, http://www.dailynews.lk/2003/12/25/fea02.html (accessed on 2 October 2005).
38 *Sunday Observer*, 21 December 2003, http://www.sundayobserver.lk/2003/12/21/fea07.html (accessed on 2 October 2005).
39 Chamuditha Samarawickrema of TNL was the presenter of the religious programmes *Näna Pahana* with Venerable Sōma and *Daham Suvanda* with Venerable U. Dhammālōka. *Sunday Observer*, 4 January 2004, http://www.sundayobserver.lk/2004/01/04/fea19.html (accessed on 2 October 2005).
40 Even before the birth of the JHU, Venerable U. Dhammālōka, the JHU MP from Colombo District, faced the camera with Sōma's weeping mother besides Sōma's dead body. *Lankādīpa*, 28 December 2003, p. 20.
41 Daya Hewapathirane, 'The Buddhist Social Reform Movement of Ven. Soma', http://shamika.50g.com/paramithaperahara/articles/27march2004.html (accessed on 2 October 2005).
42 Pujitha Wijetunge, 'Soma Thera Joins SU', *The Sunday Times*, 3 December 2002, http://www.dailymirror.lk/2002/12/03/News/7.html (accessed on 2 October 2005).
43 Pujitha Wijetunge, 'Soma Thera Joins SU', *The Sunday Times*, 3 December 2002, http://www.dailymirror.lk/2002/12/03/News/7.html
44 The Sinhala word *baṇa* is often used with reference to the teachings of the Buddha as well as to the preaching performances held in Sri Lanka. For a historical study of its religious significance see Deegalle (1997).
45 The transliteration from Sinhala and English translation of the JHU song for Sōma are mine. I have retained some crucial Pāli words in the translation to convey specific ideas embedded in the song.
46 Daya Hewapathirane, 'The Buddhist Social Reform Movement of Ven. Soma', http://shamika.50g.com/paramithaperahara/articles/27march2004.html (accessed on 2 October 2005).
47 This identification of national and religious issues is very common in the Sri Lankan Buddhist thinking. When I guided the delegation of the Buddhist Federation of Norway to the Bhikkhu Training Centre's Dahampāsāla, Venerable Hakmanē Sumanasiri responded: 'As a Sri Lankan, I feel no separation between Buddhism and the Nation. For more than two millennia Sri Lanka has developed according to Buddhism and it is now difficult to separate Buddhism from the Nation.'
48 S.K. Hennayake, 'Sri Lanka Politics: 2004 Election and JHU', http://members.tripod.com/amarasara/jhu/jhu-slpolitics-skh.htm (accessed on 5 August 2004).
49 http://www.srilankanelections.com/manifestos/HJU-EngManifesto.html (accessed on 2 October 2005).
50 *Daily Mirror*, 19 February 2004; *Spotlight on Sri Lanka*, vol. 8, no. 25 (20, February 2004); http://xi.pair.com/isweb3/spot/c0825.html (accessed on 2 October 2005).
51 The tenth anniversary souvenir of the Success (published in 2001) contains several short entries on the subject: *Āgama māruva* (a report of 'Religious Amity' conference held at IFS, Kandy on 19 August 1993), a photograph of a peaceful confrontation of a young woman who was involved in converting Buddhists to Christianity, and a poem that invokes threats of religious conversion. For more details on these issues, see also the report of the Laṅkā Bauddha Sanrakshana Sabhāwa Conference on the 'Challenges to the Buddha Sāsana' held at BMICH on 30 July 2001.
52 http://www.spur.asn.au/News_2003_Dec_31.htm (accessed on 2 October 2005).
53 http://www.spur.asn.au/News_2003_Dec_31.htm (accessed on 2 October 2005).
54 'Buddhist Monks at Election: Replies to Allegations', 15 March 2004, http://members.tripod.com/amarasara/jhu/jhu-replies1.htm (accessed on 2 October 2005).
55 http://www.srilankanelections.com/manifesto/HJU-EngManifesto.html (accessed on 2 October 2005).

56 http://www.sihalaurumaya.org (accessed on 27 April 2004). This site includes a photograph of Venerable Ellāwala Medhānanda and Venerable Kolonnāvē Sumaṅgala at the commencement of 'Pāramithā Perahera' from Kelaniya Temple on 2 March 2004.

57 For the full Sinhala version of the manifesto see http://www.jayasanka.org/dharma_rajjya.jpg (accessed on 3 April 2004) and http://www.jathikahelaurumaya.org/Index1.html. (accessed on 3 April 2004) For an abridged and incomplete English version see http://www.srilankanelections.com/manifestos/HJU-EngManifesto.html (accessed on 2 October 2005).

58 This is a further assertion of the fact that the Sri Lankan constitution agrees that the protection of Buddhism is the foremost duty of the state.

59 This notion of 'Sinhala' state can become a problem in the context of modern multi-ethnic and multi-religious Sri Lanka.

60 The emphasis here on a 'unitary state' is a clear indication of refusal to divide the country by LTTE initiated attempts.

61 http://members.tripod.com/amarasara/jhu/jhu-21qa.htm (accessed on 23 April 2004).

62 This approach to the development of Sri Lanka is very much Buddhist in nature. Leading monks like Venerable Maḍihē Paññāsīha (1997: 62) and his outspoken pupil, Sōma, preferred a person-centreed approach to the development.

63 There are several reports with regard to the status of Buddhism (Buddhist Committee of Inquiry 1956) and Sinhala people (The National Joint Committee 2001).

64 http://www.dailynews.lk/2004/04/23/pol01 (accessed on 2 October 2005).

65 Ibid.

66 Dilrukshi Handunnetti and Mandana Ismail Abeywickrema, 'Two Ministers, Deputies Named in Monk Attack', *The Sunday Leader*, 13 June 2004, http://www.thesundayleader.lk/20040613/home.htm

67 Frederica Jansz, 'Case of the Missing Monks', *The Sunday Leader*, 25 April 2004, http://www.thesundayleader.lk/20040425/issues-1.htm

68 Ranil Wijayapala and Bharatha Mallawararachchi, 'JHU to Unite with Opposition', *Daily News*, 9 June 2004, http://www.dailynews.lk/2004/06/09/pol02.html (accessed on 2 October 2005).

69 For evidence of physical abuse see http://shamika.50g.com/attacks/attack.html; http://members.tripod.com/amarasara/jhu/images/jhu-20040620–01.jpg (accessed on 2 October 2005).

70 *Daily News*, 6 August 2004, http://www.dailynews.lk/2004/08/06/new13.html (accessed on 2 October 2005).

BIBLIOGRAPHY

Abeyawardana, H.A.P. 1978. *Kadaimpot vimarsanaya*. Colombo: Ministry of Cultural Affairs.

Abeysekara, Ananda. 2001. "Identity for and Against Itself: Religion, Criticism and Pluralization." A public lecture given at Old Dominion University.

—— 2002. *Colors of the Robe*. South Carolina, SC: University of South Carolina Press.

Adhikari, Abhayaratna. 1991. *Śrī Laṅkāvē Sambhāvya Adhyapanaya hā Mahāsaṅgana*. Colombo: S. Goḍagē and Sons.

Agarwal, Bina. 1994. *A Field of One's Own*. Cambridge: Cambridge University Press.

Amunugama, Sarath. 1991. "Buddhaputra and Bhumiputra?" *Religion* 21: 115–39.

Anderson, Benedict. 1983. *Imagined Communities*. London: Verso.

Apex Body. 2003. "Text of GOSL proposals submitted to the LTTE." *The Sunday Times*, June 1, 2003.

Ariyapala, M.B. 1956. *Society in Medieval Ceylon*. Colombo: Department of Cultural Affairs.

Ariyaratne, A.T. 1987. *Peace Making in Sri Lanka in the Buddhist Context*. Ratmalāna: Sarvōdaya Vishva Lekhā Press.

—— 1989. *Collected Works*. 4 vols. Ratmalāna: Sarvōdaya Vishva Lekhā Press.

Armitage, Richard. 2003. "Comments on a possible Indian Role in the Peace Process and the ISGA Proposal." http://www.rediff.com (accessed on November 4, 2003).

Athas, Iqbal. 2003. "Situation Report." *The Sunday Times*, March 16, 2003.

Balasingham, Anton. 2003. "Communication to Prime Minister Ranil Wickremesinghe." Available from http://www.the academic.org

Bandaranaike, S.W.R.D. 1926. "Series of Six Articles by Bandaranaike." *The Ceylon Morning Leader*, May 19–June 30, 1926.

Barber, Karin. 1991. *I Could Speak Until Tomorrow*. Washington DC: Smithsonian Institution Press.

Bartholomeusz, Tessa J. 1999. "In Defense of Dharma: Just-War Ideology in Buddhist Sri Lanka." *Journal of Buddhist Ethics* 6: 1–16.

—— 2002. *In Defense of Dharma*. London: RoutledgeCurzon.

Bartholomeusz, Tessa J. and Chandra R. de Silva (eds). 1998. *Buddhist Fundamentalism and Minority Identities in Sri Lanka*. Albany, NY: State University of New York Press.

—— 2001. *The Role of the Sangha in the Reconciliation Process*. Colombo: Marga Institute.

Basic Principles. 2003. "Basic Principles for Peace and Development Draft." *The Sunday Leader*, June 8, 2003.

Bechert, Heinz. 1973. *Buddhismus*. 3 vols. Vol. 3. Wiesbaden: O. Harrassowitz.

Bechert, Heinz and Richard Gombrich (eds). 1984. *The World of Buddhism*. London and New York: Thames and Hudson.

Bond, George. 1998. "Conflicts of Identity and Interpretation of Buddhism." In *Buddhist Fundamentalism and Minority Identities in Sri Lanka*, edited by Tessa J. Bartholomeusz and Chandra R. de Silva, 36–52. Albany, NY: State University of New York Press.

Briggs, Charles. 1996. "The Politics of Discursive Authority in Research on the Invention of Tradition." *Cultural Anthropology* 11 (4): 435–69.

Buddhaputra Thera. 1965. *Pūjāvaliya*. Edited by Kiriälle Ñāṅavimala Thera. Colombo: M.D. Gunasena.

Buddhasāsana Amātyansaya. 1990. *Kolamba Bandaranaike Anusmaraṅa Jātyantara Śālāvēdi Pavatvanalada Buddha Sāsana Amātyansayē Kāryabhāraya Pilibaṅda Sammantranayē Vārtāva* (August 20–22, 1990). Colombo: Department of Government Printing.

Buddhist Committee of Inquiry. 1956. *The Betrayal of Buddhism*. Balangoda: Dharmavijaya Press.

Butalis, Urvashi. 1998. *The Other Side of Silence*. New Delhi: Penguin Books.

Carter, John Ross, and Mahinda Palihawadana. 1987. *The Dhammapada*. New York: Oxford University Press.

Collins, Steven. 1998. *Nirvāna and Other Buddhist Felicities*. Cambridge: Cambridge University Press.

ColomboPage. 2003. "LTTE Rejects Development Authority." Available from http://www.colombopage.com (April 1, 2004).

—— 2004. "Army Eases High Security Zones." Available from http://www.colombopage.com (April 1, 2004).

Da Silva Cosme, O.M. 1990. *Fidalgos in the Kingdom of Kotte*. Colombo: Harwood Publishers.

Dalai Lama. 1999. *Ethics for the New Millenium*. New York: Riverhead Books.

Dayal, Har. 1932. *The Bodhisattva Doctrine in Buddhist Sanskrit Literature*. London: Kegan Paul, Trench, Trubner.

De Queyroz, Fernao. 1930. *The Temporal and Spiritual Conquest of Ceylon*. Translated by S.G. Perera. Colombo: Government Printer.

De Silva, Chandra R. 1998. "The Plurality of Buddhist Fundamentalism." In *Buddhist Fundamentalism and Minority Identities in Sri Lanka*, edited by Tessa J. Bartholomeusz and Chandra R. de Silva, 53–73. Albany, NY: State University of New York Press.

—— 1999. "The Role of Education in the Amelioration of Political Violence in Sri Lanka." In *Creating Peace in Sri Lanka*, edited by Robert I. Rotberg, 109–29. Cambridge, MA: The World Peace Foundation.

—— 2001. "The (Mis)education of Buddhist Monks in Sri Lanka." Paper read at *Annual Meeting of the South Eastern Conference of the Association for Asian Studies 12–13 January 2001*.

—— 2002. "Comment on Ven. Akurāṭiyē Nanda's Paper" read at *International Conference on Buddhism and Conflict in Sri Lanka*, at Bath Spa University on June 28–30, 2002.

—— 2003. "Peace in Sri Lanka: Problems and Prospects." *Asia Pacific Law Review* 11 (1): 1–22.

De Silva, K.M. (ed.). 1973. *History of Ceylon*. Vol. 3. Peradeniya: University of Ceylon.

—— 1981. *A History of Sri Lanka*. Delhi: Oxford University Press.

—— (ed.). 1986. *Managing Ethnic Tensions in Multiethnic Societies, Sri Lanka 1880–1985*. Washington, DC: University Press of America.

—— (ed.). 1993. *Sri Lanka: Problems of Governance*. Delhi: Konark Publishers.

De Silva, Lynn. 1974. *Buddhism*. Colombo: The Wesley Press.

Deegalle, Mahinda. 1997. "Buddhist Preaching and Sinhala Religious Rhetoric." *Numen* 44: 180–210.

—— 1997. "Reconsidering Buddhist Preaching." In *Recent Researches in Buddhist Studies: Essays in Honour of Professor Y. Karunadasa*, edited by K. Dhammajoti, Asanga Tilakaratne, and Kapila Abhayawansa, 427–53. Colombo and Hong Kong: Y. Karunadasa Felicitation Committee.

—— 2002. "Is Violence Justified in Theravada?" *Current Dialogue* 39: 8–17.

—— 2003a. "Preacher as a Poet." In *Constituting Communities*, edited by John C. Holt, Jacob N. Kinnard, and Jonathan Walters, 151–69. Albany, NY: State University of New York Press.

—— (ed.). 2003b. *Buduṣamaya saha Śrī Laṅkāvē Janavārgika Ghaṭṭanaya*. Oslo: The Buddhist Federation of Norway.

—— (ed.). 2003c. "Bath Conference on 'Buddhism and Conflict in Sri Lanka'." *Journal of Buddhist Ethics* 10: http://www.jbe.gold.ac.uk/10/bath-conf.html (accessed on October 1, 2005).

—— 2006. "Buddhist Monks as Foot Soldiers in Political Activism in Sri Lanka." In *Can Faiths Make Peace? Holy Wars and the Resolution and Religious Conflicts from Historical and Contemporary Perspectives*, edited by Philip Broadhead and Damien Keown, 135–53. London: I.B. Tauris.

Deraniyagala, S.U. 1992. *The Prehistory of Sri Lanka*. Colombo: Department of Archaeology.

Dewaraja, L. S. 1988. *The Kandyan Kingdom of Sri Lanka 1707–1782*. Colombo: Lake House.

Dhammānanda Thera, Mädagama. 2001. *Āgam Māruva (Changing Religions)*. Kandy: Success.

Dharmadasa, K.N.O. 1979. "Sinhala Buddhist Identity and the Politics of the Kandyan Kingdom 1739–1815." In *Collective Identities: Nationalism and Protests in Modern Sri Lanka*, edited by Michael Roberts, 91–128. Colombo: Tisara.

—— 1992. "The People of the Lion." *Sri Lanka Journal of the Humanities* 15 (1 and 2): 1–35.

Dharmapāla, Anagārika. 1928. "The Unknown Co-founders of Buddhism." *The Mahā Bodhi* 36: 67–71.

—— 1965. *Return to Righteousness*, edited by W.P. Ananda Guruge. Colombo: Ministry of Educational and Cultural Affairs.

Divayina. 2002. "Report on Speech by Soosai." *Divayina*, March 6, 2002.

Edirisinghe, Rohan. 1999. "Constitutionalism, Pluralism and Ethnic Conflic." In *Creating Peace in Sri Lanka*, edited by Robert I. Rotberg, 169–87. Cambridge, MA: The World Peace Foundation.

Fanon, Frantz. 1963. *The Wretched of the Earth*. New York: Grove Press.

—— 1967. *Black Skin, White Masks*. New York: Grove Press.

Farmer, B.H. 1963. *Ceylon*. London: Oxford University Press.

Fernando, P. Edwin Ebert. 1960. "Tantric Influence on the Sculptures at Gal Vihāra, Polonnaruva." *University of Ceylon Review* 18 (1 and 2): 50–66.

Freud, Sigmund. 1981. *Group Psychology and the Analysis of the Ego*. London: The Hogarth Press.

Frydenlund, Iselin. 2005. *The Sangha and Its Relation to the Peace Process in Sri Lanka: A Report for the Norwegian Ministry of Foreign Affairs*. Oslo: International Peace Research Institute, Oslo (PRIO).

Geiger, Wilhelm. 1960. *Culture of Ceylon in Medieval Times*, edited by Heinz Bechart. Wiesbaden: Otto Harrassowitz.

Geiger, Wilhelm and C. Mabel Rickmers (trans.). 1973. *Cūlavaṃsa: Being the More Recent Part of the Mahāvaṃsa*. London: The Pali Text Society.

—— 1980. *Cūlavaṃsa: Being the More Recent Part of the Mahāvaṃsa*. Vols 1 and 2. London: The Pali Text Society.

Gellner, Ernest. 1983. *Nations and Nationalism*. Ithaca, NY: Cornell University Press.

Goldhagen, Daniel Jonah. 1996. *Hitler's Willing Executioners: Ordinary Germans and the Holocaust*. New York: Alfred A. Knopf.

Gombrich, Richard F. 1973. "Le clergé bouddhiste d'une circonscription kandienne et les éléctions générales de 1965." *Social Compass* 20 (2): 257–66.

Goonatilake, Susantha. 2001. *Anthropologizing Sri Lanka: A Eurocentric Misadventure*. Bloomington and Indianapolis, IN: Indiana University Press.

Gooneratne, Sita Padmini, H.T. Basnayake, and Senake Bandaranayake. 1984. "The Sigiri graffiti." In *Sigiriya Project: First Archaeological Excavation and Research Report*, edited by Central Cultural Fund. Colombo: Ministry of Cultural Affairs.

Gray, John. 1995. *Enlightenment's Wake: Politics and Culture at the Close of the Modern Age*. London: Routledge.

Gunasekara, B. 1900. *Rājāvaliya*. Colombo: George J.A. Skeen.

Gunawardana, R.A.L.H. 1978. "The Kinsmen of the Buddha: Myth as Political Charter in the Ancient and Early Medieval Kingdoms of Sri Lanka." In *Religion and Legitimation of Power in Sri Lanka*, edited by Bardwell L. Smith, 96–106. Chambersburg, PA: Anima Books.

—— 1985. "The People of the Lion: Sinhala Consciousness in History and Historiography." In *Ethnicity and Social Change in Sri Lanka*, edited by Social Scientists' Association. Colombo: Navamaga Printers.

—— 1990. "The People of the Lion." In *Sri Lanka: History and the Roots of Conflict*, edited by Jonathan Spencer, 45–85. London: Routledge and Kegan Paul.

—— 1995. *Historiography in a Time of Ethnic Conflict: Construction of the Past in Contemporary Sri Lanka*. Colombo: Social Scientists' Association.

Harris, Elizabeth J. 1994. *Violence and Disruption in Society: A Study of Early Buddhist Texts*. Kandy: Buddhist Publication Society.

Harvey, Peter. 2000. *An Introduction to Buddhist Ethics: Foundations, Values and Issues*. Cambridge: Cambridge University Press.

Helgerson, John. 1992. *Forms of Nationhood: The Elizabethan Writing of England*. Chicago, IL: University of Chicago Press.

Holt, John Clifford. 1991. *Buddha in the Crown: Avalokiteśvara in the Buddhist Traditions of Sri Lanka*. New York: Oxford University Press.

—— 1996. *The Religious World of Kīrti Śrī: Buddhism, Art, and Politics in Medieval Sri Lanka*. Oxford: Oxford University Press.

—— 1998. "The Persistence of Political Buddhism." In *Buddhist Fundamentalism and Minority Identities in Sri Lanka*, edited by Tessa J. Bartholomeusz and Chandra R. de Silva. 1–35. Albany, NY: State University of New York Press.

Horner, I.B. (trans.). 1954. *The Middle Length Sayings*. Vol. 1. London: The Pali Text Society.

Houtman, Gustaaf. 1993. "Sight and Insight: Globalisation, Dishabit, and the Experience of Non-Self." Paper read at *Association of Social Anthropologists' Decennial Conference*, July 26–30, 1993, at St Catherine's College, University of Oxford.

—— 1994. "Between Ruler and Yogi: Mental Culture in Colonial and Postcolonial Burma." Paper read at *The Buddhist Forum*, February 16, 1994, at SOAS, University of London.

Ilangasinha, H.B.M. 1992. *Buddhism in Medieval Sri Lanka*, edited by Sunil Gupta, *Bibliotheca Indo-Buddhica Series No. 77*. Delhi: Sri Satguru Publications.

Inden, Ronald. 1998. "Ritual, Authority, and Cycle Time in Hindu Kingship." In *Kingship and Authority in South Asia*, edited by J.F. Richards, 41–91. New Delhi: Oxford University Press.

ISGA. 2003. *Interim Self-governing Authority Proposal*. http://www.tamilnation.org/conflictresolution/tamileelam/norway/031101isga.htm (accessed on October 1, 2005).

—— 2003. "LTTE Proposal for an Interim Self-governing Authority, *Sunday Observer*, Novermber 2, 2003.

Jayatilleke, Kulatissa Nanda. 2000. *Dhamma, Man and Law*. Dehiwela: Buddhist Cultural Centre.

Jeyaraj, D.B.S. 2002. "Need for SLMC-LTTE MOU." *The Sunday Leader*, April 7, 2002.

Kantowsky, Detlef. 1980. *Sarvodaya*. Delhi: Vikas.

—— 1987. *Learning How to Live in Peace*. Ratmalāna: Sarvōdaya Vishva Lekhā Press.

Kemper, Steven. 1991. *The Presence of the Past: Chronicles, Politics, and Culture in Sinhala Life*. Ithaca, NY: Cornell University Press.

Keyes, Charles F. 1977. *The Golden Peninsula: Culture and Adaptation in Mainland South East Asia*. New York: Macmillan.

Knipe, David M. 1991. *Hinduism: Religious Traditions of the World*. San Francisco: HarperSan Francisco.

Lewis, Carrol. 1992. *Alices Adventures and Through the Looking Glass*. New York: Alfred A. Knoff, Inc.

Liyanagamage, Amaradasa. 1968. *The Decline of Poḷonnaruva and the Rise of Dambadeṇiya (circa 1180–1270 A.D.)*. Colombo: Department of Cultural Affairs.

—— 1986. "Keralas in Medieval Sri Lankan History: A Study of Two Contrasting Roles." *Kalyāni: Journal of the Humanities and Social Sciences of the University of Kelaniya* 5 and 6: 61–77.

Liyanage, Sumanasiri. 1996. "Devolution of Power and the Democratization of the State." *Daily News*, December 17, 1996.

Loy, David R. 2000. "How to Reform a Serial Killer?: The Buddhist Approach to Restorative Justice." *Journal of Buddhist Ethics* 7: 145–68.

McGowan, William. 1992. *Only Man is Vile*. New York: Farrar, Straus and Giroux.

McTernan, Oliver. 2003. *Violence in God's Name: Religion in an Age of Conflict*. London: Darton, Longman and Todd Ltd.

Macy, Joanna. 1983. *Dharma and Development: Religion as a Resource in the Sarvodaya Self-help Movement*. West Hardtford, CN: Kumarian Press.

Mahānāma Thera. 1908. *Mahāvaṃsa*. Edited by Wilhelm Geiger. London: Luzac & Company Ltd.

—— 1950. *The Mahāvaṃsa or The Great Chronicle of Ceylon*. Trans. by Wilhelm Geiger. Colombo: Ceylon Government Information Department.

—— 2002. "Statement Issued by the Mahānāyakas in Tokyo." *Daily News*, June 5, 2002.

Mahāvaṃsaya. 1967. Translated by H.S. Sumaṅgala. Kolamba: Ratnākara Pot Velanda Śālāva.

Manogaran, Chelvadorai. 1999a. "Origin of the National Conflict in Sri Lanka and Sinhalese Ethnic Nationalism." In *International Conference on Tamil Nationhood and the Search for Peace in Sri Lanka*. 160–71. Ottawa: The Academic Society of Tamil Students.

—— 1999b. "Sinhalese Settlements and Forced Evictions of Tamils in the Northern and Eastern Provinces." In *International Conference on Tamil Nationhood and the Search for Peace in Sri Lanka*, 151–59. Ottawa: The Academic Society of Tamil Students.

Manor, James. 1994. "Organizational Weakness and the Rise of Sinhalese Buddhist Extremism." In *Accounting for Fundamentalisms: The Dynamic Character of Movements*, edited by Martin E. Marty and R. Scott Appleby, 4. Chicago, IL: The University of Chicago Press.

Marapana, Thilak. 2003. "Statement in Parliament on 8 October 2003." *The Sunday Times*, October 12, 2003.

Martinesz, Rodney. 2002. "SLMC Strikes Deal with LTTE." *The Daily News*, April 16, 2002.

Meyer, Eric. 1990. "Representations of the Past and Space as Obstacles to Peace in Sri Lanka." Paper read at *Uppsala Seminar on Obstacle to Peace in Sri Lanka*.

Milindapañho: Being Dialogues between King Milinda and the Buddhist Sage Nāgasena. 1962. Edited by V. Trenckner. London. The Pali Text Society.

Milinda-Tīkā. 1961. Edited by P.S. Jaini. London: The Pali Text Society.

MOU. 2002. "Memorandum of Understanding (MOU): Agreement on a Ceasefire between the Government of the Democratic Socialist Republic of Sri Lanka and the Liberation Tigers of Tamil Eelam." *Sunday Times*, February 24, 2002.

MOU, SLFP-JVP. 2004. "Text of the Memorandum of Understanding between the SLFP and the JVP signed on 20 January 2004." *Dinamina*, January 21, 2004.

Mudiyanse, Nandasena. 1967. *Mahāyāna Monuments in Ceylon*. Colombo: M.D. Gunasena.

Nairn, Tom. 2002. *Pariah: Misfortunes of the British Kingdom*. London: Verso.

Ñāṇamoli, Bhikkhu and Bhikkhu Bodhi. 1995. The Middle Length Discourses of the Buddha. Kandy: Buddhist Publication Society.

Ñāṇānanda, Bhikkhu. 1986. *Concept and Reality in Early Buddhist Thought*. Kandy: Buddhist Publication Society.

Nanda Thera, Akurāṭiyē. 2002. "An Analysis of the Selected Statements Issued by the Mahānāyakas on the North-East Problem of Sri Lanka." Paper read at *Internationl Conference on Buddhism and Conflict in Sri Lanka*, at Bath Spa University on June 28–30, 2002; http://www.jbe.gold.ac.uk (accessed on October 1, 2005).

Narada Thera. 1978. *The Dhammapada*. Kuala Lumpur: Buddhist Missionary Society.

Nissan, Elizabeth and R.L. Stirrat. 1990. "The Generation of Communal Identities." In *Sri Lanka: History and the Roots of Conflict*, edited by Jonathan Spencer, 19–44. London: Routledge.

Norman, K.R. (trans.). 1984. *The Group of Discourses*. Vol. 1. London: The Pali Text Society.

Norwegian Communique. 2002. "Communique issued by the Royal Norwegian Government on 5 December 2002." *The Sunday Leader*, December 22, 2002.

Nyanatiloka Thera. 1980. *Buddhist Dictionary*. Kandy: Buddhist Publication Society.

Obeyesekere, Gananath. 1966. "The Buddhist Pantheon in Ceylon and Its Extensions." In *Anthropological Studies in Theravāda Buddhism*, edited by Manning Nash, 1–26. New Haven: Yale University Press.

—— 1972. "Religious Symbolism and Political Change in Ceylon." In *Two Wheels of Dhamma*, edited by Gananath Obeyesekere, Frank E. Reynolds, and Bardwell L. Smith, 58–78. Chambersburg, PA: American Academy of Religion.

—— 1978. "The Firewalkers of Kataragama: The Rise of Bhakti Religiosity in Buddhist Sri Lanka." *Journal of Asian Studies* 37 (3): 457–76.

—— 1984. *The Cult of Goddess Pattini*. Chicago, IL: University of Chicago Press.

—— 1988. *A Meditation on Conscience*. Colombo: Social Scientists' Association of Sri Lanka.

—— 1993. "Duṭṭagāmiṇī and the Buddhist Conscience." In *Religion and Political Conflict in South Asia: India, Pakistan and Sri Lanka*, edited by Douglas Allen, 135–60. Delhi: Oxford University Press.

Oldenberg, Hermann (ed.). 1982. *The Dīpavaṃsa: An Ancient Buddhist Historical Record*. New Delhi: Asian Educational Services.

Paññāsīha Thera, Maḍihē (ed.). 1990. *Buddhavaṃsaya, Sāsanavaṃsaya hā Amarapuravaṃsaya*. Maharagama: Sāsana Sēvaka Samitiya.

—— 1997. "A Country's Development: The Buddhist Standpoint." In *Prajñāprabhā*, edited by Śrī Sugata Śiṣya Sansadaya, 62–68. Maharagama: Sāsana Sēvaka Samitiya.

Paranavitana, Senarat (ed.). 1933. *Epigraphia Zeylanica*. Vol. 3. London: Oxford University Press.

—— (ed.). 1943. *Epigraphia Zeylanica*. Vol. 4. London: Oxford University Press.

—— 1956. *Sīgiri Graffiti*. Oxford.

Pathirana, Saroj. 2002. "Ranil Blessed by Buddhist Mahanayakas." *SLNet News Report*, April 27, 2002.

Pathmanathan, S. 1982. "Kingship in Sri Lanka: A.D. 1070–1270." *Sri Lanka Journal of the Humanities* 8: 120–45.

—— 1986. "Buddhism and Hinduism in Sri Lanka: Some Points of Contact between Two Religious Traditions circa A.D. 1300–1600." *Kalyāṇi: Journal of Humanities and Social Sciences of the University of Kelaniya* 5 and 6: 78–112.

Peebles, Patrick. 1990. "Colonization and Ethnic Conflict in the Dry Zone of Sri Lanka." *Journal of Asian Studies* 49 (1): 30–55.

Pico, Giandomenico. 2001. *Crossing the Divide: Dialogue among Civilizations*. South Orange, NJ: Seton Hall University.

Pieris, Paul E. 1939. *Tri Sinhala: The Last Phase 1796–1815*. Colombo: The Colombo Apothecaries Co.

—— 1995. *Sinhale and the Patriots 1815–1818*. New Delhi: Navrang.

Pirapaharan, Veluppillai. 2002a. "Interview with Pirapaharan." *Broadcast in the Sirasa* TV channel on April 10, 2002.

—— 2002b. "The Press versus Prabhakaran." *The Sunday Times*, April 14, 2002.

Ponnampalam, G.G. 1999. "The Current Political Dynamics of the Tamil National Conflict in Sri Lanka." In *International Conference on Tamil Nationhood and the Search for Peace in Sri Lanka*. May 21–22 (1999) held at Carleton University and The University of Ottawa.

Premasiri, P.D. 1972. *The Philosophy of the Aṭṭhakavagga*. Kandy: Buddhist Publication Society.

—— 1985. "Treatment of Minorities in the Buddhist Doctrine." *Ethnic Studies Report* 3 (2): 57–71.

Prematilleke, Leelananda. 1981. The Alahana Parivena Poḷonnaruva Archaeological Excavation Report (April–September 1981). Colombo: Ministry of Cultural Affairs.

Rahula, Walpola. 1959. *What the Buddha Taught*. Bedford, London: Gordon Fraser.

—— 1974. *The Heritage of the Bhikkhu: A Short History of the Bhikkhu in the Educational, Cultural, Social, and Political Life*. New York: Grove Press.

Rathana Thera, Athurāliyē. 2003. "A Buddhist Analysis of the Ethnic Conflict." *Journal of Buddhist Ethics* 10; http://www.jbe.gold.ac.uk/10/rathana-sri-lanka-conf.html (accessed on October 1, 2005).

Reed, Susan A. 2002. "Performing Respectability: The Berava, Middle-class Nationalism and the Classification of Kandyan Dance in Sri Lanka." *Cultural Anthropology* 17 (2): 246–77.

Report of Commissioners Appointed to Inquire into the Administration of the Buddhist Temporalities. 1876. In *Sessional Paper of the Legislative Council 1876–77*. Colombo: Government Press.

Reynolds, C.H.B. (ed.). 1970. *An Anthology of Sinhalese Literature up to 1815*. London: George Allen and Unwin.

Reynolds, Frank E. 1972. "The Two Wheels of Dhamma: A Study of Early Buddhism." In *The Two Wheels of Dhamma: Essays on the Theravada Tradition in India and Ceylon*, edited by Gananath Obeyesekere, Frank E. Reynolds, and Bardwell L. Smith, 1–15. Chambersburg, PA: American Academy of Religion.

Roberts, Michael. 1979a. "Stimulants and Ingredients in the Awakening of Latter Day Nationalism." In *Collective Identities: Nationalism and Protests in Modern Sri Lanka*, edited by Michael Roberts. Colombo: Marga Institute.

—— (ed.). 1979b. *Collective Identities: Nationalism and Protests in Modern Sri Lanka*. Colombo: Marga Institute.

—— 1995. *Caste Conflict and Elite Formation: The Rise of a Karava Elite in Sri Lanka, 1500–1931*. New Dehli: Navrang.

—— 2001. "The Burden of History: Obstacles to Power Sharing in Sri Lanka." *Indian Sociology, new series* 35 (1): 65–96.

Ronxi, Li (trans.). 1996. "Simhala." In *The Great Tang Dynasty Record of the Western Regions*, 323–33. Berkeley: The Numata Center.

Said, Edward. 2002. "'We' Know Who 'We' Are." *London Review of Books* 24 (20): 23–25; http://www.co.uk/v24/n20/said01_.html (accessed October 17, 2002).

Samyutta Nikāya. 1976. Vol. V. London: The Pali Text Society.

Saparamadu, S.D. (ed.). 1973. *The Poḷonnaruva Period*. Dehiwala: Tisara Prakāśakayō.

Sarvananthan, Mutukrishna. 2003. "Proposals for an Interim Self Governing Authority: ISGA Power to Elected Representatives Only." *The Sunday Observer*, November 16, 2003.

Sathananthan, S. 1999. "Peace Process in Sri Lanka: The Hidden Agenda." In *International Conference on Tamil Nationhood and the Search for Peace in Sri Lanka*, 215–29. Ottawa: The Academic Society of Tamil Students.

Schalk, Peter. 1999. "Inventing History: The Interpretation of the Concept of *Dhammadīpa* by Siṃhala-Bauddha Ethnonationalist." Paper read at *International Conference on Tamil Nationhood and Search for Peace in Sri Lanka (21–22 May 1999)*, at Carleton University and The University of Ottawa.

Schalk, Peter and Alvappillai Veluppillai (eds). 2002. *Buddhism among Tamils in Pre-Colonial Tamiḻakam and Iḻam*. 2 vols. Uppsala: Uppsala Universitet.

Scott, David. 1999. *Refashioning Futures: Criticism After Postcoloniality*. Princeton, NJ: Princeton University Press.

Seneviratna, Anuradha. 1998. *Poḷonnaruva: Medieval Capital of Sri Lanka*. Colombo: Archaeological Survey Department.

Seneviratne, H.L. 1978. *Rituals of the Kandyan State*. Cambridge: Cambridge University Press.

—— 1999. *The Work of Kings: The New Buddhism in Sri Lanka*. Chicago, IL and London: The University of Chicago Press.

Seneviratne, Sudharshan. 1983. "The Curse of Kuveni: The Veddas and the Anti-thesis of Modernization." *Lanka Guardian* 6 (1): 9–11.

—— 1996. "Peripheral Regions and Marginal Communities: Towards an Alternative Explanation of Early Iron Age Material and Social Formations in Sri Lanka." In *Tradition, Dissent and Ideology: Essays in Honour of Romila Thapar*, edited by R. Champaka Lakshmi and S. Goyal, 364–410. Delhi: Oxford University Press.

—— 1999. "Tamilaham, the Sacred Language Zone in South India: Deconstructing 'Tamil' Identity in Antiquity." Paper read at *History, Identity and Historiography*, at Goëthe Institute in Colombo on 2–3 December 1999.

Sinhala Milindapraśnaya. 1970. Edited by G. Saraṇaṅkara. Kolamba: Ratnakāra Pot Velanda Śālāva.

Sivarajah, Ambalavanar. 1996. *The Politics of Tamil Nationalism in Sri Lanka*. New Delhi: South Asian Publishers.

Siyam Mahānikāya. 1973. *Syāma Mahānikāyika Saṅghādhikaraṇa Vyavastāva saha Sāsanārakṣaka Katikāvata*.

SLMM. 2003(a). "Adjusted Proposals for Measures to be considered for preventing Clashes between the SLN and the LTTE at Sea." *The Sunday Times*, May 4, 2003.

—— 2003(b). "Initial Discussion Paper submitted by SLMM on Measures to be considered for preventing Incidents between the SLN and the LTTE at Sea." *The Sunday Times*, April 20, 2003.

Smith, Bardwell L (ed.). 1978. *Religion and the Legitimation of Power in Sri Lanka*. Chambersburg, PA: Anima Books.

Sōbhitha Thera, Māduḷuvāvē. 2003. "A Solution to the Ethnic Problem can be found within the Buddhist Tradition." *Journal of Buddhist Ethics* 10; http://www.jbe.gold.ac.uk/10/sobhitha-sri-lanka-conf.html (accessed on October 1, 2005).

Social Scientists' Association (ed.). 1985. *Ethnicity and Social Change in Sri Lanka*. Colombo: Social Scientists' Association.

Sōma, Gangoḍavila. 2001. *Misadiṭu Bindina Hañḍa: Bauddha Samājayē Mityā Viśvāsa Piḷibanda Dharmānukūla Vimasumak*. Colombo: Dayāvansa Jayakoḍi saha Samāgama.

Somaratne, G.P.V. 1984. "Jayawardhanapura: The Capital of the Kingdom of Sri Lanka c. 1400–1565." *Sri Lanka Archives* 2: 1–6.

Śrī Laṅkā Amarapura Mahāsaṅghasabhāva. 1993. *Śrī Laṅkā Amarapura Mahāsaṅghasabhāve Vyavastāmālāva*. Dehivala: Śrī Dēvī Printers.

Śrī Laṅkā Rāmañña Mahānikāya. 1989. *Śrī Laṅkā Rāmañña Mahānikāya Katikāvata*. Colombo: Department of Printing.

Stirrat, R.L. 1998. "Catholic Identity and Global Forces in Sinhala Sri Lanka." In *Buddhist Fundamentalism and Minority Identities in Sri Lanka*, edited by Tessa J. Bartholomeusz and Chandra R. de Silva, 147–66. Albany, NY: State University of New York Press.

Sumaṅgalavilasinī: Buddhaghosa's Commentary on the Dīgha Nikāya II. 1971. London: The Pali Text Society.

Suravira, A.V. 1962. *Alakeśvara Yuddhaya*. Colombo: Ratna Press.

Swamy, M.R. Narayan. 2004. *Inside an Elusive Mind Prabhakaran: The First Profile of the World's Most Ruthless Guerrilla Leader*. Colombo: Vijitha Yapa Publications.

Tambiah, Stanley J. 1976. *World Conqueror and World Renouncer*. Cambridge: Cambridge University Press.

—— 1986. *Sri Lanka: Ethnic Fratricide and the Dismantling of Democracy*. Chicago, IL and London: The University of Chicago Press.

—— 1992. *Buddhism Betrayed?: Religion, Politics and Violence in Sri Lanka*. Chicago, IL: The University of Chicago Press.

Tambiah, Stanley J. 1996. *Leveling Crowds: Ethnonationalist Conflicts and Collective Violence in South Asia*. Berkeley, CA: University of California Press.

Thambynayagam, Agnes P. n.d. "Roots of Resistance: The Role of Jaffna Catholic Schools in the Formation of the Tamil Youth Organization in Sri Lanka, 1960–72." *Unpublished Paper*.

Thapar, Romila. 1961. *Asoka and the Decline of the Mauryas*. Oxford: Oxford University Press.

The Gazette of The Democratic Socialist Republic of Sri Lanka, Part II of May 28, 2004-Supplement (Issued on May 31). 2004. *Prohibition of Forcible Conversion of Religion (Private Member's Bill) by Omalpe Sobhita*.

The National Joint Committee. 2001. *Report of the Sinhala Commission*. Colombo: The National Joint Committee.

Tilakaratne, Asanga. 1998. *Maḍihē Maha Nā Himi: Caritaya hā Cintanaya*. Colombo.

Tokyo Declaration. 2003. "Tokyo Declaration on Reconstruction and Development of Sri Lanka." *The Daily News*, June 12, 2003.

Torkelsson, Teitur. 2003. "Statement on behalf of SLMM: LTTE responsible for 90 percent Breaches of the Truce last Year." January 23, 2003.

Trenckner, V. (ed.). 1888. *The Majjhimanikāya*. Vol. 1. London: The Pali Text Society.

Turnour, George. 1889. *The Mahāvaṃsa*. Colombo: Government of Ceylon.

US Government. 2002. "Statement issued on March 11th 2002." *The Daily News*, March 12, 2002.

Valentijn, Francois. 1978. *Description of Ceylon*. Translated by Sinnappah Arasaratnam. London: The Hakluyt Society.

Veluppillai, A. 1981. "Tamils in Ancient Jaffna and Vallipuram Gold Plate." *Journal of Tamil Studies* 19: 1–14.

von Grunebaum, Gustave E. 1951. *Muhammedan Festivals*. New York: Schuman.

von Hinüber, Oskar. 1996. *A Handbook of Pāli Literature*. New Delhi: Munshiram Manoharlal Publishers.

von Schroeder, Ulrich. 1990. *Buddhist Sculptures of Sri Lanka*. Hong Kong: Visual Dharma Publications

—— 1992. *The Golden Age of Sculpture in Sri Lanka: Masterpieces of Buddhist and Hindu Bronzes from Museums in Sri Lanka*. Hong Kong: Visual Dharma Publications.

Wachtel, Andrew Baruch. 1994. *An Obsession with History: Russian Writers Confront the Past*. California: Stanford University Press.

Walshe, Maurice. 1996. *The Long Discourses of the Buddha*. Kandy: Buddhist Publication Society.

Weber, Eugen. 1976. "*Peasants into Frenchmen: The Modernization of Rural France 1870–1914*. Stanford: Stanford University Press.

Weeraratne, D. Amarasiri. 2001. "Ven. Samita as Pioneer Bhikk[h]u MP: Whither Buddha Sasana?" *Island*, December 29, 2001.

Weerawarne, Samudhu. 1999. "Dr. A.T. Ariyaratne At Close Quarters." In *People's Peace Initiative*. Ratmalāna: Sarvōdaya Vishva Lekhā Press.

Wickramasinghe, Martin. 1992. *Aspects of Sinhalese Culture*. Dehiwala: Tisara Prakāśakayō.

Wickremasinghe, Don Martino de Zilva (ed.). 1928. *Epigraphia Zeylanica*. Vol. 2. London: Oxford University Press.

Wickremeratne, Ananda. 1995. *Buddhism and Ethnicity in Sri Lanka: A Historical Analysis*. Delhi: Vikas Publishing House.

Wijesekera, O.H.D.A. 1973. "Pāli and Sanskrit in the Poḷonnaruva Period." In *The Poḷonnaruva Period*, edited by S.D. Saparamadu, 102–09. Dehiwala: Tisara Prakāśakayō.

Wilson, A. Jeyaratnam. 1974. *Politics in Sri Lanka 1947–1973*. London: Macmillan.

—— 1988. *The Break-up of Sri Lanka: The Sinhalese–Tamil Conflict*. London: C. Hurst and Company.

—— 2001. *Sri Lankan Tamil Nationalism: Its Origins and Development in the 19th and 20th Centuries*. New Delhi: Penguin Books.

INDEX

CPSIA information can be obtained at www.ICGtesting.com
Printed in the USA
LVOW081932120612
285759LV00002B/34/P